D1555153

THE PSYCHOLOGY
OF WORD MEANINGS

THE PSYCHOLOGY
OF
WORD MEANINGS

Edited by

PAULA J. SCHWANENFLUGEL
University of Georgia

A publication of the Cognitive Studies Group
and the Institute for Behavioral Research
at the University of Georgia

BF
463
.M4
P79
1991
West

 LAWRENCE ERLBAUM ASSOCIATES, PUBLISHERS
1991   Hillsdale, New Jersey   Hove and London

Copyright © 1991 by Lawrence Erlbaum Associates, Inc.
  All rights reserved. No part of this book may be reproduced in any form, by photostat, microform, retrieval system, or any other means without the prior written permission of the publisher.

Lawrence Erlbaum Associates, Inc., Publishers
365 Broadway
Hillsdale, New Jersey 07642

Library of Congress Cataloging-in-Publication Data

The Psychology of word meanings / edited by Paula J. Schwanenflugel.
        p.   cm.
    "Book is a product of a conference . . . jointly sponsored by the
Institute of Behavioral Research, the College of Education, the
Office of the Vice President for Research, and the Departments of
Psychology, Educational Psychology, Language Education, and
Linguistics"—Pref.
    Includes bibliographical references and index.
    ISBN 0-8058-0661-X
    1. Meaning (Psychology)—Congresses.   2. Word recognition—
Congresses.   3. Concepts—Congresses.   I. Schwanenflugel, Paula J.
II. University of Georgia. Institute for Behavioral Research.
BF463.M4P79   1991
401'.9—dc20   91.3444
                                                                  CIP

Printed in the United States of America
10   9   8   7   6   5   4   3   2   1

Contents

Contributors

David A. Balota is Associate Professor of Psychology at Washington University, St. Louis, MO, USA.

Benjamin G. Blount is Professor of Linguistics and Anthropology and a Research Fellow of the Institute for Behavioral Research at the University of Georgia, Athens, GA, USA.

Christine Chiarello is Associate Professor of the Cognitive Neuroscience Program in the Psychology Department at Syracuse University, Syracuse, NY, USA.

Lisa T. Connor is a doctoral student in the Department of Psychology at Washington University, Saint Louis, MO, USA.

Richard Ferraro is Associate Research Scientist of the Department of Psychology at Washington University, Saint Louis, MO, USA.

James A. Hampton is Senior Lecturer of Psychology at City University, London, England, UK.

Pei-Jung Lin is Associate Professor of Early Childhood Education at Taipei Municipal Teachers College, Taipei, Taiwan, ROC.

Barbara C. Malt is Assistant Professor of Psychology at Lehigh University, Bethlehem, PA, USA.

Margaret G. McKeown is Research Scientist at the Learning Research and Development Center at the University of Pittsburgh, Pittsburgh, PA, USA.

Gregory L. Murphy is Associate Professor of Cognitive and Linguistic Sciences at Brown University, Providence, RI, USA.

Paula J. Schwanenflugel is Associate Professor of Educational Psychology and a Research Fellow of the Institute for Behavioral Research at the University of Georgia, Athens, GA, USA.

Edward J. Shoben is Professor of Psychology at the University of Illinois, Champaign, IL, USA.

Steven A. Stahl was a Visiting Research Scientist at the Center for the Study of Reading at the University of Illinois when this chapter was written. He is currently Associate Professor of Reading Education at the University of Georgia, Athens, GA, USA.

Preface

This volume is the second publication of the Cognitive Studies Group and the Institute for Behavioral Research at the University of Georgia. These publications have originated from an annual conference organized by the Cognitive Studies Group of the Institute for Behavioral Research. The book is the product of a conference entitled The Psychology of Word Meaning, held on March 3, 1989 at the University of Georgia. The conference was jointly sponsored by the Institute for Behavioral Research, the College of Education, the Office of the Vice President for Research, and the Departments of Psychology, Educational Psychology, Language Education, and Linguistics. The participants of the conference were David Balota, Margaret McKeown, Gregory Murphy, and Edward Shoben. The other contributors to this volume were solicited through suggestions by the conference participants and organizers. I thank all the fellows of the Institute for Behavioral Research and its director, Abraham Tesser, for their support throughout this project.

P. J. Schwanenflugel

An Introduction to the
Psychology of Word Meaning

Paula J. Schwanenflugel
University of Georgia

In the past few years, cognitive scientists have made tremendous strides in the understanding of how word meaning is represented, processed, and acquired. Simultaneously, research has progressed on a number of fronts: First, our knowledge has greatly expanded regarding fairly basic issues such as the general nature and structure of word meaning (e.g., Barsalou, 1987; Cohen & Murphy, 1984; Medin & Smith, 1984) and how such structure is reflected when word meanings are combined (Hampton, 1987; Medin & Shoben, 1988). Significant advances have also been made in our understanding of how very young children come to learn the meanings of new words (Markman, 1989) and how vocabulary learning proceeds in older children and adults (McKeown, 1985; Nagy & Anderson, 1984). Our knowledge of how word meaning is processed in language understanding has been amplified by studies of word recognition in meaningful contexts (e.g., Neely, 1991; Stanovich & West, 1983; Schwanenflugel, 1991) and studies of the processing of words with varying semantic characteristics (e.g., Balota & Chumbley, 1984; Schwanenflugel, Harnishfeger, & Stowe, 1988). Moreover, as a field, we have become much more aware of the neurological contributions to the processing of word meanings (Burgess & Simpson, 1988; Chiarello, 1988). Yet, although these various advances offer the promise of a more integrated and comprehensive understanding of the psychology of word meaning, these approaches have often seemed somewhat fragmented and isolated from one another.

The purpose of this book is to provide readers with a sense of the scope of the issues that impinge upon the psychological aspects of word meaning. I do not purport to present in this single volume a complete accounting of all the topics that might need to be included to describe the state of the art of research on word meaning. There are, indeed, many relevant topics that have not been included that might have been. Instead, some representative, but disparate approaches have been included to elicit in the reader an appreciation for the wide range of processes that must be accounted for by a complete theory of word meaning. The goal of this book, then, is to provide an overview and organizing framework for researchers studying the psychological aspects of word meanings and related topics. I hope that the enterprise of studying word meaning has been furthered by an integrated presentation of these various topics in this book.

OVERVIEW OF THE CHAPTERS

Specifically, this book covers five general areas in the psychology of word meaning: general theoretical issues, conceptual combinations, vocabulary development, lexical processing, and neurolinguistic issues. What you will find for each of these topics is described below.

The first three chapters are designed to address *general theoretical issues* regarding the nature and structure of word meaning. In the first chapter, Greg Murphy deals with the very difficult issue of what exactly the relation is between concepts in general and word meaning. As he points out, very often in the psychological literature we see the terms concepts and word meanings used interchangeably. He argues that this is not accidental, for many of the same processes operating in the formation and understanding of concepts in general also operate for word meaning. He concludes that word meanings are largely built out of concepts in general.

In Chapter 2, Barbara Malt proposes that examining the extensions of words provides useful information that must be accounted for by a theory of word meaning. Extension data may have distinct advantages over the intension data that is usually collected. First, a broader range of exemplars are likely to be introduced by such data than would normally be considered in studies of word meaning. Second, it avoids the need to have subjects reflect on their conscious intuitions about word meaning and, thereby, may better assess subjects' implicit semantic knowledge. The extension data that Malt presents makes it clear that, even though people may profess that verbal labels are designed to signify items with some sort of common essence, their extensions of those labels show that they do not use words to capture such common essences.

In the third chapter, Ben Blount, Peggy Lin, and I point out that language and culture have been largely ignored in studies of word meanings and concepts. We argue that culture is at the very heart of categories, concepts, and word meanings, and deserves a central focus in theories of word meanings. We review evidence that we believe shows that culture influences not only the concepts that will be acquired but also which attributes are attended to and how the world is cut up and linguistically labeled. We place the traditional Whorfian views of the relationship between language and concepts in a more modern scientific context.

The next two chapters address problems that arise when general theories of word meaning (such as prototype theory) are used to describe the process of combining the meanings of words or *conceptual combinations*. Chapter 4 by James Hampton summarizes the research on conceptual combinations, particularly the literature on noun-noun combinations. Hampton points out that a simple logical model of conceptual combinations does not work—that is, conceptual combinations do not merely involve the overlap of the extensions of each individual noun alone. School Furniture does not encompass the simple overlap of the set of schools and the set of furniture because it would exclude highly prototypical exemplars of School Furniture such as blackboards (which fit neither in the set of schools nor in the set of furniture). He describes how mechanisms might be added to the highly successful prototype theory to account for how people combine the meanings of words.

In Chapter 5, Ed Shoben describes further complications that arise for understanding conceptual combinations in his discussion of predicating and nonpredicating adjectives. For predicate adjective combinations such as Large Spoon, it is not that the term Large merely increases the diagnosticity of the size attribute in extensions of the concept of Spoon. Such a modification model ignores the fact that attributes are correlated such that good examples of Large Spoons tend to be made out of wood rather than metal (as prototypical spoons tend to be). Theories of concepts and conceptual combinations must take into account these correlations. Moreover, for nonpredicating adjectives such as Servant Girl and Electric Shock, such a modification model (Osherson & Smith, 1982) doesn't work at all. He identifies 14 (!) different relations between nouns and their nonpredicating adjectives in such conceptual combinations. Clearly, a theory of conceptual combinations that takes into account the complexity of such nonpredicating adjective relations is a long way off.

Chapters 6 and 7 focus on *vocabulary learning,* in particular, learning the meanings of new words in the elementary school years. One traditional way in which children are taught to learn the meanings of new words is through the use of dictionaries. Perhaps not surprisingly, children have great difficulty learning the meanings of new words in this way. As Nagy and Herman (1987) put it, dictionaries "almost seem to be written in a secret code accessible only to those with the inside knowledge" (p. 29). In Chapter 6, Margaret McKeown argues convincingly that traditional dictionaries are abysmally poor tools for learning the meanings of words. She describes in detail many problems associated with traditional dictionaries and how they might be ammeliorated. However, among their many problems is that they seem to be based on an outdated Classical View of the representation of word meaning (Smith & Medin, 1981), that is, that there is a set of necessary and sufficient features that encompasses all possible extensions of words. She argues that COBUILD dictionaries, whose definitions are based around describing prototypical instances of concept use, are vastly more effective at conveying meaning to children.

In Chapter 7, Steve Stahl notes that, for the most part, children do not learn the meanings of new words from dictionaries. Instead, they learn them from hearing or reading words in context. However, the real focus of the chapter is on the relationship between vocabulary knowledge and reading comprehension in general. On one hand, low vocabulary knowledge will cause the child to demonstrate poor passage comprehension in certain instances. On the other hand, the child will be able to derive the meanings of new words from context on the basis of their comprehension of passages in which the new words are embedded. He discusses in detail both the conditions that influence the learning of word meanings from context as well as the conditions under which unknown words will detrimentally affect comprehension.

Chapters 8 and 9 address issues in the growing literature on the influence of word meaning on *lexical processing*. In Chapter 8, Dave Balota, Richard Ferraro, and Lisa Connor review the lexical processing literatures suggesting that word meaning may influence the processing of words prior to their full recognition. They suggest that words that are relatively concrete, polysemous, or that have highly available associates are recognized faster than words that do not have such characteristics. They invoke a *more-means-better* principle to explain the pervasive effects of word meaning on the processing of words. They suggest that adding a level referring to meaning analysis to an interactive activation model of the sort discussed by McClelland and Rumelhart (1981) would provide a mechanism for describing word meaning effects in lexical processing.

In Chapter 9, the focus is on concreteness effects this time in order to address the general question of why abstract words are harder to understand than concrete words. In that chapter, we see that concreteness effects in lexical processing, sentence processing, and vocabulary development are ubiquitous (although not unanimous). The relative ability of the dual-coding (Paivio, 1986), age-of-acquisition (Gilhooly & Gilhooly, 1979), and context availability (Schwanenflugel, Harnishfeger, & Stowe, 1988) views to account for these findings is evaluated. I conclude that a complete theory of word meaning will need to include some mechanism for describing concreteness effects.

Finally, in Chapter 10, Christine Chiarello makes the important point that, while many theories of word meanings may appear to work well as they stand, they cannot be the right model unless they also possess *neurological plausibility*. She points out that visual half-field studies consistently reveal different semantic processing profiles for the right and left hemispheres. Specifically, the right hemisphere seems to keep a wider range of potential meanings activated longer than the left. The left hemisphere is more responsible for meaning selection, inhibition, and integration. However, by keeping a greater variety of potential meanings activated in the right hemisphere, semantic reanalysis is possible should the wrong meaning be selected by the left. Together the hemispheres work to perform the rather errorfree semantic processing that people display. Currently, no cognitive model of word meaning proposed takes into account the differential contribution of each hemisphere.

EMERGING THEMES IN THE PSYCHOLOGY
OF WORD MEANING

As I was editing this volume, it became clear to me that there were a number of emerging themes that pervaded several chapters of the book. These should not be overlooked because they may represent a core of agreement and issues around which a full theory of word meaning may eventually be built. Here are some of the themes I noticed in no particular order of importance.

Prototypes Revisited

One theme that emerges from the book is that what has become our conventional notion of prototypes (which is illustrated nicely, I think, by the description of it in Hampton's chapter) may need to be altered somewhat. In this book, it is noted that there are at least two complications for prototype theory as it currently stands: (1) the *flexibility* problem and, (2) the *relativity* problem.

One of the problems with conventional prototype theory is that prototypes don't seem flexible enough to carry off the task of semantic processing (Barsalou, 1987). As Hampton and Shoben note, once words are placed in a combinatorial context, their meanings become radically altered. Hampton proposes a solution to this problem that suggests that we need not throw the baby out with the bathwater, however. By adding mechanisms which delete low importance and contradictory attributes from the two individual prototypes of the conceptual combination, we can preserve the original prototype notion while enabling it to account for the apparent composite prototypes that emerge in conceptual combination.

The second complication for prototype theory is the problem it has with accounting for the cultural and developmental relativity of concepts. That is, the original formulation of prototype theory seemed to suggest that prototypes emerge because of the overlap of attributes among objects and events in the world. This suggests that concepts exist "out there" rather than "in the head," as Murphy puts it. However, Malt and Schwanenflugel, et al. note that this formulation cannot account for the cultural diversity in concepts that exists. Morever, Murphy notes that children often don't acquire concepts in a domain unless they possess some sort of theory regarding how the domain works. Thus, word meaning is shaped by some sort of general cognitive determination of relevance and contrast. Murphy suggests that theories pick out concepts and attributes. Schwanenflugel et al. suggest that culture may be important.

On the other hand, we probably do not want to completely throw out the concept of prototypes. For one, its prediction of graded structures is an important one for which there is massive empirical support. Practically, as McKeown notes, concentrating on presenting prototypical instances helps us to build useful dictionaries for children. Rather, we may wish to reconsider how prototypes come about, making them more opportunistic and flexible than they currently seem to be.

How Much Episodic/Contextual Information Forms Part of Word Meaning?

Throughout the book, several of us have noted data that suggests that, when thinking about concepts, people bring in related, contextual information that seems irrelevant for understanding words presented in isolation. For example, Murphy notes that, while interpreting superordinate terms such as *musical instrument*, people tend to bring in information regarding related contextual information such as that they tend to be played on stage, that the violins are usually put together, etc. Schwanenflugel discusses data suggesting that, even when people are making simple lexical decisions, they tend to retrieve information regarding associated contextual information from prior knowledge. Similarly, Balota et al. note that the time taken to retrieve associates is fairly predictive of a word's lexical decision time, suggesting that perhaps such associates are also retrieved during lexical decision.

However, as Stahl notes, surely the task of developing word meaning is to decontextualize the meaning of a word from the contexts in which it first appeared. The issue here, then, is just how much information does word meaning encompass and just how decontextualized is it. Is word meaning merely the whole set of knowledge that we have regarding a concept? Or is it some subset of that knowledge?

We can find two distinct answers to this question in this volume. Murphy takes the position that there truly is a core around which word meanings are built. This core is picked out by the theories that people possess of a domain that decide which information is central and which information is not. In contrast, Balota et al. and Schwanenflugel take the position that perhaps word meanings never become truly decontextualized. In fact, Balota et al. suggest (as others have before them) that a model in which word meanings are cast as the accumulation of all a word's episodic traces is most appropriate.

Theories of Attributes

Another theme that surfaces in several chapters is that people have theories about concepts that tell them which attributes are likely to be important to attend to and which attributes are not important. As Murphy notes, we have theories that tell us that there is probably no thing that both writes poetry and performs photosynthesis. We may have a mistaken theory that all living things breathe. As Shoben notes, these theories may enable us to distinguish which correlations among attributes are important and which ones are not. Moreover, Hampton's composite prototype model suggests that people use these theories about attribute relations to check for the compatibility of attributes in combining concepts, making it difficult for them to know how to deal with the concepts such as "Fish that are also Birds." Regardless of whether people's theories are correct or incorrect, there is some evidence that they use them to form new concepts and to classify exemplars.

There are several notes of caution, however. First, there seems to be little being put forth regarding potential constraints on the theories that people construct to organize domains. Second, as Malt notes, it is often difficult to see what theories of attributes people are using to construct some categories. As she puts it, "It is difficult to imagine a theory of can-hood will include a tin tomato sauce can and exclude a tin cup, and at the same time, will include a cardboard orange juice can and exclude a cardboard ice cream carton; . . . " (p. 65).

The Early Availability of Word Meaning in Lexical Processing

Another theme that emerges in this book is that word meaning has its influence at a very early stage of lexical processing. The chapters by Schwanenflugel, Balota et al., and Chiarello make this very clear. Concreteness, polysemy, and associations *all* seem to have effects at the earliest point we can possibly test for them. Merely providing a letter string with a meaning (either through context or explicitly) influences how they are processed thereafter.

As Balota et al., nicely points out, these findings of early meaning influences on lexical processing suggest that models of word recognition stating that meaning is only available to the reader or listener *after* a word has been accessed (or, as they put it, after some *magic moment* in lexical access) are grossly in error. Balota et al., Chiarello, and I all agree that models of lexical processing will need to include some sort of mechanism that will enable word meaning to have an influence *prior* to the full recognition of words. Chiarello would also add that we may have to give the different hemispheres different roles in this process.

Emphasis on Later Semantic Development

The chapters by Stahl, McKeown, and I all emphasize semantic development during the elementary school years. The usual literature on semantic development typically focuses on the kinds of intuitions that very young children have about the meanings of words. However, as is noted in Stahl's chapter, the bulk of vocabulary acquisition does not occur prior to the elementary school years. Children come into school with about 6000 words and leave it with a vocabulary containing approximately 88,700 discrete word families (Nagy & Anderson, 1984). As my chapter on concreteness effects points out, much of this new vocabulary growth will consist of fairly abstract words.

The recognition of a large growth in vocabulary throughout the elementary school years suggests that more emphasis needs to be placed on the kinds of processes that are used by older children to learn the meanings of new words. The vocabulary literature suggests that induction of the meaning of words from context is one important focus that research may take. Creating better dictionaries may be another.

Whatever the mechanisms behind this growth in vocabulary development, the research makes it clear that fast-mapping is not just an ability possessed by preschoolers (Carey, 1978). Even older children learn something about the meaning of a word from a single presentation in context. This fast-mapping ability appears to be one that continues to be useful throughout the elementary school years and probably beyond.

REFERENCES

Barsalou, L. W. (1987). The instability of graded structure: Implications for the nature of concepts. In U. Neisser (Ed.), *Concepts and conceptual development: Ecological and intellectual factors in categorization* (pp. 101–140). Cambridge: Cambridge University Press.

Balota, D. A., & Chumbley, J. I. (1984). Are lexical decisions a good measure of lexical access? The role of word frequency in the neglected decision stage. *Journal of Experimental Psychology: Human Perception and Performance, 10*, 340–357.

Burgess, C., & Simpson, G. B. (1988). Cerebral hemispheric mechanisms in the retrieval of ambiguous word meanings. *Brain and Language, 33*, 86–103.

Carey, S. (1978). The child as a word learner. In M. Halle, J. Bresnan, & G. Miller (Eds.), *Linguistic theory and psychological reality* (pp. 264–293). Cambridge, MA: MIT Press.

Chiarello, C. (1988). Lateralization of lexical processes in the normal brain: A review of visual half-field research. In H. A. Witaker (Ed.), *Contemporary reviews in neuropsychology* (pp. 36–76). New York: Springer-Verlag.

Cohen, B., & Murphy, G. L. (1984). Models of concepts. *Cognitive Science, 8*, 27–60.

Gilhooly, K. J., & Gilhooly, M. L. (1979). Age-of-acquisition effects in lexical and episodic tasks. *Memory & Cognition, 7*, 214–223.

Hampton, J. A. (1987). Inheritance of attributes in natural concept conjunctions. *Memory & Cognition, 15*, 55–71.

Markman, E. (1989). *Categorization and naming in children*. Cambridge, MA: The MIT Press.

McClelland, J. L., & Rumelhart, D. E. (1981). An interactive activation model of context effects in letter perception: Part 1. An account of basic findings. *Psychological Review, 88*, 375–407.

McKeown, M. (1985). The acquisition of word meaning from context by children of high and low ability. *Reading Research Quarterly, 20*, 482–496.

Medin, D. L., & Shoben, E. J. (1988). Context and structure in conceptual combination. *Cognitive Psychology, 20*, 158–190.

Medin, D. L., & Smith, E. E. (1984). Concepts and concept formation. *Annual Review of Psychology, 35*, 113–138.

Nagy, W. E., & Anderson, R. C. (1984). How many words are there in printed school English? *Reading Research Quarterly, 19*, 304–330.

Nagy, W. E., & Herman, P. A. (1987). Breadth and depth of vocabulary knowledge: Implications for acquisition and instruction. In M. G. McKeown & M. E. Curtis (Eds.), *The nature of vocabulary acquisition* (pp. 19–35). Hillsdale, NJ: Lawrence Erlbaum Associates.

Neely, J. H. (1991). Semantic priming effects in visual word recognition. In D. Besner & G. Humphreys (Eds.), *Basic processes in reading: Visual word recognition* (pp. 264–336). NJ: Lawrence Erlbaum Associates.

Osherson, D. N., & Smith, E. E. (1982). Gradedness and conceptual conjunction. *Cognition, 12,* 299–318.

Paivio, A. (1986). *Mental representations: A dual coding approach.* Oxford, England: Oxford University Press.

Schwanenflugel, P. J. (1991). Contextual constraint and lexical processing. To appear in G. B. Simpson (Ed.), *Understanding word and sentence.* Amsterdam: North Holland.

Schwanenflugel, P. J., Harnishfeger, K. K., & Stowe, R. W. (1988). Context availability and lexical decisions for abstract and concrete words. *Journal of Memory and Language, 27,* 488–520.

Smith, E. E., & Medin, D. L. (1981). *Categories and concepts. Cambridge, MA: Harvard University Press.*

Stanovich, K. E., & West, R. F. (1983). On priming by a sentence context. *Journal of Experimental Psychology: General, 112,* 1–36.

1 Meaning and Concepts

Gregory L. Murphy
Brown University

When a child learns to call only cars by the name *car*, has he or she learned the meaning of *car*, the concept of cars, or both? Could the child have learned one without the other? Imagine an adult who calls some tree *an oak* when it is really a maple. Does this person not know the correct meaning of *oak* or is he or she confused about the category of oaks? Or do these questions amount to the same thing? The goal of this chapter is to analyze the psychological representation of word meaning and to determine its relation to concepts. In carrying out this goal, we will also need to consider philosophical views on what word meaning really is.

When discussing meaning and concepts, the first problem to address is which is which. In the psychological literature, some writers seem to randomly choose one term to use, without any clear motivation for the choice. Other writers use the terms interchangeably, perhaps in the hope that at least one of them will be correct. The issue here, of course, is not to choose one term as being "correct," but to decide what these terms mean in a theory-neutral way. By *meaning* I mean the semantic components of words, in particular. That is, meaning is the component of linguistic elements that gives them significance. This usage does not imply a commitment to any particular theory of meaning. By *concepts* I mean mental representations of coherent classes of entities. Concepts are our notions of what kinds of objects and events make up the world. These representations may or may not correspond to word meanings, and this is a large part of what we'll be worried about in this chapter.

SEMANTIC THEORIES

Let me start by very briefly considering one view of what meanings are–the view given to us by formal semantics (see Dowty, Wall, & Peters, 1981, for a good introduction). Formal semantics considers meaning to be a relation between words and the world. There are two parts to this relation. First, there is the *extension,* which is the set of all the objects that the word describes. So, the extension of *chair* would be all the chairs in the world—or, according to most theories, all the possible chairs in all the possible worlds. The second component of meaning is called the *intension* (not to be confused with *intention*). In every-day terms, the intension is the property that all chairs have in common—it's the chairness of chairs. One way to think of the intension is as a rule or property that can pick out the extension. Once you know what the (true) property of being a chair is, you can pick out all the chairs that you might encounter. Most theories of formal semantics use both of these components, which causes a serious problem for psychologists trying to apply these theories to psychology, because it seems very clear that the extension can't be anything that people know or manipulate. That is, people cannot know or represent all the chairs in the world, much less in all possible worlds. To this degree, then, it's very difficult to relate such formal semantic theories to psychological accounts of meaning (Cohen & Murphy, 1984).

This chapter focuses on the more psychologically relevant aspect of meaning, the intension. It seems likely that people could learn these intensions, or something like them, when they learn word meanings. And if you know the intension of a word, you may not have to know its complete extension, because the intension can be applied to actual objects to evaluate whether they belong to the extension. So, if you know what the intension of *chair* is, you can use it to pick out actual chairs. If intensions are part of word meanings, then we can make at least some connection between semantic theory and human language processing through them.

Virtually every theory of the psychological representation of word meaning proposes that people learn the intensions of words, with different theories disagreeing on just how the intensions are represented. For example, theories have claimed that people represent word meaning as semantic components (Clark, 1972; Katz & Fodor, 1963; Smith, Shoben, & Rips, 1974), as prototypes (Rosch, 1973, 1975), as nodes in a network (Collins & Quillian, 1969), as mental models (Johnson-Laird, 1983), and so on.

However, the philosopher Hilary Putnam (1973, 1975, 1988) has made compelling arguments against the assumption that people know the intensions of words, which is at the core of our psychological theories of meaning. The following example illustrates Putnam's argument. People have been buying oranges and lemons for many years, and most of them know what the difference is between them. However, it's conceivable that a biologist could do a genetic and morphological study of lemon trees and find out that some of the varieties that we had been calling lemons are really a rather peculiar variety of orange. This may sound a little outlandish, but such re-evaluations have actually occurred. We know that whales are not fish, even though they look and act a lot like them, and people previously thought that they were fish. Biologists have made similar surprising discoveries over the years (e.g., that "glass snakes" are really a kind of lizard), so this one is not unreasonable.

In this example, it turns out that even fluent speakers of English have been misusing the language. They have been calling a large number of oranges *lemons* for years, as if they didn't know the meaning of the word *lemon*. Although word meaning may not at first glance seem to be an empirical matter, the scientist's discovery would change people's word use and understanding of what lemons really are. So, many people who speak English apparently didn't know what the word *lemon* means—although they had a mental description of lemons, this couldn't have been the true intension of *lemon*, as it didn't actually pick out only lemons (but also some oranges). The point is, of course, that this scenario could arise for almost any natural kind word—not just lemon. So, the same kind of example could be used to show that people don't really know what *horse, cat, fruit, water, canyon, tree, silver,* or *grass* mean. It's not important that scientists haven't yet disconfirmed our notion of, say, what *silver* means—the very fact that scientists *could* disconfirm it shows that there is more to the meaning than whatever is in our mental representation of the word.

The example of the lemon is somewhat realistic, in that scientific discoveries are often changing our conceptions of things that we thought we understood. Putnam (1973, 1988) has constructed a more whimsical example that makes the point even more compellingly (my description is also based on the version of Fodor, 1987). Imagine that there is a world called Twin-Earth that is identical to the Earth in every respect but one. For example, every person on Earth has a twin there who is atom for atom identical with his or her Earth counterpart. The only respect in which Twin-Earth and Earth differ is that whereas our substance gold corresponds to an element, the thing that they call "gold" on Twin-Earth is a complicated alloy, which we can call "XYZ." Superficially, however, gold and XYZ are very similar.

Now let's consider the relationship between me and the person just like me on Twin-Earth (Twin-me). Presumably, we must have the same thoughts and mental life, because we are molecule-for-molecule identical. However, Putnam argues that our meanings are not identical. For example, we might both make the statement, "I have a gold watch." However, when I say that sentence, what I mean is that I have a gold watch, but what my twin means is that he has an XYZ watch. That is, the meaning of *gold* on Earth is the element gold, but the meaning of the same word on Twin-Earth is XYZ. Since it is XYZ that they have always called gold, XYZ is causally connected to the word *gold* in just the same way that gold on Earth is connected to the word *gold*.

Why is this a problem? Well, since Twin-me and I have identical brains and, it seems likely, identical mental representations, it seems that we should have identical meanings. However, as just pointed out, we don't. We differ in that my meaning of *gold* is not the same as my twin's. Thus, Putnam poses the following paradox: Even though we have identical mental and brain states, our meanings are not identical. For psychologists, the point is that word meaning doesn't seem to be a matter of psychology (i.e., our mental representations); the physics of Earth or Twin-Earth partly determines what the meaning is.

Putnam points out several important implications of these examples. One is that there is a *linguistic division of labor* for names describing natural kinds: We know something about the meaning of these words, but we also delegate some of the responsibility for determining their true meaning to other people—experts. To some degree, then, it's an empirical question as to exactly what a lemon is or gold is; the science of biology will tell us (eventually) what it really is to be a lemon, and we have to allocate some of the linguistic work to biologists at the same time that we're using these words.

The second implication is that people apparently don't know the intensions of words. It seems that we didn't really know the meaning of *lemon*, even though we had a mental description of lemons. And even though Twin-me and I had identical mental states, and, in particular, we had the same beliefs about gold, we had different meanings of the word *gold*. As Putnam (1973) put it in a famous quote: "Cut the pie any way you like, 'meanings' just ain't in the head!" (p. 704). Why aren't they in the head? Because there is a "right answer" to what the meaning is, and that answer is a fact about the world—not about our mental representations. So, the meaning of *lemon* is whatever lemons really are, regardless of our beliefs about them. And the meaning of *gold* depends on what gold really is on Earth (or Twin-Earth), not just on what we believe about gold.

One may feel that the Twin-Earth example is a rather récherché philosophical puzzle that has few implications for psychology. But its importance is in suggesting that meaning is not a matter of mental representations, and therefore that the study of meaning is not really part of psychology. And cases of meaning change, such as the lemon/orange example, show that Putnam's problem can have real consequences—namely, that people's mental representations of a word don't seem to determine what the word really means.

If we accept Putnam's conclusion, the psychology of meaning looks like a doomed endeavor. If meanings ain't in the head, there can't be any psychology of them. How is a psychologist to deal with this problem? To begin with, by ignoring it. Rather than directly answer the question of where meanings are, if they aren't in the head, I'm going to approach the question from the other side by asking just what is in the head. Rather than attacking Putnam's problem itself, I will initially confine myself to the question of psychological semantics: How do people represent word meanings? I'll discuss this by working through a series of questions that spell out the major possibilities. Following this purely theoretical discussion is a review of empirical evidence that bears on the question of meaning representation. Finally, the chapter ends with an attempted resolution to Putnam's problem by reviewing what has been found in the head and evaluating whether it is "meaning."

THE REPRESENTATION OF MEANING

Perhaps the first question one should ask is whether people have any knowledge at all of word meanings. Although the answer seems obviously to be "yes," there are possible arguments against it. One could argue that English is a language with a grammar and semantics regardless of whether anyone alive speaks it (Katz, 1981, expresses this view but not the psychological implication under discussion). English could be conceived of as a linguistic system apart from its speakers, just as mathematics was a valid system even before humans discovered it. To take a realistic example, there certainly is a fact of the matter as to whether a phonetic sequence is a sentence of ancient Hittite, even if there is no one alive who knows this language. The rules of the language do not have to be actually known by anyone in order to be the correct rules. Therefore, one could argue, there's no need to talk about meanings of English words being in the head, because the semantics of English exist (in some sense) independently of people.

This view of language has a certain degree of validity (though see Chomsky, 1986), but it doesn't seem to bear on the question of what speakers of a language actually know. The fact that one could imagine the semantics of English existing apart from any speakers does not entail that speakers don't know the rules of English. In contrast, people's everyday language use provides strong prima facie evidence that they know something about their language, or else their behavior would be inexplicable. Although Putnam's examples still must be accounted for, it is clear that there is something in the head that accounts both for performance in experiments (see Smith, 1978) and for normal language use.

Let us tentatively conclude then, that people have some kind of mental representation that controls their word use. What is the nature of these mental objects? One possibility is that meanings are a purely linguistic construction, just as relative clauses and phonemes are purely linguistic elements—someone who doesn't know any languages doesn't know about phonemes or relative clauses. On this view, meanings are strictly internal to the linguistic system; they aren't part of the general "language of thought" that we use to think about the world.

If we had such a theory, we could still explain the semantic relations among words. For example, we could take the Katz and Fodor (1963) framework of semantic markers as being such a theory. They suggested that word meanings can be represented as collections of semantic markers, such as [unmarried, adult, male] for the meaning of *bachelor*. If we interpret the semantic markers as arbitrary linguistic symbols, then we might have a theory of meaning that was strictly internal to the linguistic system. That is, the features could be rewritten as any arbitrary strings with no effect on the theory's explanatory power. The feature [male] could just as well have been [xyzzy] or [%3#A20!]. (By the same token, if syntacticians were to call noun phrases "LGs" instead of "NPs," this would have no effect on the explanatory power of their theories.) We could still explain semantic relations such as entailment, synonymy, and antonymy through the relations of these symbols. For example, synonymous words would have exactly the same (arbitrary) semantic markers. Opposites would be words that differ in the value of exactly one marker.

Such a theory could explain many linguistic phenomena, but it has serious problems as a psychological model. In order for people to understand how words are related to real objects in the world, they must interpret each of these components in terms of some concept that they already know. Although one could have a set of semantic markers that are purely internal to the linguistic system, these meanings couldn't refer to real objects by themselves, because they aren't connected to those objects in any way. That is, in order to identify birds with the word *bird,* the word must be connected to actual properties of birds. And in order to use the word *bird* in conversation, it must be connected to knowledge of all kinds about birds. So each semantic marker would have to be tied to a concept or subconcept that people have, so that they can connect words to the things they represent in the world. For example, the feature [xyzzy] would have to be connected to one's concept of maleness in order to accurately label someone with the word *bachelor*. It should be obvious that this view posits a semantic system that is completely redundant with the conceptual system. That is, for every semantic marker that influences word use, there must be a conceptual element that connects the marker to the world. Why not just use conceptual markers to begin with? Or to put it another way, the semantic markers don't actually supply the meaning of the word; it's the concept it's connected to that makes [xyzzy] mean maleness instead of redness or some other attribute.

In order to form a psychological model, then, it seems necessary to hook semantics up with concepts in some way. Perhaps the most straightforward way would be to suggest that meanings and concepts simply are the same thing (still ignoring Putnam's arguments for the moment). That is, perhaps every concept is a meaning, and every meaning is a concept. Unfortunately, this simple proposal won't work. Clearly, we have concepts that we don't have words for. (In fact, a few years ago, a book called *Sniglets* came out that invented words for concepts that we didn't yet have words for—such as *sniglet,* which is a word made up to fill such a lexical gap.) Many complex concepts have no conventional word associated with them (e.g., the concept of things to do at the beach when it's raining—see Barsalou, 1983). And it seems clear that children have many concepts that they haven't learned the words for yet (Clark, 1983). So every concept probably isn't a word meaning. Furthermore, it seems likely that some words don't map cleanly onto a single concept, but that they may pick out a complex construction of a number of concepts (e.g., *sniglet* or *democracy*). So, every word meaning may not be exactly one concept. In short, the simple proposal that word meanings are identical to concepts is too simplistic.

If meanings aren't equal to concepts, and yet if concepts are involved, then perhaps the best way to describe their relation is to say that meanings are built out of concepts in some way. That is, a word's meaning is constructed by mapping concepts onto the semantic component of the lexicon. This is hardly an original conclusion (e.g., Clark, 1983), but by considering and eliminating the possibilities raised earlier, we can feel more confident that there is a connection between word meaning and the conceptual system. In addition, it is clear that concepts and meanings are not exactly identical and should not be treated as interchangeable.

We can't feel too confident in this conclusion, however, because a number of writers on semantics have criticized a view similar to it. Janet Fodor (1975, p. 16) and Clark and Clark (1977, ch. 11) argued against the idea that meanings are "ideas." (In particular, Fodor focused on the notion that one's ideas are mental images. I will apply her arguments more broadly.) They claimed that different people have different ideas about things, whereas they share the same word meanings. They also suggest that one's personal idea about an object changes depending on the context, one's mood, and so on, whereas word meanings should be relatively constant. In short, "ideas" are rather ephemeral, unstable things, whereas meanings are not.

One way to generalize this argument is to say that language is a kind of social convention that we generally share. We can't make up our own word meanings any more than we can make up our own syntactic rules and think that we're still speaking English. To that degree, then, meanings can't just be our individual ideas. However, to the degree that meanings must be represented by each language user, it isn't so clear that the *psychological* basis of word meaning can't be our "ideas" or concepts (although there may also be a societal basis that could require a different kind of analysis; see below). Consider the argument that people might have different concepts about things. For example, you could have a different concept of dogs than I do (Barsalou, 1987). But if this were true, you might also use the word *dog* somewhat differently than I do. If you were to say "It's a dog's life," you might intend something different than if I said it. Rather than being a problem, this is a point in favor of the psychological theory that meanings are built from concepts.[1] Of course, you probably wouldn't have a

---

[1]Actually, this issue is somewhat more complex than the discussion admits. It may be important for *linguistics* to assume that everyone in the community shares the same word meanings, even if this is not strictly true (Chomsky, 1965). If one takes psycholinguistics to be a branch of linguistics, then the first argument might well apply to it. If one takes psycholinguistics to be a theory of performance, then the argument can be dealt with as it is in the text. Unfortunately, there is still little agreement on this matter in the field.

concept of dogs that's radically different from everyone else's, because you would soon be corrected once you started using the word *dog*. Thus, although one could imagine people's concepts diverging wildly, there are strong social constraints within a language community to prevent this from happening. If there are consistent individual or dialect differences in word use, then there should be corresponding differences in concepts.

Barsalou's (1987, 1989) research on conceptual instability is of considerable relevance to the second argument, that concepts differ even within individuals. His experiments show that many different measures of category structure have little stability across subjects from the same population, across contexts, and even within individuals across test sessions with identical instructions. Barsalou argues that it is a mistake to think of one mental structure that is "the" concept. Rather, there is a wide variety of different kinds of information connected to the representation, and which set of information gets activated in any situation depends on the person's knowledge, recent experience and the current context. If this analysis is correct, then the phenomenon noted by Fodor and others may be even more widespread than introspection indicates. But is this phenomenon an argument against using concepts to represent word meanings? Barsalou's experiments all involve linguistically described categories, including those denoted by common nouns. Therefore, his results probably have implications for linguistic processes involving those words, such as lexical selection in production and disambiguation in comprehension. And one of Barsalou's tasks required subjects to provide word definitions—presumably a task central to semantic representation. This task showed the same instability as the others (Barsalou, 1989).

In short, Fodor and others who have made this argument may be right that "concepts" are changeable and context-sensitive. However, they haven't demonstrated that the mental representation of word meaning is *not* similarly changeable and context-sensitive (and there is some evidence that it is). So, this is not a decisive argument against the conceptual representation of meaning.

I should add that it seems unlikely that our long-term concepts or word meanings change very much within short periods of time. We may emphasize one part more than others at different times: I may be disgusted with dogs or happy with dogs, but even as my attitude changes, my basic concept of what dogs are doesn't change that much. For example, as I become increasingly depressed, I don't begin to think that dogs are robots or plants, or that they can fly. Their essential nature is unchanged as a function of my mood.

There's a more serious problem with a view that meanings are built out of concepts, namely that concepts may contain considerable information that does not seem to be part of word meaning (Clark & Clark, 1977, pp. 411–412). I illustrate this issue with some experiments on categorization. This research (reported in Murphy & Wisniewski, 1989a) investigated the difference between basic concepts like *lamp, dog,* and *car* and more general concepts (called "superordinates") like *furniture, animal,* and *vehicle*. In the standard categorization experiment, subjects see a category name and a picture of an object and are asked to verify the object's category. So they might hear the word *hammer* and have to answer whether the picture was of a hammer. In our experiment (and in many others like it), subjects responded much faster to the basic concept names (like *hammer*) than to superordinates (like *tool*) (see Murphy & Smith, 1982; Murphy & Brownell, 1985; Rosch, Mervis, Gray, Johnson, & Boyes-Braem, 1976; Smith, Balzano, & Walker, 1978). Such results suggest that basic concepts are preferred by people in their thinking about the world. However, we also found a new result. What happens when the object is embedded in a scene, as in Fig. 1.1? In this case, subjects are almost equally fast at verifying superordinate and basic concepts. Apparently, some information in the superordinate concept was related to information in the scene, aiding superordinate categorization.

Figure 1.2 illustrates a different comparison. Biederman, Mezzanotte, and Rabinowitz (1982) have shown that people are faster and more accurate at identifying objects when they are in congruent scenes like the left panel of Fig. 1.2 than when they are in incongruent scenes like the right panel. We found a similar effect in our experiment, but we also found that superordinates were more affected by this inappropriate picture than basic concepts were. That is, the incongruent scene in Fig. 1.2 caused more errors in identifying the probed object as a *musical instrument* than as a *saxophone*. (And this result is not a simple matter of object priming but depends on the scene structure—see Murphy and Wisniewski, 1989a.) So, superordinates were helped by the congruent scene and hurt by the incongruent scene, relative to basic categories.

From these results, Wisniewski and I concluded that many superordinate concepts include information about whole groups of objects and scenes rather than just individual objects. For example, the concept *musical instrument* must include information such as how different instruments are held, where they are normally spatially located relative to each other, that instruments are often played

FIG. 1.1.   Stimuli from Murphy and Wisniewski (1989a). The left panel shows the scene condition and the right panel the isolation condition for the categories *hammer/tool*.

FIG. 1.2.   Stimuli from Murphy and Wisniewski (1989a). The left panel
shows the congruent scene and the right panel the incongruent scene
for the categories *saxophone/musical instrument.*

on a stage, and so on. It is just this information that accounts for the relative
speed-up of superordinate categorization in scenes. And when other objects
present in a scene are incongruent, this makes it harder to identify the superordinate category, because they contradict this information. So, although basic categories focus on the properties of individual objects, superordinates may have
much more relational information (see Murphy & Wisniewski, 1989a, for a
detailed discussion and Markman & Callanan, 1984, for developmental evidence).

Results like these raise a potential problem in relating superordinate concepts
to word meanings. Suppose the meaning of the phrase *musical instrument* is the
concept I've just described.[2] It seems that our results imply that *musical instrument* has *as part of its meaning* a feature like "they are usually played on a
stage." But, someone might argue, this is just wrong—the essence of musical
instruments is not where they occur but in their structure and functional properties. Perhaps people do know where specific instruments appear, how they're
held, when they're normally played, and so on, but this is just an association—it
can't be part of the real *meaning* of this phrase. Similarly, the way silverware is
arranged on a place setting may be something that people know, but it shouldn't
be a part of the meaning of *silverware.*

More generally, one may argue that concepts include all kinds of information
in them, information that we don't want to call word meaning. The fact that my
brother was once bitten by a dog may be stored in my memory about dogs, but it
can hardly be called part of the meaning of the word *dog,* even in my personal

---

[2]Although *musical instrument* is two words, it is a conventional phrase rather than a novel noun
phrase. Thus, it has its own lexical entry, and may be treated (loosely) as a word for the present
purposes.

lexicon. (I won't presume to speak for my brother.) So, if word meanings are based on concepts, how can we know which parts of the concept constitute word meaning? This problem is highlighted by the finding that such personal memories are apparently functionally integrated with semantic memory rather than forming two separate memory systems (McKoon, Ratcliff, & Dell, 1986).

There may not be an easy answer to this question, but a telling observation is that this problem arises not only with word meanings but also with concepts themselves (see Armstrong, Gleitman, & Gleitman, 1983). For example, people may use their knowledge of locations, spatial relations and the like to identify musical instruments, but they also realize that if they see a tuba at the bottom of the ocean, it still fits the concept *musical instrument*. That is, concepts have both central, essential attributes, and useful but less essential attributes, and the two must be discriminated. This problem is especially salient for children, in that they may see spurious correlations in the environment that they have to ignore when learning a new concept. They must realize that there's nothing in the concept of *elephant* that means that elephants must be in the zoo, even if that's the only place that they see them. In short, this problem of including just the right information is something that arises not only in learning words, but in forming any kind of concept.

One partial answer to this problem is that people form theories of a domain that tell them what kind of information is important (Carey, 1985; Keil, 1989; Murphy & Medin, 1985). People have theories of biological categories like *elephant* or of artifact categories like *musical instrument,* and these theories tell them which features are crucial to understanding each kind of object and which features are only predictive. Our theory of biology tells us that it's the physiological structure and genetics of animals that really determine what they are, not their physical location (like the zoo). The reason that building meanings out of concepts seems to have the problem of including too much information is that concepts have long been viewed as lists of associated attributes. But concepts aren't just a mass of associations—they are instead the associated information plus a theory about what makes something part of that concept. Both the associations and the domain theory contribute to concept use, but for linguistic representations, the theory seems to be central to establishing word meaning. The importance of theories becomes evident in the chapter's conclusion (see also Murphy & Medin, 1985).

A different approach to this problem would be to explicitly mark the parts of a concept that are relevant to word meaning. That is, some properties of a concept could get a special tag that identifies them as being relevant to word meaning (e.g., "makes a sound" would be tagged for the lexical item *musical instrument,* but "found on a stage" would not be). This approach seems somewhat redundant, because the parts that are crucial to meaning would also be the ones that are crucial to conceptual identity. It is the function of musical instruments (rather than the shape, location, or material of the object) that largely defines what kind of things they are, and it is also the function that is most central to the meaning of the phrase *musical instrument*. Thus, although one could consider meaning to be simply a subset of the information in a concept, it seems likely that specifying what parts of the concept are its meaning would be identical with specifying what is central to the concept itself. So it seems more parsimonious to allow the word meaning to pick out the whole concept, and to let the conceptual processes (such as theories) identify the central attributes for both.

EMPIRICAL EVIDENCE

At this stage, one might well wonder whether there is any empirical evidence that would help us to decide whether word meanings are really built out of concepts. Lyons (1977) has argued that there is no good reason to believe that concepts are the basis of word meaning. "Even if we grant that there are concepts associated with words, such that . . . when I hear the word 'table', the concept of a table will come to my mind and, if I think of a table, the word 'table' will be called up for use as required, there is no evidence to show that concepts of this kind play any part in ordinary language-behaviour" (p. 113). Lyons suggests that the only evidence available (at that time) was introspection, which is notoriously unreliable. Clearly, more convincing would be experimental evidence that using language is sensitive to variables that play an important role in concept formation and use. Although such evidence will not be knock-down proof, it will certainly establish a strong case via Ockham's Razor: If language use is determined by the same factors that influence conceptual processing, then we should assume that word meanings and concepts are part of the same psychological system rather than two independent systems that just happen to follow the same principles. In fact, there is considerable evidence of just this kind. I will describe evidence from four areas of research: prototype effects, basic-level structure, vocabulary acquisition, and conceptual combination.

Typicality Prototype

To begin with, the psychology of concepts has amassed a huge amount of evidence (e.g., Posner & Keele, 1968; Rosch, 1973, 1975) that concepts are often organized around *prototypes* (though the exact mechanism behind these results is still controversial). This means that for a given concept, we can often identify the typical, best examples of the concept and distinguish them from poor or atypical examples. North Americans generally agree that a robin is a very typical kind of bird but that an ostrich is atypical. Furthermore, many experiments have shown that the typical examples are easier to learn and then to identify and use, once the concept has been learned (see Mervis & Rosch, 1981; Smith & Medin, 1981, for reviews).

The question arises, then, as to whether typicality influences linguistic performance involving words. It does, quite strongly. For example, Rips, Shoben, and Smith (1973) showed that when subjects verify sentences like "A robin is a bird," the typicality of the example (here, *robin*) to the category (*bird*) predicts how quickly people are to verify that the sentence is true. A sentence using a less typical example like "A goose is a bird" would be verified less quickly. This result has been replicated many times (e.g., McCloskey & Glucksberg, 1979; Rosch, 1973). Using a different paradigm Rosch (1977) asked subjects to generate sentences using category names like *bird*. She then replaced the category names with names of exemplars, like *sparrow, robin,* and *turkey,* and asked subjects to rate the naturalness of the resulting sentences. The ratings declined linearly with the decreasing typicality of the new word.

One might argue that judgment tasks of this kind do not provide a natural measure of language use. However, in a case of pure language comprehension, Garrod and Sanford (1977) showed that understanding the reference of a noun phrase depended on the typicality of the noun. They presented subjects with pairs of sentences like (1) and (2) below.

(1) A robin kept getting into the house.
   The bird came in through the open door.

(2) A goose kept getting into the house.
   The bird came in through the open door.

Subjects were simply instructed to read and understand each sentence, and the reading times of individual sentences were recorded. Garrod and Sanford found that readers took longer to understand the second sentence of (2) than the identical sentence in (1). Making the connection between the anaphoric phrase *the bird* and the antecedent exemplar (*the robin* or *the goose*) depended on how typical the antecedent was of the anaphor.

In addition to the cases involving language understanding, Kelly, Bock, and Keil (1986) showed that typicality also affects language production. They found that the more typical a category name, the more likely people were to mention it first in a sentence. So, people would be more likely to say "The child's errand was to buy an apple and lemon at the fruit stand" than to say "The child's errand was to buy a lemon and apple at the fruit stand." They concluded that the sentence planning process was sensitive to the accessibility of concepts, and that typicality influences their accessibility.

These findings show that typicality effects are found in a wide variety of linguistic tasks, suggesting that lexical representations are based on conceptual structures. This argument assumes that typicality is a property of concepts, and that typicality effects in word use show the connection between words and concepts. However, one could argue that typicality is just part of word meaning. Perhaps it is part of the meaning of *apple* that it's a typical example of fruit, and it is part of the meaning of *lime* that it's an atypical fruit. There's no reason this information couldn't be stored in the lexical entry. But typicality gradation is indeed a conceptual relation—it occurs with artificial, newly learned categories that don't refer to anything familiar. For example, one of the first demonstrations of prototype effects was made by Posner and Keele (1968) using random dot patterns. These concepts didn't receive linguistic labels, but were just called categories 1, 2, and 3. Typicality differences have also been found with geometric stimuli (Franks & Bransford, 1971), strings of alphanumeric characters (Rosch & Mervis, 1975), phonetic categories (Massaro & Cohen, 1983), ad hoc categories (like *things to carry out of a burning house*, Barsalou, 1983), and personality types (Cantor & Mischel, 1979), among many others. Thus, typicality is clearly a general conceptual relation, rather than one confined to lexical items. Barsalou (1987) also notes that since context and instructions can greatly modify typicality rankings, it is unlikely that they are precomputed and simply recalled from memory as lexical entries would be. Furthermore, there are a number of theories that predict what makes items typical or atypical (see Barsalou, 1985; Reed, 1972; Rosch & Mervis, 1975), but none of these theories uses specifically linguistic relations, nor do they apply only to word meanings. So, typicality effects seem to be a property of the general conceptual system. The fact that they also appear in linguistic tasks is evidence that word meanings are based on such conceptual relations.

Basic Level Concepts

A second relevant area of concept research investigates the phenomenon of basic concepts, which was raised earlier in a different context. Rosch et al. (1976) showed that although a number of concepts can often refer to the same object, there is usually one that is preferred. So, we prefer to call something *a table* rather than *a piece of furniture*, and we prefer to call a whale *a whale* rather than *an animal* or a more specific name like a *humpback whale*. Basic concepts are at a middle level of description—they're neither too general nor too specific. This phenomenon is relevant here, because the names for basic categories differ from the names for other categories in a number of respects. First, languages usually have single-word names for basic categories, but often don't for more specific categories (like *humpback whales, dining room table,* or *racing car*) (Berlin, Breedlove, & Raven, 1973). Second, more general categories are often mass nouns, whereas basic categories are generally count nouns, across a large number of languages (Markman, 1985). For example, we have to say *a piece of furniture* or *a piece of jewelry*—we can't say **a furniture,* or **a jewelry.* We can of course say *a chair* or *a bracelet,* because these basic category names are count nouns. Third, superordinate category names are more often used to refer to groups of objects rather than to single objects, whereas the reverse is true for basic concepts (Wisniewski & Murphy, 1989). Fourth, children learn the names for basic categories sooner than they learn names for the more specific or more general categories (Anglin, 1977; Horton & Markman, 1980; Mervis & Crisafi, 1982).

Each of these examples involves people's use of the names or linguistic representation of categories. Yet, the notion of basic concepts is not inherently linguistic, and they have been investigated in artificial categories that don't have any conventional name (Mervis & Crisafi, 1982; Murphy, in press; Murphy & Smith, 1982). In short, the basic level phenomenon is a property of conceptual structure, and yet it influences language use.

Vocabulary Acquisition

The third area of research is language acquisition. In particular, vocabulary learning seems to be primarily directed by conceptual development. This influence can be seen in the order in which children acquire words. Their very first words inevitably refer to objects and events that make up their everyday lives, such as words for food, body parts, clothes, household objects, and so on (Clark & Clark, 1977, p. 302). They seldom have words for abstract concepts or concepts that cannot be perceptually identified, reflecting their cognitive abilities at the time. More specific evidence can be seen in the acquisition of words within a domain. For example, children acquire dimensional adjectives in the following order: *big-small; tall-short; high-low; thick-thin;* and *deep-shallow* (Clark, 1972, 1973). There is good reason to think that this order reflects the conceptual complexity of the concepts behind these words. For example, *big* and *small* simply refer to differences in size, with no further distinctions. *Tall* and *short* refer to size differences within one particular dimension; *thick* and *thin* require further distinctions, in that they apply only to the tertiary dimension of an object. The adjectives that are learned later refer to more complex concepts or to less salient aspects of objects. It is apparently these characteristics that predict order of acquisition rather than some purely linguistic variable (Carey, 1982; Clark, 1983).

Earlier I mentioned that children learn names for basic concepts before most subordinate or superordinate concepts. This is not merely a matter of frequency of exposure. When children are taught new words, they learn those that correspond to basic concepts much more readily than those from other conceptual levels (Horton & Markman, 1980; Mervis & Crisafi, 1982). Conceptual naturalness is clearly an important determinant of word learning.

Keil (1989) reviewed a series of studies on children's understanding of "nominal kind" words like *uncle, island, lie,* and *boil*—words that have relatively clear definitions. His studies reveal that children often begin with an incorrect notion of what these words mean, based on relatively simple, often perceptual prototypes. For example, very young children might say that any meal that consists of toast and cereal is breakfast, regardless of when it is eaten. As children get more experience with these words, they begin to understand the true dimensions underlying their use. Keil argues that children develop theories of a domain that organize concepts by picking out the dimensions and relations that are relevant to understanding the domain. Children need to acquire the theories behind kinship relations or cooking or moral terms in order to use the words correctly.

Keil discovered that the acquisition of the meaning of these terms does not occur at one specific age; the age of acquisition depends considerably on the particular domain (e.g., moral terms like *lie* are known by kindergarteners, whereas cooking terms are not fully learned until after fourth grade). So, it is not that children suddenly acquire the ability to use definitions; they must acquire the words domain by domain. Interestingly, Keil also found that when a domain used the same dimensions to define all of its members (e.g., most meal terms are defined by time of day that the meal is eaten), children acquired all of its terms at about the same age. When domains used different stimulus dimensions to define different members, there was much less consistency. In short, Keil concluded that in order for children to learn the words in a domain of nominal kinds, they must first acquire the theory that underlies the domain. If a single principle explains objects across the domain, then they can learn all the domain's words quite quickly after this.

In short, the study of word learning provides strong evidence that children's concepts underly their word meanings. (In fact, it is hard to imagine how it could be otherwise.) The acquisition of words depends on a correct understanding of the domain, and the errors that children make and the problems they face in early word use seem traceable to inadequacies in their understanding a particular domain rather than to primarily linguistic problems. Although word learning itself can influence the formation of new concepts, without the necessary conceptual basis, children cannot learn the correct word meanings. (See Carey, 1982; Clark, 1983; and Keil, 1989, for much more detailed discussions.)

Conceptual Combination

Finally, I will only mention that research on how concepts are combined to form more complex concepts provides relevant evidence (the chapters by Shoben and Hampton, this volume, give a complete review). In this work, psychologists ask how people combine concepts like *pet* and *fish* to form a new concept *pet fish*. Although this question was first raised by researchers trying to test models of concepts (Osherson & Smith, 1981), the question can also be interpreted as a psycholinguistic question, namely, how people interpret noun phrases like *pet fish, corporate stationery,* or *apple-juice seat*. And as empirical work is beginning to show, theoretical mechanisms from the psychology of concepts are quite relevant to explaining how people understand such phrases (Murphy, 1988; Smith, Osherson, Rips, & Keane, 1988). For example, typicality is again important to explaining how people interpret these phrases, as are more complex conceptual relations (Murphy, 1990).

This review shows that there is a large amount of evidence that language learning, understanding and production are dependent on conceptual relations of various kinds. If there were an entirely self-contained system of semantics in the head, we would have to view this evidence as a very large and inexplicable coincidence: There wouldn't be any reason to expect work on concepts to have any bearing on language use. But if meanings are somehow built out of concepts, then this is exactly the pattern of results that would be expected. Lyons's (1977) claim about the lack of empirical evidence for concepts underlying meaning probably reflects both the relative lack of evidence at the time of his writing and the poor development of a theory of concepts. In fact, he complains of the latter problem in saying "As the term 'concept' is used by many writers on semantics, it is simply not clear what is meant by it; and that is perhaps of itself a sufficient criticism of their use of the term" (p. 113). Now that more is known about conceptual structure and development, the possible connections between concepts and the representation of word meaning can be seen quite clearly.

STARTING TO BUILD A MODEL

What does it mean for a meaning to be built out of concepts? One possibility is that the semantic entry of a word simply points to a concept in the conceptual system. For example, a word like *lamp* may pick out a single concept. This may well be the basic relation, but more complex situations are possible, and a semantic theory should allow for them as well. For example, two different words might point to the same concept (for true synonyms). In my idiolect, *couch* and *sofa* refer to exactly the same things and so would be associated with the same concept. Some words seem to be largely disjunctive, like the baseball term *strike*. Such words may be associated with two or more different concepts (a foul ball, a swing and a miss, and a pitch through the strike zone). It has sometimes been claimed that superordinates like *furniture* or *vehicle* are largely disjunctive, and so are defined by picking out a set of more specific concepts. However, although these categories do contain a wide variety of things that can be quite different from one another (e.g., rugs, lamps and beds are all *furniture*), they are not purely arbitrary collections of objects. Therefore, it seems likely that a word like *furniture* is not simply connected to a list of concepts, but to a rather abstract concept (perhaps functionally defined), which is itself linked to subconcepts. Whether there are purely disjunctive words is still an open empirical question.

Not only may words pick out groups of concepts, they may also pick out parts of concepts or subconcepts. For example, the word *seat* might pick out one subconcept of the concept *chair*. I mention this case for completeness, but if the conceptual system is highly integrated, it may be impossible to distinguish concepts from subconcepts, as every concept may be part of some larger conceptual structure.

In short, it seems likely that there is a wide variety of relations between words and concepts. At this stage of our knowledge, we should remain somewhat neutral about what kinds of mapping between the two are possible. Many of the decisions to make here are empirical matters that cannot be stipulated in advance.

What we can propose at this stage is that word meanings are linked to nodes or subsections of the conceptual system. The relations and characteristics that seem central to our concepts are generally also central to word meanings. Thus, it seems that we may need little additional, specifically linguistic information to represent semantic structure in most domains. However, what is not yet clear is exactly the form of the links between the lexicon and the conceptual system, partly because we do not yet have a complete understanding of either.

It should also be pointed out that some aspects of linguistic meaning may not be conceptual at all. For example, the general phenomenon of connotation is one that is probably not based in the conceptual system. For example, the difference between saying *Fran died* and *Fran passed away* and the difference between the words *horse* and *steed* are probably not that they refer to different kinds of concepts. We understand that dying and passing away are the same kind of event—it is the emotions and social properties of the words that differ. In other cases, such as slang, words may be marked according to what kinds of discourse they are most appropriate for. This also does not seem to be a conceptual matter. Nonetheless, most of word meaning is not connotative, and the conceptual relations can account for much of that meaning.

REMAINING PHILOSOPHICAL PROBLEMS

The empirical data argue quite strongly that word meaning is represented at least in part by concepts. But we now have to address some of the philosophical objections to this endeavor that were raised earlier. First of all, Putnam's arguments show that the meaning of *lemon* or other natural kind terms can't just be a list of (mental) descriptions like "it's yellow, it's sour, you put it on fish," and so on. Putnam showed that none of these features is necessary for something to be a lemon. But, as is well known now, people's concepts aren't made up of necessary features either. People can and do learn ill-defined concepts, and it is widely assumed that most concepts aren't represented by perfect definitions (Smith & Medin, 1981). In short, Putnam's demonstration that meaning can't be collections of defining features doesn't show that meanings can't be constructed from concepts.

A more perplexing problem, however, is Putnam's conclusion that meaning ain't in the head. The example in which it was discovered that some things that we thought were lemons were really oranges suggests that whatever we had in our heads corresponding to the meaning of *lemon* must not have been the whole meaning. If it had been the whole meaning, then no external evidence could have made us change our minds. And the Twin-Earth examples show that two people with the same mental representations may not have the same word meaning.

What Putnam concludes is that for names of natural kinds, there is an *essence* that defines what the name is. That is, there is something about lemons, tigers, gold, and trees that makes them what they are and not something else. This essence is created by nature, and it's something for science to discover rather than something that everyone knows. "The extension of our terms depends on the actual nature of the particular things that serve as paradigms, and this actual nature is not, in general, fully known to the speaker" (Putnam, 1973, p. 711). Therefore, scientists who have a more complete understanding of a natural kind have a more accurate representation of the word meaning.

I think that there are two problems with this picture, one psychological and one philosophical. To start with the psychological problem, there isn't such a clear line between the layperson and the scientist as these examples often suggest. It's not really that people have a simple list of features in their head, and scientists have a complicated, sophisticated hypothesis (i.e., a scientific theory) about the word meaning. I've already suggested that people's concepts are embedded in theories about that domain, and in this respect, people aren't that different from the scientist. Every concept learner needs a theory to predict what features are relevant and what relations are important (Keil, 1989; Murphy & Medin, 1985; Wattenmaker et al., 1986). For example, when children learn about new kinds of animals, they use their incipient knowledge of biology to form hypotheses about what this kind of animal is like (Carey, 1985; Gelman & Markman, 1987). Sometimes our theories aren't very complicated or accurate (as in young children's theories of animacy), but this doesn't mean that they aren't important in influencing concept learning.

For example, imagine that you're learning about a new kind of object. If you discover that this thing writes poetry for a living and that it does photosynthesis, you will probably be confused. It isn't that you can't remember the two facts about this object but that you can't fit these two features together into your preconceptions about how the world normally works (Murphy & Wisniewski, 1989b). Theories about the world help concept learners sort through complex and potentially misleading information, focusing on features that are most likely to be important. Unusual examples like the combination of features above would be flagged as possibly mistaken or requiring further information.

In some sense, then, we're all like the scientists trying to understand exactly what makes something a lemon. Our own understanding of these factors may not be as sophisticated, but our theories of the world are considerably more complex and intertwined than a list of features like "it's yellow, it's sour, you put it on fish," etc. Although laypeople's theories may not be fully correct, the same is true of most scientists' theories. And as more evidence comes in, both change their theories (and meanings) accordingly. In short, if knowing a word meaning is like holding a (scientific) theory, as Putnam's example suggests, then people may have more meaning in their heads than his division of linguistic labor (Putnam, 1973) suggests.

These psychological considerations probably do not carry much weight with Putnam, however, because he would argue that the real meaning is the reality of the stuff (gold, lemons, whatever) in the world. Although scientists and laypeople may have a better or worse understanding of the stuff, that's not what the meaning is. Jerry Fodor (1987) discusses this argument in some detail, and he provides an answer that may be useful to us. Fodor distinguishes between two ways of defining mental content. *Broad content* is what the mental representation actually denotes in the world. This is the content that Putnam specifies as being the meaning of words. So, for me, *gold* refers to gold, and for Twin-me, *gold* refers to XYZ. In terms of broad content, then, my twin and I differ. *Narrow content* is content as defined by my mental representations. For example, the narrow content of the word *gold* in my mental lexicon is that it is valuable, yellow stuff that appears in jewelry, having a certain atomic weight, appearance etc. Here, however, the meaning of *gold* doesn't depend on whether it actually refers to gold (or XYZ), but only on what other representations it is connected to in my head. Note that narrow and broad content are not two separate psychological entities. Rather, they are two different ways of analyzing meaning—broad content looking outside of the person, and narrow content looking inside.

The argument, then, is whether there is any place for narrow content in an analysis of meaning. Putnam assumes that broad content is the real meaning of a word, whereas Fodor questions this assumption. He points out (1987, pp. 33–44) that the broad content of a representation has no effect whatsoever on the behavior of language users. That is, because I and my twin are identical in every respect, if you suddenly switched us so that I was in Twin-Earth and he was in Earth, we would behave and think identically. The fact that when talking about a gold watch I would now be (mistakenly) referring to XYZ and that my twin would be (mistakenly) referring to gold would have no effect whatsoever on our thought and behavior. Thus, although Fodor agrees that there is ultimately a distinction between what I know and what my twin knows, he says that for any *scientific* purpose, we are the same, since we have exactly the same causal powers. That is, we think the same thoughts, understand the same sentences and perform the same actions, even though my thoughts are (it turns out) about gold and my twin's are about XYZ. And by the same reasoning, for any scientific purpose, our mental representations are the same, since they have the same causal effects.

According to Fodor, then, narrow content is the one that is relevant to psychology (and other sciences), and by no coincidence, it is the content that is in the head (though broad content isn't, as Putnam pointed out).[3] What is narrow content, then? It "is a mental state that is semantically evaluable relative to a context [e.g., Earth or Twin-Earth]" (p. 51). For example, the narrow content of my thought that *gold is yellowish* is determined by its connection to my other concepts, including concepts of chemical elements and perceptual qualities. And when my thoughts and I are located in the context of Earth, the thoughts can be tied to actual properties of this world (i.e., the properties that give rise to those thoughts), leading to the evaluation that this particular thought is a true one.

If Fodor's response is correct (and it is by no means universally accepted; see Putnam, 1988), then the psychological study of meaning has an important place in cognitive science. That is, the psycholinguist, by studying the mental representation of word and sentence meaning is finding out some of the causal determinants of thought and behavior. Although this endeavor cannot answer questions about the ultimate meaning (i.e., the broad content) of words like *gold,* these questions are not a part of the enterprise of cognitive science; for psychology, it doesn't matter whether my concepts are in fact caused by gold or by XYZ. As Fodor points out, since behavior and thought can only be caused by states of the world that have some correspondence in the mind (i.e., their narrow content), these considerations need not be a part of cognitive science in general.

Fodor's arguments have a great deal of merit, I believe, but Putnam's claims still have important consequences for our understanding of meaning. I want to conclude, therefore, by discussing in what respects meaning still ain't in the head—keeping to the respects that are of interest to psychology. The first respect comes from something that we might call the *Reality Constraint.* In this respect, meaning ain't in the head, because it's constrained by our desire to have accurate concepts and meanings. We want our meaning of *lemon* to refer to an actual biological kind—not just to objects that happen to share some features. So, if we find that our meanings don't correspond to our best guess about the structure of reality, then we may well change our meanings. Thus, this constraint is not only a philosophical one—it has strong effects on our mental representations. (However, note that it is our perception of reality, and not reality itself, that directly causes these psychological effects.) Since I have been arguing that the mental representation of meaning is built out of concepts, it is important to see that this problem arises for concepts as well as word meanings. A biologist trying to understand a new, unnamed kind of plant would do exactly the same kind of thing as the biologists trying to understand lemon trees, which already have a name in

---

[3]Fodor's main reason for raising this issue is not our reason, but it is one worth noting. If meaning ain't in the head, then there is a real sense in which the mind cannot be embodied by the brain. For example, Twin-me and I have identical brain states (by hypothesis) but express different meanings, according to Putnam. Therefore, meaning cannot be a property of our brains, even though our words and thoughts do possess meanings. Fodor's solution states that my twin and I do share the same mental state (i.e., the narrow content), and is therefore consistent with mind-brain supervenience.

English. So, the fact that meanings are subject to this reality constraint shouldn't make us conclude that meanings can't be represented by concepts, because concepts are also subject to this constraint.

The second respect in which meanings ain't in the head we might call the *Conventionality Constraint* (Clark, 1983). What this means is that as individuals, we want our word meanings to correspond to those of the rest of the community, and so we don't just make up our own meanings. When we're trying to map our words onto concepts, we choose the particular mapping that society as a whole has chosen. I didn't decide to map the word *plumbing* onto my concept of pineapples. Instead, I did the same mapping for *plumbing* that other English speakers have done. So, it was societal behavior that directed the particular mapping I created, not something internal to me.

In these respects, meaning ain't totally in the head. But these don't seem to be particularly troublesome or puzzling kinds of constraints for psychologists. Virtually all human behavior and cognition is constrained by reality in one way or another. That's why cognition is so useful to us. Memory and perception aren't totally in the head either, but that doesn't make us want to deny that we have memories or that we form perceptual representations. Furthermore, the fact that we follow conventions in language doesn't mean that we don't have representations that correspond to those conventions in our minds. In fact, the convention wouldn't even exist unless individuals learned and represented the rule involved. Our minds are the interface between meaning as a conventional system on one hand, and actual language use (which is what the system is there for) on the other hand. So most meanings must be in the head for the language system to work. If meanings are in the head at all, I've argued that they must be built out of concepts. This is fortunate, because it gives us a place to connect up theories of semantics with research on cognition in general.

ACKNOWLEDGMENTS

The writing of this chapter was supported by NIMH grant MH-41704. I am grateful to Terry Au, Lawrence Barsalou, David Bennett, Barbara Malt, Paula Schwanenflugel and Ken Springer for very helpful comments on an earlier draft of this chapter.

REFERENCES

Anglin, J. M. (1977). *Word, object and conceptual development.* New York: Norton.
Armstrong, S. L., Gleitman, L. R., & Gleitman, H. (1983). What some concepts might not be. *Cognition, 13,* 263–308.
Barsalou, L. W. (1983). Ad hoc categories. *Memory & Cognition, 11,* 211–227.

Barsalou, L. W. (1985). Ideals, central tendency, and frequency of instantiation as determinants of graded structure in categories. *Journal of Experimental Psychology: Learning, Memory, and Cognition, 11,* 629–654.

Barsalou, L. W. (1987). The instability of graded structure: Implications for the nature of concepts. In U. Neisser (Ed.), *Concepts and conceptual development: Ecological and intellectual factors in categorization* (pp. 101–140). Cambridge: Cambridge University Press.

Barsalou, L. W. (1989). Intraconcept similarity and its implications for interconcept similarity. In S. Vosniadou & A. Ortony (Eds.), *Similarity and analogical reasoning* (pp. 76–121). Cambridge: Cambridge University Press.

Berlin, B., Breedlove, D. E., & Raven, P. H. (1973). General principles of classification and nomenclature in folk biology. *American Anthropologist, 75,* 214–242.

Biederman, I., Mezzanotte, R. J., & Rabinowitz, J. C. (1982). Scene perception: Detecting and judging objects undergoing relational violations. *Cognitive Psychology, 14,* 143–177.

Cantor, N., & Mischel, W. (1979). Prototypes in person perception. In L. Berkowitz (Ed.), *Advances in experimental social psychology.* New York: Academic Press.

Carey, S. (1982). Semantic development: The state of the art. In E. Wanner & L. R. Gleitman (Eds.), *Language acquisition: The state of the art* (pp. 347–389). Cambridge: Cambridge University Press.

Carey, S. (1985). *Conceptual change in childhood.* Cambridge, MA: MIT Press.

Chomsky, N. (1965). *Aspects of the theory of syntax.* Cambridge, MA: MIT Press.

Chomsky, N. (1986). *Knowledge of language: Its nature, origin and use.* New York: Praeger.

Clark, E. V. (1972). On the child's acquisition of antonyms in two semantic fields. *Journal of Verbal Learning and Verbal Behavior, 11,* 750–758.

Clark, E. V. (1973). What's in a word? On the child's acquisition of semantics in his first language. In T. E. Moore (Ed.), *Cognitive development and the acquisition of language* (pp. 65–110). New York: Academic Press.

Clark, E. V. (1983). Meanings and concepts. In J. H. Flavell & E. M. Markman (Eds.), *Manual of child psychology, Vol. 3: Cognitive development* (pp. 787–840). New York: Wiley.

Clark, H. H., & Clark, E. V. (1977). *Psychology and language.* New York: Harcourt Brace Jovanovich.

Collins, A. M., & Quillian, M. R. (1969). Retrieval time from semantic memory. *Journal of Verbal Learning and Verbal Behavior, 8,* 240–248.

Cohen, B., & Murphy, G. L. (1984). Models of concepts. *Cognitive Science, 8,* 27–60.

Dowty, D. R., Wall, R. E., & Peters, S. (1981). *Introduction to Montague semantics.* Dordrecht: D. Reidel.

Fodor, J. A. (1987). *Psychosemantics: The problem of meaning in the philosophy of mind.* Cambridge, MA: MIT Press.

Fodor, J. A. (1977). *Semantics: Theories of meaning & generative grammar.* New York: Crowell.

Franks, J. J., & Bransford, J. D. (1971). Abstraction of visual patterns. *Journal of Experimental Psychology, 90,* 65–74.

Garrod, S., & Sanford, A. (1977). Interpreting anaphoric relations: The integration of semantic information while reading. *Journal of Verbal Leaning and Verbal Behavior, 16,* 77–90.

Gelman, S. A., & Markman, E. M. (1987). Young children's inductions from natural kinds: The role of categories and appearances. *Child Development, 58,* 1532–1541.

Horton, M. S., & Markman, E. M. (1980). Developmental differences in the acquisition of basic and superordinate categories. *Child Development, 51,* 708–719.

Johnson-Laird, P. N. (1983). *Mental models.* Cambridge, MA: Harvard University Press.

Katz, J. J. (1981). *Language and other abstract objects.* Totowa, NJ: Rowman and Littlefield.

Katz, J. J., & Fodor, J. A. (1963). The structure of a semantic theory. *Language, 39,* 170–210.

Keil, F. C. (1989). *Concepts, kinds, and cognitive development.* Cambridge, MA: MIT Press.

Kelly, M. H., Bock, J. K., & Keil, F. C. (1986). Prototypicality in a linguistic context: Effects on sentence structure. *Journal of Memory and Language, 25,* 59–74.

Lyons, J. (1977). *Semantics* (2 Vols.). Cambridge: Cambridge University Press.

Markman, E. M. (1985). Why superordinate category terms can be mass nouns. *Cognition, 19,* 31–53.

Markman, E. M., & Callanan, M. A. (1984). An analysis of hierarchical classification. In R. Sternberg (Ed.), *Advances in the psychology of human intelligence* (Vol. 2, pp. 345–365). Hillsdale, NJ: Lawrence Erlbaum Associates.

Massaro, D. W., & Cohen, M. M. (1983). Categorical or continuous speech perception: A new test. *Speech Communication, 2,* 15–35.

McCloskey, M. E., & Glucksberg, S. (1979). Decision processes in verifying category membership statements: Implications for models of semantic memory. *Cognitive Psychology, 11,* 1–37.

McKoon, G., Ratcliff, R., & Dell, G. S. (1986). A critical evaluation of the semantic/episodic distinction. *Journal of Experimental Psychology: Learning, Memory, and Cognition, 12,* 295–306.

Mervis, C. B., & Crisafi, M. A. (1982). Order of acquisition of subordinate, basic, and superordinate level categories. *Child Development, 53,* 258–266.

Mervis, C. B., & Rosch, E. (1981). Categorization of natural objects. *Annual Review of Psychology, 32,* 89–115.

Murphy, G. L. (1988). Comprehending complex concepts. *Cognitive Science, 12,* 529–562.

Murphy, G. L. (1990). Noun phrase interpretation and conceptual combination. *Journal of Memory and Language, 29,* 259–288.

Murphy, G. L. (in press). Parts in object concepts: Experiments with artificial categories. *Memory & Cognition.*

Murphy, G. L., & Brownell, H. H. (1985). Category differentiation in object recognition: Typicality constraints on the basic category advantage. *Journal of Experimental Psychology: Learning, Memory, and Cognition, 11,* 70–84.

Murphy, G. L., & Medin, D. L. (1985). The role of theories in conceptual coherence. *Psychological Review, 92,* 289–316.

Murphy, G. L., & Smith, E. E. (1982). Basic-level superiority in picture categorization. *Journal of Verbal Learning and Verbal Behavior, 21,* 1–20.

Murphy, G. L., & Wisniewski, E. J. (1989a). Categorizing objects in isolation and in scenes: What a superordinate is good for. *Journal of Experimental Psychology: Learning, Memory, and Cognition, 15,* 572–586.

Murphy, G. L., & Wisniewski, E. J. (1989b). Feature correlations in conceptual representations. In G. Tiberghien (Ed.), *Advances in cognitive science, Vol. 2* (pp. 23–45). Chichester: Ellis Horwood.

Osherson, D. N., & Smith, E. E. (1981). On the adequacy of prototype theory as a theory of concepts. *Cognition, 9,* 35–58.

Posner, M. I., & Keele, S. W. (1968). On the genesis of abstract ideas. *Journal of Experimental Psychology, 77,* 353–363.

Putnam, H. (1973). Meaning and reference. *Journal of Philosophy, LXX,* 699–711.

Putnam, H. (1975). The meaning of "meaning." In *Mind, language, and reality (Philosophical Papers, Vol. 2)* (pp. 215–271). Cambridge: Cambridge University Press.

Putnam, H. (1988). *Representation and reality.* Cambridge, MA: MIT Press.

Reed, S. K. (1972). Pattern recognition and categorization. *Cognitive Psychology, 3,* 382–407.

Rips, L. J., Shoben, E. J., & Smith, E. E. (1973). Semantic distance and the verification of semantic relations. *Journal of Verbal Learning and Verbal Behavior, 12,* 1–20.

Rosch, E. (1973). On the internal structure of perceptual and semantic categories. In T. E. Moore (Ed.), *Cognitive development and the acquisition of language* (pp. 111–144). New York: Academic Press.

Rosch, E. (1975). Cognitive representations of semantic categories. *Journal of Experimental Psychology: General, 104*, 192–233.

Rosch, E. (1977). Human categorization. In N. Warren (Ed.), *Advances in cross-cultural psychology: Vol. 1* (pp. 177–206). New York: Academic Press.

Rosch, E., & Mervis, C. B. (1975). Family resemblances: Studies in the internal structure of categories. *Cognitive Psychology, 7*, 573–605.

Rosch, E., Mervis, C. B., Gray, W. D., Johnson, D. M., & Boyes-Braem, P. (1976). Basic objects in natural categories. *Cognitive Psychology, 8*, 382–439.

Smith, E. E. (1978). Theories of semantic memory. In W. K. Estes (Ed.), *Handbook of learning and cognitive processes, Vol. 6* (pp. 1–56). Hillsdale, NJ. Lawrence Erlbaum Associates.

Smith, E. E., Balzano, G. J., & Walker, J. (1978). Nominal, perceptual, and semantic codes in picture categorization. In J. W. Cotton & R. L. Klatzky (Eds.), *Semantic factors in cognition* (pp. 137–168). Hillsdale, NJ: Lawrence Erlbaum Associates.

Smith, E. E., & Medin, D. L. (1981). *Categories and concepts*. Cambridge, MA: Harvard University Press.

Smith, E. E., Osherson, D. J., Rips, L. J., & Keane, M. (1988). Combining prototypes: A selective modification model. *Cognitive Science, 12*, 485–528.

Smith, E. E., Shoben, E. J., & Rips, L. J. (1974). Structure and process in semantic memory: A featural model for semantic decisions. *Psychological Review, 81*, 214–241.

Wattenmaker, W. D., Dewey, G. I., Murphy, T. D., & Medin, D. L. (1986). Linear separability and concept learning: Context, relational properties, and concept naturalness. *Cognitive Psychology, 18*, 158–194.

Wisniewski, E. J., & Murphy, G. L. (1989). Superordinate and basic concept names in discourse: A textual analysis. *Discourse Processes, 12*, 245–261.

2 Word Meaning and Word Use

Barbara C. Malt
Lehigh University

INTRODUCTION

Virtually all psychological theories of word meaning, as well as many theories of meaning developed in linguistics and philosophy, have focused on describing the nature of the concepts associated with words. For instance, psychologists have been concerned with issues such as whether the knowledge involved in knowing the meaning of *bird* or *chair* is better described as a set of defining features, a prototype, or representations of individual exemplars (e.g., Smith & Medin, 1981), and whether the knowledge includes information about correlations between features (e.g., Malt & Smith, 1984; Medin, Altom, Edelson, & Freko, 1982), beliefs about missing features (e.g., Malt, 1990; Medin & Ortony, 1989; Smith, Medin, & Rips, 1984), or other types of nonfeatural information (e.g., Murphy & Medin, 1985; Rips, 1989). This emphasis on studying the concepts associated with words, in traditional terminology, constitutes an interest in the *intension,* or semantic component, of word meaning.

In contrast to their interest in intension, psychologists have tended to pay little attention to the *extension* of words, or the set of things in the world to which words refer. Thus, there has been little concern with describing the set of things to which the words *bird* or *chair* are actually applied. Nevertheless, prevailing intensional theories make several important assumptions about the nature of extensions. In this paper, I explore the relation between the intensional approach to word meaning and data about extensions. I argue that more detailed examination of the extensions of words can provide a valuable tool for understanding the intensional aspect of word meaning. I then present some observations about the extensions of words that address current issues about the nature of intension. My arguments focus on the case of common nouns, as much of the debate in the literature, as well as most of the available evidence, concerns these nouns.

Why Would Looking at Extensions be Helpful for Understanding Word Meanings?

Intensional Characterizations of Meaning Make Predictions for Extension

As just noted, most psychological theories of word meaning have focused on the nature of concepts associated with words. At the same time that the goal of these theories is to describe the concept, however, the concept itself is often described as a set of conditions that any object in the world must meet in order to be called by that word. Knowledge of the meaning of the word *bachelor,* for instance, might be described as knowledge of certain properties (such as *unmarried* and *male*) that must be true of any person in the world in order for that person to correctly be called a bachelor (e.g., Katz & Fodor, 1963; see Johnson-Laird, Herrmann, & Chaffin, 1984; Murphy, this volume). Even when concepts are not explicitly described in terms of conditions for appropriate use of the word, they often carry those conditions implicitly. Knowledge of the meaning of the word *cat,* for instance, might be described as knowledge of a set of properties associated with cathood. This knowledge presumably derives from some combination of observation of the properties of actual cats and additional information about the properties of cats (or mammals, animate beings, etc.) that might be acquired indirectly such as through schooling. The knowledge associated with the word *cat,* then, includes a description of the things in the world that the holder of the knowledge would label *cat.* In fact, the connection between a concept described in this manner and a set of entities labelled by the associated word is made explicit in many theories of categorization (which, in the psychological literature, have been closely connected to, and sometimes indistinguishable from, theories of word meaning). In these theories, a person is assumed to decide whether some entity in the world is a cat by performing some comparison of the knowledge in the mental representation with properties of the to-be-classified entity (e.g., McCloskey & Glucksberg, 1979; Smith, Shoben, & Rips, 1974).

Within psychological theories of meaning at least, then, intensional theories make clear predictions for extension. If a theory about the nature of word meaning is correct, it follows that it should be able to correctly predict what things in the world will get called by a given name. One way to test the validity of a theory of meaning is therefore to look at whether it correctly predicts naming. Several recent studies have taken advantage of this assumption in using measures involving naming choice: Keil (1986, 1987, 1989; Keil & Batterman, 1984) and Malt and Johnson (1989, 1990) have constructed descriptions of objects with combinations of properties not normally found in the world, and they have looked at naming choices for these objects (among other measures). The stimuli are designed so that at least two choices of names are possible, and the theory or theories being examined make a prediction about which name will be chosen. These studies have not, however, moved out of the laboratory world into the real world to look at choices of names for existing, familiar objects. If the prevailing theories truly capture mental representations of meaning, they should be able to predict how objects in the real world get named.

Intensional Characterizations of Meaning Make Qualitative Assumptions About the Nature of Extension

The previous observation was a very general one: that since intensional theories have implications for extension, a viable intensional theory should make correct predictions about extension. There are also more specific implications of intensional accounts for the nature of extension. All theories of intension make some assumption about what the function of nouns in a language is, and psychological theories of meaning (as well as most others) generally take the function of nouns to be to label groups of things that are in some way similar to one another. Recent psychological theories, drawing to a large degree on somewhat earlier philosophical writings, have emphasized two specific notions about the similarity captured by nouns. The first is the idea that the primary function of nouns is not to capture relatively superficial similarity based on external, visible properties. Rather, following Quine (1977) and J. S. Mill (1843), the primary function of nouns is taken to be to capture a *deep* similarity that involves many properties not readily visible (e.g., Carey, 1985; Gelman & Markman, 1986, 1987; Keil, 1989; Markman, 1989). For instance, although most mammals may have certain similarities in appearance, these shared superficial properties are not the primary reason they are treated as similar and called by the same name. Instead, they are grouped together because they share many important unseen properties such as type of body organs and method of reproduction (Quine, 1977). Thus an animal that may be superficially dissimilar to other members of the group (such as a whale) will still be called a mammal if it shares the more important unseen properties.

The second, and closely associated, idea is that of "psychological essentialism" (Medin, 1989; Medin & Ortony, 1989; see also Malt, 1990), derived in part from Putnam's (1973, 1975) philosophical analysis of the nature of word meaning. According to this idea, people hold a belief in the existence of some unifying *essence* among sets of entities in the world (whether or not one really exists). This belief has been hypothesized to play a critical role in what sets of entities are seen to be meaningful groups and thus to form a category. Categories are coherent to the extent that people can construct an explanation of their superficial similarity based on some underlying *essential* commonality (Medin, 1989; Medin & Ortony, 1989). Thus nouns, as labels for categories, should capture similarity that the average language user perceives (even if incorrectly) as due to the presence of a common essence among members.

The observations from philosophy have become part of intensional approaches to meaning in that they have influenced thinking about the nature of the concepts, as just described: Concepts are taken to fundamentally involve knowledge of deep similarity and beliefs in the existence of essences, rather than only knowledge of the relatively superficial properties on which earlier theories focused. However, while the philosophical observations have come into psychology in primarily intensional terms, the original observations were most directly ideas about extension: that nouns group together things based on deep similarity rather than on superficial similarity, and that nouns capture similarity perceived by the language user as deriving from some essence common to the category members. Thus the two psychological assumptions about the nature of the similarity involved in intensions are actually derived from two proposals about the nature of the associated extensions.

Is the idea that nouns function as suggested correct? The evidence for the proposals come primarily from discussion of a relatively small set of *natural kind* terms, and the nature of the similarity among the entities labelled by such terms has tended to be taken for granted rather than critically examined. It seems that the only way to fully and accurately assess the function of nouns in a language is to look at what sorts of entities get called by a given noun label; that is, to look at the extension of a noun. If nouns do not seem to function to group together entities in this way, or if different nouns or groups of nouns seem to capture different sorts of similarity, then theories of meaning would need to take this fact into account.

Data on Extensions May Bring to Light Facts About Meaning that Other Paradigms Do Not

If intensional theories of meaning make predictions about extension, as I have just argued, then examining extensions provides one source of data that can help confirm or disconfirm intensional theories. However, data on extensions may not be simply one more source of information to add to all the others. Data on extensions differ from other sorts of data in at least two important ways. These differences may lead them to make contributions that other kinds of data cannot.

One way in which data on extensions differ from many other sorts of data is that the exemplars of the words being studied are not chosen by the researcher. In studies involving definitions, property listings, typicality ratings, or verification times, the researcher must choose the set of exemplars (e.g., the set of members of the category *fruit*) to be tested. In studies looking at choice of labels for an object, the researcher must select or invent the entities to be labeled, and he or she typically also selects the options available as labels. In making these choices, the researcher may unintentionally overlook potential exemplars or labels that could influence the conclusions drawn from the study. For example, in property listing studies, typicality rating studies, etc., the exemplars are usually selected from norms giving all the exemplars a group of subjects generated to a category label during a fixed period of time. Even when researchers select less frequently generated exemplars, it is not clear that they have obtained the full range of entities that are normally labeled by the category name. The subjects who generate the exemplars must retrieve them from memory in some way, and the sorts of retrieval strategies they use may cause some exemplars to be generated and others not. For a word such as *can,* for instance, subjects may try to think of all the different metal containers that they call cans. In doing so, they may generate some unusual examples such as rectangular sardine cans. At the same time, though, this strategy may cause them to fail to generate other unusual examples, such as cardboard or plastic frozen orange juice cans. These exemplars then would not appear among the stimuli for the typicality ratings, property lists, etc., and information about them would not be part of the data collected. If people normally call frozen orange juice containers *can,* though, then any complete theory of word meaning would need to take data from these examples into account.

A researcher who wants to study the extension of a word will, of course, employ some strategy or strategies in trying to determine the extension of the word. In doing so, he or she may also miss some exemplars of a category. However, by having an explicit goal of obtaining as complete a sample as possible, and by using other search strategies in addition to retrieval from memory, aspects of the extension may be uncovered that would not ordinarily be noted. In uncovering these aspects, researchers may be forced to consider facts or hypotheses about the nature of the word meaning that otherwise would not have been brought to light.

A second way that data on extensions differ from many other sorts of data is their relative independence from subjects' ability to access knowledge about word meaning. Many current paradigms for studying intension rely at least in part on verbal reports from subjects about the content of their concepts or their reasons for choosing one name over another to label some object. Some researchers have directly asked for property lists or definitions of words (e.g., Ashcraft, 1976; Barr & Caplan, 1987; Malt & Smith, 1984; McNamara & Sternberg, 1983; Rosch & Mervis, 1975). Others have constructed descriptions of objects that include combinations of properties not normally found in the world, and they have looked at naming choices and/or the beliefs about meaning subjects express when asked to decide whether the objects should be called by a given label (Keil, 1986, 1989; Keil & Batterman, 1984; Malt & Johnson, 1989, 1990; Rips, 1989). The subject reports in the latter case are clearly the product of introspection into their judgment processes. The category judgments, while not requiring a verbal report of the process, are still the product of a conscious evaluation of two alternative names for an object.

At the same time that these methods are widely used, most researchers would agree that people do not necessarily have complete conscious access to their representations of meaning. For example, it is clear simply from anecdotal evidence that people have a hard time trying to define words like *truth* or *justice,* even though they may feel that they do know what the words mean. We also know from research into other aspects of language that it is possible for people to be quite unaware of the representations that underlie various language abilities. For instance, people have little conscious knowledge of either the syntax or the phonology of their native language. To return to the example of the frozen orange juice can, most people would agree that that container is something that they normally apply the label *can* to. However, if simply asked for a definition of what a can is, they most likely would not produce a definition compatible with a cardboard orange juice container, and if asked to justify their label for the container, they may have little or no insight into why they find that label acceptable. Thus there may be important aspects of meaning that cannot be studied through methods that involve direct inquiries about meaning.

One route to investigating these aspects of meaning is through studying extensions. By observing the extensions of words, cases such as the orange juice can may come to the researcher's attention. The researcher will then seek an explanation for a phenomenon that the naive language user cannot explain. To some extent, the explanation that the researcher constructs for these cases may involve the researcher's intuitions, and in that sense the analysis of extension data is not free of introspection either. However, the researcher also has available sources of information that are not available to subjects who are asked about meaning in experimental contexts. This information may include historical trends in the use of a word, observations of a pattern of use for a single word across many exemplars, and observations of patterns of use for words other than the one in question. The strategy is similar to that used in analyzing syntax or phonology, where the researcher studies a large body of observations about language use to shed light on phenomena that the naive language user produces but cannot fully explain. If what has proven true in the domains of syntax and phonology is equally true for semantics, important aspects of meaning may be brought to light that would not surface in paradigms drawing on more conscious access to knowledge about meaning.

Summary and Plan

In sum, there are at least three potential benefits to examining extensions as part of an effort to understand intension:

1. All theories of intension make predictions about extension; therefore, data on extensions can help confirm or disconfirm these theories.

2. Current theories of intension make certain specific assumptions about the function of nouns in a language; data on extensions constitute a primary source of information about the validity of these assumptions.

3. Data on extensions may provide examples of word use that are not easily retrieved from memory, and they may provide information about aspects of meaning that are not easily verbalized.

In the remainder of this paper I make some observations about the nature of extensions and try to draw some suggestions from them about the nature of intensions. I begin with comments on the available evidence about noun extensions and how it relates to current thinking about intensions. Then, I present some additional evidence about the nature of extensions that I have recently collected. From these observations I argue that certain modifications to prevailing theories may be needed. Finally, I comment about the broader implications of these observations for the study of intension.

The following discussion focuses primarily on data about the sorts of similarity that form the basis for grouping entities under a common label. I will therefore most directly be addressing the issue raised in my second point above. In doing this, though, I make use of the more general fact that intensional theories make predictions about extension (the first point). A major goal of the discussion will be to suggest that the extensional data reveal some important facts about intension that other methods may not bring to light (the third point).

SOME OBSERVATIONS ABOUT THE FUNCTIONS
OF NOUNS

What does the available evidence on extension suggest about the function of nouns in a language? As noted earlier, the idea that the primary function of nouns is to capture relatively superficial appearance-based similarity no longer plays a major role in theories of meaning. In its place is the idea that nouns (especially those used in referring to the natural world) group together entities that have a *deep* resemblance and that people may believe share some common underlying essence responsible for this deep resemblance. Although the two halves of this proposal are closely linked in the literature, it is possible to ask two separate questions in examining the extension of nouns. First, what sorts of resemblances do nouns get used to capture? Second, do people believe there is an essence shared by the set of things that the nouns name, even if in fact there is not? The first question cannot be answered by posing any sort of question to the language user. It is simply a question about what sorts of entities a noun has come to group together, through any combination of the conscious or nonconscious forces that may shape the way a noun is used in a language. The second, in contrast, must be answered by looking at the beliefs of the language user. Although extensional data therefore will not directly answer the question, knowing the right way to frame the question may depend on having a clear idea of what the extension of a noun consists of, as I argue below.

What Sorts of Resemblances Underlie Noun Use?

The basic idea of deep resemblance in psychological discussions is rather broad: It says simply that there will be a similarity among the entities called by the same name beyond the obvious properties involved in appearance, and that this similarity is more central to grouping the entities together than the superficial commonalities (e.g., Carey, 1985; Gelman & Markman, 1986, 1987; Keil, 1989; Markman, 1989). In discussions of specific cases of nouns, though, several particular interpretations about the nature of the deep similarity have been prevalent. For entities in the natural world, properties beyond appearance that have often been suggested as deep are genetic structure, atomic structure, internal structure for animals (e.g., organs and bones), and patterns of behavior or ecology (Carey, 1985; Keil, 1989; Medin, 1989; Rips, 1989; Wellman & Gelman, 1988). For nouns referring to sets of manufactured objects, an object's function has been offered as the deep property that may underlie groupings of objects with diverse appearances (e.g., Keil, 1986; Rips, 1989). In discussing what kinds of similarities form the basis for noun use, I consider whether these specific suggestions about deep resemblance fully reflect the observations.

The Deepest Deep Resemblance: Microstructure

One version of a deep resemblance that nouns might capture is set forth in Putnam's (1973, 1975) philosophical analysis of word meaning. Putnam argued that nouns function to label sets of entities that share a common underlying microstructure, such as genetic structure for animals or atomic structure for elements. Putnam did not actually propose that all current uses of a noun would perfectly reflect the underlying microstructure, since people (even scientists) trying to capture a common microstructure with their label might not fully know the microstructure. For the time being, though, I am concerned mainly with describing the kind of similarity that nouns do capture; whether or not people believe they capture a common essence is the second half of the question.

The available evidence indicates that nouns often do not function primarily to capture a common microstructure, even to the extent that current knowledge might allow. Putnam illustrated his arguments using terms for species (*tiger*) and for common elements (*gold*) and substances (*water*). A number of authors have pointed out substantial deviation from Putnam's hypothesis for these sorts of terms. For instance, species terms as currently used by biologists under one dominant model do not designate sets of animals that share a single common genetic structure. Instead, they refer to a protected gene pool, and members at extremes of the gene pool may have very different genetic endowments. The goal of designating some population by a particular species name is not to identify organisms that share a particular common structure, but rather that have a particular reproductive relationship to other populations (Mayr, 1984b; see also Lakoff, 1987). Factors other than reproductive relationships may also influence species cuts. For instance, domestic dogs can breed with both coyotes (Burt & Grossenheider, 1976) and timber wolves (Shiffer, 1987); the distinctions that are drawn are based in part on domesticity. Among birds, finer distinctions are made among the songbirds than among other birds for the sake of convenience, due to the sheer number of distinguishable songbirds (van Tyne & Berger, 1959, quoted in Boster, Berlin, & O'Neill, 1986; see also Mayr, 1984a). To the extent that the nonscientist follows the scientists in application of a species term, ordinary use of species terms like *cardinal* or *dog* will likewise not capture any single underlying microstructure. To the extent that the nonscientist may collapse similar biological species and consider them all one species (as people do with *beetle* [Dupre, 1981], or with *sparrow*), ordinary use will encompass an even greater diversity of microstructure. In sum, it seems that species terms do not necessarily label groups that share a common microstructure.

As for basic elements such as gold or copper, scientists may accept variations in atomic structure (such as isotopes) as instances of the same element as long as the variants share enough other properties with the more common form (Achinstein, 1968). Use of terms for common substances such as water show similar phenomena; scientists call some variations on H_2O (such as heavy water) a type of water (Zemach, 1976). The nonscientific use of *water* likewise does not seem to be well described simply by the presence of H_2O; the extension of *water* in everyday use will be discussed in detail later. Again, these terms do not seem to capture a single microstructure, but also to capture variations that may have certain functional properties in common. (See also Keil, 1989, ch. 3, and Lakoff, 1987, for further discussion of this issue.)

These observations suggest two main points about common microstructure as the potential basis of species term use. First, even for the terms that are the best bets to capture a common microstructure, microstructure does not seem to account for many of the observations. A number of other types of resemblances seem to be important in determining what entities get grouped together and called by a common name, including breeding relationships and relatively observable properties such as domesticity. Other factors, such as convenience, may also play a role. Second, for any one noun, there may be no single type of resemblance that explains the set of entities labeled by the noun; several factors (such as the three just mentioned for species cuts) may be important for a single noun.

Medium Deep Resemblance: Other Unseen Physical Properties

If microstructure is not a viable deep resemblance for many nouns, do many nouns capture some more general unseen physical commonalities, such as internal parts or structures above the level of microstructure (e.g., Carey, 1985;

Gelman & Markman, 1986, 1987; Keil, 1989; Markman, 1989; Quine, 1977)? Again, the best place to look for such resemblances is in nouns that refer to the natural world, since it is for these that the suggestion of deep resemblance has most often been made. Some animal terms and element terms may be based to a large extent on this sort of similarity. For instance, as already mentioned, mammals will share critical unseen properties such as the nature of reproductive anatomy with one another, and other contrasting class terms such as *reptile* and *amphibian* likewise are based on structural similarities (Conant, 1975). Similarly, instances of gold may share many properties such as melting point and softness (e.g., Putnam, 1975).

At the same time, though, there are many striking cases where nouns labeling parts of the natural world do not seem to group together a set of entities that share this sort of structural similarity with one another. *Tree*, for instance, is applied to a biologically diverse set of plants some of which have their closest relatives in species that get called bushes or cacti (Dupre, 1981; Keil, 1989). *Fish* is applied to a set of cold-blooded swimming animals that encompass great diversity in taxonomic status (Encyclopaedia Britannica, 1980a).

Many of the most frequent labels for parts of our natural world, in fact, are similar to the fish and tree groupings in the physical diversity of the things they group together. *Flower, grass, vine, bush, herb,* and *weed* all refer to groups of biologically diverse plants that have certain commonalities in size, shape, taste, prominence of blossom, or other characteristics readily available to sensory detection (Dupre, 1981; Hunn, 1985; Randall & Hunn, 1984; Wierzbicka, 1985). *Vegetable* includes entities (such as tomatoes, zucchini, and cucumbers) that are botanically fruits; others (such as potatoes and carrots) that are botanically tubers or roots; still others (such as peas) that are seeds; and others (such as lettuce and spinach) are leaves. The plants they happen to come from do not form any particular portion of a taxonomy (Encyclopaedia Britannica, 1980b). The greatest commonality they seem to share is in their role in the human diet. *Fruit,* although having a botanical use that describes a particular seedbearing organ, is used in everyday language to pick out only a subset of its botanical group: Some botanical fruits, such as tomatoes, zucchini, and cucumber, get called vegetables, while others, such as almonds, get called nuts (Random House, 1967). Many of the unseen physical properties shared by fruits are therefore also shared by entities with other names. The shared properties specific to the entities that get called *fruit* will be relatively superficial ones such as size and sweetness. It seems, then, that a substantial set of nouns referring to the natural world are based on similarity that only partially involves internal structure.

A variety of other common terms that label naturally occurring phenomena or substances of various sorts also seem to be based primarily on resemblances other than unseen physical commonalities. Disease terms such as jaundice (Goosens, 1977) and hepatitis ("Hepatitis," 1990) label a common set of symptoms that may arise from a variety of different underlying agents and that would be treated differently depending on the cause. A number of terms for common substances such as air, glass, oil, and dirt (Zemach, 1976) are applied to things with certain common superficial characteristics (such as color and texture) but varying composition.

In sum, even when looking for unseen physical properties at a grosser level than microstructure, it seems that often there is no such set of properties that forms the basis for inclusion in a category. Instead, a wide range of different types of resemblance seem to be important in determining what entities get grouped together and called by a common name. These resemblances include function with respect to humans (for fruits and vegetables) and properties such as height (for trees) and texture (for oil) that are relatively easily observed. Furthermore, as before, it seems that for any one noun, there may be no single type of resemblance that causes the entities to be grouped together; several different factors (such as both behavior and appearance for fish) may be important for a single noun.

Resemblance Outside the Natural World

As already noted, the possibility of deep resemblance has been suggested mainly for words referring to parts of the natural world. At the same time, though, nouns that do not refer to the natural world are clearly an important part of the vocabulary of urban Americans. The types of similarity that form the basis for groupings in these domains must be considered in a complete explanation of intension.

Many authors have suggested that for nouns referring to manufactured articles, function is an important factor in groupings (e.g., Malt & Johnson, 1989, 1990; Keil, 1986, 1987, 1989; Rips, 1989; Wellman & Gelman, 1988). *Toy,* for instance, labels objects with diverse internal structures (dolls of cloth, balls of rubber and plastic, playdough, clay, metal jacks and trucks, etc.) that are generally used by children for play. At the same time, though, function may not be the only factor involved even for artifacts. Kempton (1981) found shape as well as function important in determining extensions of two Spanish terms for food containers, and Labov (1973) similarly found shape relevant in naming choices for *cup* vs. *bowl* and *cup* vs. *vase.* Wierzbicka (1985) provides examples of old-fashioned cars and bicycles for which overlap in both function and appearance with their modern counterparts seems relevant to the shared name.

Although they generally have not been considered in depth, groupings other than artifact categories seem to be based on a variety of resemblances including ones endowed on the entities by human culture. For example, although a person can be a member of a religious group such as Jewish by virtue of parentage, a person can also convert, and the decision about what sort of conversions *count* is a matter of societal decree (e.g., "Shamir," 1988). Similarly, words for social positions such as *king, queen,* or *lord* seem to be based in large part on privileges or duties assigned by society. While part of being a king or queen may depend on having the right geneology or marriage, if the monarch chooses to step down, or the culture in which he or she lives abolishes the monarchy, then that person is no longer king or queen (e.g., Encyclopaedia Britannica, 1980c; Hayden, 1987; see also Keil, 1989).

In sum, these examples illustrate that a variety of similarity relations may underlie noun use in domains outside of the natural world, and many of the similarity relations are not dependent on unseen structural properties of the entities. Commonalities endowed upon entities by a culture, such as function or social privileges, may play a large role in these groupings. It also seems once again that more than one factor may be critical for a single noun, with, for example, both function and appearance, or birthright and social decree, relevant for a given noun. A general theory of intension must be able to accommodate the kinds of resemblances that these words capture, as well as resemblances of other sorts.

These observations, together with those in the preceding two sections, suggest that an interpretation of deep resemblance based primarily on hidden physical structure does not provide a full picture of the resemblances that underlie noun use, even for within the domain of the natural world. Properties such as appearance and function to humans may, in fact, be among the types of resemblances that form the basis for grouping entities together even in that domain. For nouns labeling parts of the world made by humans, a variety of additional dimensions may become important as well. In all the cases, it seems that more than one dimension of resemblance may be critical for a single noun.

Do People Believe that Nouns Capture a Common Essence, Even if the Extensions Do Not Show that They Do?

If nouns (or at least, many common ones) do not actually label sets of entities united by a common microstructure or other sort of unseen physical structure, do they label sets of entities that the average language user *believes* share a common essence? As noted earlier, a number of researchers (Keil, 1987, 1989; Malt, 1990; Medin, 1989; Medin & Ortony, 1989) have suggested that even though the things called by the category name may not share any common microstructure or other unseen physical properties, people may believe in the existence of this sort of commonality.

Psychological essentialism has been asserted primarily on the basis of subjects' verbal reports of reasons for classification decisions (Keil, 1987, 1989); subjects' judgments of sentence acceptability implying the existence of essences (Malt, 1990); logical arguments about the information that might be contained in concepts (Medin & Ortony, 1989); and intuitions about how people might choose to name an entity if they found out that it did not share the underlying trait of other things called by the same name (Putnam, 1973, 1975). Although examining existing data on extensions cannot directly tell us to what extent psychological essentialism is an important part of intension, it can provide some clues about the potential role of psychological essentialism that previous methods may not have revealed. In particular, cases such as the ones noted above, where nouns label a structurally diverse set of entities, suggest some limitations on the role of psychological essentialism.

One source of evidence about the role of psychological essentialism comes from cases of nouns used in labeling the natural world. For words like Putnam's examples of *tiger* and *gold*, and for many others such as *fish, tree, fruit,* and *vegetable,* anecdotal evidence suggests that average language users without any specialized knowledge of these categories do believe there is some sort of common underlying structure that makes all the things called by the name correctly labeled as they are. Furthermore, anecdotal evidence also supports the idea that, as Putnam suggested, people will exclude an entity from category membership if they learn that it differs in underlying structure from superficially similar category members. For instance, some people are aware that botanically, a tomato is a fruit, and they therefore believe that it should not really be called a vegetable. Similarly, many people occasionally call whales ·or dolphins fish, but when reminded that these animals bear live young and breathe above water, they agree that they should be excluded from the category (Quine, 1977). At one level, then, it does seem that psychological essentialism is an important part of the way that words get used to label entities in the world.

At the same time, however, the fact that people tend to act in this way under the described circumstances may not provide the whole picture of the relation of the belief to patterns of word use. These standard examples do not ask what people would do if they became aware that the entire category has no potential unifying structure. One such real case is that of vegetable: excluding tomatoes from *vegetable* does not make *vegetable* a biologically coherent category. As described earlier, many vegetables besides tomatoes are botanically fruits, while others are a variety of other plant parts, and the plants they come from do not form any particular portion of a biological taxonomy. Would knowing this fact lead people to feel that *vegetable* does not refer to a *real* category, and that its extension is not an appropriate use of a noun? It seems unlikely that they would. Rather, it seems that people would probably continue to use to the label *vegetable* as they always had, with some adjustment in their understanding of the nature of the category. Similarly, recognition of the genetic and structural diversity of *tree* or *fish* probably would not lead people to discard these categories, but rather to discard their naive essentialist belief about the category basis. As Gould (1983) observes in the real case of primate genetics, recognizing the lack of genetic basis for the distinction between apes and humans does not mean the categories will disappear. We will still think of apes as a group separate from humans no matter what we recognize the taxonomic relationship to be. These examples suggest that psychological essentialism is a belief people tend carry around with them about the nature of word meanings, yet it is not an unalterable belief, and it can be replaced by other beliefs without necessarily changing the sets of things that get grouped together and called by a common name.

A parallel source of evidence about the role of psychological essentialism in intension comes from examining essentialism with respect to words that do not label parts of the natural world. Although Putnam and others (e.g., Keil, 1987, 1989; Medin, 1989; Medin & Ortony, 1989) have sometimes spoken of the belief in an essence as a belief in a common microstructure or other unseen physical structure as discussed earlier, a somewhat different belief may apply in other domains. For domains such as manufactured articles, the belief may be in some more easily known commonalities such as form or function (Keil, 1989; Medin, 1989; Medin & Smith, 1984). For instance, people may believe there is some commonality in form or function among all vehicles, even if they cannot easily specify what that commonality is. Anecdotal evidence again supports this idea: Anyone who has presented Wittgenstein's analysis of the family resemblance structure of *game* to an audience knows that there can be considerable resistance to the idea that there are no defining features for use of the word *game*.

At the same time that people profess the belief, however, it seems that, as with terms for the natural world, a change in that belief will not necessarily lead to a change in the way a word is applied. After considering the standard extension of *game* and becoming convinced that there is no set of necessary and sufficient features that determine it, the audience does not propose that some exemplars should be excluded from category membership in order to create defining features. Instead, people adjust their understanding of the nature of the category. In other words, a belief in necessary and sufficient features may be given up without an accompanying preference to change the way the word is used, parallel to the case of words referring to the natural world. This observation again suggests that the beliefs people have about the nature of the resemblances may not be the primary determinant of the categories they maintain.

Summary and Conclusions from the Existing Evidence

In sum, it seems clear that many nouns do capture similarity other than that based on purely superficial characteristics. It also seems clear that people do tend to believe in the existence of some unifying underlying property among members of a category. At the same time, though, it appears that many nouns, even among those labeling parts of the natural world, may not be based primarily on resemblances of the sort most often suggested in discussions of deep similarity. Instead, they seem to involve similarities of varying sorts, including dimensions of appearance and function in human culture. In many cases, in fact, resemblances along more than one dimension may be critical for a single noun. These observations raise the question of exactly what deep resemblance consists of, and it highlights the need to better understand the sorts of resemblances that underlie calling a group of entities by a common name. Furthermore, even though people may believe in the existence of some commonality among members of a category, it is not clear that this belief is actually required in order for them to perceive the category as a useful or coherent one. It seems that at least in some cases, people may change their belief without other major consequences to their concept. This observation, like the first two, suggests that we do not yet fully understand the factors determining which entities are grouped together and given a common name.

One important question these suggestions raise is how to reconcile the possible flexibility of a belief in essence with the observations about the nature of the similarity that nouns may capture. If the belief people have about category membership is that it is determined by an underlying essence, but yet this belief is not critical to willingness to call a group of entities by a common label, then how would groupings be formed? In fact, the forces that cause a particular grouping of entities to be given a common label may be quite separate from the metalinguistic beliefs that the speaker of a language holds about how nouns in his or her language work. Over time, people may have found it useful to label a group of things *vegetable* if those things had some similarity in the kind of nutrients they provide and/or the ways they are prepared for consumption. Likewise, people may have found it useful to label a group of things *tree* if those things had similarity in their outward appearance and the ways people made use of them. These same sorts of principles of grouping may operate any time someone encounters a new entity to be named. However, language users may have little or no insight into the processes that either historically caused a group of things to be called by a common name or that they themselves would use in labeling a new entity. Language users (at least in Western cultures)—influenced by many factors such as limited exposure to biological classification, dictionary definitions that tend to oversimplify, and a general information-processing strategy that seeks cognitive economy—may develop a metalinguistic belief that nouns label groups of things that have a common underlying essence. This belief may be held relatively indiscriminately about all nouns, in the absence of any clear contradictory information. If, however, a person happens to encounter evidence or arguments to the contrary, he or she may modify that belief without any disturbance to the set of things he or she is willing to call by the noun.

The analogy to syntax and phonology that I drew earlier may again be helpful. The syntax and phonology of a language are shaped by many forces that are not apparent to speakers of a language. The speakers have knowledge that allows them to utter sentences following the rules of the syntax and phonology, but they do not have introspective access to what that knowledge is. At the same time, though, they may have developed some naive metalinguistic beliefs about how grammar or phonology works. Those beliefs can be dislodged by information to the contrary (as one might encounter by taking a linguistics course) without in any way changing the way the speakers speak their language. If a similar separation exists between metalinguistic beliefs about word meaning and other aspects of semantic representation, then it will be especially important to develop ways of tapping into knowledge that is not easily verbalized.

The observations from the literature, and the above comments, are framed in terms of their relationship to the deep resemblance idea and the notion of psychological essentialism, since these concepts have been central in recent theories of meaning. The primary purpose of the discussion is not, however, to criticize those general approaches to theories of intension. The purpose, instead, is to suggest that since psychological theories of meaning have centrally involved claims about what sort of resemblances nouns capture, it is important to consider exactly what sort of resemblances nouns do capture. It seems that we do not yet have a complete picture of the nature of the similarity that forms the basis for noun use. We need more exploration of the sorts of similarity relations that exist among the entities called by a given name.

SOME NEW DATA ON THE EXTENSIONS
OF COMMON ENGLISH NOUNS

I have recently collected some data on the extensions of various common English nouns. These observations are aimed at providing a basis for considering the kinds of similarity that nouns may capture, and hence for informing theories of intension.

Method

The data come from two sources. The first is observations of noun use collected from everyday conversations, newspapers, and other ordinary, spontaneous discourse. The second is examples elicited from subjects under instructions designed to tap into the range of entities a given noun normally refers to, rather than only the most typical or easily accessible examples. These primary data are supplemented by an important secondary type of data: examples of entities that are very similar in some way to entities called by a noun, but that are not themselves called by the same word. The data on nonexamples are critical for constraining hypotheses about why certain examples are included in the extension of a noun. For instance, a hypothesis that things get called *jacket* if they are worn on the upper body for warmth in chilly weather is immediately falsified by the observation that there are other things that have that property yet are called by other names (such as *sweater* and *sweatshirt*).

The observations from everyday language were simply collected as they were noticed. The laboratory data were collected in two separate exercises. In the first, subjects were asked to generate examples of things called by a given word by imagining that they were playing a word game. The goal of the game was to guess the same example of the target word that their opponent was thinking of. Subjects were told that the trick to the game was that their opponent was not thinking of the most ordinary, easy-to-generate examples. To win the game, therefore, they would have to try to think of as many different examples as possible of things normally called by the target word. They were given the example that, for instance, if the word were *door* they might think of not only a house door or the door to a room, but also a toaster oven door, a car door, and a garage door. Subjects saw one target word at the top of each piece of paper and simply listed the examples they guessed on the paper below it.

The second experiment was designed to elicit nonexamples for the target words. Subjects were again asked to imagine that they were playing a word game. This time, though, they were told that their opponent was going to give them the name of something similar to, but not the same as, the object s/he had in mind. Their goal was to guess the thing their opponent was thinking of. The trick, then, was to think of things that would be similar to examples of the target word, but that would be called by different names. They were given the example that, for instance, if the word their opponent gave them was *desk,* they might think of a kitchen counter, a computer table, a drafting table, or a vanity. Again, subjects saw a target word at the top of a piece of paper and simply recorded their guesses for the word on the paper below it.

The Data: Examples and Nonexamples

Table 2.1 lists some of the data collected for eight common English words through the combination of methods just described. In all cases, the examples are limited to entities that can be called by the noun alone, without any obligatory modifier or other portion of a noun phrase. Thus *ice cream sandwich* and *sandwich cookie* are not included under *sandwich,* since they are not normally called simply a *sandwich.* On the other hand, *baby's bottle* is included under *bottle,* since in normal conversation it would often simply be called a *bottle.* The examples are also all ones that do not require any particular context in order to be called by the noun; the given noun would be used as the primary label for the object in a wide range of contexts. Finally, I have avoided words for which many of the uses seem to have a primarily metaphorical relationship to the most central use of the word. (For example, I have not included *leg,* for which *leg of a race* and *leg of a table* may be metaphorically related to a human leg, or *key,* for which *answer key* and *typewriter key* may metaphorically unlock some information or action.) For discussion of metaphorical cases such as these, see, e.g., Caramazza and Grober (1976) on *line* and Green (1989) on *run.*

BOTTLE:

milk bottle
coke bottle
beer bottle
orange juice bottle
bottle of Scotch
wine, champagne bottle
ink bottle
soda bottle
baby's bottle - glass kind
baby's bottle - plastic in shape of traditional
          glass kind
baby's bottle - open cylinder with disposable plastic
          liner
bleach bottle
detergent bottle
bottle of baby powder
shampoo bottle
hamster's water bottle
hot water bottle

notes:

container

to drink out of

corked
container
plastic

has handle

squarish; shaker top

to drink out of
flat, rectangular; itself used, not just as
container

not BOTTLE:

canteen
flask
vase
keg
decanter
milk carton
salt shaker
thermos
jug
beaker
carafe

CAN:

tin can
paint can
oil can
old-fashioned milk cans
soft drink can
frozen orange juice can
cat food can
tuna can
Wood Preen can

garbage can
cheese whiz can
wd-40 can
air freshener, other sprays

notes:

large size has handle
spout
graduated top
aluminum; top only partially open
cardboard with plastic tape around rim
flat, aluminum
flat, tin
floor wax; rectangular shape with screw-on top;
metal

nozzle
spray

not CAN:

all the bottle examples
carton
cannister
tupperware container

includes round ice cream carton
metal or plastic

TABLE 2.1 (*Continued*)

JUICE: notes:

orange juice
apple juice
cranapple juice   blend
apricot juice   thick
carrot juice
vegetable juice   blend, thick; from vegetables
V-8 juice   from vegetables; spices
roast beef juice, steak juice   from meats
chicken juice   from meat
Hi-C   fruit, water, corn syrup, flavoring
bug juice   no fruit; sweeteners and flavorings

not JUICE:

cider
lemonade
water
milk
wine   extracted from grapes but fermented; used
                                                differently
other alcoholic beverages
oil   extracted from plant tissues too; different use
gravy   juices mixed with flour, etc.
vinegar
tree sap   extracted from plant tissue
maple syrup

MILK:

goat milk
human milk
cow's milk
whole milk
low-fat milk
skim milk
chocolate milk
lactose-free milk
soy milk
whale milk

not MILK:

baby's formula
light cream
heavy cream
non-dairy creamer

SANDWICH: notes:

tuna sandwich, etc.   filling between two slices of bread
bagel sandwich
club sandwich   uses roll sliced in half
English muffin sandwich
open-faced sandwich   one slice of bread; no top
pita sandwich   inserted in pocket
triple decker sandwich   3 slices of bread

TABLE 2.1 (*Continued*)

not SANDWICH:

gyro
hamberger, cheeseburger
hotdog
calzone
stromboli
burrito
enchilada

SEED: notes:

apple seeds   inside thing people eat
bird seed   sunflower, etc.; nonedible to humans
cantaloupe seed
cucumber seed
flower seeds   from decorative plant; for planting
grapefruit seeds
grass seed   from nonedible; for planting
lemon seed
poppy seed   eaten on things
sesame seed   eaten on things

not SEED:

avocado pit   nonedible; large
prune pit, etc.
walnut, acorn, nuts in general
kernels of corn   clusters; main edible part
peas
beans
flower bulb

TEA: notes:

black tea   from tea plant leaves
green tea   from tea plant leaves
sassafrass tea   from sassafrass root
camomile tea   from camomile flower
peppermint tea   blend of mint leaves and other flavorings
other teas: petals, herbs, rinds, etc.   some made with no leaves
tea with milk in it   opaque

not TEA:

boullion, beef broth
powdered soup
cocoa mix
coffee   made from bean; prepared by grind, drip, powdered
hot apple cider   extracted as a liquid

WATER: notes:

bath water
bottled water

56

TABLE 2.1 (*Continued*)

chlorinated water	
distilled water	
tap water	
fresh water	in a fresh water pond
salt water (ocean water)	
ice water	with ice cubes
pond water	
swimming pool water	
puddle water	muddy
rain water	
river water	
dish water	
stream water	
swamp water	

not WATER:

alcohol
apple juice
champagne
club soda
gingerale
lemonade
milk
iced tea
tea
orange juice
saliva
Seven-up
vodka
tears
blood
perspiration

Discussion of the Data: What Sorts of Resemblances Underlie the Extensions?

What do these data tell us about the kinds of similarity that the noun extensions are based on? A general observation in all the cases is that it is difficult or impossible to formulate any statement of the meaning of the noun that would encompass all the examples while excluding the nonexamples at the same time. Although I discuss specific cases below, the reader will probably find a brief attempt at providing definitions convincing. To the extent that no adequate definition can be found, the data support general arguments against a necessary-and-sufficient features view of meaning. Because the examples do not seem to share any common set of properties, but do seem to overlap in properties somewhat, they also support, at a general level, the idea that there is a family resemblance distribution of properties among things called by a given noun (Rosch & Mervis,

1975; Wittgenstein, 1953). There are at least two ways that a family resemblance structure could come about, though. Overlap could be on a single dimension such as appearance or function or microstructure, etc. (For example, all members of a category might overlap with one another in appearance, or they might all overlap with one another in function.) Alternatively, overlap could be along multiple dimensions within a single category. (For example, some members might overlap on appearance while others overlap on microstructure or function.) To answer the question of what kind of similarity the nouns capture, it is important to go beyond simply saying that there are overlapping sets of properties, and to look in more detail at the relations among the things called by a given noun.

Water

The case of *water* is an interesting starting point, since Putnam used *water* as one of his examples of a word that is used to capture a single underlying microstructure, and since a potential definition in terms of a microstructure is readily available. The simple definition, endorsed by Putnam and others (e.g., Wellman & Gelman, 1988, p. 113) is that *water* refers to liquid H_2O. If Putnam is correct, then *water* should be used to label substances that are composed of H_2O, at least to the best of the language user's knowledge.

Do the examples and nonexamples show that the term *water* is labeling substances composed of H_2O? The picture presented by the data indicate that the use of the word *water* is not so simple. All the things that get called *water*, except for distilled water, contain many substances besides H_2O. For instance, tap water and chlorinated water may contain minerals and various other compounds (such as chlorine or fluoride). Salt water, obviously, contains a substantial amount of salt, and dish water may contain soap and particles of food. Most striking, perhaps, is the fact that *fresh water* may, and typically does, contain many microorganisms and even visible life forms such as algae. Thus it seems that *water* is not used to pick out simple H_2O (see also Zemach, 1976).

These observations might not be too damaging to a common microstructure point of view, since one could simply say that most naturally occurring examples of H_2O will have some other things in it, and that the common basis for calling all those substances *water* is the fact that they contain a great deal of H_2O. However, the nonexamples demonstrate that this explanation is not sufficient. Lemonade, vodka, Sprite, milk, and so on, all are predominantly composed of H_2O. Like salt water, tap water, etc., they consist of H_2O with some additional substances mixed in. Apparently, *water* is not used to simply label substances that have the common property of being composed mainly of H_2O. Furthermore, since most adult Americans would probably readily acknowledge both that pond water is not pure H_2O, and that lemonade has a great deal of H_2O in it, it is highly unlikely that the divergence of *water* from instances of H_2O is due to some defect in the language users' state of knowledge.

If *water* is not used simply to group things that resemble each other by virtue of being composed of H_2O, then what is the basis for calling certain substances *water* and others by some other name? Inspection of the examples along with nonexamples suggests that there may be a number of interacting factors contributing to what things are called *water*. An important one may be the origin of the substance. Pond, river, ocean, and swamp water are all deposited in their locations by nature, and the mixtures of substances in them also come about through the forces of nature. Lemonade, alcohol, and other beverages, on the other hand, are brought into existence through human intervention, and are generally found in locations and containers as placed there by humans. Origin cannot be the whole story, though, since fluoridated tap water and chlorinated swimming pool water are mixtures devised by humans and put into human containers. Here, the use to which the substances are put may be critical. Tap water (as drinking water) is used by humans to serve the same basic cell support function that naturally occurring water forms do for many other animals, and swimming pool water is used to support swimming bodies as naturally occurring water forms do for many other animals. Again, though, simply being used in life support contexts in humans as in other animals leaves some observations unexplained. Saliva, tears, and perspiration all are similar in appearance to substances labeled water (and, in the case of tears, similar in composition to salt water), yet none are called by that name. For these cases, the extended human interest in, and study of, our own bodies may lead to a more highly differentiated vocabulary that reflects relatively fine distinctions in source and function. The finding of an expanded vocabulary for parts of a domain that are more important to a culture is pervasive (e.g., Hunn, 1985; Randall & Hunn, 1984). Finally, a similar phenomenon may be at work in the domain of beverages. Since the various beverages all play a role in human social life and have flavors and qualities that lend themselves to different uses in that social life, they may come to have a more highly developed set of names. Distinctiveness in taste or other qualities alone cannot, however, account for why the beverages have names other than *water,* since swamp water no doubt tastes distinctly different from salt water, and both from chlorinated water. Again, it is necessary to appeal to use or source in addition to other factors.

In sum, it seems that *water* labels a set of entities that may be related to one another on some or all of the dimensions of source, location, use to humans, and importance to humans. One might argue that these factors constitute a *theory* (Murphy & Medin, 1985) of what water is that is not dependent on the idea of H_2O, but instead on some other kind of knowledge, such as origin or life support function. However, it is not clear that any single theory can account for all the observations discussed above. Instead, different factors may be important for different portions of the extension of *water*. Lakoff (1987) has described the uses of the word *mother* as a *radial* structure, with a prototypical mother in the center and other uses of the word connected through different dimensions of motherhood (such as the biological aspect, the nurturant aspect, the legal or financial aspect, etc.). The uses of water may very well constitute a similar radial structure.

Seed

The word *seed* provides another case where there is a potential structural/scientific basis for use of the term, but where that basis does not seem to capture the observed pattern of use. Botanically, a seed is an embryo along with food storage tissue and a protective coat from which a new plant grows (Keeton, 1972). Most notable about the common use of *seed* is that many things that are botanically seeds are excluded from the *seed* label. Although most adults fully recognize that peas, beans, nuts, avocado pits, and kernels of corn are the parts of their respective plants that can be put in earth to grow a new plant, they do not use the label *seed* for them. What, then, does distinguish the things we call *seed* from the things that are given other names? Two relevant dimensions may be size and number. Many of the things labeled *seed* are relatively small, and are often experienced by humans in groups of several or more. In contrast, an avocado pit or peach pit and many nuts are large, and may tend to be experienced as singlets or in relatively small groups. Clearly, however, these dimensions do not provide a clear separation of seeds from nonseeds, since kernels of corn and peas are no larger than, say, lemon or orange seeds, and they tend to occur in large groups. Edibleness may also be a factor; many of the seeds are inedible, while many of the nonseeds are edible. Here, since edible entities are clearly of great importance to humans, greater differentiation in labeling can be expected, and distinctions may be made that reflect their method of preparation or use (as in the distinction between peas and beans, for instance). Again, edibleness alone is not a full explanation, since pits of various fruits are not edible yet are not called seeds, and poppy seeds and sesame seeds are edible, but fall into the seed group.

Use of the word *seed*, then, seems to be influenced by factors of botanical function, edibleness to humans, size, and usual quantity in human encounters. Like *water*, the word *seed* therefore seems to capture resemblances along at least several different dimensions, and an exemplar that gets labeled *seed* because it is similar to other seeds on one dimension may differ from other seeds on one or more of the remaining dimensions.

Milk, Juice, and Tea

Milk, juice, and *tea* are all words that refer to substances extracted from naturally occuring entities. *Milk* and *tea,* in particular, are again words whose extensions could potentially be determined by the presence of some particular composition or substance. In both cases, however, the use of the word seems to include prototypical examples that may have a particular composition or substance, and many other examples that do not share that basis. At the same time, nonexamples exist that do share the properties of the more typical instances. *Milk* might most centrally be thought of as the liquid that mammals secrete to nourish their young. This definition would explain why baby's formula is generally called *formula* instead of milk: Although it is used to nourish the young, it is not a naturally occurring secretion from the mother. It would also explain why cream is called *cream* instead of *milk:* Although it comes from the mammalian secretion, it is only a portion of it, and is extracted by human intervention for special uses other than nourishing young. At the same time, though, other substances that do get labelled "milk" are not the original secreted substance. Regular store-bought cow's milk has been homogenized, pasteurized, and has had vitamins added to it. Low-fat milk, skim milk, and lactose-free milk are only part of the original substance, and chocolate milk is the original plus an addition. Generally none of the latter four are used to nourish young, but instead have particular uses in diets or as a treat. They do, however, derive from a more typical version of milk. Soy milk, on the other hand, is called milk although it does not come from any mammalian source, but looks, tastes, and can be used much as cow's milk does. Thus factors of origin, use, and appearance all appear important in determining what is called *milk.*

The case of *tea* shows a similar pattern in the relationships of examples and nonexamples to prototypical cases of tea. There is a tea plant, from the leaves of which is brewed a standard tea. However, many other clear beverages brewed from plants and served hot are also called teas, including those made from leaves, petals, peels, stems, and/or roots of lemon, mint, roses, cinnamon, camomile, and sassafrass. In these cases, the similarity seems to be along the dimensions of appearance and use. At the same time, clear, hot brews such as beef and chicken broth are not called *tea,* perhaps because they differ in origin to a greater extent, being from an animal rather than plant source. Coffees, although from a plant source, differ from teas in being less clear in coloring, and in being prepared by grinding rather than steeping. Likewise, hot chocolate, although from a plant source, is different in appearance and is prepared from a powder that is drunk, not steeped. A simple difference in appearance cannot account for the coffee/tea distinction, since some teas with milk added are very similar in appearance to coffee, yet are still called tea.

The extension of *juice* shows similar sorts of relationships among the entities that get labeled by this word. Prototypical juices are those such as apple and orange, that are extracted from the tissues of fruits. Liquids extracted from the tissues of other plants may also be called *juice,* but apparently only if they are used as a beverage. Carrot juice and V-8 juice (a blend from several different plants) are called juices, but tree sap and olive oil, which have distinctly different uses to humans, are not. While the latter two are somewhat different in texture as well as use from the more typical juices, the physical difference is unlikely to provide a full account of exclusion, since tomato juice and apricot juice also have heavy textures and nonclear appearance. At the same time that a difference in use may be important in excluding olive oil or sap, meats are considered to have juices, perhaps because they are similar in appearance to prototypical juices. Finally, juices include blends invented by humans, such as cranapple juice, and Hi-C or other drinks that have colorings, corn syrup, and other flavorings added. However, some blends that involve juices but are not used as beverages, such as chicken gravy made with chicken juices, are not called *juice*.

For *tea* and *juice*, as for *milk*, then, a number of different factors appear important in determining the extension of the word. Origin, use, and appearance all seem to play a role, with no single one sufficient to account for the normal extension of any of the words.

Bottles and Cans

Although it is not possible to consider every case in the examples given in Table 2.1, several in particular illustrate additional relationships that may be important in determining the extension of a noun. One such relationship is historical. Consider, for instance, cans. The typical can is made of metal. Some nonmetal containers that are cylindrical are not called cans, such as round cardboard ice cream containers, which are usually called cartons or tubs. However, cardboard and plastic containers of orange juice are called cans. A likely explanation for the name in this case is that orange juice containers of a similar shape in the past were made of metal, and hence were called cans. As the material of which the containers were made changed, the function stayed the same, and the historical name persisted. A similar case seems to exist in the use of the word *bottle*. Typical bottles are glass and have a shape that involves narrowing at the top. Baby's bottles 10 to 20 years ago fit that general description. Later, baby's bottles became nonbreakable plastic, as did many other bottles. Most recently, babies are often fed their milk out of a device that is an openended cylinder with a disposable thin plastic liner that attaches inside the cylinder. This device is called a bottle. Again, a likely explanation is simply the historical connection to a more prototypical object; a baby's bottle stays a baby's bottle even as the form changes quite dramatically.

The *bottle* and *can* cases may not be rare instances, either. Parallel examples exist for other common nouns as well. For example, cartons are typically cardboard, and yogurt cartons until recently were made of waxed cardboard. As they have been changed to plastic, however, they are still called cartons. Hotel room keys used to look like typical door keys. Some hotels now use an electronic locking system that is activated by a flat piece of metal or plastic slipped into a slit in the door. These devices are called keys despite their difference in form from the previous generation of keys. Thus it seems that having a particular historical relationship to an object that more closely resembled a prototypical member of a noun's extension may be one fairly frequent type of resemblance captured by noun use.

Sandwiches

The extension of *sandwich* suggests a final consideration about the sort of similarity a noun captures. Sandwiches can be made with two pieces of bread, one piece (open-faced), three pieces (club), or with a pocket-shaped bread, a bagel, a croissant, etc. Thus, the form of sandwiches is quite variable and seems mainly to involve in some way containing a filling in a bread-like substance. However, gyros, stromboli, calzones, tacos, burritos, and enchiladas meet this general definition, yet do not get called sandwiches. These forms are from foreign cuisines and are served mainly in restaurants that have the appropriate ethnic affiliation. They appear to have retained their native names as an indication of their status as outside the set of "ordinary American" sandwiches. Again, *sandwich* is probably not an isolated case. When an object is brought into American culture from a culture with a different language, the existence of the prior label may tend to keep it from inclusion in the extension of an English word that names similar but more familiar objects.

Summary and Conclusions from the New Data

The data on extensions that I have presented highlight a number of possible similarity relationships among the entities that are called by a common name. Prominent among them are physical similarity including shape, taste, texture, size, and clarity; similarity of origin; similarity of method of preparation, and similarity of function in the culture. In addition, the factor of relative importance to the culture seems to have an impact on the potential for inclusion under a category label, since it may lead to greater or lesser differentiation in the domain and hence greater or lesser specialization of vocabulary. Finally, having a particular historical relationship to something called by a given name, and having a particular prior label in some other language, also may impact on whether or not an entity is considered to be part of the extension of the noun. These relationships are clearly not limited to the set of examples discussed above; in fact, many of the same ones were central in the observations about extension from the literature discussed earlier. As in the previous discussion, the data also strongly suggest that more than one type of resemblance may be critical for a single noun; as many as three or four appear to be relevant for some of the nouns just examined. These observations suggest again that the pattern of resemblance underlying noun use may be more varied and complex than has generally been assumed.

SIMILARITY AND INTENSION: SOME IMPLICATIONS FROM EXTENSION

As I just noted, both the observations from the literature and the analysis of my own data point to a pattern of extension that involves multiple and varied resemblances among the things called by a common name. The primary conclusion from this analysis is thus that intension cannot be based fully on knowledge of resemblance along a single dimension, especially of internal structure, or on a belief in the existence of such a resemblance. Instead, it must involve more complex knowledge or principles that allow for resemblance along the observed dimensions, even if this knowledge is not available to introspection. In closing, I offer some comments and speculations about broader implications of this conclusion for theories of word meaning.

First, it is striking that all the similarity relationships mentioned earlier are ones that have been observed and discussed at some length before, but in a literature that has remained largely separate from the psychological literature on word meaning and categorization. Anthropological investigations of the extension of category labels have shown, for many different languages, that nouns are used to refer to sets of entities that may hold varied and complex relationships to one another. Among the most important of these is the role of an entity in the culture. For instance, a category in the North American Indian language Sahaptin that corresponds roughly to the English *tree* centers on plants that are useful for firewood and building; some plants that are similar in appearance but not used in these ways are excluded from the category (Randall & Hunn, 1984). Other researchers who have documented similar sorts of relationships in a wide variety of languages include Bean (1975), Bulmer (1967), Dixon (1982), Hunn (1985), Lakoff (1987), and Tambiah (1969). In the anthropological research, the cultures and languages studied belong to traditional, nonindustrialized peoples, and it is easy to assume that their word use may differ significantly from that of an industrialized culture educated on Western science and philosophy (although see Lakoff's, 1987, analysis of the meaning of *mother* in English). The analyses above suggest, in contrast, that while scientific thought may influence some of our word use, such as leading us to exclude whales from *fish,* we are still highly influenced by many of the same factors. Our everyday use of words seems to capture a variety of similarity relations, with the function or use of an entity with respect to ourselves an important one within the natural world as well as for human-made articles. Such factors should not be discounted or assumed to be of little importance in Western languages.

Second, the potential diversity of similarity relations within a single category suggests that some caution may be needed in conclusions about the extent to which knowing category labels supports inferences. The existence of deep resemblance among members of a category has been said to be the basis for inference; by knowing that something is called *gold,* for instance, one can infer many unseen properties of the labeled object (e.g., Carey, 1985; Gelman & Markman, 1986, 1987; Keil, 1989; Markman, 1989; Quine, 1977; Smith, 1989). However, the commonalities that may be most reliably predicted by some category labels—for instance, that water includes a lot of H_2O or that cans are containers—are also true of many entities that are not members of the category in question. They are therefore not strictly inferences that depend on knowing the category label, but rather could be inferred from knowing superordinate category membership. Knowing that something has been labeled *water* or *can* will certainly allow inferences more specific to membership in the category to be drawn, but at the same time, there will be limits on the inferences that can be drawn depending on the particular similarity relations that result in a given entity being accepted as a member of a category. One can may resemble other cans in function but not very much in appearance, while another may resemble others more in appearance but less in function. Similarly, some water may be drinkable, but other water will not be; some water will support fish life, but other water will not. Of course, people may draw inferences as if all category members share some greater set of common properties than they really do; in that case, it may be of interest to understand the limits on accuracy of the inferences that people draw.

Third, the potential diversity of similarity relations among members of a category also suggests some limits on another idea closely linked with the notions of deep resemblance and belief in an underlying essence. This idea is that people have theories or background knowledge that help constrain what sets of entities they will see as coherent categories (Murphy & Medin, 1985). These theories may provide the link from the (hypothesized) underlying essence to the more superficial similarities among members of a category (Medin, 1989). The data that I have discussed are compatible at a general level with the possibility that such knowledge plays a substantial role in determining what things get labelled by a given noun. For instance, a theory or background knowledge about the nature of living things and how plants grow may provide some important constraints on what things will be called *seed*. Something made of plastic or something that is part of a plant's photosynthesis system may never be called *seed*, no matter how much it resembles a seed on other dimensions. At the same time, though, the existence of this theory may not account for some of the subtleties of what things people consider to be seeds and what things they do not. For instance, it may not account for why people call birdseed *seed* but do not call peach and date pits by the same name. It is difficult to imagine a theory of canhood that will include a tin tomato sauce can and exclude a tin cup, and at the same time, will include a cardboard orange juice can and exclude a cardboard ice cream carton; and it is difficult to imagine a theory of juice that will include both prune juice and chicken juice but exclude tree sap. The complexity of the relations that seem to be involved suggests at the very least that people may hold multiple theories that they apply at different times within a single domain. However, the kind of knowledge that underlies some uses of word, such as the historical connection between metal orange juice cans and cardboard ones, or between old-fashioned cars and modern ones, may not well fit the label of *theory*. The extent to which the idea of multiple explanatory theories captures the knowledge that underlies the groupings, versus the extent to which other types of description are required, remains to be resolved.

So far I have mainly alluded in general terms to knowledge or principles that may be involved in determining what entities will get called by a given name, and I have just suggested that one way to characterize some of this knowledge might be in terms of multiple explanatory theories about the domains. A fourth issue concerns the precise role of the knowledge in word use. One interpretation of the role of such knowledge or theories is that it is drawn upon for on-line comprehension of word use, and for on-line generation of appropriate labels for objects in the production process. This view is consistent with other theorists who have proposed that much of meaning is constructed on-line, at the moment of hearing or producing a word (e.g., Anderson & Ortony, 1975; Caramazza & Grober, 1976; Clark, 1981). The sets of extensions I have considered in this paper, however, are standard extensions that most likely occur repeatedly in comprehension for any language user, and that he or she would also produce repeatedly. Thus it is not implausible to think that for many common objects, some prior mental representation includes these particular extensions. The label of an ordinary cardboard orange juice container as a can, or of the now-common open-ended cylinder with a liner as a baby bottle, may be prestored and available for use simply by retrieval. In fact, younger members of the culture may have no actual knowledge of the historical connection that made these objects acceptable as bottles and cans. However, I would argue that the same sorts of knowledge or principles that are applied for understanding and producing labels for less standard references most likely caused the original acceptance of these particular extensions. The baby's bottle or the orange juice can when they were first introduced no doubt had a more transparent relationship to the earlier versions of these articles for the people labeling them. Thus the sorts of knowledge or principles involved in determining noun extension may operate at both the level of the individual speaker and at the level of language change within the culture.

Finally, although there is both anecdotal and experimental evidence for psychological essentialism, I have argued that such beliefs may have a limited role in how nouns come to be applied to sets of entities. Do these beliefs have any other relevance to meaning or language behavior, or are they simply beliefs with relatively little consequence? In other domains, the discrepancy between beliefs about a representation and the actual content of the representation can have a significant impact on performance in various tasks. For instance, people often believe that their memories are accurate even when the stored information contains serious inaccuracies (e.g., Harsch & Neisser, 1989; McCloskey, Wible, & Cohen, 1988; Neisser, 1981), and the discrepancy between belief and representation can cause substantial overreliance on eyewitness testimony by both those giving testimony (Neisser, 1981) and those assessing it (Loftus, 1979). The beliefs that people hold about the nature of word meaning may likewise have an impact on their performance on tasks involving questions of meaning. In attempting to define words in order to teach meaning, people may appeal to essences, and when learning meanings they may seek essences even when none exist. In drawing inferences about the reason some entity is included in a category, people may assume the presence of a shared essence with other category members in cases where no such commonality exists. A belief in the existence of clear, essence-based definitions for words may even lead to vigorous arguments about the "right" definition of a word when one person's use conflicts with another's. Metalinguistic beliefs about the nature of meaning may therefore constitute an important part of semantic representation, although much about their role in language use remains to be investigated.

CONCLUSION

The observations I have made throughout this chapter suggest the possibility of more complexity in the resemblances underlying word use than we fully recognize so far. There may also be more complexities in the beliefs people hold about meaning than we understand yet; for instance, people may express somewhat different beliefs when asked outright for definitions (Kempton, 1981) than when asked to make sentence acceptability judgments of various sorts (Malt, 1990). I have tried to argue that extension data can be a valuable resource in exploring these intricacies of the nature of word meaning.

ACKNOWLEDGMENTS

Preparation of this paper was supported by NSF grant BNS-8909360. I thank Susan Barrett, Gregory Murphy, and Paula Schwanenflugel for helpful comments on an earlier draft.

REFERENCES

Achinstein, P. (1968). *Concepts of science*. Baltimore: Johns Hopkins University Press.
Anderson, R. C., & Ortony, A. (1975). On putting apples into bottles: A problem of polysemy. *Cognitive Psychology, 7*, 167–180.
Ashcraft, M. H. (1976). Priming and property dominance effects in semantic memory. *Memory & Cognition, 4*, 490–500.
Barr, R. A., & Caplan, L. J. (1987). Category representations and their implications for category structure. *Memory & Cognition, 15*, 397–418.
Bean, S. (1975). Referential and indexical meanings of "amma" in Kannada: Mother, woman, goddess, pox, and help! *Journal of Anthropological Research, 31*, 313–330.
Boster, J., Berlin, B., & O'Neill, J. (1986). The correspondence of Jivaroan to scientific ornithology. *American Anthropologist, 88*, 569–583.
Bulmer, R. (1967). Why is the cassowary not a bird? A problem of zoological taxonomy among the Karam of the New Guinea Highlands. *Man, 2*, 5–25.
Burt, W. H., & Grossenheider, R. P. (1976). *A field guide to the mammals* (3rd ed.). Boston: Houghton Mifflin.

Caramazza, A., & Grober, E. (1976). Polysemy and the structure of the subjective lexicon. In C. Rameh (Ed.), *Georgetown University roundtable on language and linguistics*. Washington, DC: Georgetown University Press.

Carey, S. (1985). *Conceptual change in childhood*. Cambridge, MA: MIT Press.

Clark, H. H. (1981). Making sense of nonce sense. In G. B. Flores d'Arcais & R. Jarvella (Eds.), *The process of understanding language*. New York: Wiley.

Conant, R. (1975). *Reptiles and amphibians*. Boston: Houghton Mifflin.

Dixon, R. M. W. (1982). *Where have all the adjectives gone?* Berlin: Walter de Gruyter.

Dupre, J. (1981). Natural kinds and biological taxa. *Philosophical Review, 90*, 66–90.

The encyclopaedia britannica, 15th Edition (Vol. 7, pp. 330–345). (1980a). Chicago: Encyclopaedia Britannica.

The encyclopaedia britannica, 15th Edition (vol. 19, pp. 43–53). (1980b). Chicago: Encyclopaedia Britannica.

The encyclopaedia britannica, 15th Edition (Micropaedia). (Vol. X, p. 703). (1980c). Chicago: Encyclopaedia Britannica.

Gelman, S. A., & Markman, E. M. (1986). Categories and induction in young children. *Cognition, 23*, 183–208.

Gelman, S. A., & Markman, E. M. (1987). Young children's inductions from natural kinds: The role of categories and appearances. *Child Development, 58*, 1532–1541.

Gould, S. J. (1983). What, if anything, is a zebra? *Hen's teeth and horses' toes*. New York: W. W. Norton.

Goosens, W. K. (1977). Underlying trait terms. In S. P. Schwartz (Ed.), *Naming, necessity, and natural kinds*. Ithaca, NY: Cornell University Press.

Green, G. M. (1989). *Pragmatics and natural language understanding*. Hillsdale, NJ: Lawrence Erlbaum Associates.

Harsch, N., & Neisser, U. (1989). *Substantial and irreversible errors in flashbulb memories of the Challenger explosion*. Poster presented at the 30th Annual Meeting of the Psychonomic Society, Atlanta, GA.

Hayden, I. (1987). *Symbol and privilege: The ritual context of British royalty*. Tucson: University of Arizona Press.

Hepatitis. (1990, February 27). *The Morning Call*, p. D1.

Hunn, E. (1985). The utilitarian factor in folk biological classification. In J. Dougherty (Ed.), *Directions in cognitive anthropology*. Urbana: University of Illinois Press.

Johnson-Laird, P. N., Herrmann, D., & Chaffin, R. (1984). Only connections: A critique of semantic networks. *Psychological Bulletin, 96*, 292–315.

Katz, J. J., & Fodor, J. A. (1963). The structure of a semantic theory. *Language, 39*, 190–210.

Keeton, W. T. (1972). *Biological science*, (2nd Ed.) New York: W. W. Norton.

Keil, F. C. (1986). The acquisition of natural kind and artifact terms. In W. Demopoulos & A. Marras (Eds.), *Language learning and concept acquisition: Foundational issues*. Norwood, NJ: Ablex.

Keil, F. C. (1987). Conceptual development and category structure. In U. Neisser (Ed.), *Concepts and conceptual development: Ecological and intellectual factors in categorization*. New York: Cambridge University Press.

Keil, F. C. (1989). *Concepts, kinds, and cognitive development*. Cambridge, MA: MIT Press.

Keil, F. C., & Batterman, N. (1984). A characteristic-to-defining shift in the development of word meaning. *Journal of Verbal Learning and Verbal Behavior, 23*, 221–236.

Kempton, W. (1981). *The folk classification of ceramics: A Study of cognitive prototypes*. New York: Academic Press.

Labov, W. (1973). The boundaries of words and their meanings. In R. Shuy & C. S. Bailey (Eds.), *New ways of analyzing variation in English*. Washington, DC: Georgetown University Press.

Lakoff, G. (1987). *Women, fire, and dangerous things: What categories reveal about the mind.* Chicago: University of Chicago Press.

Loftus, E. F. (1979). *Eyewitness testimony.* Cambridge, MA: Harvard University Press.

Malt, B. C. (1990). Features and beliefs in the mental representation of categories. *Journal of Memory and Language, 29,* 289–315.

Malt, B. C., & Johnson, E. C. (1989). Does function provide a core for artifact concepts? *Proceedings of the eleventh annual conference of the Cognitive Science Society* (pp. 741–748). Hillsdale, NJ: Lawrence Erlbaum Associates.

Malt, B. C., & Johnson, E. C. (1990). Do artifact concepts have cores? Manuscript submitted for publication.

Malt, B. C., & Smith, E. E. (1984). Correlated properties in natural categories. *Journal of Verbal Learning and Verbal Behavior, 23,* 250–269.

Markman, E. M. (1989). *Categorization and naming in children: Problems of induction.* Cambridge, MA: MIT Press.

Mayr, E. (1984a). Biological classification: Toward a synthesis of opposing methodologies. In E. Sober (Ed.), *Conceptual issues in evolutionary biology.* Cambridge, MA: MIT Press.

Mayr, E. (1984b). Species concepts and their application. In E. Sober (Ed.), *Conceptual issues in evolutionary biology.* Cambridge, MA: MIT Press.

McCloskey, M., & Glucksberg, S. (1979). Decision processes in verifying category membership statements: Implications for models of semantic memory. *Cognitive Psychology, 11,* 1–37.

McCloskey, M., Wible, C. G., & Cohen, N. J. (1988). Is there a special flashbulb-memory mechanism? *Journal of Experimental Psychology, 117,* 171–181.

McNamara, T. P., & Sternberg, R. J. (1983). Mental models of word meaning. *Journal of Verbal Learning and Verbal Behavior, 22,* 449–474.

Medin, D. L. (1989). Concepts and conceptual structure. *American Psychologist, 44,* 1469–1481.

Medin, D. L., Altom, M., Edelson, S. M., & Freko, D. (1982). Correlated symptoms and simulated medical classification. *Journal of Experimental Psychology: Learning, Memory and Cognition, 8,* 37–50.

Medin, D. L., & Ortony, A. (1989). Psychological essentialism. In S. Vosniadou & A. Ortony (Eds.), *Similarity and analogical reasoning.* New York: Cambridge University Press.

Medin, D. L., & Smith, E. E. (1984). Concepts and concept formation. *Annual review of psychology, 35,* 113–138.

Mill, J. S. (1843). *A system of logic, ratiocinative and inductive.* London: Longmans.

Murphy, G. L., & Medin, D. L. (1985). The role of theories in conceptual coherence. *Psychological Review, 92,* 289–316.

Neisser, U. (1981). John Dean's memory: A case study. *Cognition, 9,* 1–22.

Putnam, H. (1973). Meaning and reference. *Journal of Philosophy, 70,* 699–711.

Putnam, H. (1975). The meaning of 'meaning.' In H. Putnam (1975). *Mind, language, and reality: Philosophical papers* (vol. 2). Cambridge, England: Cambridge University Press.

Quine, W. V. (1977). Natural kinds. In S. P. Schwartz (Ed.), *Naming, necessity, and natural kinds.* Ithaca, NY: Cornell University Press.

Random House Dictionary of the English Language (1967). New York: Random House.

Randall, R. A., & Hunn, E. S. (1984). Do life-forms evolve or do uses for life? Some doubts about Brown's universals hypothesis. *American Ethnologist, 11,* 329–349.

Rips, L. J. (1989). Similarity, typicality, and categorization. In S. Vosniadou & A. Ortony (Eds.), *Similarity and analogical reasoning.* New York: Cambridge University Press.

Rosch, E., & Mervis, C. B. (1975). Family resemblances: Studies in the internal structure of categories. *Cognitive Psychology, 7,* 573–605.

Schiffer, S. (1987). *Remnants of meaning.* Cambridge, MA: MIT Press.

Shamir, Americans meet on 'Who is a Jew' issue. (1988, November 19). *The Morning Call,* p. A28.

Smith, E. E. (1989). Concepts and induction. In M. Posner (Ed.), *Foundations of cognitive science*. Cambridge, MA: MIT Press.

Smith, E. E., & Medin, D. L. (1981). *Categories and concepts*. Cambridge, MA: Harvard University Press.

Smith, E. E., Medin, D. L., & Rips, L. J. (1984). A psychological approach to concepts: Comments on Rey's "Concepts and stereotypes." *Cognition, 17*, 265–274.

Smith, E. E., Shoben, E. J., & Rips, L. J. (1974). Structure and process in semantic memory: A featural model for semantic decisions. *Psychological Review, 81*, 214–241.

Tambiah, S. J. (1969). Animals are good to think and good to prohibit. *Ethnology, 8*, 424–459.

Van Tyne, J., & Berger, A. (1959). *Fundamentals of ornithology*. New York: Wiley.

Wellman, H. M., & Gelman, S. A. (1988). Children's understanding of the nonobvious. In R. Sternberg (Ed.), *Advances in the psychology of human intelligence* (pp. 99–135). Hillsdale, NJ: Lawrence Erlbaum Associates.

Wierzbicka, A. (1985). *Lexicography and conceptual analysis*. Ann Arbor, MI: Karoma Publishers.

Wittgenstein, L. (1953). *Philosophical investigations*. New York: Macmillan.

Zemach, E. M. (1976). Putnam's theory on the reference of substance terms. *Journal of Philosophy, 73*, 116–127.

3 Cross-Cultural Aspects of Word Meanings

Paula J. Schwanenflugel
Benjamin G. Blount
University of Georgia

Pei-Jung Lin
Taipei Municipal Teachers College

Cross-cultural studies of the psychology of word meaning are important for the light they may shed on the potential sociocultural, environmental, and linguistic factors involved in the development of word meanings in different cultural and language groups. There has been an explosion of research interest in the structure, process, and acquisition of word meanings and categories in the past 2 decades (see Markman, 1989; Medin & Smith, 1984, for reviews). During this relative explosion, however, cross-cultural psycholinguistic studies on the topic have been few and far between. The vast majority of studies investigating word meaning have employed English-speaking participants living in (sub)urban settings with above normal intelligence. From these studies some limited number of principles and factors have been discerned regarding how humans process, represent, and acquire the meanings of words. To the degree that other cultural or language groups have been ignored, we cannot be certain that the principles inferred from these studies present a balanced account of the factors engaged by word meaning processes.

In this chapter, we argue that a cross-cultural approach is fundamental to the development of a psychology of word meaning. First, we identify and discuss various theoretical positions on the relationship between culture, language, and word meaning. Then, we discuss the relevant evidence regarding cross-cultural variations in word meaning, and identify the factors that might begin to account for the evidence. Finally, the advantages of a cross-cultural approach to word meaning are assessed.

UNIVERSAL OR CULTURE-SPECIFIC THEORIES
OF WORD MEANING?

Although interest in language and culture in the formation of word meanings extends back into the 19th century, at least, empirical demonstrations of relationships have been relatively rare. More commonly, investigators have relied on anecdotal and illustrative examples rather than methodologically rigorous inquiry. Lack of clarity and agreement on theoretical positions has also inhibited growth of understanding. To address that issue first, a review of the literature on word meaning, language, and culture shows that at least four theoretical positions can be identified. Some standpoints are explicit statements on the relation between culture and word meaning. Others are our own abstractions from the literature. Two of the theories represent logical extremes, essentially polar opposites. Those positions serve as counterpoints for distinguishing how language and the structure of the world interact, and they provide the starting point for identifying intermediate positions. We begin our discussion on differences in theory by dealing with the two extreme positions, and then we discuss more fully the other, better developed theories on relationships between word meaning and language and culture.

Linguistic Determinism View

One position, called the Linguistic Determinism View (Kay & Kempton, 1984), is associated with the work of Benjamin Lee Whorf (1956). The Linguistic Determinism View, commonly referred to as the Sapir-Whorf hypothesis (Hoijer 1956), is usually stated in the following way: languages divide up the world in a completely arbitrary and nonuniversal fashion, and thus the meanings that words encode vary without constraint from language to language, resulting in entirely different cognitive experiences of their speakers. The principal source of that view derives from an often cited quote (Whorf, 1956).

> Formulation of ideas is not an independent process, strictly rational in the old sense, but is part of a particular grammar, and differs, from slightly to greatly, between different grammars. We dissect nature along lines laid down by our native languages. The categories and types that we isolate from the world of phenomena we do not find there because they stare every observer in the face; on the contrary, the world is presented in a kaleidoscopic flux of impressions which has to be organized by our minds—and this means largely by the linguistic systems in our minds. We cut nature up, organize it into concepts, and ascribe significances as we do, largely because we are parties to an agreement to organize it in this way—an agreement that holds through our speech community and is codified in the patterns of our language. The agreement is, of course, an implicit and unstated one, BUT

ITS TERMS ARE ABSOLUTELY OBLIGATORY; we cannot talk at all except by subscribing to the organization and classification of data which the agreement decrees. (pp. 212–214)

Whorf later goes on to say:

Languages differ not only in how they build their sentences but also in how they break down nature to secure the elements to put in those sentences. This breakdown gives units of the lexicon. . . By these more or less distinct terms we ascribe a semifictitious isolation to parts of experience. (p. 240)

These views have their intellectual antecedents in the writings of 18th century philosophers, notably Herder and von Humboldt who were concerned with the relativity of culture and held that the world was presented *through* language and thus was organized principally *by* language. A more direct influence was Sapir (1929), who stated "The worlds in which different societies live are *distinct* worlds, not merely the same world with different labels attached" (p. 209). Taken in this extreme. form, that a speaker's conception of the world is constrained isomorphically by his/her language, the very attributes or semantic primitives that comprise the set of all possible words would also vary radically from language to language (see Kempson, 1977, pp. 96–101, for a discussion of this point). Thus the concepts that speakers entertain would be a result of linguistic packaging.

Although the quotes from Whorf appear self-evident that he subscribed to a Linguistic Determinism View, the issue is not entirely clear. Reinterpretations of Worf's work (Lee, 1985; Lucy, 1985, Lucy & Wertsch, 1987) and other quotes from Whorf himself indicate that he did not subscribe to the view that the linguistic packaging of concepts made them nontranslatable across languages. Whorf's major points appear to be arguments against the simplistic view that languages are directly translatable, category for category and word for word. His linguistic analyses were accordingly designed to highlight differences in grammatical and lexical patterns and to argue that a speaker must adhere to the patterns of his/her specific language in order to be understood. Whorf's ultimate objective appears to have been the development of a meta-language for cross-language comparison, thereby avoiding the methodological problem of use of one language's system to analyze the system of another language (see Lucy, 1985 for a discussion).

Despite the entrenchment in the literature as a proponent of the Linguistic Determinism View, Whorf could more accurately be characterized as a cultural relativist, consistent with but carried further than the earlier views of Boas (1911) and Sapir (1921, 1929). Other than the misinterpreted Whorf, there do not appear to be any examples of the Linguistic Determinism View in recent decades, except in the public media where the view is sometimes encountered that the (supposed) degeneration of the English language leads to a degenerated capacity for conceptualization and understanding of the world.

Word Meaning as World Structure View

At the opposite end of the possible determinants of word meaning is a position which we call a Word Meaning as World Structure View. According to this view, the meaning distinctions that languages make and that are most often coded by words follow the basic cuts determined by the structure of objects and events in the world. These basic cuts are determined by cognitive prototypes that emerge from attributes that are shared with related objects in the category and that maximally distinguish them from unrelated objects in contrasting categories (called family resemblance). At the basic level of category structuring, where these correlations among attributes are most evident, linguistic labels are most often found and are universal in their central meaning. Thus, meaning is said to have its origin "out there," derived from the structure of the world, rather than "in the head." The existence of lexical labels that reflect those meanings is not arbitrary, but is correlated with that structure.

As in the Linguistic Determinism View, it is hard to identify proponents of the Word Meaning as World Structure View. That does, however, seem to be the position originally held by Rosch and her colleagues in their earlier work (Heider, 1972; Rosch, Mervis, Gray, Johnson, & Boyes-Braem, 1976). Their emphasis on the structure of categories rather than culture or language is unmistakable in their early work, but we must stress that Rosch later made several disclaimers to the earlier and more extreme position (Rosch, 1975a, 1975b).

A second example of Word Meaning as World Structure View can be found in the literature on ethnobiology. The work of Berlin and associates on ethnobotanical nomenclature (Berlin, 1972; Berlin, Breedlove, & Raven, 1973; Berlin & Berlin, 1983; Boster, Berlin, & O'Neill, 1986) has shown that cases of strong correspondence exist between folk and scientific systems of biological classification, suggesting that there are universals in the classificatory process. The basis for the correspondences is thought to be the basic structure of life forms. The patterns in nature, principally morphological, are so clear that it would be difficult not to recognize them (Berlin & Berlin, 1983, pg. 324). Berlin and associates, however, do not propose that all classificational systems have that basis or that they have it to the same degree. Botanical and zoological systems represent world structure, but it is an open question as to whether other domains share that organizational base. Interestingly, Boster, Berlin, and O'Neill (1986) show that the cross-cultural correspondences based on distinctive morphological traits and clusters begin to diminish if the focus is on closely related species with highly variable phenotypes. Earlier, Hunn (1982) had proposed that utilitarian issues structured as least some the classificational systems in ethnobiology.

Boster and Johnson (1989) took that view a step further by showing that knowledge and beliefs about the utility of organisms come into play and tended to override morphological features if the classifiers were highly familiar with the domain in question.

Linguistic Relativism View

The theoretical position taken in the studies by Hunn and by Boster and associates represent a modification of the Word Meaning as World Structure View. We can identify that position as an intermediate possibility for how language and culture interact in the formation of word meaning. It can be viewed as a derivative of the Linguistic Determinism View and called the Linguistic Relativism View. It was identified earlier by Roger Brown (1976), who states basically that "Structural differences between language systems will, in general, be paralleled by nonlinguistic cognitive differences, of an unspecified sort, in the native speakers of the two languages" (p. 128). The critical difference between this view and the Linguistic Determinism View is that no assertion is made about the impossibility of conceiving concepts for which one does not have single words to express. The structure of the world is allowed to play an independent, but not fully determinant, role in the meanings that persons can entertain. In generalized form, this view would hold that almost any concept can be expressed in any language. If a simple lexical equivalent is not available, phrases or sentences can be used to describe or refer. Thus, the unavailability of a particular word in a language to express a concept makes conceptualization and expression potentially more difficult for a speaker, but not impossible.

Cultural Relativism View

A second intermediate position is clearly present in the literature. In fact, in terms of breadth of topics, of number of proponents, and continuity of interest, the position is the major one in the study of word meaning and language and culture. The basis of this position is that differences across word meanings and concepts are due to differences between cultures taken as a whole. We call this position the Cultural Relativism View, although we hasten to add that we do not imply absolute relativism. The central idea is that language is only one of the many cultural factors that might make certain concepts more difficult or less likely to be expressed by words in a given culture. Regardless of similar translatability of terms from language to language or even when the cultural groups speak the same language, one can expect cross-cultural differences in the meanings of words to be the norm rather than the exception. That is the view expressed by Boas (1911), Sapir (1921), Whorf (1956), to name only a few early proponents.

As seen in the Cultural Relativism View, the cross-cultural variations in the structure of a particular word concept can be reflected in concept prototypes, category boundaries, category gradients, and even the semantic primitives that enable linguistic contrasts among objects. These differences are expected to come about because of cultural relevance and frequency of particular exemplars of words (Holland & Skinner, 1987; Kempton, 1981; Schwanenflugel & Rey, 1986) and of the salience, expertise, and beliefs associated with particular cultures (Dougherty, 1978; Frake, 1977; Lakoff, 1987; Quinn & Holland, 1987).

In sum, we have outlined four potential relationships between language, culture, and word meanings. The Linguistic Determinism View focuses on how the words of a language limit the kinds of meanings than can be conceived by its speakers. Its weaker form, the Linguistic Relativism View claims only that the words of a language assist in the development of certain kinds of meanings and not others, but do not limit the kinds of meanings that can potentially be represented by its speakers. The Word Meaning as World Structure View places the burden of word meaning on the structure of the environment which is then codified by words, with language and culture playing only a minor role, if any, in the formation of concepts. Its weaker form, the Cultural Relativism View, holds that, while the structure of the environment might play some role, there are sociocultural factors (including language) that play an equally important role in the determination of word meanings by drawing a cultural group's attention to certain relationships and attributes in the environment.

CROSS-CULTURAL VARIATIONS IN THE STRUCTURE OF WORD MEANING

There is little question that languages do not break up the world in a similar fashion. Lexical items of languages do not have a one-to-one correspondence from language to language, with each language having a direct corresponding meaning in the other language. Just a few common examples should suffice to make the point. There is no single lexical translation equivalent for the German word *Gemutlichkeit* in English. Hopi has only one word for *pilot, fly,* and *plane.* French does not distinguish between *conscience* and *consciousness* (resulting in some confusion in translation). But this simplistic level is not the one at which testing should be done. What is needed is rigorous examination of the tendencies across cultures to possess terms reflecting some basic structure of any particular category domain that is in question. The starting place for testing is with the Word Meaning as World Structure View in order to ascertain the importance of world structure as opposed to cultural variables.

Berlin and Kay (1969) have suggested that color terms demonstrate the universality of naming predicted from the Word Meaning as World Structure position. Specifically, they reported that the basic vocabularies of 20 studied languages are limited to a small set of up to 11 terms. Moreover, the languages have apparently tend to select color terms in the following order: *black* and/or *white* followed by *red* followed by *green, yellow,* and/or *blue* followed by *brown* followed by *purple, pink, orange,* and/or *green.* Languages virtually always possess terms for colors at the beginning of the list and the focal color points for the terms are similar across languages (although their boundaries may differ).

This view is further supported by the work of Heider (1972; Heider & Olivier, 1972; Rosch, 1975b) on the color system of the Dani culture. Dani has basic color terms for black (*mili*) and white (*mola*), but no single words corresponding to yellow, green, red, and so forth. She found that acquiring arbitrary color terms in her Dani subjects was fastest when the color terms were associated with focal points as defined by the English speakers and slower when they were associated with nonfocal points. Color similarity judgments between the English-speaking group and Dani group also bore a great similarity. This suggests that the labels for colors derived in English, at least, are not arbitrarily related to the structure color domain and lends support to the view that lexical items bear some systematic relationship to the domain that they are supposed to reflect.

Others, however, have argued that the color domain might be an exception to the rule because of its relative simplicity and basis in the physiology of human vision (Brown, 1977; Schonbach, 1977). However, even if physiology strongly constrains the organization of the color domain, that does not mean that any other nonarbitrary relationship between labels and the domain is invalidated. There are numerous issues in the extensive literature on color terminology, but those aside, the general position is that color terms are not arbitrarily related to the domain.

It may be instructive to consider another cognitive category that has a physiological substrate and that would seem to be as universally based as color terms, the domain of human emotions. Like colors, assertions have also been made regarding the universality of various emotions and emotion words. Izard and Buechler (1980) suggest that the basic emotions are *interest, joy, surprise, sadness, anger, disgust, contempt, fear, shame* or *shyness,* and *guilt.* (See Ekman, 1972, for a slightly different set.) However, it has been argued that there are distinguishable differences from language to language in how fundamental, even basic emotions are codified in the language. Wierzbicka (1986), for example, points out that Polish does not have a word corresponding to the English word *disgust* and that the closest corresponding word in French *degout* is tied much more closely in reference to food than the English term is and can be used in contexts where the English term is unacceptable. Similarly, the Australian Aboriginal language of Pintupi uses the word *kunta* to refer to the range of English concepts *shame, shyness, embarrassment,* and *respect* (Myers, 1976). Lutz has written extensively (1987, 1988) on the cultural construction of emotions among the Ifulak of Micronesia in the Western Pacific, arguing that the questions of what their "true feelings" are or what they really think about their feelings are not how the Ifaluk conceptualize emotions or use them strategically in their interactions with each other. It appears that even the central meanings of emotion terms vary from language to language, and it is not obvious that the terms follow any systematic structure of the domain. Consequently, languages do not appear to always codify experience along the same basic cuts that characterize the structure of the world. This is not to argue, however, that a species-specific base of fundamental emotions does not exist. Emotions have a phylogenetic history, but their ontogenetic shaping will eventually produce differential cultural codification (Blount, 1984).

If physiological bases do not fully constrain a mapping of lexical items to natural categories, neither does language structure. Not all differences in the ways that speakers structure words and their meanings are uniquely attributable to the characteristics of the language spoken. Some of it appears attributable to the cultural context in which the categories and terms are embedded. For example, Dougherty (1978; Berlin, 1978) notes that for ethnobiological terms associated with trees, most adult Americans seem to make only gross lexical distinctions between various types of trees (possessing the generic terms *tree, pine,* and *palm*), rather than more basic terms such as *oak, redwood,* and *maple,* and almost never make the further subordinate linguistic distinctions between *live oaks* and *white oaks.* In stark contrast, by the age of four, the average Tzeltal child is able to make the linguistic contrast for over a hundred different kinds of plants, trees, and grasses. Thus, which level gets coded by the lexical system of the average speaker is highly dependent on the salience and interaction with the particular domain for various cultural groups. It is argued that the basic cuts by which various cultural groups divide the world linguistically is very much relative to the expertise of the culture being studied.

Perhaps a stronger test of the Word Meaning as World Structure View would be to examine cultures that possess relatively translatable category labels as defined by their simple extensions to objects in the environment by adult speakers of the language. If adults in two cultures extend category terms to the same items, then it would also be expected that the structure of the categories should be reflected in similar ratings of prototypicality or goodness-of-example for the terms.

The structure of similar categories cross-culturally has been examined in several studies using typicality ratings. To examine the question of whether category concepts were culture-specific, Schwanenflugel and Rey (1986) compared the prototypicality ratings of instances of 12 categories for Spanish- and English-speaking monolinguals living in the South Florida region of the United States. They found considerable overall correlation between the typicality ratings of the two cultural groups (r = .64), but there was sufficient difference in the judgments to suggest nonidentical category gradients for a number of the categories. There was also considerable range in the correlations between the Spanish- and English-speakers ratings across categories (from .16 for *bird* to .94 for *body part*). Moreover, even though there was considerable overlap between the two cultures in terms of the extension of the category terms to instances to the categories, there were distinct cultural patterns in terms of prototypical exemplars for some categories. For example, for the *bird* category, domestic birds seemed to be prototypical for the Spanish speakers whereas small, wild birds seemed to prototypical for the English speakers. Thus, even for this group sharing common present environments, there were marked differences in category structure between the Spanish and English speakers.

A similar cross-cultural study has been conducted by Eckes (1985) who compared the typicality ratings of German college students for ten categories with those collected by similar groups in England and the U.S. He noted an overall correlation between the Hampton and Gardiner (1983) norms for English college students and his subjects of .69 and a .62 and .66 correlation with the American students employed in the Rosch (1975c) and the Uyeda and Mandler (1980) norms, respectively. Thus, for this somewhat different cultural group, we find a similar relationship between cultural groups for category typicality judgments.

We might expect to see a more divergent relationship in the structure of categories as the cultures become less and less similar. In order to investigate this possibility, Lin and Schwanenflugel (1990) compared typicality ratings for instances of ten categories for Chinese-speakers living in Taiwan and Americans living in the Southeastern United States. As in the Schwanenflugel and Rey (1986) study, they found a wide range in the correlations between the typicality judgments of the two cultural groups (from .06 for *kitchen utensil* to .76 for *weapon*). They also found a significantly smaller correlation in the typicality judgments of the Chinese and Americans (.51) than had been found in the Schwanenflugel and Rey study for the two cultural groups living in South Florida.

These cross-cultural differences in typicality judgments emerge fairly early in development. Lin (1989; Lin, Schwanenflugel, & Wisenbaker, 1990) replicated the procedure used by Bjorklund, Thompson, and Ornstein (1983) to investigate the understanding of category extension and structure in Chinese and American children from 5- to 12-years-of-age. Children in each culture were asked to determine whether a given item was a member of its designated category and then were asked to rate the item on a 3-point scale in terms of how good an example it was for teaching a man from outer space about the meaning of the category term. Lin was able to replicate the general finding in both cultures that category terms experience a general broadening in their boundaries with age, with adult-defined prototypical exemplars being acquired earlier than atypical exemplars (Bjorklund et al., 1983). However, overall cross-cultural correlations in children's category inclusion judgments were significant but not particularly high (.34, .27, .32., .27, for kindergartners, 2nd, 4th, and 6th grade, respectively). Their typicality judgments were very similar to cross-cultural typicality correlations displayed by adults of the culture in the Lin and Schwanenflugel

(1990) study, ranging from .45 for kindergartners, .47 for 2nd graders, .56 for 4th graders, and .58 for 5th graders. A somewhat smaller cross-cultural difference in emerging category structure has been found by Hasselhorn (1990) in his comparison of German and American children's production of category exemplars. In that study, there was an average correlation between German and American children's production frequencies of .68, .72, and .66, for 2nd, 3rd, and 4th graders, respectively. Again, the size of these cross-cultural correlations in this measure of category structure was similar to that noted by Eckes (1985) comparing German and American adults. Yet, even for these more highly similar cultures, the cross-cultural measures of category structure do not indicate identical category structures. Thus, it is clear that the category members that children acquire first and their developing category structures denote different cross-cultural category structures that emerge during the elementary school years.

Recall that the Word Meaning as World Structure View predicts that category structure emerges directly from the range of exemplars found in the category, making category prototypes psychologically more salient than other members and, thus, learned first. This would predict similar developmental patterns cross-culturally as children learn to apply their meanings to category exemplars. But, contrary to the Word Meaning as World Structure View, children do not universally learn the same prototypical exemplars of the categories first even if they do learn the prototypical exemplars as defined by the culture first.

In sum, we have discussed three cross-cultural variations in the structure of word meaning. First, there is the simple observation that linguistic labels in the form of single words do not codify the world in a similar, one-to-one fashion from language to language. Second, when linguistic labels do appear, they do not necessarily bear some systematic relationship to the structure of the domain that they are supposed to reflect. Third, even when linguistic labels have similar translation equivalents as defined by similar extensions to actual objects and events in the world, the perceived structure and acquisition of those categories varies markedly from culture to culture. Therefore, we conclude that culture and, possibly, language have pervasive effects on the structuring of word meaning.

FACTORS THAT MIGHT ACCOUNT FOR CROSS-CULTURAL VARIATIONS IN WORD MEANING

Given the cross-cultural variations in word meaning that we have discussed in the previous section, it seems important to try to discern factors that might account for them. From our review of the relatively small body of experimental literature on the cross-cultural aspects of word meaning, we have induced four potential factors that might contribute to cross-cultural diversity in word meaning: cultural prototypes, familiarity, world knowledge, and language. We discuss each of these in turn.

Cultural Prototypes

One of the factors that may partially account for cultural variation in word meaning is what we are calling *cultural prototypes*. That is, the prototypes that are generally agreed upon to be representative of the core meanings of concepts may vary from culture to culture. Rosch (1975a) has argued that the tendency to structure categories in terms of prototypes and distance from prototypes forms a universal of human categorization. If this is the case, then there should be a strong convergence in the typicality gradients only for those categories for which two cultures share similar prototypical exemplars. In contrast, when two cultures do not share similar prototypical exemplars for particular categories, there should be relative divergence in the prototypicality gradients.

Evidence for the prediction of a relationship between the similarity of the typicality gradients across cultures and the shared cultural prototypes was exhibited in a study by Schwanenflugel and Rey (1986). For their Spanish- and English-speaking monolingual samples living in South Florida, a high correlation (.74) was obtained between the number of shared prototypical exemplars and the cross-cultural typicality correlation across categories. Similarly, Kempton (1981), in an investigation of cross-cultural and subcultural differences in the prototypical exemplars and extensions of *boots* and *vessels,* noted that cultural variations in category structures were predictable from knowing an informant's category prototypes. Thus, it appears that the meanings of words and their typicality gradients may vary from culture to culture to the degree that the cultural prototypes also differ.

Cultural Familiarity

The issue of whether cultural familiarity plays a role within cultures in determining category structures, their prototypes and the resulting word meanings is not an easy one to assess. That is, does the relative availability and interaction of persons with some category instances in their environment over others influence the perceived structure of the category and, therefore, the resulting meaning of the category term? To make the issue more concrete, let's consider the category *fruit.* Most Americans have less contact with *mangos* than *cherries,* but the opposite is probably true for the average Chinese person. To what degree does the relative ubiquitousness of cherries in the American environment and the relative infrequency of mangos influence both their standing in the category in terms of prototypicality and the meaning of the category term *fruit?* If the cultural familiarity of the instances can be shown to be related to both within- and cross-cultural differences in category gradients, then it seems likely that cultural familiarity is related to differences in word meaning across cultures.

Some evidence collected within single cultures has suggested that familiarity or frequency of exemplars may not play a role in the resulting category structure or word meaning. For example, Rosch, Simpson, and Miller (1976), pitting exemplar frequency against family resemblance, did not find evidence for frequency on typicality ratings. Mervis, Catlin, and Rosch (1976) found no correlation between standard word frequency indexes and rated typicality for instance terms of common categories (see also, McCloskey, 1980).

Other evidence has been more positive regarding the relationship between category typicality and instance familiarity within cultures. Some research has suggested that persons may actually know less about (and, therefore, are less familiar with) atypical than typical exemplars of categories. Using attribute listings as a measure of instance knowledge, both Ashcraft (1978) and Malt and Smith (1982) found persons were able to retrieve fewer characteristics of atypical exemplars of categories than typical ones (but see Rosch & Mervis, 1975).

Asking persons to rate instance familiarity also tends to support a positive relationship between instance familiarity and category typicality. Hampton and Gardiner (1983) noted correlations between ranging from .27 and .82 between rated familiarity and rated typicality. Similarly, Schwanenflugel and Rey (1986) found an overall .47 correlation between rated category typicality and familiarity for Spanish-speaking and a .50 correlation for English-speaking South Floridians. Lin and Schwanenflugel (1990) found a .55 correlation between category typicality and familiarity for English-speaking Americans living in the Southeastern region of the United States, and a small, but significant .22 correlation for Chinese-speakers living in Taiwan. The smallest estimate of the relationship between category typicality and instance familiarity within a culture was reported by Barsalou (1985) who obtained a .19 correlation between the two factors.

Familiarity with instances may also play a role in the acquisition of category knowledge in children within a culture. Research examining children's understanding of category term extension in two cultures has shown that highly familiar instances in a culture tend to be acquired earlier by children than unfamiliar instances. In Lin's (1989) study, the degree to which children tended to include a given item in a category was highly related to adult judgments of the item's familiarity early in the development of a category. In that study, the correlation between children's category inclusion rates and instance familiarity decreased from .78 in kindergarten to .65 in 6th grade for American children. For Chinese children, the correlation between familiarity and category inclusion judgments also decreased from .33 in kindergarten to .16 in 6th grade. These same general trends have been shown for children's typicality ratings (Lin et al., 1990). Thus, for both cultures studied, instance familiarity is particularly influential early in the development of category knowledge.

To what degree, then, is cross-cultural variation in the familiarity of instances related to cross-cultural variation the structure of categories and potential variations in the resulting word meanings? Current evidence suggests that it may, indeed, be an important factor in accounting for both subcultural and cross-cultural variation in categories.

Several extensive anthropological investigations of particular semantic domains have pointed to familiarity as being of critical importance in determinations of category structure cross-culturally. For example, in an investigation of Mexican concepts of vessels and vessel subtypes, Kempton (1981) suggested that most of the subcultural differences in extension and prototypes that surfaced between genders, occupation, modernity and age could be partially accounted for by the relative expertise of the various subgroups with vessels. For example, experts with great experience with a wide range of vessels tended to extend their categories more in shape but less in functional dimensions, whereas nonexperts did the opposite. Also, the vessel prototypes of persons living in modern villages (having significant contact with American vessel shapes) converged more highly with the prototypes of Americans than those Mexicans living in more traditional, isolated villages. Thus, familiarity with various vessels seemed to account for much of the variation among subgroups in their concepts of vessels.

Similarly, Dougherty (1978), in her study of ethnobiological concepts of trees, plants, and grasses, noted that the relative diversity of terms possessed by Tzeltal children and adults compared to urban Americans could also be accounted for by the relative degree of reliance on, and interaction with, that particular domain in the Tzeltal culture. In contrast, the relative devolution or collapsing of the taxonomic system in Americans was thought to be attributable to the relatively minor importance of that domain for that cultural group.

Therefore, both these anthropological studies are in agreement that familiarity with exemplars in a particular semantic domain is capable of accounting for some of the diversity noted between highly varying cultures. Several psychological studies of our own have also noted that cultural familiarity can account for cross-cultural variations in category structure in comparatively more similar cultures.

One finding that consistently appears in our studies is that instances that form cultural prototypes tend to be more familiar to the culture for which they form prototypes than for the cultures for which they do not. For example, Schwanenflugel and Rey (1986) obtained familiarity and typicality ratings for instances of 12 categories from adult members of two highly similar cultures sharing the same environment (that is, Spanish- and English-speaking monolinguals living in Southern Florida). They then compared the familiarity ratings of items rated as highly prototypical by one culture but not the other (for example, *robin,* which was rated as prototypical by English- speaking but not Spanish-speaking Floridians) with the familiarity ratings of their translates. They found that items tended to be more familiar to the culture for which they formed prototypical exemplars of the categories than to the culture for which they did not form prototypical exemplars. A similar trend was obtained for two more contrasting cultures by Lin and Schwanenflugel (1990) in their comparison of category structures in Taiwanese and American adults. Thus, these findings together suggest that familiarity may be partially responsible for determining which items are weighted more heavily in prototype formation.

Another way in which the importance of cultural familiarity reveals itself is that familiarity appears to account for at least some of the overall variation in category gradients noted across cultures. For example, when Schwanenflugel and Rey (1986) statistically removed cross-cultural differences in familiarity with exemplars, the cross-cultural correlation in typicality ratings obtained in that study increased from .64 to .73. (Put another way, cultural familiarity with instances accounted for 12.3% of the variance in typicality ratings.) Similarly, Lin and Schwanenflugel (1990) found that the cross-cultural typicality correlation increased from .51 to .58 (or a 7.6% increase in the variance accounted for) when cultural familiarity with instances was controlled for statistically. Moreover, in a developmental study, Lin et al. (1990) found that, when the cross-cultural differences in familiarity with instances was removed statistically, the variance accounted for in Taiwanese and American children's category inclusion rates and typicality ratings increased 5.73% and 15.00%, respectively. Thus, each of these studies have shown conclusively that discrepancies in cultural familiarity with instances play a role in reducing the intercultural overlap in category inclusion rates and typicality gradients.

What is striking about these latter studies is the tendency for the cultural correspondence in typicality gradients to systematically increase when cultural familiarity is statistically removed. This increase in cross-cultural typicality correlations means that there may be some structure on which cultural groups agree. This finding makes it clear that cultural familiarity is not the sole determinant of typicality gradients. If familiarity was the sole determinant, then one would predict that the cross-cultural typicality correlations would actually *decrease* when cultural familiarity is partialed. Instead, these cross-cultural typicality correlations actually increased in all three studies. That is, cross-cultural variation in familiarity with instances seemed to play the role of obscuring the agreement across cultures in category structure. This finding suggests that actual structural characteristics such as family resemblance (Rosch & Mervis, 1975) may perhaps also play a role in determining category structure.

Knowledge Base

Another factor, related to cultural familiarity, that may also explain some of the cross-cultural variations in category structures is the overall contribution of knowledge base to the formation of concepts. This overall influence of knowledge base could be readily noticed in our studies of Taiwanese category structures. These days, the Taiwanese Chinese are exposed to a mixed cultural context in which the resources and knowledge of Western culture are readily available. It may be the case that the Taiwanese possess a more global perspective of the categories than Americans do.

This phenomenon can be readily observed in some of the items employed in our studies. Some culturally unfamiliar exemplars, actually never or rarely encountered in the environment by the Taiwanese, were still judged typical for their categories. For example, *subway* and *streetcar,* not parts of the transportation system in Taiwan, are available only through the media and book learning. These items were still judged to be typical exemplars of *vehicle* by Taiwanese adults and children. By contrast, some items excluded as appropriate category exemplars by American children, and rated as unfamiliar by American adults, might actually be unavailable or unknown to the majority Americans. For example, *litchi, mango, papaya,* and *pomegranate* tended to be rated as both unfamiliar and atypical by Americans, despite their relative typicality in the Taiwanese culture. Similarly, *chopsticks, wok,* and *ricecooker* are also relatively unfamiliar to Americans and but are both typical and familiar to the Taiwanese. Thus, this cultural imperialism from West to East (but not the other way around) may cause the category structures of the Taiwanese to reflect a more global perspective on the potential range of exemplars that categories might possess.

Language

Language structure, as noted by the Linguistic Determinism and Linguistic Relativism Views, may be another factor accounting for some of the cross-cultural differences in word meaning and the resulting category structure. Some languages have both explicit and implicit information in the spoken (and written) structure that conveys information regarding degree of representativeness. For example, according to Burgess, Kempton, and Maclaury (1983), the Tarahumara color terms have a system of *obligatory* postposed, bound modifiers that indicate the degree of representativeness of a particular color term. For example, the modifier [-kame] (which can be glossed as meaning something like "very") is used for colors that are viewed as prototypical examples of the color word. The modifiers [-name] (meaning something like "somewhat") and [-nanti] (meaning "slightly") are used for more peripheral and poor examples of the category. These modifiers provide very explicit information regarding category representativeness and are reflected in explicit color choices.

Chinese has a more implicit system of designating category representativeness. In our work, we found that many exemplars designated as typical by Taiwanese adults have category classifiers incorporated as part of the labeling system. We see this only occasionally for English category exemplar words. For example, the word *bluebird* indicates that the instance belongs to the bird category, but this is relatively rare and possibly arbitrary in English. In Chinese, *cardinal* is encoded as "redbird," *robin* as "paint-brown-bird," and *woodpecker* as "peck-woodbird." However, this tendency to incorporate the category term as part of the labeling system is fairly systematic and not arbitrary in Chinese. For example, in the Lin et al. (1990) study, 44.6% of the items rated by Taiwanese adults as being highly prototypical carried these category classifiers, whereas only 6.7% of the atypical items did. Moreover, the presence of these category classifiers was unrelated to the familiarity of the exemplars.

The tendency of category classifiers to be associated with typical words only is not true for all categories in Chinese, however. In some categories, category classifiers are associated with most or all of the exemplars and, in other categories, there are no classifiers at all. Comparing these categories to those for which the category classifiers *are* associated with typicality judgments, we (Lin & Schwanenflugel, 1990) have noticed an interesting relationship between language structure, familiarity, and typicality gradients. That is, for those categories with correlated classifiers, we found no correlation between category typicality and cultural familiarity. On the other hand, for those categories with uncorrelated classifiers, the correlation between category typicality and cultural familiarity was similar in size to that noted for English speakers. Thus, when the category classifiers are arbitrarily associated with category typicality (as they probably are in English), a very similar relationship between category typicality and cultural familiarity is shown. On the other hand, when the category classifiers provide the Chinese speakers with information regarding category representativeness, we find that the influence of cultural familiarity is minimized.

These indications of a positive relationship between perceived category structure and language structure fits well with the Linguistic Determinism and Relativism Views of the relationship between language and thought. These views claim that language determines or strongly influences the way one thinks of or perceives the world and that language has strong cognitive consequences. The foregoing evidence is supportive of such a proposition in two ways: First, language structure may partially determine the structural content of word meanings by providing cues to central, prototypical meanings. Second, our finding of the differential importance of cultural familiarity as a function of classifier systematicity suggests that the language structure may alter the relative influence of various other cognitive factors (in this case, familiarity) in assigning word meaning. In sum, we believe that these are the kinds of evidence that might be used to support these claims of the relationship between language, thought, and word meanings made so long ago.

A CROSS-CULTURAL CONCLUSION

In the beginning of this chapter, we argued that a cross-cultural approach is essential in charting a balanced view of the psychology of word meaning. We have summarized much evidence that we believe supports this position. We have demonstrated that culture has its influence at the very heart of categories, concepts, and word meaning. Culture affects which attributes are attended to, how the world is cut up and labeled, and the degree to which we linguistically label it.

We have noted extensive cross-cultural variation in category structure even when the cultures involved are highly similar.

We have shown that these cross-cultural differences cannot be tossed off as uninteresting, idiosyncratic "noise." Much of this cross-cultural "noise" is, we believe, highly systematic. We have isolated some factors that we hope may account for some of this cross-cultural variation: language, cultural prototypes, familiarity, and overall world knowledge. There may be others.

Lastly, we think that cross-cultural contrasts have provided us with the balance that one hopes to accomplish by using such an approach. The relative influence of the above four factors would be impossible to characterize by even a careful examination of one cultural sample alone. For example, if one were to use only American samples, the finding of a moderate correlation between cultural familiarity and category typicality would be meaningless and uninterpretable by itself. However, by systematically comparing familiarity and typicality across cultures, one can begin to see how cultural variation in familiarity can account for variation in category structures. Suddenly, that correlation between familiarity and typicality has meaning. Similarly, by a cross-cultural comparison of category prototypes, we can see that category prototypes are not strictly "out there," but are influenced by the relative interaction of the culture with the semantic domain and the culture's overall exposure to the world at large. Further, if we were to use only English as our target language, we would probably miss the importance of language structure in providing hints as to the culturally defined structure of the semantic domain.

In sum, then, we believe that a cross-cultural approach has much to offer to a developing psychology of word meaning. We hope that further research of this nature will enable us to uncover other aspects of the relationship between a culture and the meanings that its members acquire.

REFERENCES

Ashcraft, M. H. (1978). Property norms for typical and atypical items from 17 categories: A description and discussion. *Memory & Cognition, 6,* 227–232.

Barsalou, L. W. (1985). Average, ideal, and frequency of instantiation as determinants of graded structures in categories. *Journal of Experimental Psychology: Learning, Memory, and Cognition, 11,* 629–654.

Berlin, B. (1972). Speculations on the growth of ethnobotonical nomenclature. *Language in Society, 1,* 51–86.

Berlin, B. (1978). Ethnobiological classification. In E. Rosch & B. B. Lloyd (Eds.), *Cognition and categorization* (pp. 27–48). Hillsdale, NJ: Lawrence Erlbaum Associates.

Berlin, B., & Berlin, E. (1983). Adaptation and ethnozoological classification: theoretical implications of animal resources and diet of the Aguaruna and Huambisa. In R. Hames & W. Vickers (Eds.), *Adaptive resources of native Amazonians* (pp. 301–325). New York: Academic Press.

Berlin, B., Breedlove, D., & Raven, P. (1973). General principles of classification and nomenclature in folk biology. *American Anthropologist, 75,* 214–242.

Berlin, B., & Kay, P. (1969). *Basic color terms: Their universality and evolution.* Berkeley: University of California Press.

Bjorklund, D. F., Thompson, B. E., & Ornstein, P. A. (1983). Developmental trends in childen's typicality judgments. *Behavior, Research Methods & Instrumentation 15,* 350–356.

Blount, B. (1984). The language of emotions: An ontogenetic perspective. *Language Sciences, 6,* 129–156.

Boas, F. (1911). Introduction. In F. Boas (Ed.), *Handbook of American Indian languages* (pp. 1–83). Washington, DC: Smithsonian Institution.

Boster, J., Berlin, B., & O'Neill, J. (1986). The correspondence of Jivaroan to scientific ornithology. *American Anthropologist, 88,* 569–583.

Boster, J., & Johnson, J. (1989). Form or function: A comparison and expert and novice judgments of similarity among fish. *American Anthropologist, 91,* 866–889.

Brown, R. (1976). Reference: In memorial tribute to Eric Lenneberg. *Cognition, 4,* 125–153.

Brown, R. (1977). In reply to Peter Schonbach. *Cognition, 5,* 185–187.

Burgess, D., Kempton, W., & Maclaury, R. E. (1983). Tarahumara color modifiers: Category structure presaging evolutionary change. *American Ethnologist, 10,* 133–149.

Dougherty, J. W. D. (1978). Salience and relativity in classification. *American Ethnologist, 5,* 66–80.

Eckes, T. (1985). Zur internen Struktur semantischer Kategorien: Typikalitatsnormen auf der Basis von Ratings [On the internal structure of semantic categories: Typicality norms on the basis of ratings]. *Sprache & Kognition, 4,* 192–202.

Ekman, P. (1972). Universals and cultural differences in facial expressions of emotion. In J. K. Cole (Ed.), *Nebraska Symposium on Motivation.* Lincoln, NE: University of Nebraska Press.

Frake, C. (977). Plying frames can be dangerous: some reflections on methodology in cognitive anthropology. *Quarterly Newsletter of the Institute for Comparative Human Development, 1,* 1–7.

Hampton, J. A., & Gardiner, M. M. (1983). Measures of internal category structure: A correlational analysis of normative data. *British Journal of Psychology, 74,* 491–516.

Hasselhorn, M. (1990). Typizitatsnormen zu zehn Kategorien fur Kinder von der Voschule bis zur vierten Grundschulklasse [Category norms for verbal items in ten categories for children in Kindergarten and in Grades 1–4]. *Sprache & Kognition, 9,* 26–43.

Heider, E. R. (1972). Universals in color naming and memory. *Journal of Experimental Psychology, 93,* 10–20.

Heider, E. R., & Olivier, D. (1972). The structure of color space in naming and memory for two languages. *Cognitive Psychology, 3,* 337–354.

Hoijer, H. (Ed.). (1956). *Language in culture: conference on the interrelations of language and other aspects of culture.* Chicago: University of Chicago Press.

Holland, D., & Skinner, D. (1987). Prestige and intimacy: the cultural models behind American's talk about gender types. In D. Holland & N. Quinn (Eds.), *Cultural models in language and thought* (pp. 78–111). New York: Cambridge University Press.

Hunn, E. (1982). The utilitarian factor in folk biological classification. *American Anthropologist, 84,* 830–847.

Izard, C., & Buechler, S. (1980). Aspects of consciousness and personality in terms of differential emotions theory. In R. Kay, P., & Kempton, W. (1984). What is the Sapir-Whorf hypothesis? *American Anthropologist, 86,* 65–79.

Kempson, R. M. (1977). *Semantic theory.* New York: Cambridge University Press.

Kempton, W. (1981). *The folk classification of ceramics: A study of cognitive prototypes.* New York: Academic Press.

Lakoff, G. (1987). Cognitive models and prototype theory. In U. Neisser (Ed.), *Concepts and conceptual development: Ecological and intellectual factors in categorization* (pp. 63–100). New York: Cambridge University Press.

Lee, B. (1985). Peirce, Frege, Saussure, and Whorf: the semiotic mediation of ontology. In E. Mertz & R. Parmentier (Eds.), *Semiotic mediation: sociocultural and psychological perspectives* (pp. 99–128). New York: Academic Press.

Lin, P.-J. (1989). *The development of natural language categories in two cultures: The influence of familiarity.* Unpublished doctoral dissertation, University of Georgia, Athens, GA.

Lin, P.-J., & Schwanenflugel, P. J. (1990). *Cultural familiarity and language factors in the structure of category knowledge.* Unpublished manuscript, University of Georgia, Athens, GA.

Lin, P.-J., Schwanenflugel, P. J., & Wisenbaker, J. M. (in press). Category typicality, cultural familiarity, and the development of category knowledge. *Developmental Psychology.*

Lucy, J. (1985). Whorf's view of the linguistic mediation of thought. In E. Mertz & R. Parmentier (Eds.), *Semiotic mediation: sociocultural and psychological perspectives* (pp. 73–97). New York: Academic Press.

Lucy, J., & Wertsch, J. (1987). Vygotsky and Whorf: a comparative analysis. In M. Hickman (Ed.), *Social and Functional Approaches to Language and Thought* (pp. 67–86). New York: Academic Press.

Lutz, C. (1987). Goals, events, and understanding in Ifulak emotion theory. In D. Holland & N. Quinn (Eds.), *Cultural models in language and thought* (pp. 290–312). Cambridge: Cambridge University Press.

Lutz, C. (1988). *Unnatural emotions: everyday sentimentys on a Micronesian atoll & their challenge to western theory.* Chicago: University of Chicago Press.

Malt, B. C., & Smith, E. E. (1982). The role of familiarity in determining typicality. *Memory & Cognition, 6,* 622–628.

Markman, E. M. (1989). *Categorization and naming in children.* Cambridge, MA: The MIT Press.

McCloskey, M. (1980). The stimulus familiarity problem in semantic memory research. *Journal of Verbal Learning and Verbal Behavior, 19,* 485–502.

Medin, D. L., & Smith, E. E. (1984). Concepts and concept formation. *Annual Review of Psychology, 35,* 113–138.

Mervis, C. B., Catlin, J., & Rosch, E. (1976). Relationships among goodness-of-example, category norms, and word frequency. *Bulletin of the Psychonomic Society, 7,* 283–294.

Myers, F. (1976). To have and hold: a study of persistence and change in Pintupi social life. Doctoral thesis, Bryn Mawr.

Plutchik & H. Kellerman (Eds.), *Emotion: Theory, research, and experience.* New York: Academic Press.

Quinn, N., & Holland, D. (1987). Culture and cognition. In D. Holland & N. Quinn (Eds.), *Cultural models in language and thought* (pp. 3–40). Cambridge: Cambridge University Press.

Rosch, E. (1975a). Cognitive representations of semantic categories. *Journal of Experimental Psychology: General, 104,* 192–233.

Rosch, E. (1975b). Universals and cultural specifics in human categorization. In R. W. Brislin, S. Bochner, & W. J. Lonner (Eds.), Cross-cultural perspectives in learning (pp. 177–206.) New York: Sage.

Rosch, E. (1975c). Cognitive representations of semantic categories. *Journal of Experimental Psychology: General, 104,* 192–233.

Rosch, E. (1978). Principles of categorization. In E. Rosch & B. Lloyd (Eds.), *Cognition and categorization* (pp. 27–48). Hillsdale, NJ: Lawrence Erlbaum Associates.

Rosch, E., & Mervis, C. B. (1975). Family resemblances: Studies in the internal structure of categories. *Cognitive Psychology, 7,* 573–605.

Rosch, E., Mervis, C. B., Gray, W. D., Johnson, D. M., & Boyes-Brayem, P. (1976). Basic objects in natural categories. *Cognitive Psychology, 8,* 382–439.

Rosch, E. H., Simpson, C., & Miller, R. S. (1976). Structural bases of typicality effects. *Journal of Experimental Psychology: Human Perception and Performance, 2,* 491–502.

Sapir, E. (1921). *Language: an introduction to the study of speech.* New York: Harcourt, Brace.

Sapir, E. (1929). The status of linguistics as a science. *Language, 5,* 207–214.

Schonbach, P. (1977). In defense of Roger Brown against himself. *Cognition, 5,* 181–183.

Schwanenflugel, P. J., & Rey, M. (1986). The relationship between category typicality and concept familiarity: Evidence from Spanish- and English-speaking monolinguals. *Memory & Cognition, 14,* 150–163.

Uyeda, K. M., & Mandler, G. (1980). Prototypicality norms for 28 semantic categories. *Behavior Research Methods & Instrumentation, 12,* 567–595.

Whorf, B. L. (1956). Science and linguistics. In J. B. Carroll (Ed.), *Language, thought, and reality: Selected writings of Benjamin Lee Whorf* (pp. 207–219). Cambridge, MA: MIT Press.

Wierzbicka, A. (1986). Human emotions: Universal or culture-specific? *American Anthropologist, 88,* 584–594.

4 The Combination of Prototype Concepts

James Hampton
City University London

How does the meaning of a sentence relate to the meaning of the individual words within it? This question is one of the central issues in the semantics of natural language. In the absence of any strong contextual influence, the answer must be that the meaning of a sentence is *composed* or *derived* from the meanings of the individual words within it. On this view, semantics needs to provide a description of individual lexical meanings, together with combination rules for combining words into phrases, clauses, and sentences.[1]

This chapter is concerned with a particular problem in compositional semantics—namely the way in which the meaning of complex noun phrases is derived from the meaning of their component words. Shoben (this volume) describes some of the intricacies involved with different forms of adjectival modification of nouns. In forming adjective-noun phrases, a wide range of mechanisms can be seen. In fact relatively few cases are simply intersective in the way that CARNIVOROUS MAMMAL is the intersection of the classes of CARNIVOROUS and MAMMALS.

My aim in this chapter is to look at how people construct noun phrases involving two different nouns—either in a direct compound (like OFFICE FURNITURE)—or in various 'logical' combinations such as relative clause modification (A SPORT WHICH IS A GAME), negation (A SPORT WHICH IS NOT A GAME) or disjunction (SPORTS OR GAMES). The interest in such examples is that at first sight they would appear to be relatively straight forward. The

---

[1]There is obviously a further important story to be told, of how speakers and listeners use the pragmatics of the situation in which they are placed to derive *utterance meaning* from any given sentence meaning.

category of sports which are also games would seem to be simply those members of the sports category which are also in the category of games—that is the intersection of the two sets. I aim to show how people's interpretation of such apparently logical constructions is sometimes at odds with a classical interpretation in terms of Boolean set logic. For example SPORTS WHICH ARE GAMES is not coextensive with GAMES WHICH ARE SPORTS, and both categories may include items that are not judged to be GAMES *simpliciter*. The reasons for this divergence from set logic lie, I believe, in the nature of the concepts underlying the meanings of many common nouns—the so-called prototype structure of concepts. To understand the compositionality of meaning, we need to delve into the structure of the underlying lexical concepts, and look at how concepts combine.

The organization of the chapter is as follows. First, I provide a formulation of prototype theory (Rosch & Mervis, 1975), which argues that most of our everyday concepts like ART, CHAIR, or SPORT are not defined in terms of clear cut common elements, but are based instead on clustering together similar objects around a "prototype" form. As well as attempting to provide a clear specification of my understanding of this model, I provide a brief review of some of the empirical evidence supporting the theory. I then look at the important question of how conceptual combination might work if concepts themselves are inherently vague, as prototype theory would predict. There follows a summary of research that I have conducted over the last few years into the question of how people interpret different ways of combining prototype concepts, and an outline of a proposed Composite Prototype Model for forming conjunctive concepts. There are finally some concluding remarks.

PROTOTYPE THEORY—A FORMALIZATION

Prototype Theory aimed to replace the so-called "classical view" of concepts according to which all instances of a concept shared some set of defining features in common (Bruner, Goodnow, & Austin, 1956). The new theory suggested that concepts are represented in memory by some ideal prototype which represents the central tendency of the class. Taking up Wittgenstein's idea of family resemblances (Wittgenstein, 1953), Rosch and Mervis (1975) proposed that the meaning of a word such as FRUIT could be represented by a prototype of the ideal or typical fruit, and that other objects would be classified as fruit (that is correctly referred to using the word "fruit") depending on how similar they were to the prototype. Objects in the world as we perceive them fall naturally into clusters, based around the correlation of attributes across different objects. Creatures with feathers tend also to have wings, fly, have two legs and build nests. Hence we form a prototype of such creatures—a kind of *generic example*, and label it with a name—"bird". Other creatures are then considered to be birds to the extent that they have enough of the cluster of attributes that constitute the prototype of the category—effectively this means that we classify the world on the basis of *similarity,* where similarity is determined by some function of common and distinctive features (e.g., Tversky, 1977). A great deal has been written about prototype theory (see for example, Smith & Medin, 1981; and Lakoff, 1987). For the arguments which will follow, however, it is necessary to state clearly just what the theory involves.

Formally, prototype theory involves the following four axioms:[2]

A: A **prototype concept** is constituted by a set of attributes, each with a particular **weight** corresponding to its "definingness" or contribution to the concept's definition. The instantiation of the full set of attributes in an individual instance would therefore produce a prototype example of the concept. However I take the set of weighted attributes to be the basic representation of the concept, rather than any particular instances, since an instance would also be likely to instantiate many other irrelevant attributes, not defining for the concept. There may also be incompatibilities amongst the set of attributes defining the prototype, so that not all attributes can be instantiated at the same time. For example furniture can have a number of different functions, while apples can have a number of different typical colors. An attribute set is thus a more flexible representation than is an instantiated prototype.

B: A **similarity scale** is defined for the domain of possible instances based on the set of weighted attributes. For example, within the domain of creatures, objects can be placed on a scale of similarity to BIRDS. Usually a linear combination rule is assumed, such as the sum of attributes possessed by an item, weighted by the definingness of each attribute for the prototype, and also weighted by the degree to which the attribute is typically true of the item. Other nonlinear functions would however be possible within the general prototype framework.[3]

C: Ratings made by subjects of item "representativeness" or "**typicality**" are monotonically related to the similarity scale. (Below a certain level, items will be seen as merely *related* to the concept, rather than being representative or unrepresentative of it.)

D: A **criterion** is placed on the similarity scale such that membership in the category is positive for items with similarity above criterion, and negative for items below criterion.

---

[2]Other commentators (e.g., Osherson & Smith, 1981) have proposed a role in the theory for an actual prototype, or for a spatial representation of the similarity space around the prototype. Neither of these additional assumptions seem to play any role in the theory, and so may only serve to confuse the issue. The formalization presented here expresses my own understanding of the theory (see Hampton, 1979).

[3]If nonlinear rules are allowed, then the prototype theory in fact becomes a highly general framework which incorporates classical conjunctive definitions as a special case, and can also accommodate interactive cue models.

Two quick points can be made about this characterization. First, note that the use of a criterion in (D) means that items can vary in rated typicality without necessarily varying in the probability with which they are judged to belong in the class. Membership and typicality are both derived from the underlying similarity scale, but are not identical. So, for example thrushes and ostriches may differ widely in their typicality as birds, but yet a (reasonably well-educated) group of people may all consistently categorize both kinds of creatures as birds. In this case the range of similarity within the category does not fall low enough to come within the range of variation of the criterion—unless extinct species like the pterodactyl or the archeopterix are considered.

Second, note that while the model can readily account for disagreement and uncertainty in category membership judgments, it does not require that all categorization is unclear (or 'fuzzy' to use Zadeh's [1965] term). If both the criterion in (D) and the similarity measure in (B) are highly stable for a particular concept, or else if there are no items in the world corresponding to points in the similarity space that are near the criterion (as in the BIRD category), then there may be no items whose membership is fuzzy. The degree of fuzziness in categorization for a particular concept will therefore come from four sources:

—the variability across subjects and across situations of the weights attached to different attributes (leading to variability in perceived similarity),

—the variability across subjects and situations in the degree to which an item (or subclass of items) is assumed to possess each attribute,

—the variability across subjects in where the criterion is placed (a commonly observed individual difference), and

—the availability in the world of borderline instances.

PROTOTYPE THEORY—THE EVIDENCE

The evidence for this model of concepts came from four main sources. To start with, the categories named by common nouns like FRUIT, SPORT, or CHAIR, show effects that can not readily be explained with a classical common-element definition. First, they often show *fuzziness* in category membership decisions. There are items at the borderline of the category which cannot be easily classified as in or out of the set. Tomatoes are a well-known case, where classification as a fruit seems to be a matter of debate, and as McCloskey and Glucksberg (1978) demonstrated experimentally, similar fuzzy boundaries can be seen in a wide variety of semantic categories, both as disagreement between different subjects, and, more significantly, as inconsistency within the same subject on different occasions. It is important to note that the classification is not fuzzy simply because of uncertainty or a lack of information about an instance—tomatoes are, after all, a very familiar part of our diet—but because of an inherent vagueness in the category definition itself, as captured by the prototype theory. The second aspect of categories that suggests a prototype structure is the variation in *typicality* or representativeness amongst category members. Apples are just much more typical as fruits than are olives. If all category members have the same attributes in common, they why should this be? There has subsequently been much research devoted to the question of what determines typicality of category items (e.g., Barsalou, 1985; Hampton & Gardiner, 1983), and one strong determinant for common natural categories does turn out to be the degree to which an item possesses the attributes shown by other category members (Rosch and Mervis, 1975, developed a "family resemblance score" based on this notion, which they found to correlate well with rated typicality).

The remaining two sources of evidence come from a consideration of the attributes themselves. First, when subjects are asked to describe the meaning of a term like BIRD, by listing different descriptive attributes, they appear to make no distinction between attributes which are common to the whole set (such as two legs and feathers) and those that are only true of typical birds (such as flying). The most commonly listed attributes may often be true of only the more typical members of a category. Second, when one looks through all the attributes generated, and ignores those which are not common to all category members, it is frequently not possible to construct a sufficient common element definition out of the remaining attributes (Hampton, 1979; McNamara & Sternberg, 1983; Rosch & Mervis, 1975).

Prototype theory has had considerable success, both in application to other domains (Cantor et al., 1980; Hampton, 1981) and in the demonstration of a wide range of psychological measures that are sensitive to typicality differences in category items. However, surrendering the neat logic of the classical common element definition left a serious gap in the theory of concepts, and it was to this flaw that Osherson and Smith (1981) drew attention in a highly influential article, in which they challenged the whole basis of prototype theory as a theory of concepts.

COMBINING CONCEPTS

With a classical theory of concept definitions, one can define the conjunction of two sets either extensionally (that is, in the external world of things)—as the set intersection of the two categories of exemplars—or intensionally (in the internal world of ideas)—as the concept defined by the set union of the two sets of defining attributes. For example, within the general domain of people, the concept of British Sportsman can be defined extensionally as the intersection of the set of British people, and the set of Sportsmen, or intensionally as the set union of the defining features of being British and the defining features of being a

Sportsman. Conjunction thus involves grouping together the two sets of defining attributes to make a new, more specific, set, and with common element definitions the two aspects—the extensional and the intensional—are in perfect accord. How could this process work however, if we give up common element definitions, and only have similarity-based prototypes to work with? Prototype theory itself had no answer.

Initially an answer was sought using the notion of Fuzzy Logic, developed by Zadeh (1965) for representing the vagueness of natural language sentences such as "John is tall" or "There is a pile of sand." The limits of size for tallness, or for constituting a pile, are naturally vague, and fuzzy logic provided a way of giving truth values to vague statements and explained how those truth values were changed by logical operators such as negation, conjunction and disjunction. The basic premise was to suppose that truth was a continuous variable that could be represented by some number between 1 (for True) and 0 (for False). One could therefore speak of a fuzzy *set* such as TALL MEN which had clear cases at its centre, and continuous gradation of degrees of membership, where degree of membership for any instance P in a fuzzy set S could be equated with the truth value of the proposition "P is a member of the set S." It seemed a natural extension of the approach then to use fuzzy logic to model the logic of vague categorization statements. Just as "John is a tall man" may be true to a *varying* extent, as a function of John's height, so "X is a FRUIT" could be considered true to a varying extent as a function of X's similarity to the prototype definition of FRUIT. The proposition "A tomato is a fruit" might then be represented as having a truth value of 0.6, for example. (No mechanism was ever suggested for actually specifying numerical truth values as a function of any empirical measure, but one could clearly do so.)

As a brief example of this approach, consider the case of conjunction. Given that proposition p is true to extent c_p and that q is true to extent c_q, how true is the proposition $p\&q$ (both p and q)? Zadeh chose combination rules for conjunction that would yield a classic truth table definition in the case where the values of c_p and c_q are restricted to be simply TRUE (1) or FALSE (0). Two such rules that he proposed for conjunction were:

The Minimum rule—$p\&q$ is as true as the least true of p or q considered separately.

The Product rule—the truth of $p\&q$ is found by multiplying the individual truth values of p and q. This rule he termed 'interactive'.

In both these rules, if either c_p or c_q has a value of zero, then so does the conjunction. Hence statements with clear-cut truth values will produce the standard truth table definition for conjunction—something that is false if either of the component statements is false, and true otherwise. Evidence for the rules was provided by Oden (1977) in a study in which he showed that people's judgments of the combined truth of two independent category statements (such as "A penguin is a bird and a tomato is a fruit") could be predicted from the individual judged truth values of each statement, and a fuzzy logic conjunction rule.

Initially, fuzzy logic was seen as a direct way of representing the degree of similarity of an instance to a prototype concept. Thus both differing typicality *and* fuzzy boundaries were to be captured by the value of c_p for some p such as "Instance X is in category C." Unfortunately for this general approach, Osherson and Smith (1981, 1982) were able to demonstrate quite neatly that fuzzy logic would not work as an account of the typicality of instances in conjunctions of semantic categories. This effect is illustrated by the so-called "guppy effect." Osherson and Smith pointed out that although the guppy is a poor example of a pet, and a poor example of a fish, yet it is a good example of a pet fish. None of Zadeh's fuzzy logic rules for conjunction can allow this, since neither the minimum nor the product rules can assign truth values to a conjunction that are higher than those of a constituent proposition. One therefore has to abandon at least the notion that typicality judgments can be captured by a fuzzy logic formalism. In any case, fuzzy truth values may not be well suited to represent instance typicality, since as I argued earlier, the use of a criterion for determining set membership in the prototype approach means that it is quite consistent for items to vary in typicality even though they are equally clear members of the set, and thus have equal truth value for the proposition "X is in set C."

The problem (as a number of researchers realized at about the same time) was that fuzzy logic operates on sets of items in categories, without any recourse to the semantic "intensional" information in the concept definitions. When words are combined, then there is frequently an interaction between their semantic contents, such that the complex concept no longer shares all the attributes of its constituent concepts. Pets are typically furry, home-based objects, while fish are typically scaly creatures living in the wild. Since one cannot be at the same time furry and scaly, or home-based and live in the wild, the conjunctive concept PET FISH can only have one or the other attribute—that is, some attributes are kept, and some are lost. Pet fish are scaly and home-based rather than furry wild creatures. Guppies have just these attributes and so they are good examples of pet fish, whereas they lack the furriness of pets, and the wildness of fish, and so are not good examples of either category alone.

The theoretical move away from a fuzzy logic applied to extensional set membership and towards intensional attribute-based concept definitions leads prototype theory to make a more radical prediction. It is normally taken as a given of rational behavior that people will only allow an item to belong in a conjunction of two categories if it also belongs in both categories individually. That is, the conjunction of concepts involves the set intersection of the two categories. However, if we abandon the extensional approach to combining prototype categories, as exemplified by fuzzy logic, then this logical constraint on conjunction will no longer hold. The intensional approach says that we take the two sets of attributes for, say, Pet and Fish, and then combine them interactively to create a new set of attributes—a composite prototype as I have termed it (Hampton, 1987, 1988b)—for the concept Pet Fish. If membership in the Pet Fish category is then determined as for other prototype concepts, by similarity to the prototype, (defined by some function of possession of the attributes in the composite prototype) then what is to prevent inconsistencies of classification? The guppy effect shows how some items, like guppies, may possess more of the attributes of the composite prototype than they do of either original constituent set. Unless the criterion for membership in the conjunction is set very high, this will mean that people may allow some items to be in the conjunction which were not in either one, or even both, of the constituent sets.

Osherson and Smith (1982) found this a disturbing corollary of prototype theory—sufficiently disturbing to cast doubt on the adequacy of the theory as an account of concept use. Theories of concepts that embody apparently "irrational" combination mechanisms are a threat to the need for an account of our ability to reason logically, and the normative use of concepts (Hampton, 1989). The only way to use the intensional combination of attribute information to produce a set intersection of the categories, is the classical system of having defining attributes, which are common to all category members—a solution that Osherson and Smith (1982) therefore argued for. They suggested that prototypes may be involved simply in the determination of typicality within a category, while some "core" of defining features would be involved in any operation involving the logic of set membership (a position which has had considerable support: e.g., Armstrong, Gleitman, & Gleitman, 1983; Miller & Johnson-Laird, 1976; Keil & Batterman, 1984; Smith, Shoben & Rips, 1974).

EXPERIMENTAL EVIDENCE

It was against this background, that I decided to collect some data on how people actually judge membership and typicality in conjunctive and other kinds of set combinations. In an earlier study (Hampton, 1982) following up some work in the anthropological literature (Kempton, 1978; Randall, 1976) I had shown that the set relation corresponding to natural language categorization, was not in fact class inclusion as one might suppose. Thus when people claim that the following statement is true:

(1) A chair is a type of furniture

they do not thereby imply the logical proposition:

(2) For all x, if x is a chair, then x is furniture.

Examples like carseats, and ski-lifts show that natural language categorization is based on intensional information, and not on extensional set inclusion. Typical chairs possess enough of the prototypical attributes of furniture to make (1) *generally true*. It is in this sense of "generic truth" that many natural language statements are understood.[4] It may then be quite possible that other apparently extensional statements are treated intensionally with similar "inconsistent" results. To this end I set out to examine the logical consistency with which people normally interpret a number of other common language constructions—noun-noun compounds, relative clause qualification, disjunction using "or," and negation with relative clauses. The following sections briefly review the results of these studies.

NOUN-NOUN COMPOUNDS

If one interprets PET as a noun, then the phrase Pet Fish is an example of a noun-noun compound. The traditional linguistic treatment of such compounds (e.g., Levi, 1978; Shoben, this volume) is that the first noun is a modifier, while the second is the head noun. It is the head noun that defines the class in which the concept falls, while the modifier selects a particular subset of that class.[5] For instance an OCEAN DRIVE is a particular kind of drive, a CAR REPAIR is a kind of repair, and so forth.

Compound noun phrases have received a lot of attention of late (Murphy, 1988; Medin & Shoben, 1988), as they provide good examples of noncompositional combinations of word meanings—that is, examples where the result of the combination can not be predicted solely in terms of the constituent meanings. Consider the following pairs:

(3) A hand wound
  A gun wound

The "mediating relation" specifying how the concept WOUND is modified in the case of hand is the *PATIENT* role—wound done **to a** hand, and in the case of gun it is *INSTRUMENTAL*—wound done **with a** gun. It may then be tempting to propose that the word HAND looks for a patient role to fill whereas GUN looks

---

[4]The same is true of property statements. People readily agree that "Birds can fly" is true, regardless of knowing of counterexamples like penguins and ostriches.

[5]A similar treatment may be given of many adjective-noun compound noun phrases, with the exception of privative adjectives like *fake*, or *former*, and those that function as privatives, as in the case of *stone lion*, or *chocolate coin*—for an illuminating treatment see Franks (1989).

for an instrumental. However they can easily be reversed, as in the following pair of compounds:

(4) A hand repair
A gun repair

Here it is now the hand that is the instrument, and the gun that is the patient of the head noun.

Even though it is readily apparent from this kind of example that the role of the modifier noun is highly flexible and context dependent (see Cohen & Murphy, 1984), most treatments see the head noun as relatively fixed in meaning. However such need not be the case. If the modifier acts to change enough of the default attributes of the head noun class, then it should be possible that an item that is not normally similar enough to the head noun prototype to belong to the head noun class, could nevertheless be similar enough to the modified concept to belong in the category defined by the noun-noun compound. Hampton (1988b, experiment 1) showed evidence for this semantic interaction. Subjects were asked whether items were examples of furniture, and also if they were examples of school furniture, garden furniture, church furniture, and so forth. There was a significant tendency for some items to be included in the compound categories which had been excluded from the head noun category on its own. Blackboards are not furniture, but are considered to be school furniture. What is more, in a follow-up test, subjects assented that it was possible for both the following statements to be true:

(5) School furniture is a type of furniture

(6) Some school furniture is not furniture

It is clear therefore that for subjects in this task, categorization of a class as a subtype of another class did not bring with it the extensional implication of class inclusion.

RELATIVE CLAUSE CONJUNCTIONS

Given that most noun–noun compounds are not simple intersections of the two noun categories (school furniture is not the intersection of schools and furniture), they may not provide the best testing ground for studying the conjunction of prototype categories.[6] I therefore looked for a more obviously conjunctive natu-

---

[6]Pet Fish is perhaps an exception to the more common type of noun-noun compound where the modifier noun has no set overlap with the head noun.

ral language phrase, and chose relative clauses for a further set of experiments. The phrase "Sports which are also Games" seems at first blush to be uncompromisingly the subset of sports which also happen to belong to the class of games. As such the phrase should be equivalent to the converse phrase "Games which are also Sports," since extensionally both phrases pick out the intersection of the sport and game categories.

How do subjects rate items in these categories? The basic method used to study this question was to present them with a list of objects. At the head of the list was a category name—either a simple category such as SPORTS, or a conjunctive category like "GAMES which are also SPORTS." Their task was to work down the list of items deciding if each was in the category or not. They were additionally asked to rate category members for their typicality in the category, and to judge the relatedness of non-members to the category.[7] The experiment has been done both within subjects (where subjects first rate the list of items as Sports, then as Games, and then in the conjunction), and also between subjects (with different subject groups providing each of the judgments) with essentially the same result. The basic finding was that subjects overextended the conjunctive categories to include in them items which were judged not to belong to one of the two constituent categories. For example they would rate CHESS as a GAME but not as a SPORT, but would later judge it to be a SPORT which is a GAME (or a GAME which is a SPORT). Seven different pairs of categories were examined, with similar results in each case.[8]

The overextension could be tested in three ways. First, individual subjects' sets of three category judgments for each item were analyzed and shown to have a much higher frequency of inconsistent overextended responses than would be expected by chance alone (even allowing for the unstable nature of category judgments close to the category boundary). Second, category membership scale values were calculated for each item, based on the rating scale and ranging from most typical member, through to least related nonmember. This scale can be thought of as an operationalization of the similarity-to-prototype scale. Membership scale values for the conjunction were in the majority of cases intermediate between membership for one category and membership for the other. Indeed a very regular relationship obtained between the three sets of item means, suggesting that a geometric mean of the two constituent membership values could accurately predict the membership value for the conjunction. A final way of

---

[7]Further studies by Chater, Lyon, and Myers (1990) have repeated the experiment without this additional rating task, with very similar results.

[8]BIRDS were not overextended as a category, but probably because of a lack of examples whose membership in the category could be considered vague. The fact that BIRDS form a clear-cut category is more a matter of biological accident, than anything else—other natural kinds like FISH and INSECT are vaguely defined in laymen's concepts, and it is also possible to invent novel birdlike creatures whose membership in the category of BIRDS could be fuzzy.

testing the overextension was to apply a probability model to the pattern of positive or negative categorization judgments, using data from different groups of subjects for each classification judgment (Hampton, 1990). Once again, the probability of an item being classed in the conjunction was generally predictable by a geometric average of the two constituent category probabilities.

The conclusion drawn from these studies was that when a noun occurs modified by a relative clause, or is itself a modifier in such a clause, the semantic interpretation of the concept is modified. More specifically the original concept is liable to lose some of its prototypical default features, through conjunction with another concept. The result is that some items will be more similar to the conjunction than to the simple concept, and hence may be included in the conjunction category although not included in the simple concept category.

I return to this account in the final section which presents a model for composite prototype formation for conjunctive concepts.

DISJUNCTION

I have so far tried to argue that categorization statements in language are not tied to a class inclusion logic, and that conjunctions of semantic categories do not follow the logic of set intersection. In a further set of studies (Hampton, 1988a) I considered the disjunction of semantic categories. If people are asked to consider whether an item falls into either of two categories, will they follow the logical rule of set union—that is, give a positive answer to all and only those items that they would place in one or the other category (or both) considered individually?

The short answer is again no. The experimental procedure was once again to ask people to judge category membership and to rate typicality or relatedness, first for a list of items as members of one category, then as members of the other category, and finally as members of either (using expressions such as TOOLS OR INSTRUMENTS, or FRUITS OR VEGETABLES). A between-groups experiment was also carried out using the same tasks. In order to demonstrate the effects of intensional representation on classification judgments, it is necessary to choose categories to be disjoined that are close together in the same semantic domain. We may then expect on the basis of the previous results that subjects would be inclined to judge membership in a disjunction such as HERBS or SPICES, on the basis of some overall average membership in the two constituent categories. For a disjunction, a good example of either category is sure to be a member, regardless of membership in the other category, so one would expect any deviation from a simple linear averaging to be in the opposite direction from the case of concept conjunction. When the data were collected and analyzed, it was indeed found that both degree of rated membership in the disjunction, and probability of a positive response, could be accurately predicted by a regression equation involving the two component category membership values, and a negative interaction term. That is membership in a disjunction could be predicted with an equation of the general form of (7).

(7) disjunction $= c_1 + c_2.A + c_3.B - c_4.A.B$

where A and B represent degree of membership in the constituent categories, c_1 is a constant, and c_2, c_3 and c_4 are positive constants. Note that (7) has the same form as the rule for calculating the probability of a disjunction of two events (8).

(8) $p(A \text{ or } B) = p(A) + p(B) - c.p(A).p(B)$

where c is a positive constant reflecting the degree of interdependence between the two events.

In terms of responses to individual items, the effect of the semantic interaction was to lead to a pattern where some items were included in the disjunction which had been rejected from both categories individually, while others were excluded, even though they had been included in one of the constituent categories. Examples of the former case of overextension occurred with cases like FRUIT or VEGETABLES, where the two categories being combined were close to being contrasting sets, which together covered most of the domain. In such a situation, a number of other edible plant stuffs—like nuts, herbs, rhubarb, etc.—were not included in either category alone, but were included in the disjunction. As one subject put it—"I don't really think it is a Fruit, and I don't think it is a Vegetable, but I feel it has to be in one category or the other." That overextension was not just an effect of statistical dependence between the decisions was shown by the fact that for many decisions the probability of a positive disjunction response was greater than the sum of the two constituent response probabilities (breaking the constraint on disjunctions of probabilities—see (8) above).

Examples of underextension—the exclusion of items from the disjunction which belonged to one or other constituent category—could often be attributed to a contextual effect operating between the two categories. Considering HOUSEHOLD APPLIANCES on its own, subjects were prepared to give equal weight to all machine-like artifacts in the home as category members. When disjoined with KITCHEN UTENSILS, the feature "used in the kitchen" appeared to affect the overall decision, to the extent that items like electric toothbrushes were no longer considered to belong.

NEGATION

The final study in this series investigated the effect of negation on complex categorization (see Hampton, 1990). In order to test the effect of the word "NOT" on the interpretation of noun phrases, it is necessary to place the phrase in some clearly defined domain. One cannot go around asking people to what extent a bicycle is an example of the category "Not a Fruit," since the category has no prototype. The problem could be easily solved by using the relative clause constructions studied earlier. By placing the NOT operator in the relative clause modifier, the presumed scope of the negator could be clearly specified. In an unpublished study (Hampton, 1990) subjects were thus asked to categorize items as SPORTS, GAMES, and then as SPORTS WHICH ARE NOT GAMES, or GAMES WHICH ARE NOT SPORTS. The analysis of mapping constituent membership onto membership in the complex noun phrase category was then carried out in the same way as for conjunctions and disjunctions.

For the mean membership ratings, the pattern was very much consistent with the earlier results. By placing a negative sign in front of membership in the negated category, the results for conjunctions (A which are B) could be translated into results for complement conjunctions (A which are not B). The form of the regression equations thus took the form (9):

(9) A which are not B $= c_1 + c_2.A - c_3.B + c_4.A.B$

where the sole change from conjunction is the negating of the constants affecting the B term.

As regards the "inconsistency" and overextension observed for conjunctions, the same pattern was observed for complements, with in some cases a more extreme degree of overextension. Items were included in the category "A which are not B" which had either been left out of category A, or which *had been* included in category B. For example, in a between-groups study, a majority of each group was in favor of including DESK LAMPS in each of the following categories:

(10) HOUSEHOLD APPLIANCE that is FURNITURE
      FURNITURE that is a HOUSEHOLD APPLIANCE
      HOUSEHOLD APPLIANCE that is NOT FURNITURE
      FURNITURE that is NOT A HOUSEHOLD APPLIANCE.

It was also found for the complement sets, that there were some items that were much more likely to be included in the complex sets, than in *either* of the two constituent sets (if one assumes membership in NOT B to be 1 minus membership in B). This *double overextension* was very rare in the case of unnegated relative clause conjunction, where items which were overextended for one category were almost always very typical examples of the other category. Double overextension is the phenomenon that would be predicted by the "guppy effect" discussed in the introduction. Since guppies are purportedly better examples of PET FISH than of either PET or FISH, then for items near the borderline one might expect degree of membership to follow a similar pattern. Failure to find it for simple conjunctions may of course reflect the materials used for those experiments.

AN INHERITANCE MODEL FOR COMPOSITE
PROTOTYPES

The relationship between category membership in individual concepts and in different logical combinations of them appears to be a very regular one, at least for the range of categories used in the studies. The temptation might then be to try to revive a version of fuzzy set logic to account for the results. Given appropriate scaling factors, the data approximate reasonably well to Zadeh's "interactive" or multiplicative combination rules, by which degrees of category membership are combined in the same way as event probabilities. Indeed Zadeh himself (Zadeh, 1982) made a similar proposal.

There are at least two problems with using an extensional fuzzy logic approach. First, Osherson and Smith (1982) were able to demonstrate that no general fuzzy logic function can deal with concept conjunction. The degree to which pairs of categories allow the "guppy effect" seems to depend on the degree of overlap between them. Pets and fish are categories with very low overlap (most pets are not fish, and most fish are not pets). Other categories with much higher overlap, like Sports and Games, will show little or no double overextension. The combination function needs to reflect the overlap between the categories.

The second problem relates to an unexpected phenomenon that appeared in the studies described above on conjunction. When two categories are combined in conjunction with a relative clause, it turned out that one of the categories tended to have a much stronger effect overall than the other. For example the extent to which an activity is a SPORT had much more influence than the extent to which it is a GAME in determining its degree of membership in the conjunctive categories "SPORTS WHICH ARE GAMES" or "GAMES WHICH ARE SPORTS." This pattern of **dominance** was found in most of the category pairs studied, and was replicated in different studies with different lists of category items. An extensional account would have to explain the effect in terms of some extensional aspect of the category—such as its set size. However set size does not appear to predict the dominant category.

On the basis of these arguments against the extensional approach, the following intensional model was developed, which has the advantage of readily explaining why double overextension depends on semantic overlap, and also why some categories should dominate others.

THE COMPOSITE PROTOTYPE MODEL

The model makes the following initial assumptions:

1. Concepts are represented as sets of attributes, in much the same way as Rosch's prototype theory proposed. The attributes may however be intercon-

nected by **higher level** "theory driven" relations. Malt and Smith (1983) and Murphy and Medin (1985) pointed out that as well as knowing that birds have wings and can fly, we also know that having wings is an enabling condition for flight. That is, there are higher levels of understanding, such as a naive physics of flight, which provide additional semantic relations between concept attributes. Such relations will typically involve notions like CAUSE and ENABLEMENT, as for example in:

(Pets live in homes) CAUSES (Pets need litter trays)
or
(Pets are tame) ENABLES (Pets are cuddled)

2. The attributes are associated with a quantitative "degree of definingness" which I will term **Importance.** Those attributes which are most central or criterial for category membership will be the most important, and those that are least relevant to the categorization of any item will be the least important.[9]

3. At the top end of the scale of attribute importance there may be some attributes which are so important as to be **necessary** for category membership.[10] For example HAS GILLS may be treated as a necessary attribute of FISH.

4. Attributes are **organized** in such a way that at least some of them are represented as particular sets of values on particular dimensions. Obvious examples would be dimensions such as COLOR and SIZE. Smith et al. (1988) make a similar proposal in their concept modification model. For example the fact that Pets are domesticated may be represented as a dimension (or frame–slot) labeled HABITAT taking a particular value [DOMESTIC].

5. There is a "**consistency**" checking procedure which can tell whether different values for a dimension are incompatible with other values for that dimension, and also with other attributes in the prototype. This procedure will make use of the higher level attribute relations—for instance to determine that if a bird has a value of [20 kilos] for the dimension WEIGHT, it is unlikely to take the value [FLIES] for the dimension MEANS OF LOCOMOTION.

---

[9]The notion of importance has been proposed in many contexts—e.g., as definingness (Smith, Shoben, and Rips, 1974), as cue validity (Murphy, 1982) or as centrality (Barsalou & Billman, 1989)—and should be thought of as reflecting in an intuitive way the relative likelihood of an item belonging to a category given that it does or does not have the particular attribute. No formal definition is attempted at this stage.

[10]The concept of necessity employed here does not need to imply the philosophical notion of analyticity (that is, that the attribute is necessarily true of the concept, *by virtue* of the concepts meaning alone). It could for example reflect the interconnection of the attribute to others in the prototype through higher order relations, so that lack of the attribute involves a concomitant lack of many others.

So far the model bears strong similarity to the prototype model, with some additional refinements in terms of higher order relations between attributes, necessity of the most highly weighted attributes, and consistency among attribute values.

A conjunctive concept is then represented semantically by a composite prototype which is formed from the two constituent concept prototypes according to the following rules (a genealogical metaphor of attribute inheritance will be used—with the constituent concepts as mother and father, and the conjunctive concept as offspring):

6. Initially the "genotype" composite prototype is formed as the **union of the sets of attributes** from both "parent" concepts. Thus initially the concept PET FISH will have all the attributes of both PET and FISH prototypes.

This new set of attributes is then modified, and assigned importance values according to the following rules:

7. Where an attribute is maximally important for at least one parent concept (i.e., a Necessary attribute), it will also be maximally important for the offspring, regardless of the importance value for the other parent. For example if HAS GILLS is necessary for FISH, then it will also be necessary for PET FISH. This places a **Necessity Constraint** on attribute inheritance.

8. For other attributes, the importance of each attribute for the offspring is determined as a **monotonic positive function of importance** for each parent— for example a simple average of the two constituent concept importance values could be taken. To take the PET FISH case again, supposing that LOVABLE is fairly important for PETS and irrelevant for FISH, it will be of intermediate importance for PET FISH.

9. Those attributes with **low importance** as determined in (8) above are dropped from the representation (or filtered out in the process of constructing it). Thus, if LOVABLE is now of relatively low importance, a subject may simply exclude it from the prototype for PET FISH.

10. A consistency checking procedure is applied to the new set of attributes. Where there are incompatible attributes, a choice has to be made to delete certain attributes. This provides a **Consistency Constraint.**

—Where the conflict of attributes is between a necessary attribute of one parent and a nonnecessary attribute of the other, the necessary attribute will always win. This has the effect of predicting that any attribute which is considered to be "impossible" for one parent—that is any attribute which conflicts with a necessary attribute of the parent—will also be impossible for the off-spring. For example if PETS typically breathe air, but this is inconsistent with living underwater, which itself is necessary for the concept FISH, then breathing air will not be possible for PET FISH.

—Where the conflict is between two necessary attributes, then the process of constructing the prototype fails, and the conclusion is drawn that the conjunction is an empty set—a "logical impossibility." So, if asked to describe a FISH that is also a BIRD, subjects may say that such a creature is not possible since FISH must have GILLS, while BIRDS must have LUNGS. If the subject is pressed to continue into the realm of science fiction, or if the linguistic context is supportive of a nonliteral interpretation, then one or other of the necessary attributes will be deleted. Hence one can arrive at interpretations for phrases such as ROBOT CATS, or STONE LIONS (see Franks, 1989), or speak more loosely of WHALES as FISH that are also MAMMALS, or perhaps (very loosely) of PENGUINS as BIRDS that are also FISH.

—Where the conflict involves two non-necessary attributes, then the choice of which to delete will depend on their relative importance, on the overall consistency that can be achieved with respect to the other inherited attributes, and on the context in which the phrase is being used.

It should be noted that, as stated, the model is far from a complete theory of conceptual modification. In particular, a great deal more specification is needed for the consistency checking process—how is information about the incompatibility of attributes represented and accessed during this stage? It is also worth noting however, that the proposed model could be applied to the conjunction of well-defined concepts with a core of common element defining features, with the desired results. The necessity constraint would ensure that all defining features of each concept remain critical for the conjunctive concept, and the consistency constraint would ensure the correct identification of nonoverlapping sets. Well-defined concepts would therefore require no different treatment in the model, and would behave intersectively.

EVIDENCE FOR THE MODEL

To test the model, some recent experiments (Hampton, 1987) obtained attribute listings for the same pairs of categories studied in the conjunction experiments described earlier. Each attribute was then rated by subjects for its importance in defining each of the parent concepts, and for its importance in defining the conjunctive concept (on an intuitive scale ranging from "necessarily true of all possible examples of the concept" through "very important" to "not usually true" and "necessarily false of all possible examples of the concept"). The resulting data were then analyzed to test the predictions of the model.

In brief, the pattern of attribute inheritance shown by the subjects' judgments of importance supported the model well. Importance for the conjunction was predictable as a linear weighted average of importance for each constituent (see (8) in the model above), with Multiple R for the regression equations averaging around 0.8. As a result there were a number of attributes which although important for a parent concept were judged relatively unimportant for the conjunction (i.e., were not inherited). There was also clear evidence that with very few exceptions, attributes that were considered either necessary, or impossible, for either parent concept were also considered necessary or impossible respectively for the conjunction. To demonstrate the effects of consistency, an additional analysis was run on the conjunction PETS WHICH ARE BIRDS, in which each attribute that was distinctively true of one category or the other, was rated for consistency with the attributes of the other category. For example, distinctive attributes of BIRDS were singing and migrating. The extent to which each of these attributes (among others) was consistent with the attributes of being a PET was rated by subjects, and then entered into a regression predicting importance for the conjunction. Obviously singing is much more consistent with being a pet than is migrating. Indeed it was found that degree of consistency predicted additional variance in the conjunctive importance measure, over and above that predicted by importance for the two constituent concepts.

OVEREXTENSION AND DOMINANCE

How does the model explain the pattern of typicality and membership ratings obtained in the categorization studies of conjunction? I shall consider three aspects—the "guppy effect" of double overextension, the more pervasive phenomenon of the overextension due to compensatory averaging of constituent typicalities, and finally the dominance relation between pairs of categories.

The start of the whole project was the claim by Osherson and Smith that GUPPIES are better PET FISH than they are either PETS or FISH alone. The Composite Prototype model accounts for this phenomenon by showing how attributes of the parent concepts fail to get inherited as a result of the necessity constraint and the consistency constraint. The typical pet fish just doesn't have many of the attributes normally associated with pets or fish alone. In more detail, consider a few of the attributes of pets and fish and how they are inherited by the conjunction:

PET	FISH	PETFISH	GUPPY
HABITAT:			
Domestic	Sea, lake, river	Domestic	Domestic
EDIBILITY:			
Not eaten	Often eaten	Not eaten	Not eaten
BREATHING:			
With lungs	With gills	With gills	With gills
LIMBS:			
Four legs	Fins	Fins	Fins

Attribute overlap:		
Guppy–Pet	= 2
Guppy–Fish	= 2
Guppy–Pet Fish	= 4

Pet fish inherit habitat and not being eaten from the pet concept, because the attribute values for PET are more criterial for PETS than are the attribute values of FISH criterial for being a FISH. On the other hand, the possession of gills and fins is more critical for fish-hood than is the possession of lungs and legs for pet–hood. Hence the composite prototype for PET FISH is a hybrid—having some attributes and lacking others of each parent. Instances like guppies and goldfish will obviously have more attributes in common with the pet fish prototype than they will with either pets or fish alone—hence they are considered more typical as pet fish.[11]

As regards overextension through compensation, this phenomenon is a clear prediction of the intensional approach. So long as the necessary attributes are not together sufficient to determine category membership, but the definition also relies on a similarity metric defined over "characteristic" attributes (i.e., the prototype view), then intensional combination of attributes will tend to lead to inconsistency in the treatment of conjunctions. Strict set intersection requires (as in Zadeh's minimum rule, but not in his product rule) that if membership falls below criterion for either concept, then degree of membership in the other can have *no positive influence at all* on the degree of membership in the conjunction. If this requirement is not met, then inconsistency will result. For example Zadeh's original product rule would lead to serious underextension, since an item

---

[11]Smith et al.'s (1988) selective modification model is a simpler version of this type of approach, whereby adjectival modification works by simply changing the default value of a single attribute (see Shoben, this volume). In keeping with Osherson and Smith's (1982) position however, they restrict their model to making predictions about typicality judgments, reserving serious doubts about its ability to account for set membership judgments. In fact, any intensional modification model will necessarily result in a representation for a conjunctive concept that is different from that of the head noun, or modifier alone. Hence the guppy effect falls naturally out of *any* model proposing intensional conceptual combination, given a few simple assumptions about how typicality is derived from attribute overlap.

lying above criterion for two categories (e.g., c(A) = c(B) = 0.6) would be very likely to be excluded from the conjunction (c(AB) = 0.36). Rescaling the conjunction by lowering the membership criterion could remove the underextension, but only at the expense of increasing overextension. Thus if the criterion is set now at 0.35 for the conjunction, items with c(A) = 1.0 and c(B) = .4 would have to be included in the conjunction.

The dominance effect was the observation that some categories exert a much stronger influence on conjunctions than do others. SPORTS was dominant with respect to GAMES, and BIRDS with respect to PETS. The model outlined above can account for dominance very naturally, if it is assumed that some concepts have a greater number of salient and important attributes than others. In such a case, the concept with the higher number of important attributes would tend to contribute a greater proportion of the attributes that constitute the final composite prototype for the conjunction—because of the necessity constraint, and because of the average importance rule. Consider the case of two concepts X and Y, with features as below:

Concept X	Concept Y
f1	f1
f2	f4
f3	f5
	f6
	f7

Suppose the simplest case—that the composite concept is created without any consistency problems arising, so that the composite prototype for the concept 'X that is a Y' has all the features of both concepts—that is f1 through f7.

Now the degree to which an instance is typical of the conjunction will depend on the number of features f1 through f7 that it possesses. Knowing its typicality as an X will tell us about the degree to which it possesses 3 of those 7. On the other hand knowing its typicality as a Y will tell us about its possession of 5 of the 7. It follows that typicality of items for concept Y will be a better predictor of typicality in the conjunction than will typicality in concept X, other things being equal. In other words, the more semantic specification a concept has, the more dominant a part it will play in the final composite.

There is a second possible mechanism within the model for accounting for dominance. If one concept has stronger higher order links between attributes than the other, then the conflict resolution process would favor such a concept simply because one could not remove one attribute from the composite without affecting the others to which it is linked. Dominance should therefore depend both on the relative number of important attributes, and the degree of internal coherence that results from inter-attribute links.

The attribute rating study (Hampton, 1987) found good evidence for the first account, and some indirect evidence for the second. The categories identified as dominant in the experiments on categorization (Hampton, 1988b) did indeed have a significantly higher average importance across all attributes, and a significantly higher number of important attributes than those that were non-dominant. In addition, the regression weight in the equation predicting importance for the conjunction from importance for each constituent also reflected the dominance of the categories. The importance of an attribute for the dominant category was a better predictor of conjunctive importance than was importance for the non-dominant category. Since this analysis applies to individual attributes, it could not be explained simply in terms of the relative numbers of important attributes for each concept. This second effect could reflect the coherence effect, although it can only be taken as indirect evidence at present.

NONCOMPOSITIONAL EFFECTS

So far the story has been of a relatively simple mechanism, by which the only attributes found in representations of conjunctive concepts have been derived through inheritance from one or other parent. The picture is however not quite so simple. In the attribute inheritance study, there were a small number of *emergent* properties that subjects listed as important for the conjunction, but which were absent in the parent concepts. For example, PET BIRDS talk and live in cages— both attributes that are conspicuously absent in pets and birds when considered as separate categories. One way for such attributes to appear is through the retrieval of additional information from memory. The use of the noun phrase PET BIRD when first encountered may indeed set off the process of creating a new composite prototype. (Consider the novel concepts of PET SCORPION or GLASS BICYCLE.) But it is also possible that the phrase will identify a concept that is already available in memory—either as a result of an earlier encounter with the concept, or even as a result of direct experience with a number of instances of the conjunctive category. Someone when faced with the concept Black Politician may retrieve one or two familiar instances, and then base a prototype on their perceived common attributes.

A second possible source of emergent attributes would be from the coherence constraint as applied to the creation of the composite concept. If a particular inconsistency is identified, then one way to resolve it may be to make an additional modification to the concept. Suppose, while travelling in Georgia, that you hear of a PET SKUNK for the first time. The behavior of skunks is not in every respect compatible with a home environment. The problem can be resolved however with a surgical intervention, which you may then decide to add to your composite prototype as a likely attribute.

FINAL REMARKS—TESTING CONCEPTS TO DESTRUCTION

This chapter has focused on a specific research program aimed at showing that prototype theory can provide a solid basis from which to build an account of how the meaning of compound noun phrases is composed from the meanings of constituent parts. I have argued that the rejection of the classical approach to concept definition predicts inconsistency in categorization, and that just such inconsistencies do occur. It should of course be understood that these results do not preclude the possibility of people responding in a logically consistent way if they chose to do so. Rather than reflecting a nonnormativity in behavior, I would argue that the results reflect the flexibility inherent in the interface between language and the world. Natural language uses phrases such as "A is a kind of B" or "X is an A which is not a B," which appear in their syntactic form to entail class inclusion or set intersection and complementation. However because meanings are combined *intensionally,* and because concepts have prototype structure, the result is quite frequently non-Boolean. There are many other circumstances in which we operate in an intensional mode. The so-called "conjunction fallacy" demonstrated by Tversky and Kahneman (1983) is one example. The moral is that semantics has to be studied through analysis of the intensional meaning of terms. Attempts to build extensional model-theoretic accounts in which word meanings are tied to the sets of objects to which they refer in a model of a possible world will fail to capture the interesting interactions that occur in people's use of words in combination.

As a postscript, I describe a pilot study in which subjects were asked to combine the uncombinable. The idea of the study was to exaggerate the conflict resolution part of the model by requiring subjects to imagine objects that combined two highly different categories, with no overlap in normal experience. There should then be plenty of opportunity for emergent attributes to be produced as subjects struggled to find a consistent composite prototype to represent the new type of object.

For example, subjects were asked to describe attributes for the following objects:

—A teapot that is a computer
—A bicycle that is a stove
—A fruit that is a kind of furniture
—A fish that is also a vehicle

Subjects were encouraged to use drawings to help illustrate the typical appearance of such an object.

Apart from being too idiosyncratic for easy analysis, the study did provide some points of interest. For example, there was clear evidence of conflict resolution (something for which there was a pressing need in most instances!) achieved through the invention of new attributes, not seen in either parent alone. Thus the need for the FISH-VEHICLE to be directable at will led some subjects to postulate control wires implanted in the fish's brain, while others had the fish conditioned to respond to particular signals. One problem with FRUIT-FURNITURE was that fruit decays, while furniture should be relatively durable. The resolution was achieved by either replacing the furniture once a week (inheriting the attribute from FRUIT) or else by developing strains of fruit that were stable for very long periods (taking an attribute of FURNITURE). Others had the fruit still attached to a vine, so that it could be prevented from decay by still being alive. Again the process of maturation of the fruit would be extremely slow.

The impossible objects study brings out the similarity between the process of concept combination and the construction of scenarios, or mental models. People take one of the objects and try to adapt it to reflect as many of the attributes of the other concept as possible. Changes are introduced, and the consequences of those changes are then *propagated* through the object to see what else would be entailed. A fish that is a vehicle would have to be able to carry people or things (a highly important attribute of vehicles). Hence some kind of compartment or attachment must be added. Some subjects put a saddle on the back of the fish, others slung a basket underneath like a hot-air balloon would have, while still others surgically implanted a pressurized compartment within the fish. One can see that as each change is implemented, the subject has to think through the consequences, and make further adaptations. Different people will end up with quite different answers to the problem. Such processes are obviously an extreme form of concept modification, likely to be seen only in creative design and planning decisions (see for example Barsalou, Usher, and Sewell, 1985). In less exaggerated form, however, they appear to be at work in everyday language understanding, whenever we hear a novel combination of words, and have to construct a new concept of what is being referred to.

CONCLUSION

In this chapter I have argued for the interactive nature of conceptual combination. The result of considering two concepts in conjunction can only be properly explained with reference to the intensional semantic contents of those concepts, together with higher-order mechanisms for determining coherence and conflict amongst the attributes of the composite prototype. More generally, the results on intransitivity of categorization, and inconsistencies in the treatment of conjunction, disjunction and negation all point to the common conclusion that the way in which we use noun terms in common parlance only approximates to the corresponding interpretation of such constructions in set logic. To the extent that our concepts are defined around prototypes, with a corresponding fuzziness about just what a term should refer to, the same fuzziness carries over into our interpretation of logical connectives like relative clause constructions, or the phrase 'A or B'. Most critically, the demonstration of the range of effects described here provides strong evidence for the lack of "core" common element definitions for a considerable number of concepts.[12] The widespread occurrence of non-normative effects of the kind that Osherson and Smith (1981) originally identified as false predictions of the prototype model, must be seen as the best kind of support for that model. I have tried to show how the basic prototype model has to be extended in order to take account of the more complex range of effects thrown up by the study of conceptual combinations.

REFERENCES

Armstrong, S. L., Gleitman, L. R., & Gleitman, H. (1983). What some concepts might not be. *Cognition, 13,* 263–308.

Barsalou, L. W. (1985). Ideals, central tendency, and frequency of instantiation as determinants of graded structure in categories. *Journal of Experimental Psychology: Learning, Memory, and Cognition, 11,* 629–654.

Barsalou, L. W., & Billman, D. (1989). *Systematicity in concepts.* Unpublished manuscript. Georgia Institute of Technology.

Barsalou, L. W., Usher, J. A., & Sewell, D. R. (1985). *Schema-based planning of events.* Paper presented at the Annual Convention of the Psychonomic Society, Boston, November.

Bruner, J. S., Goodnow, J. J., & Austin, G. A. (1956). *A study of thinking.* New York: Wiley.

Cantor, N., Smith, E. E., French, R., & Mezzich, J. (1980). Psychiatric diagnosis as prototype categorization. *Abnormal Psychology, 89,* 181–193.

Chater, N., Lyon, K., & Myers, T. (1990). Why are conjunctive categories overextended? *Journal of Experimental Psychology: Learning, Memory & Cognition, 16,* 497–508.

Cohen, B., & Murphy, G. L. (1984). Models of concepts. *Cognitive Science, 8,* 27–58.

Franks, B. (1989). Concept Combination: Towards an account of privatives. *In* G. Dunbar, B. Franks, & T. Myers, (Eds.), *Papers from the 1989 Edinburgh round table on the mental lexicon.* Edinburgh: Edinburgh University, Centre for Cognitive Science.

Hampton, J. A. (1979). Polymorphous concepts in semantic memory. *Journal of Verbal Learning and Verbal Behavior, 18,* 441–461.

Hampton, J. A. (1981). An investigation of the nature of abstract concepts. *Memory and Cognition, 9,* 149–156.

Hampton, J. A. (1982). A demonstration of intransitivity in natural concepts. *Cognition, 12,* 151–164.

Hampton, J. A. (1987). Inheritance of attributes in natural concept conjunctions. *Memory and Cognition, 15,* 55–71.

Hampton, J. A. (1988a). Disjunction of natural concepts. *Memory & Cognition, 16,* 579–591.

Hampton, J. A. (1988b). Overextension of conjunctive concepts: Evidence for a unitary model of

---

[12]Or at least it shows a failure to use such common element definitions (should they exist) when doing categorization tasks.

concept typicality and class inclusion. *Journal of Experimental Psychology: Learning, Memory and Cognition, 14,* 12–32.

Hampton, J. A. (1989). Concepts and correct thinking. *Mind and Language, 4,* 35–42.

Hampton, J. A. (1990). *Conceptual combination: Conjunction and negation of natural concepts.* Unpublished manuscript. City University, London.

Hampton, J. A., & Gardiner, M. M. (1983). Measures of internal category structure: A correlational analysis of normative data. *British Journal of Psychology, 74,* 491–516.

Keil, F. C., & Batterman, N. (1984). A characteristic-to-defining shift in the development of word meaning. *Journal of Verbal Learning and Verbal Behavior, 23,* 221–236.

Kempton, W. (1978). Category grading and taxonomic relations: A mug is a sort of cup. *American Ethnologist, 5,* 44–65.

Lakoff, G. (1987). *Women, fire and dangerous things.* Chicago: University of Chicago Press.

Levi, J. (1978). *The syntax and semantics of complex nominals.* New York: Academic Press.

Malt, B. C., & Smith, E. E. (1983). Correlated properties in natural categories. *Journal of Verbal Learning and Verbal Behavior, 23,* 250–269.

McCloskey, M., & Glucksberg, S. (1978). Natural categories: Well-defined or fuzzy sets? *Memory and Cognition, 6,* 462–472.

McNamara, T. P., & Sternberg, R. (1983). Mental models of word meaning. *Journal of Verbal Learning and Verbal Behavior, 22,* 449–474.

Medin, D. L., & Shoben, E. J. (1988). Context and structure in conceptual combination. *Cognitive Psychology, 20,* 158–190.

Miller, G. A., & Johnson-Laird, P. N. (1976). *Language and perception.* Cambridge, MA: Harvard University Press.

Murphy, G. L. (1982). Cue validity and levels of categorization. *Psychological Bulletin, 91,* 174–177.

Murphy, G. L. (1988). Comprehending complex concepts. *Cognitive Science, 12,* 529–562.

Murphy, G. L., & Medin, D. L. (1985). The role of theories in conceptual coherence. *Psychological Review, 92,* 289–316.

Oden, G. C. (1977). Integration of fuzzy logical information. *Journal of Experimental Psychology: Human Perception and Performance, 3,* 565–575.

Osherson, D. N., & Smith, E. E. (1981). On the adequacy of prototype theory as a theory of concepts. *Cognition, 11,* 35–58.

Osherson, D. N., & Smith, E. E. (1982). Gradedness and conceptual conjunction. *Cognition, 12,* 299–318.

Randall, R. A. (1976). How tall is a taxonomic tree? Some evidence for dwarfism. *American Ethnologist, 3,* 543–553.

Rosch, E., & Mervis, C. B. (1975). Family resemblances: Studies in the internal structure of categories. *Cognitive Psychology, 7,* 573–605.

Smith, E. E., & Medin, D. L. (1981). *Categories and concepts.* Cambridge, MA: Harvard University Press.

Smith, E. E., Osherson, D. N., Rips, L. J., & Keane, M. (1988). Combining prototypes: A selective modification model. *Cognitive Science, 12,* 485–527.

Smith, E. E., Shoben, E. J., & Rips, L. J. (1974). Structure and process in semantic memory: A featural model for semantic decisions. *Psychological Review, 81,* 214–241.

Tversky, A. (1977). Features of similarity. *Psychological Review, 84,* 327–352.

Tversky, A., & Kahneman, D. (1983). Extensional versus intuitive reasoning: The conjunction fallacy in probability judgment. *Psychological Review, 90,* 293–315.

Wittgenstein, L. (1953). *Philosophical investigations.* New York: Macmillan.

Zadeh, L. (1965). Fuzzy sets. *Information and control, 8,* 338–353.

Zadeh, L. (1982). A note on prototype theory and fuzzy sets. *Cognition, 12,* 291–297.

5 Predicating and Nonpredicating Combinations

Edward J. Shoben
University of Illinois

During the past 15 years, there has been a great deal of interest in categorization. This work has ranged from the early work in how people classify a particular exemplar as a member of a particular category (Rosch, 1975; Smith, Shoben, & Rips, 1974) to more recent concerns about how categories are structured and learned (Armstrong, Gleitman, & Gleitman, 1983; Medin & Wattenmaker, 1987). Medin (1989) provides a useful summary of this work.

Despite the large volume of work on categorization *per se,* there has been very little work on another aspect of concepts: how concepts are combined (although see Gleitman & Gleitman, 1970; Murphy, 1990). In some cases, such combinations seem relatively transparent; a *red truck* is a truck that is red. For many such *predicating* adjectives, this kind of interpretation comes readily to mind. However, there is another type of combination that does not so readily admit such an interpretation. For example, a *criminal lawyer* is not usually a criminal. This latter combination uses a *nonpredicating* adjective, one that cannot accurately be paraphrased as *The noun that is Adjective.*

From these examples, one might be tempted to claim that combinations involving predicating adjectives are easy to interpret and those involving nonpredicating adjectives are difficult to interpret. I believe that such a contention would be at best only half-correct. How we comprehend predicating adjectives is a very difficult problem. Our objective in the present chapter is to suggest that it is fruitful to make such a division between *predicating* and *nonpredicating* adjectives and to place some constraints on the nature of any viable theory of their comprehension.

An understanding of conceptual combinations is important for several reasons. First, even a perfect understanding of how concepts are represented in memory would not tell us much about how they are used. Many are used in combination with other concepts and the myriad of combinations into which concepts can enter is itself an interesting reflection of the complexity of the human understanding system. Second, combinations themselves reflect an interesting aspect of how much we know about the world. We know, for example, that *rain forest,* and *rain cloud* both have meaning (although the relation between the nouns is different in the two cases) but that *rain desk* and *rain temper* do not. More subtly, we know that a *mountain town* is likely to be small, but a *mountain river* need not be.

In this chapter, I begin by examining predicating adjectives and showing that an understanding of even these most simple of combinations is indeed a difficult problem. I then move on to a discussion of nonpredicating adjectives and consider some ways by which people might arrive at the proper interpretation of them. Finally, I offer some speculations about the similarity of the two types of combinations and how it might be advisable to look for a uniform theory of how we process conceptual combinations.

PREDICATING ADJECTIVES

Predicating adjectives are deceptively simple. A *red apple,* for example, means an apple that is red. Similarly, a *pet fish* is a fish that is also a pet. One might be tempted to use a kind of set-theoretic logic in trying to account for membership decisions in such combined categories. More specifically, one proposal is to adapt fuzzy set theory (Zadeh, 1965) to combinations. According to one such version, the degree to which an exemplar belongs to a combined category is a function of the degree to which it belongs to each of the constituent categories. To use the example of *red apple,* the degree to which something is a *red apple* is a function of its membership in the category *apples* and its membership in the category *red things.* To exclude such things as fire engines and golden delicious apples, the function is usually the minimum (or *min*) function: Membership of an exemplar is determined by the minimum of its membership in each of the constituent categories.

Although such an approach seems inherently reasonable, Osherson and Smith (1983) noted several problems with it. Most notably, it seemed that there were some exemplars that were better members of the combined categories than of either of the constituent categories. According to the *min rule,* such a result is impossible. For example, a *guppy* is an excellent example of a *pet fish.* Yet, a guppy is a relatively poor example of a fish and a poor example of a pet. According to the *min rule,* such examples should not exist. Osherson and Smith (1983) provide other examples. In addition, they performed an experiment in which they asked subjects to determine how good a picture of various types of apple was of five categories: an apple, a red apple, a brown apple, a red thing, and a brown thing. In contrast to the predictions of the *min rule,* Osherson and Smith found that subjects judged a picture of a brown apple to be a better example of a brown apple, than of either a brown thing or an apple. Although they also obtained other results that were incompatible with the *min rule,* this one was clearly the most striking.

THE MODIFICATION MODEL

Osherson and Smith (1983) proposed a modification model to account for their data. According to this model, concepts are stored as dimensions and values on those dimensions. Table 5.1 provides an example for the concept *apple,* and its combined concepts *red apple,* and *brown apple.* It is assumed by the model that concepts have dimensions and a range of acceptable values on those dimensions. These values correspond at least roughly to frequency in the world. Additionally, each dimension is associated with some level of diagnosticity: The degree of importance of that dimension for that particular concept.

The formation of conceptual combinations in the model, such as *red apple,* involves changing the values on the color dimension and increasing the diagnosticity of that dimension. Thus, as Table 5.1 indicates, all of the color values have been shifted to *red,* and the diagnosticity of the color dimension has been increased by some amount. Aside from these two changes, the representation, according to the model, is identical for *apple* and *red apple.*

The model identifies concepts by matching stored representations to those presented. Goodness of match is determined by comparing values on each di-

TABLE 5.1
Diagnosticities and Dimensions (Underscored) and Number of Votes on Each for Apple

Apple	*Picture of Red Apple*	*Picture of Brown Apple*
.5 Color		
40 Red	50 Red	
10 Yellow		
Brown		50 Brown
.25 Shape		
45 Round	50 Round	50 Round
5 Cylindrical		
Square		
.10 Texture		
45 Smooth	50 Smooth	50 Smooth
5 Rough		
Bumpy		

mension weighted by diagnosticity. Thus, for example, if one is presented with a picture of a typical apple, then it will be one that is round, smooth, and red. As a result, we can compute, according to the modification model, the degree to which it will match all of the representations shown in Table 5.1. The rule for similarity is that, for each dimension, the values that mismatch are subtracted from those that match and weighted by the diagnosticity. More formally, the model adopts the contrast rule first proposed by Tversky (1977). The similarity between any two concepts is the number of shared attributes reduced by the number of unshared ones, as described by Equation 1.

$$S(a,b) = f_a(a\ b) - f_b(a - b) - f_c(b - a) \qquad (1)$$

Here, $S(a,b)$ is the similarity between a and b, and $f_a(a\ b)$ is the number of attributes shared by the two concepts, $f_b(a - b)$ is the number of attributes possessed by a that are not possessed by b and $f_c(b - a)$ is some function of the attributes possessed by b but not possessed by a. All functions are assumed to be monotonic. The modification model in fact assumes that all of these functions are identical.

Let us begin with the representation for *apple*. According to Table 5.1, 40 of the values match on the color dimension, and 10 mismatch. Weighted by the diagnosticity, this gives a value of (.5) (40–20) or 10. For shape, 45 values match our picture of a round, smooth, and red apple, and thus the similarity in terms of shape is (.25) (45–10) or 8.75. Finally, for texture, the similarity is (.1) (45–10) or 3. Summing over all three dimensions, the overall similarity is 21.25.

Comparing the picture to *red apple*, the values are identical except on the color dimension. As Table 5.2 indicates, all of the values match and, because of

TABLE 5.2
Diagnosticities and Dimensions (Underscored) and Number of Votes on Each for Red Apple

Red Apple	Picture of Red Apple	Picture of Brown Apple
2 Color		
50 Red	50 Red	
Yellow		
Brown		50 Brown
.25 Shape		
45 Round	50 Round	50 Round
5 Cylindrical		
Square		
.10 Texture		
45 Smooth	50 Smooth	50 Smooth
5 Rough		
Bumpy		

TABLE 5.3
Diagnosticities and Dimensions (Underscored) and Number of Votes on Each for Brown Apple

Apple	Picture of Red Apple	Picture of Brown Apple
2 Color		
Red	50 Red	
Yellow		
50 Brown		50 Brown
.25 Shape		
45 Round	50 Round	50 Round
5 Cylindrical		
Square		
.10 Texture		
45 Smooth	50 Smooth	50 Smooth
5 Rough		
Bumpy		

the increased diagnosticity, the similarity of color is 2 (50) or 100. Summing over all three dimensions, the overall similarity of the picture of a red apple to the concept *red apple* is 112.25. Not surprisingly, the picture is not very similar to the concept of *brown apple*. The mismatch on all color values (see Table 5.3) yields a similarity of -100 (when weighted by diagnosticity) and the overall similarity is -87.75.

If one assumes that the judged similarity rating is some monotonic function of this similarity, then the modification model is now able to predict violations of the *min* rule. Our similarity analysis has just indicated that an object can be more similar to a combined concept, *red apple*, than to the simple concept *apple*. In fact, Osherson and Smith have shown that the modification model can provide a satisfactory account of people's judgments of a number of simple and combined concepts.

COMPLICATIONS FOR THE MODIFICATION MODEL

Although the modification model can account very nicely for violations of the *min* rule, it suffers from several problems. As Medin and Shoben (1988) noted, the modification model makes no provision for correlated attributes. Thus, for example, when one changes from *apple* to *red apple*, the only attribute that changes is the attribute for color. Now in this particular case, such an assumption may be tenable, although one could argue that *green apple* and *yellow apple* would make such an assumption false. Green apples are more likely to be used for cooking than ordinary apples (yellow apples less so). Green apples are also more likely to be tart (yellow apples less likely). Medin and Shoben used the example from the category spoons. They noted that the modification model makes some rather specific predictions concerning the transitivity of similarity relations. For example, Medin and Shoben (1988) noted that people judged *metal spoons* better examples than *wooden spoons* of the category *spoons*. According to the modification model, such a result means that there are more votes on the value metal than on the value wooden for the *materials* dimension. This finding implies for the modification model that a *metal spoon* should be a better example than a *wooden spoon* of a *small spoon*. The same result should also hold for the category *large spoon*. Formally, we can express these ordinal relations as equations. Thus, these two predictions are:

$$ws(S) < ms(S) => ws(SS) < ms(SS), \qquad (2)$$

$$ws(S) < ms(S) => ws(LS) < ms(LS), \qquad (3)$$

where $ws(S)$ is the typicality of a wooden spoon as a spoon and $ms(SS)$ is the typicality of a metal spoon as a small spoon. Because the size votes on metal and wooden spoons are identical according to the modification model, this model also predicts the outcome in equation 4.

$$ws(SS) < ms(SS) => ws(LS) < ms(LS). \qquad (4)$$

In addition to these three predictions, there are three others that are in some sense the complement of the first three:

$$ws(LS) < ws(SS) => ms(LS) < ms(SS), \qquad (5)$$

$$ws(S) < ws(SS) => ms(S) < ms(SS), \qquad (6)$$

$$ms(S) < ms(LS) => ws(S) < ws(LS). \qquad (7)$$

Let us consider equation 6 in more detail. Spoons have some distribution of votes on the dimensions of size and materials. If a wooden spoon is less typical of a spoon than it is of a small spoon, then a metal spoon must show the same relation because a metal spoon differs from a wooden one only on the materials dimension. Medin and Shoben (1988) performed an experiment in which they asked subjects to judge the goodness of example of combined concepts, such as "How good an example of the category *small spoon* is a *metal spoon?*" Contrary to the predictions of the modification model, Medin and Shoben found numerous violations of these predictions of the model. In fact, they found that the predictions held less frequently than even chance would expect.

To provide one example, the results for the *spoon* category are given in Table 5.4. Note here that *metal spoons* and *small spoons* are considered better examples of the category *spoon*, but *metal spoons* are not judged as better examples of *large spoons* and *small spoons* are not better examples of *wooden spoons*. One interpretation of these results is that people take advantage of correlated at-

TABLE 5.4
Typicality Ratings for Combinations of Spoons

Typicality as Spoons

Large	5.42
Small	7.58
Wooden	4.77
Metal	7.54

Typicality as Combinations

	As Wooden Spoon	*As Metal Spoon*
Large	7.74	4.68
Small	2.44	7.44

tributes. Wooden spoons tend to be large as they are usually used in food preparation. Metal spoons, on the other hand, are most commonly used for consumption. The modification model, as currently constituted, has no way of accounting for correlated attributes.

Put more generally, this model has no way of incorporating the kind of knowledge that we have about relations among attributes. In our argument about why wooden spoons tend to be large, it might be noted that one might explain such a finding by reference to our theories about spoon use. Spoons that are used for eating should be small enough to fit comfortably in the mouth, yet hold a reasonable amount. Thus, such spoons typically are neither demitasse spoons nor serving spoons. Moreover, such spoons should be pleasant to look at and unlikely to injure; they are thus usually metal. In contrast, spoons used for cooking are more functional. They can be larger and now the concern is not scratching the mouth but scratching the cooking vessel. Thus, our theories about the way such an implement is used (Murphy & Medin, 1985) arguably play an important role in how we think about what constitutes a typical combined concept.

One question that remains is how general is this correlation among attributes. Both proponents of the modification model (Smith & Osherson, 1987) and its detractors (Medin & Shoben, 1988) have used a limited and nonrandom sample. As with any variant on the method of single cases (Clark, 1973), the generality of the results is limited to the representativeness of the materials.

It seems that the correlated case is more general for a number of reasons. First, some properties are inherently correlational: Changing the construction material from lead to aluminum will necessarily make the object lighter and less likely to oxidize, for example. Such correlations are an intrinsic part of the meaning of these two metals. Second, some properties are correlational because of people's beliefs. For example, made in Japan is usually considered of higher quality than made in the Philippines, although that relation is not intrinsically true. Finally, most properties are correlational because of our knowledge about the world. Upon reflection, it would indeed be remarkable if the color or size of an object was uncorrelated with every other attribute. One example is the concept *tropical fish*. Suppose we consider whether certain attributes change their values when one moves from a *tropical fish* to a *large tropical fish*. At least in the author's mind, a large tropical fish is (a) more likely to dig in the sand, (b) more likely to be a good parent, (c) less likely to be peaceful, (d) more likely to have its colors fade with age, (e) more likely to be oviparous rather than viviparous, (f) more likely to mate for life, (g) more likely to require more acid water, (h) more likely to require soft water, and (i) more likely to require live food in its diet. The point of all this is to illustrate that it is often difficult to think of an attribute that is *not* correlated with a dimension like size.

COMBINATIONS AND THEIR "SIMPLE" COUNTERPARTS

Given that most predicating adjectives specify a value on a particular dimension, then it is instructive to examine what happens to judgments of typicality of concepts that are so modified. More specifically, can we expect the typicality of an item to its combined category to correlate with its typicality to its simple category? One might assume, for example, that the noun might dominate the adjective-noun combination in this circumstance as it does in others (Hampton, 1988). Considering the categories birds and song birds leads one to place some credence in such an account. Robin is a good example of both and pigeon is a good example of neither. In fact, it seems that the combined category restricts the range of acceptable exemplars such that pigeon is a moderately good example of bird and a poor example of song bird. Poor examples of bird, such as penguin and goose are not members of the category song birds at all. In contrast, examination of birds and farm birds yields a quite different result. Chicken, for example, is a good example of farm bird but a poor example of a bird. In fact, most good examples of farm bird are very poor examples of bird and vice versa.

Although such linguistic arguments are useful, it remains to be demonstrated that subjects perform in accordance with our intuitions. Accordingly, Douglas Medin and I performed an experiment in which subjects were asked to judge the typicality of eight exemplars in each of ten categories. Half of the categories for each subject were simple ones, like games and weapons and half were combined categories like board games and military weapons. The categories were counterbalanced such that no subject got both games and board games, for example. All exemplars had been pretested so that all exemplars were judged to be members of both the derived category and the corresponding simple one.

The results of primary interest were the correlations between the ratings of typicality of the simple category and its corresponding derived category. For example, for the category games, we correlated the typicality ratings assigned to monopoly, clue, and checkers with those assigned to those same games in the category board games.

Perhaps the most striking result was that results varied tremendously according to category. Although the average correlation was near zero, the range was extreme. For example, the correlation between the board game exemplars and game exemplars was .79. At the same time, the correlation between beverage exemplars and alcoholic beverage exemplars was $-.80$. Finally, there was no relation between the typicality assigned to vegetable exemplars and that assigned to raw vegetable exemplars ($r = -.02$). The exemplars are given in Table 5.5.

TABLE 5.5
Exemplars for Simple and Combined Categories
Ordered by Typicality as a Simple Concept with Typicality as a Combination in Parentheses

Games and Board Games

1. Monopoly (1)
2. Risk (4)
3. Clue (5)
4. Checkers (2)
5. Stratego (6)
6. Shutes and Ladders (8)
7. Trivial Pursuit (3)
8. Chinese Checkers (7)

Beverages and Alcoholic Beverages

1. Vodka (7)
2. Whiskey (5)
3. (Rum (6)
4. (Gin (8)
5. Beer (1)
6. Champagne (4)
7. Wine (2)
8. Wine cooler (3)

Vegetables and Raw Vegetables

1. Green Beans (6)
2. (Corn (8)
3. Lettuce (3)
4. Cucumber (2)
5. Spinach (5)
6. Celery (1)
7. Cauliflower (4)
8. Squash (7)

Examination of the exemplars given in Table 5.5 provides a clue to understanding why this correlation is so variable. The direction of the correlation depends on the way in which the conceptual combination is formed. If the combination selects a typical attribute of the simple category, then the correlation between the exemplars of the simple category and those of the combined category is relatively high. For example, most representative exemplars of the category games are board games. In contrast, the correlation between exemplars of the combined category and exemplars of the simple category is low when the conceptual combination is formed by selecting an atypical attribute of the simple category. For example, most good examples of beverages (coffee, tea, milk) are nonalcoholic. Thus, good examples of alcoholic beverages tend to be poor examples of beverages. Finally, when the attribute selected is neither typical nor atypical, then the correlation between the two exemplar contexts is near zero. For vegetables and raw vegetables, the correlation is near zero as many good examples of vegetables are rarely raw (corn, peas) while many good examples are often raw (lettuce, cucumber). Similarly, many poor examples of vegetables (squash) are rarely raw, whereas others frequently are (cauliflower).

Thus, the combined category may or may not bear a particular relation to its simple category. Although the results of this study are certainly far from definitive, it appears that the determining factor is the adjectival component. Thus, if the adjective (as in board games) selects a typical value on one of the dimensions of the noun category, then the typicality gradient of the combined category may mirror the gradient of the simple category. On the other hand, if the adjective selects an unusual value of the simple category (alcoholic beverages) then the typicality gradient of the combined category may be very different from the gradient of the simple category.

One future extension of this work is an examination of the typicality gradients for a category and two combined categories that are derived from the same simple category. For example, using the simple category *bird,* one might examine the typicality gradients for *song birds* and *huntable birds*. If the analysis in terms of common values on a dimension is correct, then the typicality gradient for *song birds* should resemble the gradient for *birds* very closely because most birds sing. At the same time, the typicality gradient for *huntable birds* should not resemble the typicality gradient for *birds* because most birds are not huntable.

Thus, for predicating adjectives, it seems that the relation among the attributes is of primary importance. Consistent with Osherson and Smith's modification model, red apples may indeed be a great deal like apples, as most apples are red. At the same time, as Medin and Shoben (1988) pointed out, there are a great many cases where changing one of the attributes changes many others as well. Moreover these relations among attributes appear to be central in determining whether the gradient of typicality will be similar or dissimilar between a combined category and the one from which it was derived.

Thus, it seems clear that the relation between the parts of these simple combinations is not nearly as straightforward as one might believe. Any adequate model of the processing of these combinations must take into account the problem of correlated attributes.

NONPREDICATING ADJECTIVES

It is clear from the preceding discussion that relatively simple solutions to the question of how predicating adjectives are comprehended are far from satisfactory. Specifically, approaches based on changing one value in the representation for a concept are not likely to succeed, even for the simplest (such as large and small) of predicating adjectives. At a minimum, the evidence for correlated attributes would seem to suggest a region or subcategory of the noun.

The problem of nonpredicating adjectives, those that cannot be paraphrased as "An N that is A," is doubly complicated because the determination of the meaning is a difficult task in and of itself. There are no morphological cues, as there are with predicating adjectives. Thus, for example, a *lemon peel* is the peel of a lemon where the peel is an integral part of the lemon. In contrast, *flu virus* implies a causal relation such that a virus causes the flu. These types of combinations have received relatively little attention from cognitive scientists. There was some early work in linguistics (Gleitman & Gleitman, 1970; Postal, 1974). Perhaps the most interesting analysis has been provided by Levi (1978). In addition to providing a taxonomy of nonpredicating adjectives, she also provided a derivational analysis consistent with then standard generational theory. Here, our major concern is with the taxonomy she provides.

RELATIONS AMONG COMPONENTS

Levi delineated 10 categories of nonpredicating combinations in addition to a group of combinations that she classified as "nominalizations," such as *presidential power*. Douglas Medin and I elected to try to classify all of the nonpredicating adjectives without worrying about the nominalizations (many of which were cross-classified as one of the 10 categories).

Our own taxonomy used 14 categories, the first ten of which are taken from Levi. These categories and examples are given in Table 5.6. Categories A and B are causals where N causes Adj and Adj causes N respectively. *Electric shock* and *flu virus* are examples. Categories C and D are possessives that can be paraphrased as N has A and A has N, respectively. *Picture book* and *lemon peel* are examples. Categories E and F reflect a compositional or making relation, but this pair of categories is not parallel in the same way that the first two pairs are. Category E can be paraphrased as "makes" as in *heat lamp*. Category F can be paraphrased as "comprised of" or "made from," as in *daisy chain*. Category G

TABLE 5.6
Types of Nonpredicating Adjectives

A. N causes Adj FLU VIRUS	H. N uses Adj GAS STOVE
B. Adj causes N HEAT RASH	I. N located Adj URBAN RIOTS
C. N has Adj PICTURE BOOK	J. N for Adj NOSE DROPS
D. Adj has N LEMON PEEL	K. N about Adj TAX LAW
E. N makes Adj HONEY BEE	F.' N derived from Adj OIL MONEY
F. N made of Adj SUGAR CUBE	I.' Adj located N MURDER TOWN
G. Adj is N SERVANT GIRL	H.' N used by Adj FINGER TOY

reflects the "is" relation as in *servant girl*. Category H combinations can be paraphrased as "uses" as in *oil lamp*. Category I combinations are locatives, as in *mountain stream*. Category J combinations can be paraphrased as "for," as in *industrial equipment*.

Beginning with category K, we begin to deviate substantially from Levi's taxonomy. In this class of combinations, we have included many of her nominalizations with the paraphrase "about." Examples here are *tax law* and *murder mystery*. Our remaining categories are all related to earlier ones and consequently are designated with a prime. Combinations from category F', for example, can be paraphrased as "derived from," as in *oil money*. Combinations from category H' are the inverse of the "use" relation in category H. For example, a *finger toy* is a toy used by the fingers as opposed to a *gas stove* (category H) which is a stove that uses gas. Finally, inverse locatives, category I' are combinations such as *murder town* that indicate the location of the adjective, as opposed to category I combinations that indicate the location of the noun.

THE COMPLEXITY HYPOTHESIS

Our first hypothesis was that some of these categories were conceptually more complex than others. More specifically, some relations, such as categories I and J, can be marked by case endings in some languages. One could analogously argue that category K combinations resembled ablatives. In contrast, causals, such as categories A and B seemed much more complex to us. The concept of

causality develops much later in children than does the concept of simple possession (categories C and D) and it is therefore a reasonable hypothesis that
causality is more complex for adults to comprehend as well.

Medin and I consequently performed an experiment in which we asked subjects to read simple sentences, each of which concluded with a conceptual
combination of the type discussed earlier. All consisted of a nonpredicating
adjective and a noun. To make the number of stimuli manageable, we restricted
our combinations to those that we judged fell into the categories A through K. As
a check on comprehension, subjects answered a true–false question after reading
the sentence. The sentence was presented in two parts. For example, subjects
pressed a space bar on a computer terminal and read "The serviceman was aware
of the dangers of." After they had comprehended this segment, they pressed a
space bar and read "electric shock." They pressed the space bar again and the
question was displayed to which they responded by pressing one of two keys.
The primary dependent variable of interest was the time required to read the
conceptual combination, "electric shock" in this example.

Contrary to expectations, the results provided no support for the complexity
hypothesis. Overall, the mean comprehension time was 1201 msec, but the mean
time for the comprehension of the two causals was 1200 msec. There were some
interesting asymmetries, however. The *have* relations, such as picture book
(group C) and lemon peel (group D) were nearly the most different pair of the
ten: 1164 and 1295 msec, respectively. At the same time, the causals, flu virus
(group A) and heat rash (group B) were very similar on average, 1209 and 1190
msec, respectively. So too were the make relations, honey bee (group E) and
sugar cube (group F), 1142 and 1156 msec, respectively.

Thus, not only did we fail to observe any evidence in support of the complexity hypothesis, but we also failed to find any consistency among pairs of combinations that shared some similarity of relation. Although the groups differed
from each other in overall analysis of variance, structural variables appeared not
to account for the differences we observed.

THE TYPICALITY HYPOTHESIS

At the same time, although the types of combinations did not seem to vary
tremendously, there were marked variations in the examples that we selected for
each category in how rapidly they were comprehended. Although space limitations preclude us from examining all of them, examination of several is illustrative of the range of magnitude that were found.

Table 5.7 shows the mean comprehension times for "made of" relations,
group F. Interestingly, many of the times are very fast and, with one exception,
mountain range, all of the times are faster than 1225 msec. The slowest time of
all, mountain range, was over 100 msec slower at 1343 msec. Such a result is

TABLE 5.7
Mean Comprehension Times for Group F

Floral wreath		1167
Mountain range		1343
Chocolate bar		1124
Sugar cube		1015
Paper money		1223
Student committee		1134
Cable network		1101
Plastic toy		1142
	Mean	1156

somewhat surprising in that mountain range is certainly a common combination. An even more extreme result can be seen in the analysis of the results for group G (the "is" relations). Here, seven of the eight combinations were comprehended in less than 1170 msec. The extreme item (finger lakes) required over 1500 msec. on average. Such results suggest an alternative explanation for our findings: Perhaps it is naive to think that some types of combinations will be inherently more difficult than others any more than we might expect nouns to have inherently longer lexical decision times than verbs. In contrast to this approach, it may be that combinations are like schemata and take various values. Moreover, some values may fit better than others. If we assume that comprehension time is a function of how well the value fits the existing slot, then, as in other aspects of categorization, we should find that good examples of a certain type of combination should be comprehended more readily than poor examples.

Although one would need a new experiment to provide a rigorous test of this schema hypothesis, we can reach a preliminary evaluation of it by examining the data from this experiment. We have already noted that *mountain range* and *finger lakes* are outliers within their own respective categories. One can argue that these are different by looking at how other examples in each category are paraphrased. For example, in category G, examples can be paraphrased as Noun is (a) Adj, as in *the season is winter*, or *the plant is a cactus*. However, the paraphrase rule fails for *the lakes are fingers* (?). Thus, according to the schema hypothesis, *finger lakes* is difficult to comprehend because it does not fit the schema well.

A similar argument can be made for *mountain range*. Other examples in category F can all be paraphrased as Noun is made out of (comprised of) Adj. For example, *The toy is made out of plastic* is a suitable paraphrase for *plastic toy*, just as *the committee was comprised of students* is an appropriate paraphrase for *student committee*. However, *the range was made out of (comprised of) mountains* is not an acceptable paraphrase for *mountain range*.

Two other categories have outliers that are useful to look at in evaluating our hypothesis. The category that has the most extreme outliers is category K. As we see in Table 5.8, there are six examples (such as *tax law* and *sports magazine*)

TABLE 5.8
Mean Comprehension Times for Group K

Tax law		1214
Financial report		1260
Adventure story		1125
Sports magazine		1164
Sex scandal		1119
Oil crisis		1146
Historical drama		1510
Idological debate		1751
	Mean	1286

that are comprehended in between 1119 and 1260 msec. All of these examples can be paraphrased as Noun about Adj or Noun concerning Adj. However, there are two exceptions: *Historical Drama* and *Ideological Debate*. At first blush, these two examples might seem to fit the proposed paraphrase quite well. However, the fit is only syntactic in nature. The drama, for example, is not really *about* history; it is only based on history. Similarly, the *ideological debate* is a debate about some topic that reveals a difference in ideology among the participants, not a debate about ideology *per se*. Thus, these last two examples do not fit the frame very well and thus it is not surprising that comprehension times, as shown in Table 5.4, are in excess of 1500 msec.

The last category we shall consider is category D. In general, all examples (see Table 5.9) can be paraphrased as Adj has Noun, as in *A lemon has a peel* or *A family has antiques*. However, if one divides the examples into those where possession is of a concrete and inalienable part (*lemon peel* and *tire rim*), then the mean comprehension time is 1192 msec. For the remaining six that do not meet these criteria, the mean time is 1330 msec. This result suggests that good examples of this category should include inalienable possession.

As we noted at the outset of this discussion, it is clear that additional empirical work needs to be done before a full evaluation of the schema hypothesis can be

TABLE 5.9
Mean Comprehension Times for Group D

Student power		1187
Lemon peel		1068
Tire rim		1317
Municipal property		1454
Party members		1350
Family antiques		1389
Maternal instincts		1232
National resources		1365
	Mean	1295

made. At the same time, examination of these outliers among the various tax-onomic categories does suggest that such an explanation of our results is at least plausible.

One possibility that should be addressed is that our combinations are so frequent that they constitute single lexical entries, much like idioms. Thus, a proponent of such a view might attribute our results to variability in the degree to which such combinations are lexicalized. Thus, *finger lakes* is less likely to be lexicalized than *servant girl* and consequently it is not surprising that *finger lakes* takes longer to comprehend.

There are at least two reasons to doubt such an account: one theoretical and one empirical. First, allowing large numbers of combinations to be lexicalized leads to a kind of combinatorial explosion of the number of concepts that must be represented in memory. For example, we now need entries not only for *bird*, but also for *song bird, family bird, summer bird, grain bird, urban bird, sea bird, plastic bird, fruit bird, chocolate bird, home bird, city bird,* and *paper bird.* These 13 examples do not begin to exhaust the possible combinations of the noun *bird.* A similarly long list can be constructed for many other common nouns. Assuming that half of these combinations are lexicalized would thus require a six-fold increase in the storage requirements of the memory system.

The empirical argument is that many of the outliers discussed above are highly common (and thus presumably likely to be lexicalized) items. Although one might reasonably argue that *finger lakes* is not terribly common, the same cannot be said about *mountain range* and *historical drama.* Yet these latter two examples had two of the slowest reading times in the study. Thus, although there are no frequency norms for these kinds of combinations, it does not appear that a simple lexicality argument will account for the results.

PROCESSING NONPREDICATING COMBINATIONS

The crucial question of course, is how people arrive at the correct interpretation. One possibility is that people know what kinds of relations certain nouns are likely to enter into. For example, one might notice that the noun *law* tends to enter into combinations involving "about," such as *tax law, divorce law,* and *admiralty law.* Similarly, certain adjectives tend to be found in certain combinations as well; for example, *mountain* tends to be a locative, as in *mountain stream.* However, there are exceptions to both of these generalizations: *Rural law* and *mountain range* are examples. Despite these exceptions, we cannot rule out the possibility that knowledge of possible combinations is involved in the com-prehension of conceptual combinations. However, there is as yet no evidence that requires such an interpretation.

In the absence of such evidence, we can make the default assumption that people try all such possible interpretations in parallel. The interpretation that provides the best match is the one that is selected. Context plays an important role in specifying the interpretation selected. Thus, for example, *oil money* may mean one thing in the context of "With winter approaching, the New Englander wondered if he had enough *oil money*," and quite another in "The recent acquisitions to the Houston art gallery were financed by *oil money*."

How rapidly the interpretation is selected depends not only on the degree of contextual support, but also on how well the interpretation matches the selected frame. Consequently, as suggested earlier, we might expect even novel combinations that match their schema well (such as *plum alcohol*) will be comprehended faster than those that do not (such as *folk remedy*). Both examples here are category F (derived from or made out of). Alcohol made from plums is easily obtained, but the remedy is not derived from folk, but rather from folklore and thus does not fit the schema as well.

At this juncture, such an analysis is clearly speculative. Moreover, the importance we have placed on these structural variables should not be taken to imply no role for other aspects of language. For example, it is undoubtedly the case that common combinations are going to be comprehended more rapidly than novel ones. It is easier to understand *paper doll* than *paper cow* although the type of combination is identical.

THE RELATION BETWEEN PREDICATING AND NONPREDICATING COMBINATIONS

We are a long way from a coherent theory of conceptual combination. For predicating adjectives, it is tempting to analyze the combination in terms of a simple modification of the noun category. We have tried to indicate that this analysis has many problems and that any adequate theory must take into account the relations among attributes of the concept. We suggested instead that item-specific information, such as exemplars are likely to be present in memory.

Nonpredicating adjectives are qualitatively different from their predicating counterparts. Whereas all predicating adjectives may be interpreted as "A N that is Adj", the interpretation of nonpredicating adjectives is neither trivial nor easy. Based on Levi's (1976) earlier linguistic work and some of our own, there are roughly a dozen or more kinds of nonpredicating combinations. We suggested that such categories had good examples and bad examples and that this variability accounted, at least in part, for variations in comprehension time.

What we are far from is a unified theory. Perhaps, given the qualitative differences between predicating and nonpredicating adjectives, we should not aim for a unified theory. However, the dualistic alternative implies that we make a psychological distinction between the two types of combinations and process them differently. At least on intuitive grounds, it seems unlikely that combinations must first be analyzed into predicating and nonpredicating ones and only then can comprehension routines be applied. More likely, in our view, is that there are common routines for both. One might be tempted to argue, for example, that people try to analyze these combinations in terms of the rules for predicating adjectives. Only if such rules fail to find a suitable interpretation do we analyze the combination as a nonpredicating adjective.

Although such a successive discrete stage model has its appeal, we doubt it will prove satisfactory for two reasons. First, similar models of other processes have not fared too well in recent years. One of the best known was Clark and Lucy's (1975) account of indirect requests. Clark and Lucy (1975) assumed that people initially processed requests such as "Can you pass the salt?" literally. Only after failing to reach a sensible interpretation did they arrive at an indirect approach. Subsequent work by Gibbs (1984, Gibbs & Nayak 1989) and others has indicated that many indirect interpretations are reached as rapidly as direct ones. Second, it seems implausible that in processing *corporate lawyer* one must first reject the possibility that the lawyer is obese.

As a final speculation, it may be that predicating adjective are just another class of nonpredicating ones, in the sense that "A noun that is Adj" is similar to "A noun that uses Adj" as in *oil lamp*. The comprehension of combinations must then be a matter of determining both the correct class of combination and determining the correct meaning.

ACKNOWLEDGMENTS

Preparation of this chapter was supported in part by Grant BNS86-08215 from the National Science Foundation. Support for writing this chapter was also provided by a University Scholars grant from the University of Melbourne. I would like to give special thanks to Douglas Medin with whom I collaborated on the research reported in this chapter. Others who commented on earlier drafts of this chapter were James Hampton, V. M. Holmes, and Roger Wales.

REFERENCES

Armstrong, S. L., Gleitman, L. R., & Gleitman, H. (1983). What some concepts might not be. *Cognition, 13*, 263–308.

Clark, H. H. (1973). The language-as-fixed-effect fallacy. *Journal of Verbal Learning and Verbal Behavior, 12*, 335–359.

Clark, H. H., & Lucy, P. (1975). Understanding what is meant from what is said: A study in conversationally conveyed requests. *Journal of Verbal Learning and Verbal Behavior, 14*, 56–72.

Gibbs, R. (1984). Literal meaning and psychological theory. *Cognitive Science, 8*, 275–304.

Gibbs, R., & Nayak, N. (1989). Psycholinguistic studies on the syntactic behavior of idioms. *Cognitive Psychology, 21*, 100–138.

Gleitman, L. R., & Gleitman, H. (1970). *Phrase and Paraphrase*. New York: Norton.

Hampton, J. (1988). Overextension of conjunctive concepts: Evidence for a unitary model of concept typicality and class inclusion. *Journal of Experimental Psychology: Learning, Memory, and Cognition, 14*, 12–32.

Levi, J. N. (1976). *The syntax and semantics of nonpredicating adjectives in English.* Bloomington: Indiana Linguistics Society.

Levi, J. N. (1978). *The syntax and semantics of complex nominals.* New York: Academic Press.

Medin, D. L. (1989). Concepts and conceptual structure. *American Psychologist, 44*, 1469–1481.

Medin, D. L., & Shoben, E. J. (1988). Context and structure in conceptual combination. *Cognitive Psychology, 20*, 158–190.

Medin, D. L., & Wattenmaker, W. (1987). Category cohesiveness, theories, and cognitive archeology. In U. Neisser (Ed.), *Concepts and conceptual Development: The ecological and intellectual factors in categories* (pp. 25–62). Cambridge: Cambridge University Press.

Murphy, G. L. (1990). Noun phrase interpretation and conceptual combination. *Journal of Memory and Language, 29*, 259–288.

Murphy, G. L., & Medin, D. L. (1985). The role of theories in conceptual coherence. *Psychological Review, 92*, 289–316.

Osherson, D. N., & Smith, E. E. (1983). Gradedness and conceptual combination. *Cognition, 12*, 299–318.

Postal, P. (1974). *On raising: One rule of English grammar and its theoretical implications.* Cambridge, MA: MIT Press.

Rosch, E. (1975). Cognitive representation of semantic categories. *Journal of Experimental Psychology: General, 104*, 192–233.

Smith, E. E., & Osherson, D. N. (1987). Compositionality and typicality. In S. Schifter & S. Steele (Eds.), *The 2nd Arizona Colloquium on Cognitive Science.* Tucson: University of Arizona Press.

Smith, E. E., Shoben, E. J., & Rips, L. J. (1974). Structure and process in semantic memory: A featural model for semantic decisions. *Psychological Review, 81*, 214–241.

Tversky, A. (1977). Features of similarity. *Psychological Review, 84*, 327–352.

Zadeh, L. A. (1965). Fuzzy sets. *Information and Control, 8*, 338–353.

6

Learning Word Meanings from Definitions: Problems and Potential

Margaret G. McKeown
LRDC, University of Pittsburgh

Philosophers, psychologists, and linguists have long struggled with the issue of what word meaning is and how to represent it. Although the issue seems far from resolved, this situation has not daunted lexicographers and their forebears, who have been rendering definitions for individual words for at least 24 centuries (Wierzbicka, 1985).

A definition can be seen as an attempt to capture the essence of a word's meaning by summarizing all of its applications and possible applications. There are compelling practical reasons for such attempts. A collection of summaries of word meanings offers valuable recourse to language users who reach the limits of their word knowledge.

The focus of the research described in this chapter is how to capture word meaning in a definition so that it is a useful introduction to the word for young learners, particularly students from about 4th grade through junior high school, when learning the meanings of words beyond a basic oral vocabulary dominates language development. Two major assumptions underlie my interest in useful definitions for young learners. The first is that definitions *can* be a source of independent word learning, with the qualification that a definition should be viewed as an initiating event in learning about a word rather than the primary mode for that learning. (However, definitions probably do serve as the primary mode of vocabulary instruction in the majority of classrooms.)

The second assumption is that, although definitions may be potentially useful for learning word meanings, young students typically do not learn much from definitions in their traditional format. Evidence of this comes from research by Miller and Gildea (1985) and Scott and Nagy (1989, 1990). Miller and Gildea found that 5th and 6th graders who studied dictionary definitions were frequently unable to generate sentences that used the words appropriately. Of 208 sentences composed with unfamiliar words, 63% were "judged to be odd" (p. 18). Miller and Gildea report such examples as the definition for *transitory*, "passing soon; lasting only a short time," producing sentences such as "The train was transitory." The most frequent error was something that the researchers called "kidrule." It seemed that what students often did was to select a fragment of the definition that was familiar to them and use that as the word's entire meaning. For example, from the definition for *accrue*, "to come as a growth or result," one student wrote, "We had a branch accrue on our plant."

The tendency for students to interpret fragments of a definition as the complete word meaning was supported in Scott and Nagy's (1989) research. In this study 4th and 6th graders were presented with definitions and then tested on three types of sentences, one that used the target word appropriately, one that was based on a fragment that was inconsistent with the full word meaning, and one that used the word incorrectly with no semantic overlap. Although students responded correctly to the appropriate and grossly inappropriate sentences about 80% of the time, they selected the fragment sentences as correct about half the time. Nagy and Herman (1987) summed up what young students must often experience in using the dictionary, saying that definitions "almost seem to be written in a secret code accessible only to those with the inside knowledge" (p. 29).

The research that is the basis for this chapter involved my investigation of the characteristics of typical dictionary definitions that prevent them from being useful to learners and development of solutions in the form of better definitions. The project included analyzing definitions in order to describe the obstacles to learning in a systematic way, creating revised definitions based on principles that emerged from the analysis, and testing the effectiveness of traditional and revised definitions with target learners.

Before discussing the problems that I found with definitions, it seems appropriate to consider the rationale underlying traditional dictionary definitions and the standing of that rationale in current lexicography. Thus, the first section of this chapter establishes a lexicographic context for research on definitions. The second section focuses on the three phases of my research, analyzing, revising, and testing definitions. A final section forecasts two directions in which this work might extend.

A LEXICOGRAPHIC CONTEXT FOR RESEARCH ON DEFINITIONS

This section begins with discussion of the basis for traditional dictionary definitions and how those forms developed. The discussion illustrates that certain principles underlie the forms that definitions take, but that there are no hard and fast rules. Then the kinds of complaints that lexicographers have about some of these principles are examined, along with alternatives to the traditional dictionary format that have been put forth by lexicographers.

Why Definitions Are the Way They Are

The following description of the derivation of formalized dictionary definitions is drawn primarily from Landau (1984) and Hanks (1987), although the same general principles are highlighted in other lexicographic descriptions, such as Benson, Benson, and Ilson (1986a), Jackson (1988), and Zgusta (1971).

Definitions in dictionaries created before the 18th century tended to be informal, discursive explanations. More formalized definitional practice is traced to the time of Samuel Johnson's dictionary in the mid-18th century. The basis of traditional rules of lexicography are the Aristotelian notions of defining an entity through genus and differentia; that is, by first identifying the class to which something belongs, and then how it differs from other members of the class. A classic example is *bachelor,* defined as "a man who is unmarried."

Several notions beyond this classic definition structure influenced the formalization of definitions. One very influential idea from 18th century philosophy was Leibniz's notion that two expressions are synonymous if one can be substituted for the other. Following Leibniz, lexicographers established a principle of substitutability, whereby a definition was to be formulated so that it could be directly substituted for the word in any context.

Two other principles that were added a little later were reductionism, that a definition should be created by isolating and describing minimal units of meaning, and the notion that a definition should set forth necessary and sufficient conditions so that it allows one to identify all and only the things referred to by the word being defined.

Overriding all others, however, is the granddaddy influence of dictionary definitions—space restrictions. Landau (1984) says that "almost every defining characteristic common to dictionaries can be traced to the need to conserve space" (p. 140), and Summers (1988a) calls space problems "the most horrendous constraint" of lexicographers (p. 13).

Lexicographic Alternatives

Although the principles outlined have shaped lexicography for the past nearly two centuries, they are all controversial to some extent. For example, most lexicographers agree that it is "preposterous" to have definitions completely conform to the principle of substitutability (e.g., Benson et al., 1986a; Zgusta, 1971). The notion of defining minimal units is a source of much disagreement because it comes down to the idea of whether variations in the use of a word are mistaken for distinct meanings, an issue that is discussed at greater length in a later section. Regarding the standing of this collection of principles in current lexicography, one lexicographer has ᴗaid that they have led to "some remarkable convolutions in dictionary prose style" (Hanks, 1987, p. 120). Examples of such convolutions might include the following definition for *sympathy* from *Merriam Webster's New Collegiate Dictionary* (1977): "an affinity, association, or relationship between persons or things wherein whatever affects the one similarly affects the other," or the definition for *accrue:* "to come by way of increase or addition."

Currently, alternative approaches to dictionary-making are being explored by lexicographers, ranging from radical restructuring of the dictionary to new approaches to portraying meaning. Moves to restructure the dictionary derive from the problem that dictionaries must be arranged alphabetically to allow ready access, but this arrangement does not reveal how word meanings stand in relation to one another. Semantic connections among words has been conceived as an important component of how word meanings are represented in memory (see for example Collins & Loftus, 1975; Miller & Johnson-Laird, 1976). Semantic relationships in one's mental lexicon reflect the structure of vocabulary; meanings of words fall into various relationships, whether described as categories, networks, fields, or in terms of synonymy, antonymy, and hyponymy. Thus for a description of word meanings to be complete, it should attend to the relational properties of language. A description of the language that includes relationships allows a learner to "see the semantic boundaries of words" (Jackson, 1988, p. 221).

Roget's *Thesaurus* was originally created to deal with the inherent limitations of alphabetical arrangement of dictionary entries. A recent attempt to organize the lexicon in terms of semantic relationships, or lexical fields, is the *Longman Lexicon of Contemporary English* (Longman, 1981). An important difference between the *Lexicon* and Roget's volume is that the *Lexicon* includes a dictionary type entry for each word, including definitions, examples, and grammatical information.

The advent of the computer has excited possibilities in the area of organizing the lexicon semantically. A computerized dictionary allows immediate access to the word of choice via electronic search. This eliminates the search problem presented by printed dictionaries, which can be solved only through alphabetization.

Other alternatives to traditional dictionaries include new approaches to defining, or more accurately, portraying word meaning, as some do not include definitions as such. Most prominent in this category are learner's dictionaries, which are created for the advanced foreign language learner. Learner's dictionaries first appeared in 1935 (Summers, 1988a), but two recent versions have made notable departures from traditional defining techniques.

One of these is the *Longman Dictionary of Contemporary English* (LDOCE) (1987), which uses a strictly controlled vocabulary of 2000 words to define all entries. Although the controlled vocabulary approach has been criticized for, among other things, resulting in sometimes long and clumsy definitions, it often results in a surprising clarity. For example, consider *Longman's* definition for *delicate:* "needing careful handling, esp. because easily broken or damaged," in contrast to that of *Merriam Webster:* "calling for or involving meticulously careful treatment."

The other recent and notable learner's dictionary is the *Collins COBUILD*[1] *English Language Dictionary* (1987), which represents an even greater departure from traditional lexicography. This dictionary provides discursive explanations for the words rather than definitions in the traditional sense. The words are presented in a typical structure, and typicality of use is a driving force behind how the words are explained. The dictionary strives to present meanings in ordinary English that sounds natural when read aloud. For example, *COBUILD* explains *delicate* as follows: "Something that is delicate is fragile and needs to be handled carefully." A further example for *accrue,* shows how verbs are typically treated: "If you accrue things or if they accrue, you collect them or allow them to accumulate over a period of time."

Learner's dictionaries contain two other features that are an important part of complete word knowledge but are not used to advantage in traditional dictionaries. One is example sentences, which do appear in virtually all dictionaries, but receive particular attention in learner's dictionaries. This attention is evident in the inclusion of an example for nearly every entry versus occasional examples in traditional desk dictionaries for native speakers, and in the space allotted in the front of the dictionary to discussion of the role of examples and how examples were selected or constructed to serve a learner's goals.

The other aspect of word knowledge included in learner's dictionaries is collocations, which is the company in which words customarily appear; for example, speakers of English typically say *make an effort,* but not *make an exertion;* and send *warm regards,* but not *hot regards* (Benson, 1989). Some collocational information appears in traditional dictionaries, but it is sparse and not presented systematically. The recent learner's dictionaries have made efforts to improve the presentation of collocations.

In addition to greater efforts to include examples and collocations in dictionaries, another alternative to traditional lexicography has been efforts to create reference texts whose primary information is either examples or collocations instead of definitions. In terms of examples, this effort seems to have gone only as far as testing whether entries consisting solely of examples would be more successful than traditional dictionary entries. The result suggested, however, that a mix of definitions and examples was more facilitative (Summers, 1988b).

There have been dictionaries created, however, based solely on collocations. There exist, in fact, two types of collocational, or combinatorial, dictionaries.

---

[1]COBUILD stands for Collins Birmingham University International Language Database.

One type is meant as a practical reference tool for the learner, such as *The BBI Combinatory Dictionary of English* (Benson, Benson, & Ilson, 1986b). The information it provides is exemplified by the entry for *collection:*

> **collection** n. 1. to take up a ~ (of money) 2. to break up a ~ 3. an art; coin; private; stamp ~

The other type of dictionary that highlights collocational information is actually a theoretical description of language intended for a specialized audience, primarily linguists and lexicographers (Benson, 1989). The purpose of these dictionaries, which are called "explanatory combinatorial" dictionaries is to describe, rigorously and exhaustively, the information conveyed by individual lexical units. Thus, for example, the definition for *cups* would include that they are "a kind of thing that people make . . . they are made for people to use repeatedly for drinking hot liquids from such as tea or coffee . . . they are made of something rigid, smooth, and easy to wash . . ." (Wierzbicka, 1985). Collocations are an important part of the full lexical descriptions offered in these dictionaries.

The attitude toward traditional dictionary definitions expressed in the lexicographic literature seems to support the view that the current format is not completely satisfactory. A reading of the lexicographic literature also demonstrates that, although there is productive activity in creating alternatives to portraying word meaning, there is a dearth of empirical work to examine the effects of the information on understanding word meanings (Crystal, 1986). Possibly the only exception is the work sponsored by Longman, mentioned earlier, to discern the effectiveness of examples versus definitions. An important component of my research is testing the effectiveness of definitions.

DEFINITION PROBLEMS AND SOLUTIONS

This section focuses on my efforts to systematically describe why dictionary definitions are not effective for young learners and to develop more effective alternatives. I begin with a description of my analysis of definitions; I then present the principles for creating definitions that arose from the analysis and were used for revising definitions. Finally, testing of dictionary versus revised definitions is reported.

The Problems with Definitions: An Analysis

The analysis of definitions involved considering how a young learner might try to make sense of the information presented in a definition. In essence, it is an attempt to simulate the process of a learner's interaction with a definition that takes into account an understanding of how features of written language (e.g., ambiguous terms, clarity of relationships among pieces of information) may cause processing to proceed or to break down. To simulate that process I hypothesized how a learner might access the meaning and select the appropriate sense of the defining terms, call forth relevant background knowledge, decide where emphasis should be placed, and integrate various pieces of information toward forming a coherent representation of the word. Analysis of a definition yielded hypothetical representations of the word's meaning that a young learner might be likely to establish.

In the research reported here, definitions were taken from two student dictionaries, which were selected because of their wide use in elementary classrooms, the *Scott Foresman Intermediate Dictionary* (1979) and *Webster's Elementary Dictionary* (1980). However, for the analysis of definitions, all words were also checked in standard dictionaries, primarily *Merriam Webster's New Collegiate Dictionary* (1977). Comparing definitions between standard and student dictionaries quickly shows the great similarity between the two. Definitions in student dictionaries are most often abbreviated versions of standard definitions with some substitutions for the more difficult defining vocabulary.

Four categories of problematic definitions were derived from the analysis. In this section of the chapter, those categories are described and exemplified.

Weak Differentiation.   A definition that exhibits weak differentiation places the defined word within a broad, easily identifiable semantic domain but fails to distinguish it within the domain. Thus the definition provides a representation for the word that, although not incorrect, overshoots the target concept by seeming to include cases that are not covered by the concept. A general rule of thumb for lexicographers, according to Landau (1984), is that a definition should capture the essence of the thing defined; that is exactly what a weakly differentiated definition fails to do. For example, consider the definition given in both the *Scott Foresman* (SF) and *Webster's Elementary* (WE) dictionaries for *conspicuous:* "easily seen." This definition weakly differentiates *conspicuous* from the general domain of "visible." Unless it is dark or you have poor vision, nearly everything is easily seen. *Conspicuous* is a strong form of "easily seen," because the word is more specialized than that. In contrast, consider the definition from *Collin's COBUILD Dictionary* (CO): "Something that is conspicuous is more noticeable and more likely to be looked at than the other things or people around, usually because of their size, color, or position."

Another example of weak differentiation shows that definitions in this category may include wording that goes beyond the general domain, but which seems likely to be insufficient for communicating the word's distinctiveness. Consider the definition for *covet:* "to wish for greatly or with envy" (WE). This phrasing—with optional envy—provides weak differentiation from generic wishing. Yet *covet* implies a special, very potent form of wishing: that the thing wanted either belongs to someone else or that you want it for yourself and no one else—a kind of possessiveness. This quality is captured by the phrase "inordinately or culpably" in the standard *Merriam Webster* (MW) definition, implying wishing for something so strongly that you would be willing to take the wished-for-thing away from someone else. But the definition provided in the student dictionary, even though it does contain accurate modifiers of wishing, is likely to lead young learners to think along the lines of "I covet a Barbie doll for Christmas." One reason for the hypothesis that this definition will not differentiate from general wishing is that the notion of making wishes is a very salient one for youngsters, and the additional information in the definition is not strong enough to lead them beyond the familiar conception of wishing.

Vague Language.   A vague definition uses wording that has low explanatory power, especially for young learners. It either does not provide for a representation of the word, or it offers competing representations that do not seem compatible and can not be readily unified into a single concept. As an example, consider the following definition for *typical:* "being a type; representative" (SF). First of all, discussion of "representative" can be omitted, because learners who are seeking the meaning of *typical* are unlikely to be familiar with *representative.* The main issue with this definition is, what might "being a type" mean to a young learner. A safe bet is that it would not mean much. The best a learner might manage would be to ask "a type of what?" It is unlikely that a young student would be able to make enough sense of this definition to develop any representation at all.

A definition can also be vague by offering an array of diverse possibilities for a word's meaning. An example is the definition for *impress:* "to have a strong effect on the mind or feelings of" (SF). Consider the possibilities: having a fight with someone, learning something interesting, seeing a horror movie, or a surprise party could all have a strong effect on a person's mind or feelings. The potential implications are so diverse that a learner would have great difficulty establishing a coherent conception of the word. This type of vague definition has features similar to weak differentiation in that it might be seen as providing a "broad domain," but the domain, which in this case is that of producing strong feelings, is so broad as to be meaningless; it encompasses too many diverse concepts.

Likely Interpretation.   A definition has a likely interpretation if it seems to lead to a single, accessible representation for a word's meaning which is incorrect. This problem occurs when the intended sense of the words used to define are less likely to be accessed by young learners because an unintended sense is more familiar. For example, consider the definition for *devious:* "straying from the right course; not straightforward" (SF). This definition has a likely interpretation of literal nonstraightness; crooked walking or getting lost.

Another even more blatant example of a likely interpretation is the definition for *jaded:* "worn out; tired; weary" (SF). This definition does not seem to allow any interpretation except that of a physical tiredness, which of course is not an accurate representation for *jaded*.

Landau (1984) cites as a principle of good defining that words used in a definition should be used unambiguously. Similarly, Zgusta (1971), who is a major figure in lexicography, cautions that "particular care should be taken of the fact that the words used in a lexicographic definition will themselves be polysemous" (p. 257) and that they should be disambiguated by the context. This principle is violated in the case of likely interpretations. In many definitions there is no context to disambiguate the words—as in the examples presented here, the definitions consist only of sets of polysemous expressions.

Disjoint Components.   Definitions with disjoint components give multiple pieces of information but offer no guidance in how they should be integrated, or at what intersection of the pieces the meaning of the target word lies. For example, consider the definition for *exotic:* "foreign; strange; not native" (SF). A learner might wonder what relationship to draw among the parts; is something exotic if it is strange but not foreign, or only if it is both foreign and strange? And what role does "not native" play, as it is virtually the same as "foreign"? Hanks (1987), who is one of the lexicographers on the COBUILD project, refers to this approach to definitions as the "multiple-bite strategy." The definition of *exotic* presented in COBUILD gives an indication of the relationship among the pieces: "Something that is exotic is strange, unusual, or interesting *because* it comes from a distant country."

The effect of disjoint definitions on the learner is similar to that of vague definitions in that the learner may be offered an array of directions to pursue in establishing a representation of the word's meaning. The distinction between the two types is that, in vague definitions, there is one piece of information offered with several possible interpretations, while in definitions with disjoint components, the problem stems from the presentation of several pieces of information with no unifying relationship.

Another variation of disjoint components deserves note because it represents a controversy in lexicography and linguistics in general. The controversy has to do with the distinction between the meaning of a word and the contexts in which words occur (See for example Anderson & Nagy, 1991, versus Johnson-Laird, 1987). In lexicography the controversy centers on the tendency to define words by discriminating many senses of the word that actually represent its use in different contexts.

On one side of the controversy, lexicographers argue that it is a mistake to interpret different applications of a lexical unit as different senses (Regan, 1987), and that a lexicographer's obligations include making a clear distinction between lexical meaning and variations in the contexts in which a word can be used (Gouws, 1987).

Moon (1987) faults lexicographers for too often defining and analyzing the context, and looking for diversity rather than unity: "We look too hard around the word we are working on, and not hard enough at what it means in itself, or what it adds to the context" (p. 182). The result, says Moon, is that meaning of the target word is dissipated.

On the other side of the controversy, Allen Walker Read (1981) argues that "an ideal dictionary would have a definition for every citation" (p. 88). The bulk of lexicographic practice seems to be on the side of Read's contextualist position. For instance, consider that the entry for *give* in *Merriam Webster* presents 43 separate senses!

Moon's notion about looking for diversity rather than unity and the effect of weakening a word's meaning through overdiscrimination of senses suggests the implications that this practice may have for dictionary users, particularly younger users. Consider, for example, the entry from *Webster's Elementary* for the word *delicate:*

> (1) pleasing because of fineness or mildness (a . . . flavor). (2) able to sense very small differences (a . . . instrument). (3) calling for skill and careful treatment (a . . . operation). (4) easily damaged. (5) sickly (a . . . child). (6) requiring tact.

This treatment of the words seems to very much weaken its meaning. Imagine a young learner trying to get a sense of the word from this conglomerate of information. All the senses have been particularized to a context, and no overall essence of the word has been captured. For example, consider "easily damaged": Lots of things can be damaged easily; anyone who has ever had a minor car accident has likely found how easy it is to run up several hundred dollars worth of damage to a car. But it would be unusual to hear a car described as delicate. It seems that "ease of damaging" is an attribute of something delicate, but the word does not mean that. Similarly with "sickly": if we say a child is delicate, we often mean she looks frail because of sickness, but it seems a safe bet that few users of the word equate *sickly* with *delicate*. Considering how a learner might build a representation of this word from the information given brings to mind the story of the blind men and the elephant—any one of the senses gives a very small and not wholly accurate picture of the concept.

Moon's suggestion of looking for unity in creating definitions seems likely to lead to definitions that are more coherent and therefore more helpful to users. But what form this "looking for unity" might take is not straightforward in all cases. In some cases it is not so difficult to imagine uniting senses of a word into a description of a core meaning. For example, in the case of *delicate*, something like "describes things that must be handled gently, often because they are fragile or small and light" could be the basis for understanding the essence of the word.

The more difficult cases to solve are the most basic words, such as *give*. Although *give* may well have a core meaning, the expression of a core meaning that unites its uses may be too vague to be communicative. For example, *Mer-

riam Webster, in one of its synonym paragraphs that describes the shared meaning among words such as *give, donate,* and *present,* describes *give* as "applicable to any passing over of anything by any means." That seems an accurate rendering of something like a core meaning, but it may be too vague to assist a user in developing a representation for the word.

Even if the treatment of a word fails to cover 43 different senses, it is my contention that moving toward unity in describing meaning will yield definitions that most facilitate a learner's understanding of a word. It has been my experience that young learners are much more able to extend the application of a newly learned word than to bring coherence to discrete pieces of information. Youngsters' ability to extend concepts was demonstrated during a research study to teach vocabulary (Beck, Perfetti, & McKeown, 1982; McKeown, Beck, Omanson, & Perfetti, 1983). The 4th grade students rather readily understood what it meant to "devour a book," although the definitions and examples of *devour* that they had worked with in instruction all involved consumption of food.

In contrast, youngsters' difficulty with discrete pieces of information was shown in a study designed to investigate students' ability to learn word meanings from context (McKeown, 1985). Here students were often hindered rather than helped by the presentation of two contexts simultaneously. Trying to bridge the slight variations in the application of a word offered in the two contexts tended to lead them astray. For example, many students were unable to select *ordinary* as the meaning of the target word when given sentences that described mundane items in a store and usual kinds of people.

Before the discussion of problem categories closes, a couple of notes about the nature of the categories are appropriate. First, definitions sometimes exhibited more than one problem type and thus could be put into multiple categories. For example, the disjoint definition discussed earlier for *exotic,* "foreign, strange, not native," might lead students to interpret *strange* as unpleasantly odd, and thus could be placed in the likely interpretation category as well. Second, no claim is made that these categories are exhaustive. They may not capture all the problems that definitions exhibit; however, all of the definitions examined fell into one of the categories described.

Principles for Writing Definitions

From the identification of problematic features of definitions and consideration of how those features might affect young learners, I developed several principles for creating definitions that are maximally comprehensible for young learners. These principles have guided my revision of definitions.

Identify Unique Role of the Word. The creation of a definition should begin with consideration of the essence of the word and its unique role in the language: why do we have such a word; when do speakers use *this* word and none other?

Identifying a word's uniqueness can be done by considering situations in which the word is particularly appropriate and analyzing the features of those situations. For example, *conspicuous* is not used merely to describe something that one can readily see; it is reserved for labeling something to which one's eye is immediately drawn because it is dissonant with the rest of the context.

After such features are identified, the definition can be developed to explain how the features fit together to create a particular meaning space, conveying where within the bounds of the defining words the target word lies. The revised definition for *conspicuous* reads: "describes something that you notice right away because it stands out."

Characterize the Word.   For a definition to be optimally helpful for developing a representation for a word's meaning, it should be as particular as possible. It should pinpoint a word's meaning by explaining its characteristic or prototypical use. The downside to pinpointing a word's meaning is that the resultant definition may not capture all possible applications of a word. But in trying to be all inclusive, the explanatory strength of a definition is too easily lost.

A good route to characterizing a word is to take a tentative or existing definition and try to generate cases that would fit the definition as written but are beyond the scope of the target word. Then the definition can be refined to eliminate those interpretations. For example, the definition for *tamper*, "to interfere in a secret or incorrect way," (WE) would seem to allow application to simply meddling in someone else's affairs, as a busybody. The definition was revised to read: "to secretly change something so that it does not work properly or becomes harmful." Another example, which seems particularly lacking in explanatory strength, is the definition for *shrewd*, "having a sharp mind; showing a keen wit; clever; keen; sharp" (SF). This promotes the concept of general mental acumen; yet *shrewd* typically refers to a kind of calculating cleverness that is used to one's own advantage. The revised definition characterizes *shrewd* in the following way: "able to size up a situation quickly and use it to get what you want."

Make Meaning Accessible.   An explanation of a word's meaning should be framed to bring meaning to the surface so that it is accessible for a young learner. For example, why should learners be forced to interrogate their lexicons to figure out what "one associated with another" means in the definition of *ally* (WE)? The revised definition renders the phrase as: "*someone who helps you* in what you are trying to do, especially when there are other people who are against you." Similarly, defining *typical* as: "combining or showing the special characteristics of a group or kind" (WE) makes the meaning rather inaccessible. The revised definition tries to provide access to the notion of "showing characteristics of a group or kind" as follows: "describes something that is a good example of a person or thing because it shows what that person or thing is usually like."

Although the examples given use simpler vocabulary in the revised definitions, making meaning accessible means more than simplifying terms. Consider that the dictionary definition presented for *typical* could be simplified to read "showing the special qualities of a group," but the meaning would probably still be difficult for young learners to access. Making meaning accessible means developing a more straightforward way to communicate a concept. Clarity, rather than simplicity, is the key.

Arrange for Attention to the Whole Definition.   Often, when faced with new or difficult language or contexts, young learners will select a fragment that is familiar and base their interpretation on that fragment, however inappropriate (McKeown, 1985; Miller & Gildea, 1985; Scott & Nagy, 1990). The selection of a fragment from a definition may be even more likely when the definition contains words that allow different levels of interpretation—as youngsters are most likely to make literal interpretations—or when the definition is based on a word that has particular saliency for young language users.

In order to lessen the chances of interpretation based on a fragment, definitions should be phrased to avoid emphasizing words that are particularly salient for young learners, in order to direct attention to the whole definition. The effect of strong terms may be diffused, for example, by changing their position in the definition. For instance, defining *meticulous* as: "extremely or excessively *careful* about small details" may give students the idea that the word relates to being cautious about danger. The revised definition tries to mitigate that association to *careful* by beginning the definition "neat and careful."

TESTING THE EFFECTIVENESS OF DEFINITIONS

Two tasks were designed to evaluate students' ability to use the dictionary and revised definitions. The first was a sentence task in which students were presented with a word and its definition and asked to write a sentence using the word. This task was used for two reasons. First, because it is a familiar task in the vocabulary learning domain, it provides a common ground for understanding the results it yields. Second, because Miller and Gildea's study (1985) employed a sentence task, using such a task would enable me to compare their findings with what students in my study were able to do with dictionary definitions and to examine how revised definitions would fare under the same conditions.

The sentence task, however, is quite limited for finding out what students understand about a word's meaning. When students are asked to use a word in a sentence, the implicit task is to construct a sentence that is uniquely appropriate for the target word so that its meaning—and thus the student's understanding of the word—is transparent. But that is not the way sentences are naturally constructed. In response to the sentence task, students often use a more natural mode of sentence generation, using the target word but not revealing its features. For example, the sentence, "The car is conspicuous" may be adequate for some circumstances of communication, but the situation referred to by the sentence is not unique enough to *conspicuous* to reveal the student's understanding of the word.

Let us put the limitations of the sentence task aside for the moment, and examine the results from the task. Twenty-four 5th graders participated in this task. The students were presented with a definition and then asked to write a sentence using the defined word. Each student responded to 12 words, 6 presented with dictionary definitions and 6 with revised definitions. The sentences were scored either acceptable or unacceptable based on a judgment of whether the situation described by the sentence was clearly appropriate for the meaning of the word. For example, acceptable sentences for *devious* included: "A thief will be devious with you"; and "He was devious when he put frogs in her bed." Unacceptable sentences included: "Some drivers devious of the road"; and "He is blind so he is devious." The two former sentences were generated from the revised definition, "using tricky and secretive ways to do something dishonest," the latter two from the dictionary definition, "straying from the right course; not straightforward."

Nearly a third of the sentences were judged unscorable because they were of the "natural" type described earlier. For the remaining 218 sentences, the dictionary definitions yielded 25% acceptable sentences and 75% unacceptable sentences, while the revised definitions yielded 50% of each sentence type. Thus there were significantly more acceptable sentences and fewer unacceptable sentences generated from the revised definitions.

The extent of the advantage in favor of the revised sentences was due to the overwhelming proportion of unacceptable sentences generated from dictionary definitions; the revised definitions did not fare all that well in absolute terms, with only a 50/50 ratio of acceptable to unacceptable sentences. It should not be too surprising that the revised definitions did not look better than this. The sentence task is not a particularly revealing one, as discussed above. Thus a second task was developed in an attempt to reveal more clearly what students understood from the definitional information.

For this second task, a definition was read aloud to students as they followed along, and then students responded briefly in writing to two questions about the use of the word. Nonwords replaced real words in this task in order to control for prior knowledge. For example, for *conspicuous* (presented to students as *calliguous*), the questions were: "what can you think of that would be conspicuous?" and "what might make a person conspicuous?" and for *prudent* (*tordent*): "what is something that should be done in a prudent way?" and "when might you tell someone to be prudent?" Sixty 5th graders participated, and again they each responded to six dictionary and six revised definitions.

The data for this second task were scored by sorting the responses for each word into three categories, *good, acceptable,* and *unacceptable.* Good responses were those that represented a clearly appropriate and characteristic use of the word. This included responding to "What can you think of that would be conspicuous?" by naming things that were visually unusual and in contrast with the rest of the context, and to the question "How might someone tamper with something?" by describing making a change to an object that was obviously intended to bring harm.

Acceptable responses were ones that suggested uses that could not be called incorrect but did not represent a strong application of the word; the use could be appropriate for the word, but did not seem uniquely so. For example, responses to "what might be conspicuous?" that merely named things that could well stand out, such as trees or someone's clothes, but not describing what might make those objects conspicuous. Unacceptable responses were those that presented clearly inappropriate uses of the word, or when students could not respond.

As Fig. 6.1 illustrates, revised definitions yielded a considerably higher proportion of *good* responses and considerably fewer *unacceptable* responses. An equivalent amount of responses was judged *acceptable* for both definition types.

A striking characterization of the distinctions between the dictionary and revised responses is that in many cases the responses to the dictionary definitions matched the misinterpretations anticipated by the analysis of definition problems. In contrast, responses to the revised definitions went a long way toward capturing the essence of the words.

For example, students who worked with the dictionary definition did seem to interpret *covet (covin)* as simple wishing. Based on the definition *to wish for greatly or with envy,* when asked "what would you say to a friend who covets something?" students gave answers such as: "I hope you get what you want"; "I might be able to get it for you as a birthday or Christmas present"; "You can go to the store and buy one." Responses to the revised definition—*to want to have*

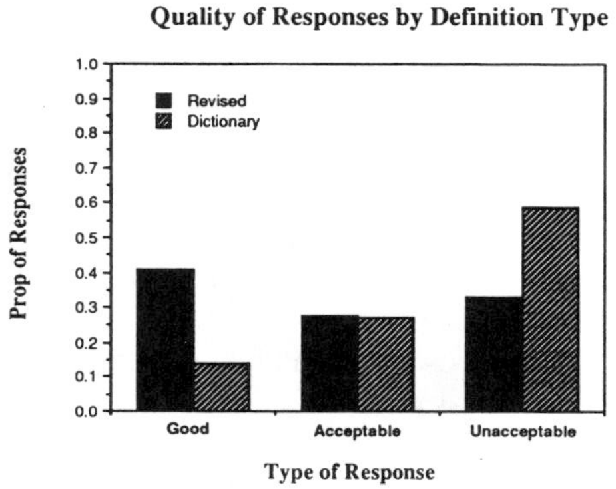

Quality of Responses by Definition Type

FIG. 6.1. Proportion of good, acceptable, and unacceptable responses to revised and dictionary definitions.

something even though it belongs to someone else—often evidenced the more culpable kind of wishing that covet typically implies. For example: "Give it back"; "Please do not touch, that is not yours"; "It is not nice to want something that is not yours."

A similar pattern emerged for *tamper (kember)*. The dictionary definition—*to interfere in a secret or incorrect way*—led to answers to the question "how might someone tamper with something?" that implied rather benign interference, akin to "butting in." Sample responses included: "if you're telling your friend a secret and someone will tamper"; "talk when others are talking";"they might find out a secret and tell everyone about it." Responses to the revised definition—*to secretly change something so that it does not work properly or becomes harmful*—revealed a more sinister kind of interference. For example, "take wires out of a car"; "loosen a chandelier to make it fall"; "an airplane, someone could mess around with the motor."

Even some of the more subtle differences in definitions yielded striking differences in response. For example, for *prudent,* the dictionary definition seemed to emphasize making plans: *planning carefully ahead of time; sensible; discreet.* And the result was that 50% of the students responded either that "planning a vacation" or "planning a party" was something that should be done in a prudent way. Responses to the revised definition—*thinking things over carefully before making decisions*—showed a much richer set of ideas. For example: "when you are taking a test"; "thinking if you want to go to college"; and one I find particularly appealing—"a test, a report in ink, a project where you only get one piece of paper."

The results suggest that the revised definitions helped students to understand the typical uses for the words and to avoid some of the pitfalls inherent in the dictionary definitions. The dictionary definitions, on the other hand, led students to make some of the misinterpretations anticipated by the analysis of definition problems. For example, students did seem to interpret *covet* as simple wishing, to view *tampering* as nosiness, and to interpret *devious* as a physical nonstraightness.

BEYOND REVISING AND TESTING DEFINITIONS

I envision two directions in which the work on revising definitions can extend. One draws on the instrumentation and methodology developed for revising and testing definitions for the purpose of examining the processes involved in establishing representations of word meaning. The other concerns the practical application of notions about comprehensible definitions for young learners.

The motivation for undertaking a study of word learning processes is that situations in which students are asked to respond to definitions can provide a rich source for investigating word learning processes. An activity designed to have students think aloud as they create a sentence or answer questions about a word's use may reveal how learners manipulate semantic information to make it meaningful to themselves. Examples of what such a task might uncover were obtained in a follow-up discussion I had with some 5th graders I had worked with. The students were asked, in a group setting, to talk about what the definitions were telling them—what ideas came to mind about what the words meant. In this discussion, one strategy that was quite apparent was the tendency to generate an example of a situation that might fit the word. For instance, in responding to the definition for *improvise,* students said, "if you need a jewelry box, you could make it out of sticks"; and "you could use a butter knife for a screwdriver." In telling what she understood *tamper* to mean, one child said "like change your report card by erasing it and putting in an A." Blachowicz, Guastafeste, Wohlreich, & Fisher (1990) have also used a think-aloud condition to gain insight into how 4th graders select a definition entry that best fits a context sentence.

Interactions in which students are asked to use and think about definitional information might lead to notions about how appropriately different learners use outside knowledge in trying to understand a new word, or how learners handle semantic similarities and differences in establishing representations of related but distinct word meanings. These issues stem from earlier work that investigated how 5th grade learners establish word meaning from contexts (McKeown, 1985). In that research, lower ability learners were found to have difficulty in distinguishing the kind of outside information that was relevant to the task of deriving the meaning of a word from a context. These students would often bring in information that seemed somewhat related to the context as a whole, but was not applicable to figuring out what the word meant.

An example of using outside information inappropriately comes from a student who was asked whether the nonword *renby* could mean *smile* in the sentence: "Tony wanted to join the noisy renby." The student responded, "Yes, it could mean smile; when he want to join something he could smile and be all happy." The notion that the student is trying to apply, that someone might feel like smiling about joining something, is not used appropriately in evaluating how *smile* relates to the context. It is anticipated that this earlier work with context may lead to the development of models of how learners use definitional information to construct an understanding of word meaning.

The other direction in which the work on definitions leads concerns how notions of comprehensible definitions can be applied to help students in learning situations. The most immediate application is that it offers a tool to teachers for helping students make sense of definitions. An understanding of some of the problems definitions exhibit and the kinds of interpretations students make could help teachers devise ways to convert problematic definitions into more comprehensible terms.

The broader and more obvious area of application is student dictionaries and glossaries in school textbooks. These references could be more functional if the task of defining words for young learners were seen as more than parroting standard dictionary definitions and abbreviating them or substituting a few easier terms.

Creating more functional dictionaries might best be accomplished within a new orientation that would embody a somewhat different purpose, as well as a new defining style. There are notions discussed in the lexicographic literature that coincide with such a reorientation, though not specifically for student dictionaries. Jackson (1988), in a discussion of the earliest dictionaries, refers to them as "hard word" dictionaries, because they were written expressly to help people with unfamiliar words. Jackson then ponders "whether there might be a justification for hard word dictionaries today" (p. 114). A related comment comes from Quine (1973), who objects to "clutter[ing] a . . . dictionary with idly compulsive definitions of words that all speakers of the language know" (p. 249). His recommendation involves omitting from a dictionary words that could not be defined by simpler words, thus constituting a "basic English that is used but not mentioned" (p. 249).

I suggest that the notion of a hard word dictionary is particularly appropriate for young students. It might be conceived of as a learner's dictionary for native speakers. Jackson (1988) says that recent learner's dictionaries have paid great attention to "tailoring the[ir] content and presentation . . . to the needs and abilities of their users" (p. 189). It seems that dictionaries for students sorely need to consider the needs and abilities of their young users. Tailoring content for young learners might include eliminating the most basic words, or at the very least eliminating excessive treatment of such words (Even the *Scott Foresman Intermediate Dictionary,* for example, presents 10 senses of *give.*). Implementing this new orientation would then leave space for fuller treatment of words that would be most beneficial to students in enriching their vocabulary. Within this new orientation, this fuller treatment would take the form of definitions from which students could most readily learn about the unfamiliar words, definitions that characterize a word's use and are phrased in language that makes meaning easily accessible to young learners.

A FINAL COMMENT

The definitions that have been highlighted in this chapter, both those of the learners' dictionaries—especially COBUILD—and those resulting from my revisions, focus on prototypical or characteristic use. To a great extent, the nature of these definitions coincides with current theories of word meaning, which emphasize a central meaning, often expressed as a prototype or exemplar, as the basis for knowledge of individual words. Earlier semantic theories portrayed word meaning in terms of a set of features that were considered necessary and sufficient for distinguishing a word from all other words, but that view is no longer generally held to be a good description of the way word meaning is represented in the mental lexicon (see for example Smith & Medin, 1981).

The "classical" view embodying necessity and sufficiency has the same roots as the traditional dictionary format in which meanings are portrayed by defining a general category and the features that distinguish the word from all other members of the category. The research presented here suggests that perhaps it is appropriate to consider applying the more current views to the way words are defined in dictionaries, or at least creating alternatives to the traditional format that offer learners information most useful for representing word meaning.

ACKNOWLEDGMENT

The work reported in this paper was supported by a Spencer Fellowship from the National Academy of Education.

REFERENCES

Anderson, R. C., & Nagy, W. E. (1991). Word knowledge. In P. D. Pearson (Ed.), *Handbook of reading research* (2nd Ed., pp. 690–724). New York: Longman.

Beck, I. L., Perfetti, C. A., & McKeown, M. G. (1982). Effects of long-term vocabulary instruction on lexical access and reading comprehension. *Journal of Educational Psychology, 74*(4), 506–521.

Benson, M. (1989). The structure of the collocational dictionary. *International Journal of Lexicography, 2*(1), 1–14.

Benson, M., Benson, E., & Ilson, R. (1986a). Lexicographic description of English. *Studies in language* (Vol. 14). Netherlands: John Benjamins.

Benson, M., Benson, E., & Ilson, R. (1986b). *The BBI combinatory dictionary of English: A guide to word combinations.* Amsterdam and Philadelphia: John Benjamins.

Blachowicz, C. L., Guastafeste, P., Wolreich, J., & Fisher, P. J. (1990, April). *Observing dictionary users: Teachers look at fourth grade students.* Paper presented at the American Educational Research Association, Boston, MA.

Collins, A. M., & Loftus, E. F. (1975). A spreading-activation theory of semantic processing. *Psychological Review, 82,* 407–428.

Collins COBUILD English language dictionary. (1987). London: Collins.

Crystal, D. (1986). The ideal dictionary, lexicographer, & user. In R. Ilson (Ed.), *Lexicography: An emerging international profession* (The Fulbright Papers Proceedings of Colloquia volume 1, pp. 72–80). London: Manchester University Press.

Gouws, R. H. (1987). Lexical meaning versus contextual evidence in dictionary articles. *Dictionaries, 9,* 87–96.

Hanks, P. (1987). Definitions and explanations. In J. M. Sinclair (Ed.), *Looking Up* (pp. 116–136). London: Collins.

Jackson, H. J. (1988). *Words and their meaning.* New York: Longman.

Johnson-Laird, P. N. (1987). The mental representation of the meaning of words. *Cognition, 25,* 189–211.

Landau, S. I. (1984). *Dictionaries: The art and craft of lexicography*. New York: The Scribner Press.

Longman dictionary of contemporary English. (1987). New York: Longman.

Longman lexicon of contemporary English. (1981). New York: Longman.

McKeown, M. G. (1985). The acquisition of word meaning from context by children of high and low ability. *Reading Research Quarterly, 22*, 263–284.

McKeown, M. G., Beck, I. L., Omanson, R. C., & Perfetti, C. A. (1983). The effects of long-term vocabulary instruction on reading comprehension: A replication. *Journal of reading behavior, 15*(1), 3–18.

Miller, G. A., & Gildea, P. M. (1985). How to misread a dictionary. *AILA Bulletin*. Pisa: AILA (International Association for Applied Linguistics).

Miller, G. A., & Johnson-Laird, P. N. (1976). *Language and perception*. Cambridge: Harvard University Press.

Moon, R. (1987). Monosemous words and the dictionary. In A. P. Cowie (Ed.), *The dictionary and the language user*. Lexicographica Series Maior #17, (173–182). Tubingen: Max Niemeyer Verlag.

Nagy, W. E., & Herman, P. A. (1987). Breadth and depth of vocabulary knowledge: Implications for acquisition and instruction. In M. G. McKeown & M. E. Curtis (Eds.), *The nature of vocabulary acquisition* (pp. 19–35). Hillsdale, NJ: Lawrence Erlbaum Associates.

Quine, W. V. (1973). Vagaries of definition. In R. J. McDavid & A. R. Duckut (Eds.), *Lexicography in English*. Annals of the New York Academy of Sciences volume 211, (pp. 247–252). New York: New York Academy of Sciences.

Read, A. W. (1981). The relation of definitions to their contextual basis. *Papers of the Dictionary Society of North America* (pp. 88–99). Terre Haute: Indiana State University.

Regan, V. (1987). A dialogic perspective on the variability of lexicographical meaning. *Dictionaries, 9*, 76–82.

Scott Foresman intermediate dictionary. (1979). Garden City, NY: Doubleday.

Scott, J., & Nagy, W. E. (1990, April). *Definitions: Understanding students' misunderstandings*. Paper presented at annual meeting of the American Educational Research Association, Boston, MA.

Scott, J., & Nagy, W. E. (1989, December). *Fourth graders' knowledge of definitions and how they work*. Paper presented at annual meeting of the National Reading Conference, Austin, TX.

Smith, E. E., & Medin, D. L. (1981). *Categories and Concepts*. Cambridge, MA: Harvard University Press.

Summers, D. (1988a). English language teaching dictionaries: Past, present, and future. *English Today, 14*, 10–16.

Summers, D. (1988b). The role of dictionaries in language learning. In R. Carter & M. McCarthy (Eds.), *Vocabulary and language teaching* (pp. 111–125). New York: Longman.

Webster's elementary dictionary. (1980). Springfield, MA: Merriam-Webster.

Webster's new collegiate dictionary. (7th ed.). (1977). Springfield, MA: Merriam-Webster.

Wierzbicka, A. (1985). *Lexicography and conceptual analysis*. Ann Arbor: Karoma Publishers.

Zgusta, L. (1971). *Manual of lexicography*. The Hague: Mouton, Prague: Academia.

7

Beyond the Instrumentalist Hypothesis: Some Relationships Between Word Meanings and Comprehension

Steven A. Stahl
University of Georgia

That vocabulary knowledge is strongly related to reading comprehension is among the most robust findings in the reading literature. From research in areas as diverse as readability (Dale & Chall, in press) and psychometrics (Thorndike, 1973–74), extremely strong correlations have been reported between measures of word knowledge and measures of comprehension. In a paper that had a strong influence on the resurgence of interest in vocabulary knowledge, Anderson and Freebody (1981) proposed three hypotheses to explain these correlations.

The most direct was an *instrumentalist* hypothesis, which proposes that the presence or absence of vocabulary knowledge causes or hampers reading comprehension. This hypothesis suggests that teaching word meanings would directly improve comprehension, as would mechanical substitutions of known words for unknown ones. A second hypothesis, the *general aptitude* hypothesis, suggests that vocabulary and comprehension are only indirectly related, through common links to aptitude. Vocabulary knowledge is one of the strongest predictors of overall intelligence, and intelligence relates to comprehension (Anderson & Freebody, 1981). Therefore, the vocabulary-comprehension correlations are artifacts of an ability-comprehension relationship. The third hypothesis, the *general knowledge* hypothesis, suggests a similar indirect relationship between vocabulary knowledge and comprehension, but through their common relationships to general knowledge. People who know the meanings of words like *bunt* and *shortstop* tend to know more about baseball than those who do not. People with greater topic knowledge also comprehend text better (for a review, see Anderson & Pearson, 1984).

Mezynski (1983) added one more hypothesis to Anderson and Freebody's

(1981) list, the *speed-of-access* hypothesis. This hypothesis suggests that it may not be whether a person "knows" a word that is the crucial variable in the relationship between vocabulary and reading comprehension, it is how easily the word can be accessed for use in comprehension. All comprehension processes, vocabulary retrieval as well as other processes, share limited cognitive resources. Nonautomatic access to word meanings may impair other comprehension processes by consuming some of these resources that would have been otherwise available for micro- or macroprocessing, for example.

All four of these hypotheses capture some aspect of the vocabulary-comprehension relationship. The aptitude hypothesis gets support from the strong correlations between general vocabulary and general intelligence and reading comprehension. O'Brien (1986) and Stahl, Hare, Sinatra, and Gregory (1990) both found a measure of general vocabulary to be a better predictor of passage comprehension than knowledge of vocabulary specific to the passage. This suggests that it is more than knowledge of specific words that affects comprehension. Yet, as is discussed later, the connections between aptitude and vocabulary may not be as clear-cut as they appear.

The general knowledge hypothesis has not fared as well. The basic premise that passages will contain vocabulary specific to their topic and these words will be better known by people with greater topic knowledge is unassailable. But in general, vocabulary and prior knowledge seem to function separately. Freebody and Anderson (1983b), Stahl and Jacobson (1986), Stahl, Jacobson, Davis, and Davis (1989), and Stahl, Hare, Sinatra, and Gregory (1990) all found that vocabulary knowledge and prior knowledge had specific effects on comprehension, but that these effects did not interact with each other.

The speed-of-access hypothesis has also received support. Beck, Perfetti, and McKeown (1982) found that, as a result of instruction, children could access the meanings of words they had been taught faster than words they had not been taught, suggesting that students learned the words well enough so that the words were available for complex processing tasks. Word frequency, which presumably measures how often children encounter words in text, also has strong relationships with timed recognition measures, both of reaction time measures involving isolated word recognition and with fixation duration during reading (Just & Carpenter, 1987; Nagy, Anderson, Schommer, Scott, & Stallman, 1989). These findings suggest that as readers encounter a word over and over, it becomes easier for them to access the word's meaning. Presumably faster lexical access aids comprehension or, at least, does not impede it.

The Instrumentalist Hypothesis.   As an educator, I have been most interested in the instrumentalist hypothesis, because it, or variations of it, suggests that one can improve comprehension by teaching words. This hypothesis has received support from both well-designed research studies such as those of Beck, McKeown, and their colleagues (Beck, Perfetti, & McKeown, 1982; McKeown,

Beck, Omanson, & Perfetti, 1983; McKeown, Beck, Omanson, & Pople, 1985); Kameenui, Carnine, and Freschi (1982); and Stahl (1983), among many others, and from research syntheses, such as the meta-analytic review conducted by Stahl and Fairbanks (1986). Stahl and Fairbanks, for example, found that some forms of direct instruction of word meanings had a significant effect on the comprehension of passages containing taught words and on comprehension in general. They found that a child at the 50th percentile in a group that was pretaught word meanings performed as well as a child in the 82nd percentile of the control group on measures of comprehension of passages containing taught words and as well as a child at the 63rd percentile on standardized measures of comprehension, not necessarily containing taught words.

Not all vocabulary instruction improved comprehension, however. Instead, Stahl and Fairbanks suggest that for vocabulary instruction to have a significant effect on comprehension, it needed (a) to include both definitional and contextual information about to-be-learned words, (b) to involve students in active, meaningful processing of the words and their meanings, and (c) to provide multiple exposures to meaningful information about each word. This means that relatively complex treatments appear to be needed for vocabulary instruction to improve comprehension. Simply drilling children on definitions or having them look up words in dictionaries had little or no effect.

However, there are powerful arguments against an instrumentalist hypothesis in its strongest forms, or, at least, against the implication derived from the instrumentalist hypothesis that direct instruction of word meanings will necessarily improve comprehension. One arises from Nagy and Anderson's (1984) findings that printed school English contains 88,700 discrete word families. If children learn about half of these over the school years, and if they enter school with about 6000 words already known (and these seem to be supportable assumptions), then they would be learning 3000 words per year. Because this is far more words than could be taught through direct instruction the vast majority of these words must be learned by children in the context of reading. The 300 to 400 or so words that reasonably could be taught to children through direct instruction might add a significant amount of new word meanings to those already being acquired through context, especially for poorer readers who learn considerably fewer than 3000 new words per year. But direct instruction, at least not instruction as extensive as appears to be needed in order to be effective, cannot logically account for the majority of word learning.

Thus, vocabulary instruction can significantly improve comprehension but cannot account for all of the words ordinarily learned. The vocabulary instruction that appears successful, given our current research designs, is very extensive and time consuming. However, as I discuss throughout this chapter, extensive instruction may not be needed for all words in all situations. What is needed is a means for teachers to better estimate when words need extensive instruction and when less extensive instruction would be equally useful.

Changing Perspectives

Another problem with the body of instructional research is in the measures used in it to assess comprehension. In the majority of the studies that found an effect on comprehension for rich and elaborate vocabulary instruction (e.g., Beck et al., 1983; McKeown et al., 1983, 1985; Kameenui, Carnine, & Freschi, 1982; Stahl, 1983) the criterion passages contained a high percentage of unknown words, typically 10% or higher. In many of the studies that failed to find such an effect, the percentage of taught words was much lower (e.g., Ahlfors, 1979). Yet, as I mentioned earlier, a reader typically encounters between one and a half and three unknown words per hundred running words, a considerably smaller percentage than used in these studies. Large percentages of unknown words were used to simulate the effects of long-term vocabulary instruction, after which, presumably, larger percentages of words would have been taught.

To understand the effects of these larger percentages on comprehension, one must understand how an unknown or partially known word affects comprehension. This involves looking at the vocabulary-comprehension relationship from a different perspective, that of the individual word's effect on understanding the individual passage. From this perspective, all four vocabulary-comprehension hypotheses seem too general. Each examines the overall effect of knowing word meanings (in general) on comprehending passages (again, in general). Each loses important distinctions about word knowledge, such as how well a person knows a word, or the types of knowledge a person has about particular words. Each also loses distinctions about reading comprehension, such as the type of task used to measure comprehension.

In real-world comprehension, a person rarely approaches a task with a total absence of knowledge about a word. In fact, it took me a great deal of reading to come up with the passages below and with *micturition* and *minatory* as examples of words that I—and perhaps the reader of this report—did not know. I chose two passages of roughly 75 words each for my examples because for a school-age child, experiencing one unknown word per 75 words is typical. Therefore, the experience of a well-educated reader reading these passages should be analogous to that of a typical school-age child reading appropriate materials. In addition, a person having no comprehension of what he or she read is also rare. Instead, a reader is going to get some information about a text's meaning, no matter how difficult the text might be. Consider then, these passages and how the two italicized words affect your comprehension.

> "Oh, all right," I grumbled. I turned off the water and went into the living room to do my stretches. Peppy didn't understand why I wasn't limber and ready to go as soon as I got out of bed. Every few minutes she'd give a *minatory* bark from the back. When I finally appeared in my sweats and running shoes, she raced down the stairs, turning at every half landing to make sure I was still coming. (Paretsky, *Blood Shot*, 1988, p. 28).

Then I am in the short passage leading to the kitchen at the rear. I find the men's room door. I am hit by the salt stink of a public bathroom. Mr. Schultz stands at the urinal with his legs apart and his hands on his hips so that the back of the jacket wings out, and his water arcs from him directly into the urinal drain, thus making the rich foaming sound of a proud man at his *micturition*. (Doctorow, *Billy Bathgate*, 1989, p. 300)

If you are like me, you had not seen either *micturition* or *minatory* before reading these passages. Yet, in neither case did you have difficulty understanding what you were reading, and, indeed, you might not have taken notice of either word had you been reading it in the original book rather than in a paper on word meanings.

Although it is clear that one unknown word in a short passage will not cause comprehension breakdown, it is not clear exactly what effects an unknown word might have. Larger models of reading appear to focus on either word recognition processes (such as Adams, 1990) or comprehension processes (such as Kintsch & van Dijk, 1978). Vocabulary knowledge is somewhere between these two perspectives, so we must look at both to understand the role of word meanings in comprehension. To examine the role of partial word knowledge in comprehension, I first look at lexical knowledge from a bottom-up view, focusing on the interactions between orthographic and contextual knowledge in comprehending and in learning word meanings. Then I shift the focus to look at the effects of unknown words on comprehension of larger units of text. Finally, I try to speculate about what implications the role of word knowledge has for instruction and for the other three hypotheses.

WORD MEANING, ORTHOGRAPHY, AND CONTEXT

The model of word recognition illustrated in Fig. 7.1 is taken from Adams (1990), but most interactive models of reading (e.g., Just & Carpenter, 1987) make similar predictions. Adams proposes that four interconnected processors act upon written words. The orthographic processor contains our knowledge of spelling patterns and uses that knowledge to identify words. The phonological processor contains parallel information concerning our knowledge of sounds in spoken words. The meaning processor contains information about word meanings and how they relate to each other. The context processor contains our ongoing information about the text, derived from our comprehension.

In this model, visual information from the printed page first goes to the orthographic processor, which takes the information available from visual perception and matches it with a reader's knowledge of spelling patterns. While doing this, it receives and shares information with the phonological and meaning processors. The phonological processor reinforces information directly available

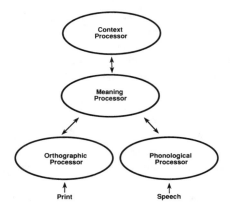

FIG. 7.1.   Adams' (1990) model of the reading process.

from orthography, as well as information incoming from the meaning processor. The meaning processor contains our store of word meanings, which takes and provides information to the orthographic processor about possible word meanings. The context processor, in turn, takes and provides information to the meaning processor, allowing the meaning processor to choose among alternatives.

It is the meaning processor that concerns us most, because this is where the vocabulary store is acted upon. Adams (1990) views the meaning processor as an interconnected network of concepts, similar to the semantic networks proposed by Collins and Loftus (1975). Network models have their proponents and detractors (see Smith & Medin, 1984). For the purpose of this chapter, however, the exact format of the storage is not important. What is important are the interconnections between this processor and other processors. In the model shown, the meaning processor gives and receives information from two other processors, the context processor and the orthographic processor. The context processor is where Adams (1990) suggests that ongoing processing of sentences occurs. She suggests that as comprehension (begging, for the moment, the question of exactly what comprehension is) occurs, information available from context is available for the meaning processor to help decide the meaning of an unknown word.

Learning from Context and Comprehension

In Adams's model, if a word is totally unknown, as *micturition* and *minatory* were to me, the meaning processor would have no information available to activate. The meaning processor would simultaneously get stimulation from both the orthographic processor and the phonological processor, providing information about the word's spelling and pronunciation, and the context processor, providing information about ongoing comprehension. Within the orthographic processor, some sort of representation of *micturition* would be formed, involving the reinforcement of links between already represented spelling patterns. This would be available the next time the word is encountered.

The two contexts presented earlier differ significantly in the richness of information provided about these two unknown words. For *minatory*, the context simply does not provide any relevant support for a reader to infer that *minatory* means "threatening." Yet, as I stated earlier, the word should cause little comprehension difficulty. The main point of the paragraph in which the word appears is that the unnamed first person is preparing to take her dog for a walk. The only portion of the message that would be missed relates to the nuance of the dog's bark. The point of the sentence, that the dog is communicating her impatience, is available from context.

In the case of *micturition*, if the context were completely comprehended, the information from the context processor would include information about bathrooms, that the use of a urinal was involved, and so forth. This would suggest strongly that micturition relates to urination (which, in fact, it does). But the reader probably would not stop and substitute *urination* for *micturition*. Instead, *micturition* would be tied (weakly, since this is only the first encounter) to roughly the same concepts as *urination* might be. Probably, both *micturition* and *urination* might be accessible from the same concepts (although *micturition* would be harder to access because of the weakness of the links), but *urination* and *micturition* would not be *directly linked* but connected only through their *common linkages*. Omanson, Beck, McKeown, and Perfetti (1984) found that readers are more likely to process incompletely a proposition containing an unknown word than to substitute a synonym for that word and continue normal processing. Thus the information about *micturition* would be tied weakly to orthographic representation and be available for the next encounter with the word.

Studies of children's derivations of word meanings from context, in which subjects are given sentences containing nonce words and are asked to give tentative definitions for words after each new sentence, suggest that, at first, children tend to integrate thoroughly the word's meaning with the context in which it appears (Elshout-Mohr & van Daalen-Kapteijns, 1987; McKeown, 1985). Children with high verbal ability begin to decontextualize the word's meaning, drawing elements from different exposures together to create a flexible representation of the word's meaning (see also Nelson & Nelson, 1978). Children with low verbal ability tend either to create a new meaning from each context, not integrating meanings across contexts, or tend not to distinguish well between information that overlaps between contexts and information that does not. McKeown (1985) noted that low-ability students may carry the topic of one sentence to the other sentence, rather than isolating the portions of word meaning common to both.

It is probably not desirable to substitute a synonym for words encountered in context in real-world comprehension. Often contexts contain misleading information about the word's meaning, information that may interfere with comprehension the next time the word is encountered. If, on a first encounter, a reader wrongly associates one word with another, this misassociation might interfere not only with ongoing comprehension but it might also interfere with comprehension the next time the reader encounters the word. Consider what word you might substitute for *minatory* in the sentence provided earlier. In my informal survey of adults, "threatening" was never offered as a potential meaning for *minatory*. Let's say a reader infers logically from the context of the sentence that minatory means "short." However, the second time the reader encounters minatory is in the sentence "He gave her a minatory glance." In this case, the use of minatory is meant to suggest that the "he" is contemplating villainy. Substituting "short," although it would yield a plausible meaning, would nonetheless cause the reader to lose the nuance of this second sentence. Contexts are misleading a good proportion of the time, and without recourse to a dictionary the reader does not really know whether the initial encounter or the second encounter or both was misleading. So it is not usually a wise strategy for a reader to commit to any particular synonym for an unknown word encountered in context.

DIFFERENCES IN CONTEXTS

The Effects of Overlap

Because the information in the case of *micturition* from the context processor strongly overlaps with the actual, intended meaning of the word, the presence of an unknown word here is not likely to impair comprehension markedly. This is not always the case. Context can be more or less congruent with a word's meaning. When the meaning of the word is not congruent with that expected from the context, subjects have difficulty using the context effectively to learn the meaning of the unknown word. In the *minatory* passage, as in the passages studied by Shatz and Baldwin (1986) and Beck, McKeown, and McCaslin (1983), the meaning of the word was not easily discerned from context.

If the information available from context overlaps strongly with the intended meaning, it is more likely that a person will learn the meaning of that word from context. In a series of studies, Nagy and his colleagues (Nagy, Anderson, & Herman, 1987; Nagy, Herman, & Anderson, 1985; Herman, Anderson, Pearson, & Nagy, 1987) found that the congruence of the context with the tested meaning of the word influences the likelihood of learning an individual word from context, as did a number of factors, including the conceptual difficulty of the word. Thus a naive reader, reading both *Billy Bathgate* and *Blood Shot,* would be more likely to learn the meaning of micturition than minatory.

If there is a strong overlap between the information and the meaning of the word, it also is less likely that particular word will disrupt comprehension, or, if it does, that it will do so in a different manner than will a word with less overlap. When an unknown word is encountered, the process of searching for its meaning will take some time, time that may or may not interfere with comprehension, depending on the demands of the rest of the task. But if the information about the word is incongruous, it might send the readers down a garden path, which either will lead to a breakdown of comprehension or require resource-consuming repairs.

Some evidence for this notion comes from the effects of revisions that make text more "considerate," or the context more congruent with the word's intended meaning. Herman, Anderson, Pearson, and Nagy (1987), Konopak et al. (1987), and Konopak (1988) found that such revisions improved both comprehension and learning words from context. Such revisions include apposition of an explicit definition, clearly signaling relations between target words and other words in the passage, or elaborated explanations placed around the target word. As will be discussed below, many readers cannot take advantage of such elaborations when they are provided. In natural language, however, such appositions and elaborations are rarely provided because words are chosen for their appropriateness to the topic, and authors do not ordinarily feel they have to define them.

Richness of Information

Related to the issue of overlap is the richness of the information provided by contexts. Some contexts will use a word in passing; others, such as the micturition passage, will provide a great deal of information around that word. If one assumes, as Adams (1990) does, that information about word meanings is stored as part of a network of interrelations between concepts, then the richer or more elaborate the information provided about the word's meaning, the more likely it is that the word will be recalled and used. With richer contexts, it is also less likely that an unknown word will interfere with comprehension.

A word like *minatory,* if encountered only in the one context presented earlier, might be only known as a type of bark. *Micturition,* on the other hand, may be accessible from a number of related concepts, including *bathroom, urinal, Dutch Schultz* (the referent of "he" in the passage), and so forth.

Each connection from one exposure would be weak, and, in the model described by Adams (1990), weak connections are more difficult to access. Even with weak connections, a reader having a multiplicity of such connections would be more likely to access a word's meaning than a reader with fewer equally weak connections (Just & Carpenter, 1987). Thus, even with a single exposure, a word encountered in a richer context is more likely to be learned than is one encountered in a less-rich context, as was indeed found by Herman, Anderson, Pearson, and Nagy (1987).

Together the amount of overlap between the word and the context and the richness of the context produce two complementary effects. First, a word in a rich and congruent context is less likely to impair comprehension than a word in a less-rich or less-congruent context. Second, a word in a rich and congruent context is more likely to be learned from that context.

Taxonomies of Context Cues.   One approach to describing many of these variations has been the use of taxonomies of context cues. A number of such taxonomies have been developed largely to teach the use of context to children. However, the evidence is scant that teaching children taxonomies of context cues improves their ability to derive word meanings from context (see Graves, 1986). Such taxonomies may be useful in helping them describe richness of contextual support. Sternberg and Powell (1983) have developed a model of learning from context that suggests that variation in learning from context is due to three factors—(a) processes of knowledge acquisition, (b) contextual cues in the text, and (c) moderating variables. Processes of knowledge acquisition include selective encoding, selective combination, and selective comparison. Individual variations in these abilities are expected to underlie differences in learning word meanings. Contextual cues, such as temporal cues, spatial cues, and so forth refer to the information given in the text about the target word. Presumably the more different types of cues given, the easier the word is to learn, all other factors being equal. Moderating variables include the number of occurrences of the unknown word, the variability of contexts containing the unknown word, the importance of the unknown word to understanding the context, the helpfulness of the context surrounding the unknown word, the density of unknown words, and the usefulness of previously known information.

Directiveness of Contexts.   The taxonomy of Sternberg and Powell (1983) was developed for teaching students to better utilize context. The more intuitive approach of Beck, McKeown, and McCaslin (1983) might be better suited for helping teachers make decisions about the need for instruction of words in context. They defined four general types of contexts, *directive,* or contexts that direct a highly specific meaning for an unknown word; *general directive,* or contexts that suggest a general meaning, *nondirective* or neutral contexts; and *misdirective,* or contexts that may mislead a reader about a word's meaning. Of the two passages used in this report, the context in the minatory passage would be classified as misdirective and the context in the micturition passage would be directive.

Beck, McKeown, and McCaslin's (1983) approach mixes the factors of overlap and richness discussed earlier. In general, a directive context is going to have a high degree of overlap between a word's meaning and a rich context. A misdirective context, on the other hand, will generally have a low overlap in a rich context. It is the richness of the context that strongly suggests an incorrect meaning. Following the same analysis, a generally directive context would have a strong overlap in a sparse context and a nondirective context would be low in both richness and overlap. The bipolar dimensions of richness and overlap seem to have more heuristic value, but the scale of Beck et al. (1983) may be as useful for making instructional decisions. All other factors being equal, one might elect to teach a word in a nondirective or misdirective context before teaching one in a directive or even generally directive one. The other factors, which may or may not be equal, include the importance of the unknown word, as well as differences in the abilities of students.

Importance of the Unknown Word

The amount of information a reader gets about a word's meaning may also relate to the word's importance to the passage as a whole. Importance may affect learning from context in at least two ways. First, a reader may devote more attention to learning an unknown word if it is an obstacle to understanding an important concept than if it is relatively unimportant.

Second, as in the case of *micturition,* the word relates directly to the *major* idea of the chapter from which it was taken, that Dutch Schultz was shot while in the bathroom. The details in the passage elaborate that macrostatement, and thus elaborate micturition. If a word is located in a proposition relatively lower in importance, fewer words in the passage will elaborate on that proposition, and thus the person will receive less information about the new word. Because the information provided is less elaborate, the word is less likely to be learned. Of the two context examples used in this paper, in the micturition example, the word was tied to ideas important to the meaning of the entire passage; in the minatory example, the unknown word was relatively incidental.

Summary of Differences Between Texts

There seem to be three significant differences among texts that affect both learning from context and comprehension—(a) the overlap between the information in the context and the word's meaning, (b) the richness of information available in the context, and (c) the importance of the word in relation to the rest of the passage. These factors all have complementary effects on learning from context and comprehension. As it becomes more likely that a word will be learned from context—through a greater overlap of information, richer contexts, or because the proposition that the word is attached to is more important—that word is also less likely to affect comprehension.

For making decisions about instruction, the more important a word is to the content, the more important it would seem to be to teach explicitly the word's meaning. The greater the overlap between the word's meaning and the information available from context and the richer that information is, or the more directive the context is, the less extensive that instruction needs to be. If a word's meaning is adequately directed from the context, discussion of a definition may be enough. If the meaning is not accessible from context, more extensive instruction may be needed.

This is true only for words that represent concepts already in a reader's concept store. For words representing concepts new to the reader, extensive instruction will always be required. Polysemy and homonymy will also affect instructional decisions. The presence or absence of prefixes, suffixes, and roots are also important distinctions among words, but morphology is not discussed in this paper.

DIFFERENCES AMONG WORDS

Conceptual Complexity

It would seem that unknown words representing concepts new to the reader would create different problems than words representing known concepts. Information from a single context could not adequately describe a complex concept that a student does not know prior to reading. Thus, a student might be less likely to learn from context a word like *osmosis* than a word like *pusillanimous*. This is especially a problem in content area textbooks, in which complex concepts are often defined with an appositive, such as:

The colonists wanted their *independence,* or freedom from another's power.

If a student did not know the meaning of *independence,* such a context would not be adequate to learn it. Indeed, Nagy, Anderson, and Herman (1987) found that conceptual difficulty affected the probability of learning a word from context, and that there "was simply no learning from context for words at the highest level of conceptual difficulty" (p. 255).

However, it appears difficult to distinguish the conceptual complexity of words beyond the grossest levels. Nagy, Anderson, and Herman (1987) could only reliably distinguish between words which were closely tied to a content schema (e.g., *tributary, capillary*) and words in more general use. They could not reliably distinguish different levels of complexity in general words. Bill Nagy and I could not, after many tries and refinement of scales, establish interrater reliability above .5 in ranking the conceptual complexity of general terms. P. Durkin (1990) who did find sets of words which she could rank reliably as more or less complex, found that complexity did not make a difference in an intentional learning from context task.

What appeared to be conceptual complexity in Nagy, Anderson, and Herman's (1987) study may be how much words are tied to a particular content schema. Words which are part of a complex knowledge domain, such as "River Systems" or "The Human Circulatory System," as in Nagy, et al.'s study, may need to be learned as part of that schema or through elaborate use of examples, nonexamples, superordinates, and so forth (see Frayer, Fredrick, & Klausmeier, 1969). Words in more general use may be learned through a variety of techniques, as discussed later.

A high percentage of schema-related words, of course, would strongly affect comprehension, because they would carry a higher percentage of the content. However, the higher the percentage of such words, the more a person's knowledge of the domain would affect their comprehension. This can be seen very clearly by comparing an article in a professional journal or book such as this and an article on the same topic in a popular magazine. The article in the professional journal would contain a higher percentage of schema-related words, or jargon, than that written for the layman. Of course, the jargon carries very specific meanings to the professional, but confusion to anyone outside of the field.

Polysemy and Homonymy

Two related concepts useful for examining the effects of unknown words on comprehension are polysemy and homonymy. Polysemous words are words that are orthographically identical but share related, although separate meanings. An example would be *line* as in "to get in line" or a "line of Kings." Both uses are derived from the core meaning, that of a line such as this: ——————. (Sometimes, a picture indeed is worth a thousand words.) Homonyms share the same spelling but different meanings with different derivations, as in *line,* meaning to "line one's pockets." In this case, *line* is derived from *linen,* not a straight line.

One could write passages containing enough polysemous words and homonyms so that they were completely ambiguous (for an example, see Anderson & Pearson, 1984), but in the ordinary case, it is unclear whether polysemy or homonymy creates genuine comprehension difficulties. Context could (and certainly does) disambiguate polysemous words. In fact, Anderson and Nagy (in press) have argued that all words are polysemous, because their meanings change in every unique context in which they appear. If so, some amount of acceptance of polysemy would be part of ordinary processing of word meanings. However, reports from nonnative speakers of English suggest that polysemy can create specific problems (Imai, personal communication, December 1989).

DIFFERENCES BETWEEN READERS

In addition to differences among texts and among words, there are a number of differences between readers that affect both learning from context and comprehension. Differences in the amount of prior vocabulary knowledge certainly affects both word learning and comprehension. Such differences may affect children's ability to comprehend the information in the context that supports the unknown word's meaning. Differences in topic knowledge as well as differences in ability and in working memory have been discussed in the literature as well.

Differences in Prior Word Knowledge

Children with low vocabulary knowledge may not gain the same benefits from context as children with high vocabulary knowledge. For such children, even explicit definitions used as appositives, the most directive of contexts, may not be useful if they do not know the meanings of the definitions themselves. Because children with low vocabulary knowledge tend not to know a great many words, including some that are used to define other words, they might not be able to take advantage of such definitions. For example, Shefelbine (1990) found some low-ability students misunderstood *gaucho* in the sentence, "Gauchos, the cowhands of South America, learned to chase the birds on cow ponies."

> One student, who did not know the meaning of "cowhand" on the pretest, incorrectly inferred from the passage that they were Indians who hunted rheas . . . The same student then used his understanding of cowhands to define "gauchos" as "cowhands, a type of Indian." A second student who thought cowhands were ponies, concluded that gauchos were "cow ponies, ponies to chase birds." In four other instances, inappropriate responses for cowhands were used to define gauchos. One of the more inventive, but still logical interpretations saw cowhands as being the front feet of a cow." (p. 90)

Even for better readers, definitions might be misunderstood. Miller and Gildea (1987) asked children to make sentences for unknown words from definitions and found that these sentences often showed serious misunderstandings of the sentences. For example, for the following definition of *redress:*

> 1. set right; repair; remedy: *when King Arthur tried to redress wrongs in his kingdom.*

One student wrote,

> The *redress* for getting well (when) you're sick is to stay in bed.

As discussed earlier, the more explicit the information that contexts provide about a word's meaning, the more likely the word is to be learned *and* the less likely that it will disrupt comprehension. Yet even the most explicit contexts, when definitions are put in apposition, will not aid comprehension for students who do not understand the defining terms and/or do not flexibly apply the information from varied sources to gain a more accurate representation of the word's meaning and to aid ongoing comprehension.

In general, students must be able to use the elaborated contexts to make sense of the unknown words. In the case of *redress,* a student focused on a "sickness" instantiation of *remedy,* rather than on the broader meaning. The student may have had only partial knowledge of *remedy,* and this partial knowledge may have interfered with the learning of *redress* (see McKeown, this volume; Scott & Nagy, 1990).

Children who know more word meanings also tend to read more than do children with lower vocabulary knowledge (for review, see Stanovich, 1986). More exposure to text translates into exposure to more words, meaning more partial and full meanings of words are available. Thus, in Stanovich's terms, "the richer get richer," and children who know more, learn more, exacerbating the differences between high- and low-verbal children over time.

Can vocabulary instruction reduce these differences? Possibly, possibly not. On one hand, vocabulary instruction may account for a larger percentage of words that children with low vocabularies learn over the course of the school year. Estimates of the number of words a child ordinarily will learn from context range from 1000 to 5000 new words (Graves, 1986). For a child at the low end of this range, the 300 to 400 words taught through direct instruction will be more significant than for a child at the upper end.

On the other hand, children with low vocabulary knowledge are in a double bind. Because they are less likely to know words in the context, making contexts less useful, they may need more intensive instruction to learn each new word. More intensive instruction is going to take time away from other activities, including the wide reading that will not only better allow them to solidify their vocabulary gains but also will itself lead to greater vocabulary growth.

Differences in Topic Knowledge

One might also assume that greater topic knowledge would enable students to be more efficient at learning from context. Two studies that examined this question, Barnes, Ginther, and Cochran (1989) and Stahl (1989), failed to find clear effects of prior topic knowledge on learning word meanings from context. These studies both manipulated prior knowledge through some form of preteaching. While such manipulations seem to affect comprehension (e.g., Stahl & Jacobson, 1986), a better test of the effects of prior knowledge on learning word meanings might be to examine preexisting prior knowledge. Herman et al. (1987) did find a significant effect for subjects' reported prior knowledge on learning from context.

Greater prior knowledge may affect learning from context in three ways. First, readers with more prior topic knowledge may be able to devote more available resources to examining unknown words, because they presumably will have less difficulty connecting information in the text to an already existing knowledge base (Anderson & Pearson, 1984). Second, readers with more prior knowledge would be more likely to understand the information elaborating the unknown word and thus be able to get greater benefit from context, Third, readers with more prior knowledge would be more likely to have partial knowledge of the unknown word. This may be the case in the Herman et al. (1987) study, because the words tested tended to be related to the topic, such as *pulmonary, circulatory,* and *capillary* for the topic "Circulation" and *levee, runoff, tributary,* and *turbulent* for the topic "River Systems." Shore, Durso, Dayton, Coggins, Davis, Beasley, and Gloria (1987) found that adults could learn words for which they had partial knowledge faster than words for which they lacked such knowledge. In the case of the Herman et al. (1987) study, the context may have served to add enough information to already existing word knowledge of subjects with high topic knowledge. Subjects with low topic knowledge, lacking that partial knowledge, needed more exposure to both words and topic to learn them.

Therefore, topic knowledge might influence word learning to the extent that the to-be-learned words are tied to the topic. Words like *circulatory, tributary,* and so forth, which are closely tied to a specific topic, would seem to be influenced more by topic knowledge. This could be because persons having prior knowledge of the topic might have had some exposure to the target words. Or it could be that persons with greater topic knowledge have a richer existing conceptual store to tie the words to as they are encountered. Words that are more general, or that can appear in texts dealing with a number of different topics, may not be related to topic knowledge at all.

Differences in Ability

A number of different studies have examined the relationship between readers' ability and learning word meanings from context. Here the results seem to form a consistent pattern. Studies in which children were asked to *derive* word meanings, that is, studies in which children were told prior to reading that they were expected to come up with a definition of a word they were to read in context, have found clear differences between students of high and low verbal ability in deriving word meanings from context (see Elshout-Mohr & van Daalen-Kapteijns, 1987; McKeown, 1985). Of studies examining *incidental* vocabulary learning, or studies in which students were not told that they would be tested on words they read in context, the majority of studies did not find such ability differences (Nagy, Anderson, & Herman, 1987; Nagy, Herman, & Anderson, 1985; Stahl, 1989).

Even though this pattern seems clear, its interpretation is not. First is the question of whether the derivation task or the incidental task is more appropriate. The incidental task seems to mirror what presumably happens "naturally." The derivation task may be inherently more susceptible to ability effects since studies which have used it, such as McKeown (1985) and Elshout-Mohr and van Daalen-Kapteijns (1987) have used constructing a definition as their criterion measure. Such a measure may require more verbal ability than a multiple choice test. In addition, as noted before, it seems likely that readers do not ordinarily derive a synonym for words encountered in context, but instead might recall the associations between the word and information in the context. Thus, the derivation task may add an extra layer of complexity. This layer may account for the strong individual differences found.

But the question should be kept open, if for no other reason than the impossibility of accepting a null hypothesis. In addition, of the incidental learning studies, Herman, Anderson, Pearson, and Nagy (1987) did find significant ability differences in learning words from context.

This question, if left open, leads to other interesting questions. If ability does, in fact, influence learning word meanings from context, does it mean that one should train directly the ability to derive word meanings from context, as suggested by Sternberg and Powell (1983)? The results of such training have been ambiguous at best, with relatively few studies finding that training children in context cues affects word learning (see Graves, 1986 for review). If ability does not directly affect learning from context, then are the differences in word knowledge due to differences in the amount of reading done by good and poor readers, rather than ability, as suggested by Stanovich (1986)?

One final point: It is also not clear how much verbal ability influences word learning and how much of it is influenced by word knowledge. Verbal ability is partially measured by measures of vocabulary knowledge (or measures strongly correlated to them, such as reading comprehension measures), so it is possible that differences in verbal ability merely represent differences in breadth or depth of a student's vocabulary knowledge. A student with broader or deeper vocabulary knowledge might know more about the words in a defining context, even if a nonce word were the target word, as in the McKeown (1985) and Elshout-Mohr and van Daalen-Kapteijns (1987) studies. In Shefelbine's (1990) study, in which a nonverbal measure was used to measure ability, no relationships were found between ability and intentional learning of word meanings from context.

Working Memory

Yet another difference in readers that might affect learning from context may be differences in working memory capacity. Working memory is defined in terms of both memory capacity and processing ability. This has been measured in a number of studies by a reading span test, in which subjects read increasingly longer sets of sentences and are asked to recall the last word of each sentence (Just & Carpenter, 1987). Presumably, people with longer reading spans can hold larger proportions of text in working memory, and thus have more information from larger contexts available for learning a word's meaning. Daneman (1988) has found that learning from context has a moderately high correlation with differences in working memory, $(r = .66)$, higher than correlations with age or grade. She suggests that differences in working memory, which appear to develop with age, may underlie developmental differences in efficiency of learning from context, such as those found by Werner and Kaplan (1952).

It is, however, unclear exactly what the reading span test is measuring. Because it includes both capacity and processing in its definition, differences in reading span may reflect no more than differences in basic verbal ability, which brings us back to the problems discussed earlier.

Summary of Differences Among Readers

In short, children who know more words can learn more words. They can do this for two reasons. First, they are more likely to know the meanings of the words in the context, and thus get richer contextual information about each unknown word. A child who has low vocabulary knowledge to begin with may not be able to take full advantage of a rich and elaborated context. Second, children who know more words are likely to read more, and reading more means that they are exposed to more words.

The effects of differences in topic knowledge, verbal ability, and working memory are less clear. Topic knowledge might affect words closely related to the topic, but it is not clear whether topic knowledge itself aids in learning new words or merely reflects prior exposure to targeted words. Verbal ability seems to affect children's ability to derive word meanings, but not their ability to learn them incidentally from text, but whether the incidental or derivation tasks are better measures of word learning is not clear. It is equally unclear whether measures of working memory reflect something different from verbal ability.

AS A WORD IS LEARNED

All of this concerns the effects of various factors on one exposure to a word in context. With additional exposures, a richer understanding of the word's meaning is obtained. This happens two ways. First, there is nearly always an overlap between information received from different exposures. It would seem that the greater the overlap between exposures (and presumably the greater the overlap in each exposure between the context and the intended meaning), the more likely the word is to be learned. The repeated exposures to this overlapped information would strengthen it, making it the core of the word's meaning. The stronger the association, the easier it is to access it once the orthographic representation of the concept is activated (Just & Carpenter, 1987). These areas of overlap would also become the default interpretation, or how the reader evokes the concept in the absence of constraining context, as is discussed below. Second, broader contextual information would increase the number of links to other concepts, making the word easier to access. Beck, Perfetti, and McKeown (1982) found that increased amount of practice during vocabulary instruction led to faster access.

Words that received the most practice were responded to on semantic decision tasks as rapidly as were common words, but words receiving less practice were responded to significantly slower. There were no differences in accuracy between the two types of words. On sentence decision tasks, the results were similar. Thus, it seems that even once accuracy is achieved, increased practice with words can lead to gains in speed of access. (McKeown, Beck, Omanson, and Pople [1985] found that, beyond a certain limit, increased numbers of exposures in vocabulary instruction did not improve speed of access, suggesting that there is a ceiling to this effect.)

Access Speed and Comprehension.   Whether these increases in access speed necessarily lead to improved comprehension is unclear, however. First, as discussed earlier, word frequency is strongly related to a variety of reaction time measures. And word frequency (or more precisely, word family frequency) appears to be related to passage comprehension (Ryder, 1989). Evidence for this relation has also been found in instructional studies, but here the evidence is less consistent. Beck, Perfetti, and McKeown (1982) and McKeown, Beck, Omanson, and Pople (1985) found differences in effects for words receiving more and those receiving less practice on some measures of comprehension, but not others.

However, a large number of exposures may not be sufficient for a reader to access efficiently a word's meaning if the exposures contain limited information. In a series of studies, Jenkins and his colleagues (Jenkins, Pany, & Schreck, 1978; Pany & Jenkins, 1977) found that drilling children on the connection between a word and its synonym (For example, "debris means trash") was very effective in getting children to recall the synonym, but did not affect comprehension. In this case, children received a great deal of practice making a single connection between a new word and already known information. To be useful for comprehension of text, to-be-learned words seem to need a number of different connections to known words and concepts. In her review of the effects of vocabulary instructional methods on comprehension, Mezynski (1983) found that those methods that did improve comprehension all taught words in rich and varied contexts. Often these successful methods provided fewer exposures than the unsuccessful methods such as those used by Jenkins and colleagues.

The effects of access speed would seem to vary depending on two dimensions of the text—percentage of difficult words and difficulty of the comprehension task in general. Slowness in accessing one word might not interfere with comprehension. Slow access to a great many words would slow comprehension down in general, leading to loss of information. Because all processes must compete with each other for limited cognitive resources, excessive difficulty with accessing word meanings would consume resources ordinarily used by other processes.

Also, as the comprehension task itself becomes more difficult, either because the topic is unfamiliar and the reader has to construct new knowledge structures or because the task demands are themselves high or because the passage is poorly or ambiguously written, the presence of known but difficult to access words is likely to affect comprehension to a greater extent. This is also likely specifically to affect development of a microstructure, because this may be more resource intensive.

VOCABULARY KNOWLEDGE AND COMPREHENSION

To this point, I have discussed operation of the context processor rather generally, without specifying the mechanisms with which it works. For the earlier arguments, it was necessary simply to understand that the context contributes information about a word's meaning and that information becomes easier to access again if matched with information already in the meaning processor.

The information from context also appears to choose which information about a word's meaning is salient. For example, for the sentence "Nurses have to be licensed," the context highlights the "medical professional" aspects of the concept *nurse*. For the sentence, "Nurses are often beautiful," the context highlights that *nurses* are often female and young. Anderson, Pichert, Goetz, Schallert, Stevens, and Trollip (1976) found that the word "doctor" was a better retrieval cue for the first sentence than for the second, while the reverse was true for the word *actress*. They suggest that each context causes a particular instantiation for each word (see also Anderson & Nagy, in press). This instantiation consists of the information about the word salient to the context, which in turn, feeds back into the context processor, adding to information about the context, and thus aiding continuing comprehension. The same process may resolve ambiguities about polysemous words, as discussed before.

Thus, the richness of information available from the context may lead to a more precise instantiation of each word, and thus to richer information available in the context processor to instantiate the next word.

Microprocessing and Macroprocessing

The ongoing sentence comprehension represented by the contextual processor of Adams (1990) has at least two components, microprocessing and macroprocessing. Microprocessing involves the combination of individual words into propositions and propositions into a coherent representation of the text, or a microstructure. Macroprocessing involves the development of a gist representation of the context of the text. In a number of models (e.g., Just & Carpenter, 1987; Kintsch & van Dijk, 1978), the reader strategically applies reduction strategies to the developing microstructure to develop the macrostructure, in interaction with schema-driven macroprocesses. Our research (Stahl & Jacobson, 1986; Stahl, Jacobson, Davis, & Davis, 1989; Stahl, Hare, Sinatra, & Gregory, 1990) and that of others (Freebody & Anderson, 1983b; Ryder, 1989) suggest that vocabulary difficulty has its greatest effect on microprocessing, while prior topic knowledge affects macroprocessing most strongly. These two processes seem to be separable, at least by observing the effects of different factors, but in reality they interact in a number of ways. Because our focus is on vocabulary effects on comprehension, these higher level interactions are not discussed here.

In three different designs and these five studies, using three different passages, vocabulary knowledge and prior knowledge appear to have independent effects. Further, vocabulary knowledge appears to have effects on those measures that seem to involve the construction of a microstructure involving the relations between individual propositions in a text—a sentence verification task (Freebody & Anderson, 1983b; Stahl & Jacobson, 1986), recall of the order of events (Stahl et al., 1989, Studies 1 & 3), exact replacement of function words in a cloze task (Stahl et al., 1989, Study 2), and the number of propositions recalled (Stahl et al., 1989; Stahl et al., 1990), especially the number of details recalled (Stahl et al., 1990).

Prior knowledge also affected the recall of central and supporting propositions in the Stahl et al. (1989) and in the Stahl et al. (1990) study. Prior knowledge also had unique effects on measures of gist comprehension or comprehension of the relative importance of information, such as a summarization task (Freebody & Anderson, 1983b), construction of a gist statement in recall (Stahl et al., 1990), and an importance rating task (Stahl et al., 1989, Study 3). In the last three cases, however, these effects were relatively small. Further, the tendency of subjects to give irrelevant preteaching to recall facts that matched that preteaching in the Stahl et al. (1989) study and for subjects who claim more interest in the topic of baseball to recall more numbers such as a pitcher's E.R.A. and career strikeouts in the Stahl et al. (1990) study suggests that differences in prior knowledge can also direct readers' attention to different information within the text (Reynolds & Anderson, 1982; Reynolds, Standiford, & Anderson, 1979).

How Vocabulary Difficulty Might Affect Microprocessing

When a reader encounters an unknown word, there seem to be two possible strategies available. The reader may decide to invest cognitive effort in discovering the meaning of the unknown word. This might involve a resource-intensive examination of the context. This is the presumption of researchers who have attempted to train students in the deliberate use of context to determine the meanings of unknown words. Training of explicit use of context cues does not seem to be consistently successful (see Graves, 1986, for review). In natural reading situations, readers are unlikely to devote limited resources to deriving word meanings from context. Instead, they are likely to take what limited information is available from the automatic use of context and proceed with reading. If so, they are likely to use an incomplete representation of the proposition containing the unknown word in the microstructure.

Omanson, Beck, McKeown, and Perfetti (1984) tested these two models using data from their training studies. They examined the recall protocols taken from subjects recalling passages containing 11% unfamiliar words. They presumed that if subjects would use context to derive the meaning of the unknown word, the resulting proposition would contain a rough synonym for the unknown word and would be otherwise processed normally. If the subjects formed an incomplete proposition, they would process the proposition only once, when it was encountered, and that proposition would be less likely to be recalled than it would be if all the words were familiar. They found that the second model, in which the unknown word was processed incompletely, better characterized their data than a model in which synonyms were substituted for unknown words.

Yet, their study may overstate the effects of lack of vocabulary knowledge. The target passages contained a very high amount of unknown words. Assuming that about half of the words in a typical passage are function words, the 11% of the total words in Omanson et al.'s (1984) analysis represents close to 25% of the content words of the passage.

It is unclear what percentage of unknown words is needed to disrupt comprehension. In the Stahl et al. (1989) study significant effects were found with a substitution of one out of six content words. However, Freebody and Anderson (1983a) found a one to three ratio was necessary to significantly disrupt comprehension. In any case, the passage used by Omanson et al. (1984) contained a fairly high percentage of unknown words. This high a percentage may have disrupted comprehension to a point that information was not available from context. Without the information available from ongoing comprehension, readers may have had no choice but to use incomplete representations. Whether they would do so with more realistic proportions of unknown words has yet to be demonstrated.

These models, of course, concern totally unknown words. In reality, most unfamiliar words are not totally unknown. Instead, they might be in a "twilight zone" in which the reader has some information about their meaning, but not full enough meaning to express it in a definition or use it productively and confidently in a sentence. Curtis (1987) has found that readers do not need this full knowledge to answer multiple choice questions typical of a vocabulary test. As the foregoing analysis suggests, they also might not need such knowledge in typical comprehension activities. Instead, more general recognition of the word and a notion of what semantic domain it belongs to may to be enough for a word not to interfere with comprehension, depending on the importance of the word within the passage and the overlap and richness of the context.

Shore et al. (1987) found that "Twilight zone" words were easier to learn than totally unknown words. This was especially true if the words were presented organized by semantic fields.

How Vocabulary Difficulty Might Affect Macroprocessing

While the studies cited earlier found that vocabulary difficulty largely affected development of a microstructure, words in those studies were chosen to be general terms, usable in a side variety of contexts. Other words tend to be associated with a restricted range of semantic fields, such as *tributary* for "river systems" or *capillary* for "circulatory system" or *bunt* with "baseball." In these cases, acquisition of word meanings seems to be inseparably connected with acquisition of knowledge in the semantic field. Knowledge of the word *capillary* might mark an individual as more highly knowledgeable about a subject matter. Stahl et al. (1990) found that subjects who knew more baseball terms, such as *bunt, shortstop,* and so forth tended to be more knowledgeable about baseball and that this knowledge affected their comprehension.

Encountering a term, such as *bunt* or *tributary* or *capillary,* would, at least for a reader with knowledge in the corresponding fields, activate that knowledge. Activation of appropriate knowledge has been found to improve comprehension if the knowledge is focused on the concepts central to understanding the passage (Stahl et al., 1989). However, such activation may be inappropriate if the concepts are tangential to understanding. In that case, activation of knowledge may lead the reader to make bridging inferences between the semantic domain implied by the term and the actual intended meaning of the passage. If these inferences are inappropriate, comprehension will suffer. This may be one reason why metaphorical passages are difficult to understand.

IMPLICATIONS FOR VOCABULARY INSTRUCTION

The view of the effects of vocabulary difficulty on comprehension from the word level taken here suggests that the effects that an individual unknown or partially known would have on comprehension will depend on a number of different factors. An unknown word will be more likely to impair comprehension if (a) there is a relatively small overlap between information in the context and the word's meaning, (b) if the context is relatively sparse in information, (c) if the word is relatively important to the text, and/or (d) if the word represents a complex concept new to the reader. In addition, if children have less vocabulary knowledge, they are less able to take advantage of the overlap and richness of the information in the context, for both comprehension and learning word meanings from context. Finally, vocabulary difficulty is more likely to impair comprehension if the task is one involving microprocessing, such as recalling details from a text, than if the task involves macroprocessing, such as getting just the gist of the message. Conversely, if there is a wide overlap, with a rich context, the word is relatively unimportant, and so on, vocabulary difficulty will be less likely to impair comprehension. By itself, a difficult word will have little effect on comprehension.

Why Has Only Extensive Vocabulary Instruction Improved Comprehension?

If the purpose of vocabulary instruction is to provide enough knowledge for a reader to comprehend a passage containing a taught word, from the analysis thus far it would seem that how much knowledge is required depends on the word's context and on the comprehension task. Full knowledge may be necessary for certain comprehension tasks, such as metaphor (see Readence, Baldwin, Rickelman, & Miller, 1986), but in most cases, partial knowledge combined with information incoming from the context processor is sufficient. Some authors (e.g., Kameenui, Dixon, & Carnine, 1987) have argued that for most circumstances, relatively brief vocabulary instruction is all that is needed to teach words well enough for comprehension. In the *micturition* and *minatory* cases, a simple definition appears to be enough for comprehension to continue. Yet the research consistently shows that full and elaborate methods are necessary to improve comprehension.

One way of explaining this contradiction is to look at the comprehension tasks used to measure the effects of vocabulary instruction. As noted earlier, the majority of studies that found an effect for vocabulary instruction on comprehension used passages that contained high percentages of unknown words. Yet a high percentage of unknown words may distort the effects of word knowledge by making the task of reading excessively difficult. If too many words are unknown, this may interfere with the feedback between the meaning processor and the context processor, making comprehension beyond the simplest level impossible.

In the case of comprehension breakdown, readers may take information from their prior knowledge to construct what they can from the text. In the studies cited earlier, this can be a gist statement ("This passage is about . . . ."). Yet enough word meanings are usually known to avoid comprehension breakdown. Instead, ongoing comprehension continually adds and acts on information available in the context processor. An unknown word might impair comprehension somewhat, especially of the proposition in which it is located, but information from context should enable ongoing comprehension, at least in a typical case of one and a half to three unknown words per hundred. The conundrum for the researcher interested in the effects of vocabulary instruction or vocabulary difficulty on comprehension is that, on one hand, one needs to have a certain percentage of unknown words in a target passage to overcome the beneficial effects from context, but, on the other hand, with too large a percentage of unknown words, the process observed may be markedly different than that which usually occurs.

It has been argued however that one needs to use passages with a high density of unknown words in order to gauge the effects of long-term vocabulary instruction (e.g., Stahl, 1983). Over the long term, a great many words have been taught and a passage containing these words might look like those used in the studies cited before. This argument has merit. Indeed, using such contrived passages may be the only way of demonstrating that vocabulary instruction affects comprehension. Yet one must be aware of the limitations of such use.

How Extensive Does Instruction Have to Be?

Many of the same factors used to analyze context, word, and reader differences in the effects of vocabulary knowledge on comprehension can be used in deciding how intensive or extensive instruction needs to be. Many of the approaches discussed in the literature for teaching word meanings assume, explicitly or implicitly, that a reader needs to have full knowledge of a word's meaning to comprehend it in text. Indeed, providing full knowledge may be the only way of improving comprehension in a text with 10% of the words unknown. Given a certain degree of support from context, instruction need only provide partial knowledge, or instruction may not be needed.

How is one to decide whether or not instruction is needed, or how extensive that instruction should be? Many of the factors discussed here could be part of that decision-making process. First, if a word represents a concept that is new to a child, that is, a concept that the child does not already have experience with or know any other words for, this word will require extensive instruction. This instruction might include providing examples and nonexamples of the concept, giving superordinate and subordinate terms, and so on, possibly including concrete experiences (for one approach, see Frayer et al., 1969; also Wixson, 1986).

If a word represents a known concept, then one should examine the context in which it is set. If the proposition the word is in is relatively important, then the word should receive more extensive attention, even if the context is relatively directive. Wixson (1986) tested this hypothesis directly, finding that students instructed on words contained in propositions central to the story answered correctly significantly more questions about that central information than students instructed on words located in noncentral propositions. Students instructed on words located in noncentral information, suggesting that vocabulary instruction can misdirect a students' comprehension as well as direct it. If a word is relatively unimportant to the passage, teaching it might increase students' attention to that unimportant information.

If the context is relatively directive (that is, there is a strong overlap between the information in the context and the word's meaning and the information is relatively rich), then again the word might not need to be taught, since the context may provide enough information without such instruction. However, it should be cautioned that students with low vocabulary knowledge might not be able to take advantage of a rich context if they do not know the meanings of surrounding words as well. These students might especially require specific instruction in word meanings.

This analysis, therefore, suggests that extensive instruction is required (a) if the concept represented by the word is not known by the student, (b) if the proposition the word is in is relatively important, and (c) if the context is nondirective or misdirective. Instruction might not be needed if the proposition containing the word is relatively unimportant and the context is relatively directive. In between these extremes, words need more or less extensive instruction.

What do we mean by more or less extensive instruction? In the rich and extensive instruction given by Beck and her colleagues (e.g., Beck et al., 1982), an average of 17 minutes of instruction was provided per word taught, including drill on definitions, discussion of whether the word would fit into a particular sentence context, having students generate their own contexts, and so on. Such instruction produced powerful effects on their comprehension measures.

Less extensive instruction might consist minimally of providing a definition orally and discussing one or two sentences for each taught word. One such minimal approach, "Possible Sentences," involves providing a list of target and known words, briefly discussing the target words, and having students generate sentences that possibly could be in the text they are about to read that contain at least two of the words on the list. After reading, students discuss whether the sentences could or could not appear in the text. Such an approach produced significant effects on recall of facts in science material in two separate studies (Stahl & Kapinus, 1990).

There is evidence, however, that definitional drills, a traditional model of vocabulary instruction, are not effective. For example, Jenkins, Pany, and Schreck (1978) found that drilling children on definitions failed to improve comprehension on a number of measures. This may be because, as discussed earlier, readers do not merely substitute a synonym when meeting a newly learned word. Instead, they bring to bear information from a number of previously encountered contexts. Even the most abbreviated vocabulary instruction should include both definitional and contextual information.

Approaches to vocabulary instruction that have been found to improve comprehension have exposed students to a breadth of information about each words' meaning, not just a synonym or definition (see Stahl & Fairbanks, 1986). In addition, effective approaches must provide students with a number of different exposures to words in different contexts. Such different exposures allow a reader to have a number of different connections to other known words, as well as a sense about which of these connections are the most salient. To be useful, vocabulary knowledge needs to be flexible. Nitsch (1978) found that children who learned word meanings in one context were best at understanding those words in the contexts in which they were learned. Children who saw the words in multiple contexts, however, were better able to recognize the words in novel settings.

Nagy (1988) has argued that all of these conditions can be satisfied through learning from context. Indeed, they can be, and most vocabulary is learned from context and learned apparently well enough. But as Carroll (1964) pointed out, good vocabulary instruction should mimic the effects of context learning, except it should do so more efficiently.

FOUR HYPOTHESES

This report began with the hypotheses engendered by Anderson and Freebody's (1981) seminal paper on vocabulary knowledge. This review suggests that the "truth" captured by each of these hypotheses depends on the particular contexts in which a word is found, the way the task of comprehension is defined, and the amount and types of knowledge a person has about a word. It is possible within the literature to find support for each hypothesis and to find situations where each is irrelevant.

In the explosion of research since the Anderson and Freebody (1981) paper, we have resolved some of what might be called "first generation" questions about vocabulary knowledge and its effects on reading comprehension. We have also found that it is necessary to move beyond these initial hypotheses, and to begin to examine the conditions in which a person's knowledge of word meanings influences comprehension (microprocessing or macroprocessing) in different contexts (directive to misdirective, important to unimportant). Much of this report is speculative, but it is speculation to be useful in defining a next step for vocabulary research.

ACKNOWLEDGMENTS

I would like to thank Marilyn Adams, Bill Nagy, and Mike Shand for their comments on an earlier version of this paper, and Fran Lehr for her editorial assistance. This paper was written while the author was visiting the Center for the Study of Reading at the University of Illinois, Urbana-Champaign. I am grateful for its support.

REFERENCES

Adams, M. J. (1990). *Beginning to read: Thinking and learning about print.* Cambridge, MA: MIT Press.
Ahlfors, G. (1979). *Learning word meanings: A comparison of three instructional procedures.* Unpublished doctoral dissertation, University of Minnesota, Minneapolis.

Anderson, R. C., & Freebody, P. (1981). Vocabulary knowledge. In J. T. Guthrie (Ed.), *Comprehension and teaching: Research reviews* (pp. 77–117). Newark, DE: International Reading Association.

Anderson, R. C., & Nagy, W. E. (1991). Word meanings. In P. D. Pearson (Ed.), *Handbook of reading research* (2nd ed.). (pp. 690–724). New York: Longman.

Anderson, R. C., & Pearson, P. D. (1984). A schema-theoretic view of basic processes in reading comprehension. In P. D. Pearson (Ed.), *Handbook of reading research* (1st ed., pp. 255–291). New York: Longman.

Anderson, R. C., Pichert, J. W., Goetz, E. T., Schallert, D. L., Stevens, K. V., & Trollip, S. R. (1976). Instantiation of general terms. *Journal of Verbal Learning and Verbal Behavior, 15,* 667–679.

Barnes, J. A., Ginther, D. W., & Cochran, S. W. (1989). Schema and purpose in reading comprehension and learning vocabulary from context. *Reading Research and Instruction, 28,* 16–28.

Beck, I. L., McKeown, M. G., & McCaslin, E. S. (1983). All contexts are not created equal. *Elementary School Journal, 83,* 177–181.

Beck, I. L., Perfetti, C. A., & McKeown, M. G. (1982). Effects of long-term vocabulary instruction on lexical access and reading comprehension. *Journal of Educational Psychology, 74,* 506–521.

Carroll, J. B. (1964). Words, meanings, and concepts. *Harvard Educational Review, 34,* 178–202.

Collins, A. M., & Loftus, E. F. (1975). A spreading activation theory of semantic processing. *Psychological Review, 82,* 407–428.

Curtis, M. E. (1987). Vocabulary testing and vocabulary instruction. In M. G. McKeown & M. E. Curtis (Eds.), *The nature of vocabulary acquisition* (pp. 37–51). Hillsdale, NJ: Lawrence Erlbaum Associates.

Dale, E., & Chall, J. S. (in press). *Readability: A review of the research.* New York: Teacher's College Press.

Daneman, M. (1988). Word knowledge and reading skill. In M. Daneman, G. E. McKinnon, & T. G. Waller (Eds.), *Reading research: Advances in theory and practice* (Vol. 6). New York: Academic Press.

Doctorow, E. L. (1989). *Billy Bathgate.* New York: Random House.

Durkin, P. M. (1990, December). Vocabulary acquisition in context reconsidered: The effects of word type and exposure level on the learning of unknown words. Paper presented at the annual meeting of the National Reading Conference, Miami Beach, FL.

Elshout-Mohr, M., & van Daalen-Kapteijns, M. (1987). Cognitive processes in learning word meanings. In M. G. McKeown & M. E. Curtis (Eds.), *The nature of vocabulary acquisition* (pp. 53–72). Hillsdale, NJ: Lawrence Erlbaum Associates.

Frayer, D. A., Fredrick, W. C., & Klausmeier, H. J. (1969). *A schema for testing the level of concept mastery.* (Working Paper No. 16). Madison: Wisconsin Research and Development Center for Cognitive Learning.

Freebody, P., & Anderson, R. C. (1983a). Effects on text comprehension of differing proportions and locations of difficult vocabulary. *Journal of Reading Behavior, 15,* 19–40.

Freebody, P., & Anderson, R. C. (1983b). Effects of vocabulary difficulty, text cohesion, and schema availability on reading comprehension. *Reading Research Quarterly, 18,* 277–294.

Graves, M. F. (1986). Vocabulary learning and instruction. In E. Z. Rothkopf & L. C. Ehri (Eds.), *Review of Research in Education* (Vol. 13, pp. 49–89). Washington, DC: American Educational Research Association.

Herman, P. A., Anderson, R. C., Pearson, P. D., & Nagy, W. E. (1987). Incidental acquisition of word meaning from expositions with varied text features. *Reading Research Quarterly, 22,* 263–284.

Jenkins, J. R., Pany, D., & Schreck, J. (1978). *Vocabulary and reading comprehension: Instructional effects* (Tech. Rep. No. 100). Urbana-Champaign: University of Illinois, Center for the Study of Reading. (ERIC Document Reproduction Service No. ED 160 999).

Just, M. A., & Carpenter, P. A. (1987). *The psychology of reading and language comprehension.* Boston: Allyn & Bacon.

Kameenui, E. J., Carnine, D. W., & Freschi, R. (1982). Effects of text construction and instructional procedures for teaching word meanings on comprehension and recall. *Reading Research Quarterly, 17,* 367–388.

Kameenui, E. J., Dixon, R. C., & Carnine, D. W. (1987). Issues in the design of vocabulary instruction. In M. G. McKeown & M. E. Curtis (Eds.), *The nature of vocabulary acquisition* (pp. 129–145). Hillsdale, NJ: Lawrence Erlbaum Associates.

Kintsch, W., & van Dijk, T. A. (1978). Toward a model of text comprehension and production. *Psychological Review, 85,* 363–394.

Konopak, B. C. (1988). Effects of inconsiderate vs. considerate text on secondary students' vocabulary learning. *Journal of Reading Behavior, 20,* 5–24.

Konopak, B. C., Sheard, C., Longman, D., Lyman, B., Slaton, E., Atkinson, R., & Thames, D. (1987). Incidental versus intentional word learning from context. *Reading Psychology, 8,* 7–21.

McKeown, M. G. (1985). The acquisition of word meaning from context by children of high and low ability. *Reading Research Quarterly, 20,* 482–496.

McKeown, M. G., Beck, I. L., Omanson, R., & Perfetti, C. A. (1983). The effects of long-term vocabulary instruction on reading comprehension: A replication. *Journal of Reading Behavior, 15,* 3–18.

McKeown, M. G., Beck, I. L., Omanson, R., & Pople, M. T. (1985). Some effects of the nature and frequency of vocabulary instruction on the knowledge and use of words. *Reading Research Quarterly, 20,* 522–535.

Mezynski, K. (1983). Issues concerning the acquisition of knowledge: Effects of vocabulary training on reading comprehension. *Review of Educational Research, 53,* 253–279.

Miller, G., & Gildea, P. (1987). How children learn words. *Scientific American, 257*(3), 94–99.

Nagy, W. E. (1988). *Teaching vocabulary to improve comprehension.* Neward, DE: International Reading Association, Urbana, IL: National Council of Teachers of English.

Nagy, W. E., & Anderson, R. C. (1984). How many words are there in printed school English? *Reading Research Quarterly, 19,* 304–330.

Nagy, W. E., Anderson, R. C., & Herman, P. A. (1987). Learning word meanings from context during normal reading. *American Educational Research Journal, 24,* 237–270.

Nagy, W. E., Anderson, R. C., Schommer, M., Scott, J. A., & Stallman, A. C. (1989). Morphological families and word recognition. *Reading Research Quarterly, 24,* 262–282.

Nagy, W. E., Herman, P. A., & Anderson, R. C. (1985). Learning words from context. *Reading Research Quarterly, 20,* 233–253.

Nelson, K., & Nelson, K. E. (1978). Cognitive pendulums and their linguistic realization. In K. E. Nelson (Ed.), *Children's language* (Vol. 1). New York: Gardner Press.

Nitsch, K. E. (1978). *Structuring decontextualized forms of knowledge.* Unpublished doctoral dissertation, Vanderbilt University, Nashville, TN.

O'Brien, D. G. (1986). A test of three hypotheses posed to explain the relation between word knowledge and comprehension. In J. A. Niles & R. V. Lalik (Eds.), *Solving problems in literacy: Learners, teachers, and researchers. Thirty-fifth yearbook of the National Reading Conference.* Rochester, NY: National Reading Conference.

Omanson, R. C., Beck, I. L., McKeown, M. G., & Perfetti, C. A. (1984). Comprehension of texts with unfamiliar versus recently taught words: Assessment of alternative models. *Journal of Educational Psychology, 76,* 1253–1268.

Pany, D., & Jenkins, J. (1977). *Learning word meanings: A comparison of instructional procedures and effects on measures of reading comprehension with learning disabled students* (Tech. Rep. No. 25). Urbana-Champaign: University of Illinois, Center for the Study of Reading. (ERIC Document Reproduction Service No. ED 134 979).

Paretsky, S. (1988). *Blood Shot.* New York: Dell Publishing.

Readence, J. E., Baldwin, R. S., Rickelman, R. J., & Miller, G. M. (1986). The effect of vocabulary instruction on interpreting metaphor. In J. Niles & R. V. Lalik (Eds.), *Solving problems in literacy: Learners, teachers, researchers. 35th Yearbook of the National Reading Conference.* Rochester, NY: National Reading Conference.

Reynolds, R. E., & Anderson, R. C. (1982). Influence of questions on the allocation of attention during reading. *Journal of Educational Psychology, 74,* 623–632.

Reynolds, R. E., Standiford, S. N., & Anderson, R. C. (1979). Distribution of reading time when questions are asked about a restricted category of text information. *Journal of Educational Psychology, 71,* 183–190.

Ryder, R. J. (1989, March). *The effect of word frequency on text comprehension.* Paper presented at the annual meeting of the American Educational Research Association, San Francisco.

Scott, J., & Nagy, W. E. (1990, April). *Definitions: Understanding students' misunderstandings.* Paper presented at the annual meeting of the American Educational Research Association, Boston.

Shatz, E., & Baldwin, R. S. (1986). Context clues are unreliable predictors of word meanings. *Reading Research Quarterly, 21,* 439–453.

Shefelbine, J. (1990). Student factors related to variability in learning word meanings from context. *Journal of Reading Behavior, 22,* 71–97.

Shore, W. J., Durso, F. T., Dayton, T., Coggins, K. A., Davis, D. L., Beasley, R., & Gloria, A. (1987). *Effects of prior word knowledge on improving receptive and expressive vocabulary.* Norman, OK: University of Oklahoma, Department of Psychology, Cognitive Processes Laboratory.

Smith, E. E., & Medin, D. (1984). *Categories and concepts.* Cambridge, MA: Harvard University Press.

Stahl, S. A. (1983). Differential word knowledge and comprehension. *Journal of Reading Behavior, 15,* 33–50.

Stahl, S. A. (1989). Task variations and prior knowledge in learning word meanings from context. In S. McCormick, & J. Zutell (Eds.), *Thirty-eighth Yearbook of the National Reading Conference.* Chicago: National Reading Conference.

Stahl, S. A., & Fairbanks, M. M. (1986). The effects of vocabulary instruction: A model-based meta-analysis. *Review of Educational Research, 56,* 72–110.

Stahl, S. A., Hare, V. C., Sinatra, R., & Gregory, J. F. (1990, April). *Defining the effects of prior knowledge and vocabulary difficulty on text comprehension: The retiring of No. 41.* Paper presented at the annual meeting of the American Educational Research Association, Boston.

Stahl, S. A., & Jacobson, M. G. (1986). Vocabulary difficulty, prior knowledge, and text comprehension. *Journal of Reading Behavior, 18,* 309–324.

Stahl, S. A., Jacobson, M. G., Davis, C. E., & Davis, R. L. (1989). Prior knowledge and difficult vocabulary in the comprehension of unfamiliar text. *Reading Research Quarterly, 24,* 27–43.

Stahl, S. A., & Kapinus, B. A. (1990, April). *The effectiveness of "Possible Sentences" as a technique for teaching science vocabulary.* Paper presented at the annual meeting of the American Educational Research Association, Boston.

Stanovich, K. E. (1986). Matthew effects in reading: Some consequences of individual differences in the acquisition of literacy. *Reading Research Quarterly, 21,* 360–407.

Sternberg, R. J., & Powell, J. S. (1983). Comprehending verbal comprehension. *American Psychologist, 38,* 878–893.

Thorndike, R. L. (1973–74). Reading as reasoning. *Reading Research Quarterly, 9,* 135–147.

Werner, H., & Kaplan, E. (1952). The acquisition of word meanings: A developmental study. *Monographs of the Society for Research in Child Development, 15.*

Wixson, K. K. (1986). Vocabulary instruction and children's comprehension of basal stories. *Reading Research Quarterly, 21,* 317–329.

On the Early Influence of Meaning in Word Recognition: A Review of the Literature

David A. Balota
F. Richard Ferraro
Lisa T. Connor
Washington University

The prominent view of visual word recognition theorists is that readers must first match the visual stimulus to some internal representation before meaning of the stimulus word becomes available. Very simply, a word must be recognized before its meaning can be accessed. For example, in Morton's classic logogen model (Morton, 1969), word recognition devices (logogens) must receive sufficient activation via featural detectors before the word is identified. The meaning of the word does not become available before this theoretical threshold has been reached (see Becker, 1980; Forster, 1979; Norris, 1986, for similar views).

The notion that recognition must precede meaning access would appear to be a reasonable assumption, i.e., how could a reader access the referent of a word without first determining the identity of the word that was presented? In the present chapter we challenge this assumption. We first present a brief review of the tasks available that provide the major data bases for the available models of word recognition. Based on the studies reviewed in this section, we suggest that theorists do not have available an adequate measure of recognition processing that is *unequivocally* devoid of meaning access. We then turn to a review of the literature to determine whether there are any studies available that provide compelling evidence that meaning can contribute to the word identification process. Finally, we present a brief discussion of a theoretical framework that predicts a meaning-level influence in word identification.

Before turning to a more detailed discussion of these issues, there are two points that need to be noted. First, the emphasis in the present discussion is on studies that involve isolated word recognition or word recognition in neutral or unrelated contexts. When words are presented in associatively/semantically related contexts, performance in word recognition tasks is facilitated compared to when words are presented in neutral or unrelated contexts. Such *priming* effects would appear to indicate that meaning access, via a related context, has taken place before word recognition is completed. Although there are alternative accounts of such priming effects (see Neely, 1990, for a review), such effects and the accompanying theories are only minimally related to the present thesis. Clearly, the fact that meaning can be accessed via a related context does not presuppose that meaning of a word in an isolated context can influence the word recognition process. It is this latter issue that is the focus of present discussion.

The second point that needs to be discussed is an operationalization of the terms word identification and word access. Here we equate word identification with the processes that lead up to and include the decision to execute a response (i.e., *the Magic Moment*, see Balota, 1990). Word access involves accessing an internal representation that corresponds to a word. For example, in Morton's logogen model, lexical access would be reflected by activation at a lexical representation that may or may not be sufficient to exceed the threshold needed to execute a response, whereas, lexical identification would be reflected by the activation at a lexical representation that is sufficient to execute a response.

Here, as in all interpretations that we are aware of, lexical identification is primarily operationalized via three major tasks; lexical decision, pronunciation, and threshold identification. Hence, we operationalize lexical identification as (a) the time it takes, after stimulus presentation, for the subject to produce a sound that triggers a voice-operated relay (pronunciation), (b) the time it takes, after stimulus presentation, to produce a word/nonword response that triggers a microswitch (lexical decision), or (c) the stimulus conditions (e.g., duration, intensity, etc.) necessary to identify a stimulus (threshold identification). Because these three tasks provide the major data base for current models of word identification, it is necessary to briefly specify any limits that are inherent in these tasks concerning their use as windows into the magic moment of word identification.

LEXICAL DECISION, PRONUNCIATION, AND THRESHOLD IDENTIFICATION: THE TOOLS OF THE TRADE

On the surface, these three tasks would seem to be faithful reflections of word identification. For example, making a lexical decision would appear to involve the point in time when an internal representation has been sufficiently matched by stimulus-driven information. Thus, the button press in the lexical decision task (LDT) would appear to be a reasonable reflection of word identification. Likewise, it would appear that naming a word simply involves a match between stimulus-driven processing of the stimulus word and some lexical representation. Once this match is completed, the appropriate sequence of motor codes is engaged for output. Thus, the onset of pronunciation would also appear to be a reasonable reflection of word identification. Finally, with respect to the threshold identification task, the stimulus duration needed to identify a briefly presented stimulus word would appear to reflect the amount of stimulus information needed to surpass the lexical threshold. Hence, accuracy at a given stimulus duration may be used as a metric for the ease of word identification. Although at first glance these three tasks are tantalizingly simple, there are aspects of the tasks that question whether they can be used as sources of data to build *premeaning* access models of word identification. We shall now turn to a brief discussion of these aspects.

Lexical Decision Performance

First, let us consider the LDT. It is now clear that the LDT cannot be viewed as a faithful reflection of only processes leading up to and including word identification (e.g., Balota & Chumbley, 1984; Balota & Lorch, 1986; Besner & McCann, 1987; Chumbley & Balota, 1984; de Groot, 1983; Keefe & Neely, 1990; Lorch, Balota, & Stamm, 1986; Neely, 1990; Neely & Keefe, 1989; Neely, Keefe, & Ross, 1989; Seidenberg, Waters, Sanders, & Langer, 1984; West & Stanovich, 1982). The major problem with this task is very simple. The LDT is not only a word identification task but is also a discrimination task, in which subjects are forced to discriminate words from nonwords. Often one finds that variables that presumably only influence word identification processes are confounded with the discrimination component of this task. For example, consider the finding that high-frequency words produce considerably faster lexical decisions than low-frequency words. Here, manipulations of stimulus frequency/familiarity are *confounded* with a type of information, familiarity, that would be available to the reader, and very helpful in making the word/nonword discrimination, i.e., words are more familiar than nonwords. Specifically, compared to high-frequency words (e.g., *CAKE*), low-frequency words (e.g., *SHAM*) are more similar to, and therefore more difficult to discriminate from, nonwords (e.g., *ROLM*) on the relevant familiarity dimension. A similar discrimination *confounding* occurs in semantic priming studies. Briefly, if there is a relationship between the prime and the target then the target must be a word, however, if there is no relationship between the prime and the target then the target can either be a word, primed by an unrelated word, or a nonword. Hence, the discrimination is more difficult on unrelated trials, thereby slowing response latency (see, e.g., Balota & Lorch, 1986).

The major point to note concerning the LDT is that there is often a confounding between the manipulation of interest and the information that subjects can use to make the word/nonword discrimination. Subjects are very sensitive to such confoundings (see Chumbley & Balota, 1984), and these confoundings can produce exaggerated influences of variables, thereby misdirecting theories of word recognition. Most importantly, for the present discussion, these confoundings cause concern regarding the utility of the LDT as an unequivocal reflection of lexical identification without meaning access.

Pronunciation Performance

The pronunciation task does not involve the problem of subjects making a discrimination between words and nonwords, and therefore, there should be little contribution of contaminating decision processes on overall response latency. However, even in the pronunciation task a variable could potentially play a role at many different loci in this task. Specifically, in pronouncing a word, the reader not only has to recognize the stimulus but also has to output the recognized word. Thus, a variable could have an impact on identification processes and/or on processes after identification that are tied to the output of the response. Consider the impact of word frequency. Balota and Chumbley (1985) used a delayed-pronunciation task to tease apart the impact of frequency on word identification from its impact on output processes. In the delayed-pronunciation task, subjects are given sufficient time to recognize the word and then are presented a cue to pronounce the word aloud. If frequency only influences the identification stage in this task, then one should not find a frequency effect after subjects have had sufficient time to recognize the stimulus. However, Balota and Chumbley found that subjects still produced a significant frequency effect in this task, even though they were given up to 1400 ms to recognize the stimulus (also see Connine, Mullennix, Shernoff, & Yelen, 1990).

More recently, Balota, Boland, and Shields (1989) have demonstrated that prime-target associations can influence both onset latencies and production durations in a delayed-pronunciation task. For example, in one of their experiments, they reported that subjects were both faster to begin their production of two related words, compared to two unrelated words, even though they had 1400 ms to recognize the stimuli (also see Dallas & Merikle, 1976; Midgley-West, 1979). Interestingly, Balota et al. also found that the production durations were shorter for related words than unrelated words.

The important point for the present discussion is quite simple. Because variables appear to influence processes *after* subjects have sufficient time to recognize the stimulus, one cannot unequivocally use data from the pronunciation task as a metric of processes that lead up to word identification, and hence, take place *before* meaning access.

Threshold Identification Performance

Possibly, the threshold identification task is a pure measure of lexical identification. This task presumably taps the amount of stimulus information necessary to surpass some lexical threshold to make the correct stimulus identification. Unfortunately, there is again an inherent problem that often produces interpretive difficulties when this task is employed.

Consider the perceptual problem a subject encounters while attempting to identify a highly degraded stimulus. The subject may be able to determine that the word is short and most likely begins with the letters *th*. Because the subject is typically not penalized for guessing, the subject proceeds to make a *best guess* at the target identification. Now, what types of information might the subject use to make such a guess? One obvious piece of information may be frequency information. That is, when presented with such a guessing situation, the subject may be more likely to guess the high-frequency word *thread* over the low-frequency word *thump* (see Catlin, 1973). If frequency influences threshold identification in this situation, one cannot conclude that frequency only influences lexical identification, but one must also consider its influence on the guessing biases that subjects may bring into the experimental situation. This concern with threshold identification is a general methodological concern in perceptual studies and falls under the general heading of *sophisticated guessing*. The point is quite simple, one cannot infer that a variable is influencing lexical identification in the threshold identification task, without taking into consideration all the potential guessing biases that subjects may bring into the experimental setting. The use of preexisting memory information to maximize accuracy in a perceptually degraded situation will most likely not be highly related to the processes that are involved in fluent word identification.

In sum, the *tools of the trade* in word recognition research that theorists use to build models that assume mandatory word identification before meaning access have characteristics that do not allow unequivocal interpretation of the data obtained from these tasks. The important point here is that if one cannot disentangle word identification from meaning access, then it may be more fruitful to consider a framework that might allow meaning to contribute to word identification.

On the other hand, it is possible that there is no evidence available even from lexical decision, pronunciation, and threshold identification tasks that indicate that meaning can contribute to word identification processing. If this were the case then one might at least feel cautiously comfortable with the extant models. We now turn to an evaluation of the relevant literature.

THE CONTRIBUTION OF MEANING TO WORD IDENTIFICATION: A REVIEW OF THE LITERATURE

As noted earlier, it is important to operationalize word identification. Here, as in the vast majority of word recognition studies, we shall operationalize word identification as the ability to (a) name a word aloud, (b) discriminate words from nonwords, or (c) identify a degraded stimulus. Hence, we will be using the above-criticized tasks in developing our review, and acknowledging caveats in interpretations along the way. The important point is that models of word recognition have also relied on these tasks and have come to the conclusion that meaning does not influence word identification. We are simply evaluating the relevant literature regarding this theoretical predisposition.

In the present review we address the four following areas: (a) the influence of pre-existing meaning representations (e.g., concreteness, contextual availability, and polysemy) in word identification; (b) associative reaction time as a task and as a predictor of lexical decision/pronunciation performance; (c) the influence of attaching meaning to previously nonlexical strings; (d) meaning access without word identification. A summary of the findings concerning each of these four areas along with a description of the tasks and potential confounds is displayed in Table 8.1.

The Influence of Pre-existing Meaning Representations on Word Identification

The studies reviewed in this section address whether there are meaning-level characteristics of words that influence word identification. Consider, for example, *concreteness* effects in word identification. If one could provide evidence that concrete words are recognized faster, or slower, than abstract words, then this would suggest that the fact that a word can be the object of a sense verb (i.e., *touch, see, hear, etc. . . .*) is sufficient to modulate word identification. This would be an example of a meaning-level variable (semantic class) participating in word identification processes.

Before we turn to this literature, it should be noted that a major difficulty in this area, along with other areas reviewed below, is whether there has been a confounding between the target variable (e.g., *concreteness*) and some other variable that may influence task performance. Gernsbacher (1984) has pointed out that many of the studies that have addressed meaning variables in isolated word recognition have not adequately controlled for the *familiarity* of the stimulus. Hence, this will be a general theme cutting across the studies reviewed in this and the following sections.

(1) Concreteness Effects

The question of whether there are differences in word recognition for semantically abstract versus concrete nouns has been prominent in the word recognition literature. In fact, the concrete/abstract distinction has been the most widely investigated dimension regarding semantic effects in word identification. Despite the widespread interest in this area, at least until recently, the results in this area have been equivocal. We first describe studies involving threshold identification and then turn to studies involving lexical decision and pronunciation performance.

It should be noted that in most studies discussed in this section concreteness has been confounded with imageability (see Boles, 1983, 1989). Because these

TABLE 8.1
The Contribution of Meaning to Word Identification: A Review of the Literature

Study	Task	Effect	Potential Confounds
The Influence of Preexisting Meaning Representations on Word Identification			

1. Concreteness Effects

Study	Task	Effect	Potential Confounds
Winnick & Kressel (1965)	TI[a]	A[b]rt = C[c]rt	RB,[d] CA,[e] I[f]
Paivio & O'Neill (1970)	TI	A rt < C rt	repetition of items, CA, RB
Richards (1976)	TI	C rt < A rt	FNM,[g] I, RB
Boles (1983)	word/digit report; word identification in left/right visual fields	familiarity of word had more impact than I or C	RB, CA
Boles (1989)	TI/incidental learning	In Expt. 1, main effects for I and interaction with visual field primarily for intentional learning instructions	FNM, RB, CA
Rubenstein, Garfield, & Millikan (1970)	LDT	C rt < A rt	stimulus problems (see Clark, 1973), CA, I
James (1975)	Expt. 1 & 2 (LDT)	C rt < A rt for LF words; C rt = A rt for HF words	FNM, I
James (1975)	Expt. 3 & 4 (Naming)	C rt + A rt for both LF & HF words	FNM (E1 - E3), (although familiarity manipulated episodically in E4)
Richardson (1976)	LDT/Naming	A rt = C rt	FNM, CA
deGroot (1989)	LDT	replicated James (1975), E1 & E2	FNM, CA
Day (1977)	LDT	C rt < A rt only in left visual field; C rt = A rt only in right visual field	FNM, CA, repetition of items, I
Kroll & Mervis (1986)	LDT	E1 & E2: conditions blocked and mixed, C rt < A rt; E3: conditions blocked A following C (C rt < A rt); conditions blocked C following A (C rt = Art)	FNM, CA, I
Bleasdale (1987)	Expt. 1 (Naming)	C rt < A rt	CA
	Expt. 2-4 (LDT)	C rt < A rt	

(continued)

TABLE 8.1 (*Continued*)

Study	Task	Effect	Potential Confounds
Marshall & Newcomb (1980)	RA (U)[h]	C %E < A %E	FNM, WFNM[i], CA, RB
Coltheart, Patterson, & Marshall (1980)	RA (U)	C %E < A %E	FNM, CA, RB
Richardson (1975a)	TI	C %E < A %E	FNM, CA
Richardson (1975b)	TI	C %E < A %E	FNM, CA
Shallice & Warrington (1975)	RA (U)	C %E < A %E	FNM, CA, RB
Shallice & Warrington (1980)	RA (U)	C %E < A %E	FNM, CA, RB
Seymour (1990)	selective interference (Naming)	C rt < A rt	FNM, CA, RB
Coltheart (1980)	RA (U)	similar to Day (1977)	FNM, CA, RB
Saffran, Bogyo, Schwartz, & Marin (1980)	RA (U)	C rt < A rt	FNM, CA, RB
Gernsbacher (1984)	LDT	main effect for familiarity (F), no main effect for C, no F x C interaction	CA
Schwanenflugel, Harnishfeger, & Stowe (1988)	LDT	C rt < A rt	CA
Schwanenflugel, Harnishfeger, & Stowe (1988)	LDT	C rt = A rt (contextual availability unconfounded)	--------------------------

2. Polysemy Effects

Study	Task	Effect	Potential Confounds
Rubenstein, Garfield, & Millikan (1970)	LDT	homograph rt < non-homograph rt	item sampling (see Clark, 1973), CA, FNM
Rubenstein, Lewis, & Rubenstein (1971b)	LDT	homograph rt < non-homograph rt	item sampling (see Clark, 1973), CA, FNM
Jastrzembski (1981)	LDT	words with more entries faster than words with few entries in dictionary	meaning metric not adequate, CA, FNM
Jastrzembski & Stanners (1975)	LDT	(see Jastrzembski, 1981)	(see Jastrzembski, 1981)

(*continued*)

TABLE 8.1 (*Continued*)

Study	Task	Effect	Potential Confounds
Kellas, Ferraro, & Simpson (1988)	LDT	ambiguous word rt faster than unambiguous word rt, ambiguous words demand less attentional resources than unambiguous words	CA
Kellas, Simpson, & Ferraro (1988)	LDT	(same as above)	CA
Millis & Button (1989)	LDT	words with many meanings responded to faster than words with few meanings	CA

Associative Reaction Time as a Task and as a Predictor of Lexical Decision and Pronunciation Performance

deGroot (1989)	LDT/Naming	HF C words responded to faster than LF C words. C better predictor than frequency	FNM, CA
Chumbley & Balota (1984)	LDT	speed to produce associate of target word good predictor of LDT	FNM

The Impact of Adding Meaning to Previously Nonmeaningful Strings

Whittlesea & Cantwell (1987)	letter detection	letters in nonwords given meaning detected better than letters in nonwords not given meaning	-------------------------
Forster (1985)	LDT, masked repetition priming	obsolete words assigned meaning produce more repetition priming than obsolete words not given meaning	-------------------------

Failure to "Recognize" Words that have Activated Meaning Representations

Balota (1983)	TP[j] (LDT)	priming even though primes were presented below subjects' threshold	-------------------------
Carr & Dagenbach (1990)	TP (LDT)	(see Balota, 1983)	-------------------------

(*continued*)

TABLE 8.1 (*Continued*)

Study	Task	Effect	Potential Confounds
Dagenbach, Carr, & Wilhelmsen (1989)	supra-TP (LDT); masked priming (LDT)	(see Balota, 1983)	-----------------------
Fowler, Wolford, Slade, & Tassinary (1981)	TP (LTD)	(see Balota, 1983)	-----------------------
Marcel (1983)	TP (LDT)	(see Balota, 1983)	-----------------------

Further Impacts of Meaning on Early Perceptual Processing

Schendel & Shaw (1976)	line segment detection	line segment from a letter detected better than line segment presented alone	-----------------------
Weinstein & Harris (1974)	line segment detection	line segment in three-dimensional forms better detected than line segment in two-dimensional forms	-----------------------
Virzi & Egeth (1984)	name target word or target word color	report colors/words that were not present in desplay (illusory conjunctions at meaning level)	-----------------------

TI[a] = Threshold Identification
A[b] = Abstract Words
C[c] = Concrete Words
RB[d] = Response Bias
CA[e] = Contextual Availability not measured
I[f] = Imageability
FNM[g] = Familiarity Not Masured
RA (U)[h] = Reading Aloud (Untimed)
WFNM[i] = Word Frequency Not Measured
TP[j] = Threshold Priming

two factors are highly correlated, unless otherwise specified, one can assume that the concreteness effects also involve contaminated imageability effects. Of course, for the present discussion, an imageability effect would also support the notion that underlying referential information was modulating word recognition. Therefore, at this level, the contamination of concreteness and imageability does not strongly constrain our arguments regarding meaning influences in word recognition.

Concreteness Effects in Threshold Identification Studies. Winnick and Kressel (1965) investigated the influence of word frequency and concreteness on threshold identification performance. The independent variable in this study was the number of 10 ms exposures that subjects required before they correctly identified the target word. The results indicated that there was no difference between the number of exposures needed to identify abstract and concrete words; both required 9.65 exposures.

Paivio and O'Neill (1970) investigated imageability/concreteness, word frequency, and the meaningfulness of target words in a threshold identification task. In their study, the stimuli were originally presented for 10 ms and then incremented by 5 ms exposure durations until the subject could correctly identify the target word. The results revealed main effects of frequency, imageability/ concreteness, and meaningfulness. Thresholds for abstract words were lower than for concrete words. However, further analyses indicated that familiarity, as reflected by untimed familiarity ratings by a different group of subjects, was correlated with concreteness, and that concreteness of the stimulus did not account for any variance above-and-beyond the influence of familiarity. However, even with the impact of familiarity partialled out, the correlation between meaningfulness and mean threshold identification, although reduced, was still significant.

A third study of recognition thresholds was conducted by Richards (1976). Richards used the same procedure that Paivio and O'Neill used and found main effects of both word frequency and concreteness across two experiments, with no interactions. Unlike Paivio and O'Neill, Richards found that concrete words had lower identification thresholds than abstract words. Unfortunately, Richards did not control for the familiarity of his stimuli.

A fourth series of experiments has been reported by Boles (1983, 1989). Boles was interested in the influence of imageability, concreteness, and familiarity on word identification in left and right visual fields. The visual field variable is important because it is possible that abstract words only have a single verbal-based representation, whereas, concrete words (and/or high imageable words) have both a verbal-based and an image-based representation, consistent with arguments by Paivio, among others, concerning dual codes. (We return to this issue below.) In the Boles (1983) study, words were presented for 100 ms for an identification response. The results of a series of five experiments yielded an impact of only word familiarity. Thus, Boles concluded that imageability and concreteness did not influence word identification nor did these variables interact with visual field of presentation, and therefore, involve different hemispheric representations.

More recently, however, Boles (1989) has modified this position. In this work, Boles has found that memory instructions can mediate these semantic effects. In his first experiment, subjects participated in a threshold identification study under intentional memory instructions. The results yielded main effects of familiarity and imageability, along with evidence that imageability modulated the right visual field advantage reported in this literature. That is, the right visual field advantage was smaller for high-imageable stimuli compared to low-imageable stimuli. In the second experiment, subjects were given incidental learning instructions. The results of this study yielded main effects of concreteness and imageability that were in large part eliminated when familiarity of the stimuli was partialled out. Hence, Boles argues that imageability effects and their interaction with visual field can be obtained under intentional learning instructions in a threshold identification task, but not under incidental learning instructions. It should also be pointed out, that concreteness did not have an influence on threshold identification above and beyond familiarity and imageability in any of the Boles studies.

In sum, it is difficult to reach a firm conclusion regarding the threshold identification studies. Beyond the inconsistencies in the data, a further problem is the potential for response biases to play a role in performance. For example, it is possible that when presented a degraded stimulus, subjects are more likely to guess that a concrete word was presented rather than an abstract word. Although interesting, such a response bias would not support an influence of concreteness on word identification. On the other hand, one could argue that simply because concreteness does not account for any variance above-and-beyond the impact of familiarity in threshold identification studies, as Paivio and O'Neill and Boles found, this does not necessarily discount the impact of concreteness on word identification. It is possible that subjects use concreteness in both ratings of familiarity and the processes involved in threshold identification. We now turn to studies that involve response latency measures.

Concreteness Effects in Lexical Decision and Naming.   An early study that explored the effect of concreteness along with a number of other variables (e.g., word frequency and polysemy) in lexical decision performance was conducted by Rubenstein, Garfield, and Millikan (1970). These researchers proposed that word frequency exerted its influence on lower-order processes while concreteness exerted its influence on higher-order processes. They found main effects of word frequency and polysemy as well as an interaction between concreteness and polysemy. Interestingly, they found that latencies for homographs having one concrete meaning and one abstract meaning were actually shorter than for homographs where both meanings were considered concrete. Because frequency, word length, number of meanings, and relative frequency of meanings were equated across the two sets of homographs, these results would appear to provide evidence for a true meaning effect. Therefore, at this level, it would appear that two semantic variables (concreteness and polysemy) work in consort to modulate word identification performance.

In an often-cited paper, James (1975) also manipulated word frequency and concreteness in a LDT. The results of his first experiment yielded main effects of frequency and concreteness along with an interaction between the two variables. The interaction indicated that low- and medium-frequency abstract words produced slower response latencies than concrete words at the same frequency levels, whereas there was no impact of concreteness for high-frequency words. This pattern was replicated in his second experiment when the lexical decision list contained nonwords that were homophones of words (e.g., *brane*). James eliminated any influence of concreteness in his third experiment when only nonpronounceable nonwords (e.g., *ebnra*) were presented within the list. Of course, this would be predicted because subjects could simply base their discrimination in the LDT on the acceptability of the orthographic code instead of relying on word identification processing.

James also eliminated the concreteness effect in his fourth experiment. This experiment involved two parts. In the first part, subjects were presented the target words in a sentence generation task; in the second part they received the same targets in a LDT. In this experiment, the concreteness effects were eliminated in lexical decision performance. Overall, the results from the James' study indicate that concreteness can modulate word identification for medium- to low-frequency words when subjects cannot rely on orthographic regularity or a high degree of familiarity (due to the earlier sentence completion task) to make lexical decisions. Clearly, the constraints of the LDT are extremely important in interpreting James' results, as he readily acknowledged.

Richardson (1976) addressed concreteness, imageability and lexical complexity effects in both pronunciation and lexical decision tasks. In Richardson's study, lexical complexity simply involved a distinction between suffixed and nonsuffixed nouns. Across three different tasks (pronunciation, lexical decision with pronounceable nonwords, and lexical decision with nonpronounceable nonwords) there were no effects of concreteness, imageability, or lexical complexity, even though there were large effects of word frequency and length in letters. Interestingly, however, it should be noted that non-suffixed concrete words were pronounced 29 ms faster than abstract words when collapsing across imageability levels. In addition, a difference of 28 ms was found between concrete and abstract words in the LDT that contained pronounceable nonwords. However, consistent with the James' study, only a 7 ms effect of concreteness was attained for the LDT when nonpronounceable nonwords were used. Unfortunately, it is difficult to interpret these effects because they were not directly tested by Richardson and the power to detect such effects was relatively low—each experimental condition had only ten subjects, with 10 observations per subject per cell.

Recently, deGroot (1989, Experiment 4) replicated the interaction between concreteness/imageability and word frequency in lexical decision performance with pronounceable nonwords that was reported by James. In addition, in her Experiment 5, she reported a pronunciation study that also produced a significant effect of concreteness/imageability that was additive with the effect of frequency. Thus, deGroot argues that the interaction between concreteness and frequency may be limited to the LDT. More importantly, the deGroot study indicates that concreteness/imageability can influence both lexical decision and pronunciation performance.

Day (1977) addressed whether concreteness effects in the LDT would be modulated by their visual field (and hence hemisphere) of encoding. As noted above, this is an intriguing extension of dual coding theory. Day reported three lexical decision experiments, all with pronounceable nonwords. The results of these experiments were quite clear. In each experiment, Day reported an interaction between concreteness and visual field, such that when the words were presented to the right visual field (left hemisphere) there was no impact of concreteness, whereas, when the words were presented to the left visual field (right hemisphere) concrete words produced faster lexical decisions than abstract words. Hence, the Day results suggest that not only does concreteness influence lexical decision performance, but it has a specialized right hemisphere impact.

More recently, Kroll and Merves (1986) also addressed the possibility that concrete and abstract words differ in their representational format. In order to test the dual-representation assumption, in their first experiment, Kroll and Merves presented pure lists of concrete words or pure lists of abstract words. The notion was that subjects may be able to attend to the different representational formats for the abstract and concrete words. The results of this experiment indicated that concrete words produced significantly faster (by items but not by subjects) lexical decisions than abstract words. Like James (1975) and Day (1977), these authors found that concrete words produced faster response latencies than abstract words. One might argue based on the results of this experiment that subjects were attending to the different representational formats of the concrete and abstract words. However, in a second experiment, where concreteness involved a within-subjects manipulation, a similar effect of concreteness was found. Hence, Kroll and Merves could not attribute the results of the first experiment to simply attending to different representational formats because a similar result was found when mixed lists were used. Interestingly, in both experiments Kroll and Merves reported an interaction between frequency and concreteness of the same nature reported by James (1975) and deGroot (1989), i.e., the concreteness effect was largest for low-frequency words. In their final experiment Kroll and Merves again blocked abstract and concrete words in a LDT, but now subjects received both blocks in a counterbalanced order across subjects. The results indicated that when subjects were given a pure list of concrete words first and then a pure list of abstract words, there was a large impact of concreteness. However, when abstract words preceded concrete words, there was no impact of concreteness. Instead of attributing these sequencing effects to selectively attending to different representational sources due to exposure to either only abstract or only concrete words, Kroll and Merves suggested that these effects may simply reflect strategic post-lexical effects in the LDT. Even if these results are due to strategic processes, it is clearly the case that subjects can be induced to utilize the concreteness dimension, in a speeded task, thereby suggesting that this is a readily available source of information, and that the recognition of this dimension can, at least, modulate a major task that provides data for models of word identification, i.e., lexical decision performance.

Like Kroll and Merves, Bleasdale (1987) investigated the effects of concreteness in order to address differences in representational formats, i.e., single vs. dual representational systems. Bleasdale employed a priming paradigm in both the pronunciation task and the LDT. As noted earlier, because we are primarily interested in isolated word recognition processes, it is beyond the scope of the present discussion to detail the influence of related versus unrelated contexts. However, Bleasdale's study is pertinent because in each of the four experiments, there was a neutral context condition (i.e., the neutral prime was BLANK) and an unrelated context condition. There is no *a priori* reason to expect such nonrelated contexts to differentially influence word identification processes for concrete and abstract words. Hence, one can use the concreteness effects in the neutral and unrelated prime conditions to determine whether there is any concreteness effect for *isolated* word recognition. In this light, the Bleasdale results are highly consistent and informative. In the first experiment, which involved a pronunciation task, there was a 10 ms advantage for concrete words over abstract words in the neutral prime condition and a 19 ms advantage in the unrelated prime condition. Although this difference was not directly tested, there was a main effect of target concreteness in this experiment and did not interact with prime context. A similar pattern was found in the three subsequent experiments that employed the LDT. That is, concrete words produced faster response latencies than abstract words by 27 ms for the neutral and 12 ms for the unrelated conditions in Experiment 2, 18 ms for the neutral and 26 ms for the unrelated conditions in Experiment 3, and 23 ms for the neutral and 26 ms for the unrelated conditions in Experiment 4. There are two further aspects of the Bleasdale study that are important to note here. First, the study appeared to produce an effect of concreteness in the pronunciation task; a task that does not involve the binary decision component. Second, the stimuli appeared to be well-controlled on dimensions that have been confounded in the past studies (see Gernsbacher, 1984; Schwanenflugel, Harnishfeger, & Stowe, 1988). Before turning to a discussion of these confoundings, we briefly describe some intriguing results regarding concreteness effects in *acquired* and *developmental dyslexics*.

Concreteness Effects in Acquired and Developmental Dyslexics.   Individuals who have specific reading disabilities due to brain trauma are referred to as acquired dyslexics, whereas, individuals who have specific deficits in reading performance that cannot be attributed to specific brain trauma are referred to as developmental dyslexics. Interestingly, there is evidence from both groups of subjects that the concreteness dimension may modulate isolated word recognition performance.

First, consider the performance of the group of acquired dyslexics that has been referred to as *deep dyslexics*. One hallmark symptom of this disorder is the inability to pronounce nonwords. Interestingly, these individuals produce a number of semantic errors in isolated reading such that they often report an

associate to the presented word instead of the target word itself. More importantly, however, for the present discussion, concrete nouns are the most spared of all
word types, with abstract words, adjectives, adverbs, and function words producing the most errors (Marshall & Newcombe, 1980). The concreteness effect
has now been reported in a number of studies (Coltheart, Patterson, & Marshall,
1980; Richardson, 1975a, 1975b; Shallice and Warrington, 1975, 1980). Thus,
these results suggest that a brain trauma can selectively interfere with an individual's ability to recognize, i.e., read aloud, abstract words.

Interestingly, Seymour (1990) has recently reported a selective interference
with the production of abstract words in a developmental dyslexic. In a case
study reported by Seymour, subject *JB* showed a dramatic difference in vocal
reaction time for abstract and concrete words in a reading aloud task. Abstract
words took nearly twice as long to say aloud as concrete words. Moreover, error
rates for reading abstract words were more than twice as high as for concrete
words.

Although there are a number of different accounts of the concreteness effect in
dyslexics, one of the more interesting accounts is that there is a selective breakdown in right hemisphere performance in these subjects (see Coltheart, 1980;
Saffran, Bogyo, Schwartz, & Marin, 1980). This, of course, is quite consistent
with Day's (1977) finding, reviewed earlier, that abstract words produced considerably slower lexical decisions when presented to the right hemisphere, but not to
the left (see however, Boles, 1983, 1989).

Unfortunately, as in studies outside the area of the dyslexia literature, stimulus
selection factors make it difficult to draw strong conclusions from the data. That
is, in many of the studies familiarity and contextual availability, see discussion
below, have not been adequately controlled. Moreover, because most of the
studies involved untimed reading, response biases may play a role. Thus, although suggestive and, in large part, consistent with studies with normal subjects
reviewed above, one must be cautious in extending results obtained with these
patients to general models of word recognition performance.

Concreteness Effects and Contaminating Variables.   Gernsbacher (1984) reviewed the inconsistent patterns of data in the word recognition literature regarding the impact of concreteness and word frequency. She argued that one variable
that appeared to be consistently confounded in these studies was item familiarity.
In order to demonstrate the importance of familiarity in these past studies,
Gernsbacher reported two lexical decision experiments (one with pronounceable
nonwords and one with nonpronounceable nonwords) in which she factorially
crossed familiarity with concreteness. Familiarity produced a significant effect,
but concreteness did not, and there was no evidence of an interaction. Hence, it
appears that familiarity may have been modulating performance instead of concreteness in, at least, some of the above studies. This argument is also consistent

with the arguments by Paivio and O'Neill and Boles, reviewed earlier, who suggested that there was no impact of concreteness above-and-beyond familiarity in threshold identification performance.

However, there are two points to note here regarding the problem of familiarity. First, it is not clear precisely what subjects use to rate items on a familiarity dimension. As noted before, it is possible that subjects may use a type of meaning information, e.g., *concreteness,* that is also used in lexical identification. By partialling out familiarity, one may also be inadvertently partialling out correlated meaning variables. Second, and more importantly, there is one study (Bleasdale, 1987) that indicates that one consistently finds a concreteness effect when familiarity is well-controlled. Thus, even if one argues that familiarity ratings do not involve access to meaning representations, which we believe is a rather tenuous argument, there is at least some evidence for concreteness effects that cannot simply be dismissed as familiarity effects.

More recently, Schwanenflugel, Harnishfeger, and Stowe (1988) have also challenged the observation that concreteness *per se* modulates word recognition performance. Schwanenflugel et al. suggest that, in addition to familiarity, concreteness is correlated with a dimension they refer to as *contextual availability.* These authors argue that it is important to access contextual information for the necessary integration that occurs across words in comprehension. Moreover, they argue that abstract words will, in general, have less contextual availability than concrete words. In their first experiment, they nicely demonstrated that when concreteness is confounded with contextual availability, concrete words produce faster response latencies in an LDT than abstract words, however, when concreteness is decoupled from contextual availability, there is a significant effect of contextual availability, but no effect of concreteness. In the second experiment, they found that contextual availability accounted for a significant proportion of the variance, independent of the impact of rated familiarity and word frequency. Moreover, the results of this analysis indicated that concreteness did not predict a significant proportion of the variance in lexical decision performance after contextual availability, familiarity, and frequency were partialled out. A similar pattern was found in their third experiment which involved a sentence context manipulation. Here, we again focus on the results of the neutral context condition. The results of this condition nicely replicate the results of their second experiment, i.e., concreteness does not have an impact above and beyond contextual availability.

As with familiarity ratings, one must ask what types of information subjects use in making contextual availability ratings. It may in fact be the case that subjects access the concreteness dimension when making contextual availability ratings. Although this would appear to be *a priori* less likely than in the case of familiarity ratings, it is still a possibility. However, it should also be emphasized here that even if contextual availability ratings include a concreteness dimension, the Schwanenflugel et al. study nicely demonstrates that contextual availability ratings predict word identification performance *above-and-beyond* any influence of concreteness.

Overall Conclusions Regarding Concreteness Effects.   Several generalizations can be made concerning the reviewed literature. First, stimulus selection factors qualify the conclusions regarding concreteness effects discussed in all studies, with the exception of Boles (1983, 1989), Bleasdale (1987), Gernsbacher (1984), and Schwanenflugel et al. (1988). Even the later studies must be interpreted with caution. For example, Bleasdale argues that he controls his stimuli on the familiarity dimension, and handles the context availability issue via his contextual manipulations. Bleasdale argues that contextual availability cannot adequately explain the priming results obtained in his study. In all four experiments conducted by Bleasdale, the Target Concreteness by Prime Context interaction failed to reach significance. If contextual availability is the crucial factor then one would expect greater facilitation for abstract words and this was not the case. Clearly, however, it would have been useful to obtain contextual availability ratings for the Bleasdale stimuli to address whether there are influences of concreteness above-and-beyond contextual availability.

Although there are concerns in this area whether concreteness if the only factor that is modulating performance, the results from this area suggests that some type of semantic variable does influence isolated word recognition. Even if, as Schwanenflugel et al. have argued, contextual availability is the crucial factor in studies that have produced concreteness effects, then there is still evidence that a semantic variable influences isolated word recognition. Moreover, as already noted, the fact that untimed familiarity and contextual availability ratings predict speeded word recognition performance does not preclude a concreteness effect impact in normal word identification, unless one has evidence concerning the specific dimensions that subjects actually use to rate words on familiarity and contextual availability dimensions.

(2) Polysemy Effects

Just as the impact of concreteness has played an important role in word recognition research, there is also a considerable literature base that has addressed the impact of multiple meanings on word recognition. Most of this literature deals with the issue of multiple versus direct access of ambiguous word meanings (e.g., Balota & Duchek, 1991; Seidenberg, Tanenhaus, Leiman, & Bienkowski, 1982; Swinney, 1979; Tabossi, 1988), and involves the presentation of contextual constraints to direct the language processing system to a specific meaning of an ambiguous word. However, there are also a series of studies that simply address the impact of the sheer number of meanings available for a given word on word identification. If there is evidence that words with multiple meanings (e.g., *yard*) are recognized differently than words with only a single meaning (e.g., *paper*), this could be viewed as suggesting that meaning is participating in the word recognition process.

One of the first investigations concerning how polysemy influences word recognition was reported by Rubenstein, Garfield, and Millikan (1970; see also Rubenstein, Lewis, & Rubenstein, 1971). These authors found that homographs presented in isolation produced faster lexical decisions than nonhomographs. Rubenstein et al. argued that ambiguous words involve lexical representations for each meaning, and hence, assuming a parallel access model, can be recognized more quickly. Unfortunately, Clark (1973) pointed out that the Rubenstein et al. results can easily be attributed to peculiarities of a few of the list items that Rubenstein et al. utilized. That is, Clark (1973) conducted statistical tests to determine whether the results would generalize beyond the specific language sample employed. The results of Clark's analyses were quite clear. Effects that had been significant (i.e., the homography effect) in the original analyses across subjects did not produce significant effects across items (see Forster & Bednall, 1976, for a similar observation and discussion of this stimulus sampling problem).

Jastrzembski (1981; Jastrzembski & Stanners, 1975) found that the number of available meanings associated with a word can be a strong predictor of lexical decision performance beyond simple word frequency. Using the meaning metric of number of dictionary entries, Jastrzembski found that words possessing many (greater than 10) meanings produced faster lexical decisions compared to words possessing few (less than 4) meanings. Although these results are intriguing, there are two reasons for concern. First, the metric used in the Jastrzembski studies was the number of dictionary entries. Clearly the word *FUDGE* is polysemous. However, based on the number of dictionary entries, *FUDGE* possesses approximately 13 entries. It is difficult to imagine that subjects have knowledge of much more than 2 or 3 such meanings. A second concern about the Jastrzembski studies is that again familiarity of the stimuli appear to be confounded. This was nicely demonstrated by Gernsbacher (1984) who found that number of dictionary entries did not predict performance above-and-beyond familiarity. Again, however, one must question what types of information subjects rely on to make untimed familiarity ratings. It is at least possible that meaningfulness may play a role in such familiarity ratings.

There are three recent studies that provide more compelling evidence that the number of meanings available for a given word can influence word identification performance. First, Kellas, Ferraro, and Simpson (1988) found that ambiguous words presented in isolation in a LDT produced faster response latencies than unambiguous words. The stimuli used in this study were well-controlled for familiarity, frequency of occurrence, bigram frequency, number of syllables, and number of letters. Moreover, the results of this study indicated, via the use of a dual-task methodology (i.e., the response latency to detect a tone), that ambiguous words also demanded less attentional resources for processing as early as 90 ms after stimulus presentation. This general pattern was replicated in a second experiment in which attentional load was manipulated via a short-term memory load of 7 digits. These attentional effects have also been extended to an elderly sample (Kellas, Simpson, & Ferraro, 1988). Thus, it appears that the attentional resources demanded in word recognition are relatively less for ambiguous words compared to unambiguous words. Moreover, these meaning effects occur very early (i.e., at least as early as 90 ms) in word recognition.

Millis and Button (1989) have also reported evidence that polysemy can influence isolated LDT performance. In this study, the impact of polysemy was found when it was operationally defined as the number of meanings subjects can access from their memory. This metric was assessed in the following manner. One group of subjects generated meanings for the stimulus set, and a second group of subjects participated in a LDT with a selected set of target stimuli. The results indicated that, compared to words that only produced few meanings, words that produced many meanings in the meaning generation task, produced significantly faster response latencies in lexical decision performance. Because Millis and Button both (1) directly obtained measures of meaning availability from their subjects and (2) equated familiarity across their high- and low-meaningful stimuli they avoided both concerns that were raised before with the Jastrzembski (1981) study.

Finally, we should note that recent work in our own lab has extended this pattern to the pronunciation task. That is, one might argue that number of meanings may influence lexical decision performance because meaningfulness is a relevant dimension in this task. However, we have found that pronunciation is also significantly influenced by the number of meanings available, with the same set of highly controlled stimuli used by Kellas et al. described earlier.

Conclusions Regarding the Impact of Polysemy in Word Recognition.   Just as in the case of the impact of concreteness, we find that the early work on polysemy needs to be cautiously interpreted in light of stimulus confounds. However, the more recent work which controls for such confounds appears to suggest that polysemy can produce a reliable impact in both lexical decision and pronunciation performance. These results provide further support for the notion that meaning, now reflected by the sheer number of meanings available, can participate in isolated word recognition performance.

On the other hand, one might argue that these results may only reflect the fact that each meaning of a word has a unique lexical representation. Hence, based on a race horse model, one would predict that polysemous words that have multiple lexical representations would produce faster response latencies than words with only single lexical representations. Such a model does not need to assume any direct influence of meaning representation on word recognition. There are, at least two responses to this argument. The first response is simply based on parsimony. That is, we are unaware of any data that demands that words with multiple meanings also have multiple lexical representations. Although such redundancy is possible, it might be computationally inefficient. Second, and more importantly, if one assumes that lexical representation is based on meaning representation then one loses the strict distinction between the lexicon and the system that represents meaning. As noted, this is precisely the distinction that we are concerned with.

Finally, it should be noted that one of the important lessons to be learned from this area is that the metric used to assess meaning availability is crucial in determining an impact of polysemy. That is, simply the number of dictionary entries appears to be an inappropriate measure, while the number of meanings generated by a sample of subjects from the target population seems to be a more powerful predictor of performance (see Kellas, Ferraro, & Simpson, 1988; Millis & Button, 1989, for a more detailed discussion of this issue).

Associative Reaction Time as a Task and as a Predictor of Lexical Decision and Pronunciation Performance

The time a subject takes to produce an associate to a given stimulus word should reflect processes involved both in word recognition and in meaning access. Moreover, because accessing meaning representations for a given stimulus word is also highly relevant to processes involved in language processing, performance in this task may provide interesting insights into more "normal" word processing demands.

First, consider the impact of concreteness/imageability in an associative reaction time task. DeGroot (1989) recently reported that concreteness/imageability significantly predicted associative response latency, above-and-beyond the impact of word frequency. Specifically, subjects were faster to produce an associate to target words that had relatively high concreteness/imageability ratings compared to targets with relatively low concreteness/imageability ratings. In fact, in deGroot's experiments, the effect of concreteness was much stronger than the impact of frequency, which produced only a minimal effect. Thus, in a task that may more faithfully reflect processes involved in processing words in a similar fashion as in language processing; frequency had relatively little effect, compared to the rather large effect of a meaning variable, i.e., concreteness/ imageability.

Chumbley and Balota (1984) argued that a second use of associative word response latency is to use performance in this task as a predictor of performance in other word recognition tasks. If indeed associative response latency predicted performance in presumably pure word identification tasks, then one could argue that the time taken to access meaning is a predictor of word identification. The results of the Chumbley and Balota study indicated that lexical decision performance could be nicely predicted from the speed to produce an associate to a given target word from a different group of subjects after the influence of lexical variables (e.g., frequency, length, and naming performance) had been partialled out. Balota and Chumbley (1984) found a similar pattern. In this latter study, the time taken to produce the category name for a given exemplar nicely predicted lexical decision performance, after variables related to lexical access had been partialled out. Thus, it appears that the time to access a meaning of a word predicts performance in the LDT.

In sum, the results of the data reviewed in this section indicate that when subjects are asked to access meaning via an associative response latency task that performance in this task (1) is highly influenced by a meaning variable, i.e., concreteness/imageability, and (2) nicely predicts lexical decision performance, after variables that are related to current notions of lexical identification have been partialled out.

The Impact of Adding Meaning to Previously Nonmeaningful Strings

There are two studies in the literature that are quite intriguing because they appear to indicate that providing meaning for a previously nonmeaningful string can influence word recognition processes, above-and-beyond the impact of simple exposure to the stimulus. First, consider the study by Whittlesea and Cantwell (1987). These researchers were interested in, among other issues, the impact of meaning on the word-superiority effect. In their third experiment, they presented subjects with 24 pronounceable nonwords; half of which were assigned meaning and half were presented in a simple letter checking task to equate visual processing. The meanings assigned to the nonwords represented *lexical gaps*, i.e., meanings in which there were no obvious lexical representations, e.g., *WALEN— the sound a dam makes before breaking.* After the subjects received the meaning assignment and visual processing tasks, they participated in a Reicher- (1969) type letter detection task, in which the nonwords were presented for 30 ms and immediately followed by a pattern mask. The subject's task was to identify as many letters as possible from the masked nonword. The results indicated that subjects could report significantly more letters from nonwords that were assigned meaning compared to nonwords that only received visual processing.

It is important to note here that mere exposure to the stimuli does not appear to be the critical factor modulating performance in the letter identification task. For example, one might argue that the meaning assignment conditions may have an impact via an increase in familiarity compared to the visual control condition. Hence, one may not need to appeal to an impact of meaning on letter identification. However, a comparison across Experiments 2 and 3 diminishes the plausibility of this account. In the first part of Experiment 2 subjects only received the meaning assignment task for half of the stimuli. The remaining half of the stimuli did not receive any visual processing until the letter identification task. In Experiment 2, the meaning superiority effect was 15%, i.e., the difference in the probability of identifying a letter from a nonword that was assigned a meaning versus the probability of identifying a letter from a nonword that was not assigned a meaning. In Experiment 3, subjects received the same meaning assignment task used in Experiment 2, but, as noted above, also received a visual processing task for the remaining nonwords. The meaning superiority effect was not substantially reduced in this third experiment, i.e., it was still 12%. Hence, it appears that mere exposure to the stimuli is not the potent factor in producing the meaning superiority effect, but rather it appears to be the impact of meaning assignment.

Forster (1985) has also reported an impact of meaning assignment on nonword performance. In this case, Forster presented obsolete words such as *holimonth* (defined as, *a month of holidays*) in a masked repetition priming task. These stimuli were used because they were actually words, and hence, have the orthographic constraints of lexical items. However, these words were so obsolete that it was unlikely that any of the subjects knew their corresponding meanings.

In order to fully understand the Forster study, it is necessary to first briefly describe the masked repetition paradigm. On each trial subjects were presented the following sequence. First, an unrelated word was presented for 500 ms, second either the repetition prime or a visually unrelated prime was presented for 60 ms, and finally the target was presented for 500 ms. Because the prime stimulus is both forward masked by the first unrelated word and backward masked by the target, Forster has argued that this paradigm provides a pure measure of lexical access processing.

Forster first demonstrated that the obsolete words did not produce any repetition priming effect. This was consistent with other findings by Forster that have indicated that there is little if any masked repetition priming for nonword stimuli in the LDT. Of course, this would be expected because nonwords presumably do not have lexical representations. After this was demonstrated, the obsolete words were then assigned meaning. Now, the results yielded large repetition priming effects. Presumably, the assignment of meaning produced lexical representations. Of course, one could also argue that simply an increase in familiarity was producing this effect. However, there were aspects of this study that decrease the plausibility of this argument. Specifically, the stimuli were repeated across several blocks of trials. If familiarity was modulating the effect then one would expect the effect to diminish as subjects became more and more familiar with the stimuli. However, this was not the case. The masked repetition priming effect remained quite constant across blocks after meaning was assigned to the stimuli. Thus, the Forster results appear to reflect an all-or-none impact of meaning availability.

In sum, both the Whittlesea and Cantwell study and the Forster study indicate that providing meaning for previously meaningless letter strings can influence early word processing, i.e., letter identification and masked repetition priming in lexical decision performance. We would suggest that it is at least possible that these results support the notion that meaning was participating in the word identification process. Of course, there is an alternative account. That is, it is possible that the effects are not simply due to meaning but rather are due to *lexicalization*. That is, by providing a meaning for a stimulus one is not only providing a meaning but also providing a lexical representation. Hence, the effects may only indirectly be due to meaning *per se*. However, there are aspects of both studies that suggest that the effects are not simply due to lexicalization. That is, as discussed earlier, it does not appear that mere visual exposure to the stimuli was modulating the effects. A lexically-based account would predict that such visual exposure would modulate performance in both studies. Hence, it appears that there must be a factor above-and-beyond visual exposure and lex-icalization. We suggest that this factor is the association between the letter string and meaning. Of course, one might argue that lexicalization is the same as associating meaning to a nonword string. However, if one makes this argument then this would appear to weaken the distinction between lexical identification and meaning access, and, as noted before, this distinction is one of our major concerns with current models of word identification.

Failure to "Recognize" Words that have Activated Meaning Representations

If we assume that lexical decision and naming performance are accurate reflections of word recognition without meaning access, then a discussion of studies of threshold semantic priming is relevant. In threshold priming studies (see for example, Balota, 1983; Carr & Dagenbach, 1990; Dagenbach, Carr, & Wilhelmsen, 1989; Fowler, Wolford, Slade, & Tassinary, 1981; Marcel, 1983), subjects are first presented a threshold-setting task, in which stimuli are present-ed for brief durations (e.g., 10 or 15 ms) and followed by pattern masks. In the first session, the researcher attempts to determine the threshold at which subjects are at chance levels of performance at making discriminations between the pre-sentation of a stimulus word versus the presentation of a blank field. After subjects participate in this session, they participate in a semantic priming LDT with the primes presented under the threshold conditions that were defined in Session 1. The interesting finding in these studies is that one still finds evidence for semantic priming even though the primes are presented so briefly that sub-jects are at or near chance presence/absence detection thresholds.

What is the importance of this finding? These results suggest that meaning has been accessed, even though subjects cannot make a discrimination between the presence of a word and the presence of a blank stimulus field. Thus, if we assume that lexical decision and naming performance can be used as metrics for lexical access without meaning access then these data are problematic. Clearly, if subjects cannot discriminate between the presence and absence of a stimulus, it is unlikely that they could discriminate between words and nonwords or be able to name the stimulus aloud. Thus, these results suggest that meaning has been accessed (as indicated by the threshold semantic priming effects), even though word identification processing has not been sufficient to perform one of the tasks that have been used to build models of *pre*meaning word identification.

It should be noted that there is some debate in the literature concerning whether researchers who have purported to have obtained threshold priming effects have provided adequate estimates of presence/absence detection thresholds (see Holender, 1986, and the accompanying commentaries for a detailed discussion). Although important, this debate does not strongly compromise the present arguments. That is, as noted, even if subjects were not at a detection level threshold in the earlier-cited studies, it is unlikely that subjects were at a level of visual analysis that would yield accurate lexical decision or pronunciation performance. Specifically, if subjects have difficulty indicating whether something or nothing was presented on a given trial, then it is unlikely that they could make a lexical decision or correctly pronounce a stimulus word under such highly masked conditions. This obviously runs counter to the suggestion that these tasks are a reflection of a *pre*meaning access component of word recognition. It appears that meaning can be accessed very early and without the full visual record of the stimulus available for conscious report.

Further Impacts of Meaning on Early Perceptual Processing

We turn now to three studies that have demonstrated the impact of meaning variables on simple line detection, and on illusory conjunctions. Although these studies do not exclusively deal with lexical processing, they are of interest because they demonstrate influences of meaning variables on measures of early perceptual processing, and hence, further bolster the plausibility of such effects.

Schendel and Shaw (1976) reported an interesting study in which they found that subjects could more accurately recognize a line segment when it was part of a meaningful letter of the alphabet compared to when the same line segment was presented in isolation. These authors wanted to provide evidence that would extend and generalize the word-superiority effect reported by Reicher (1969) and Wheeler (1970). Schendel and Shaw operationally defined "context" as a specified letter of the alphabet (H, N, R, Z, etc.) and the "target" as either a horizontal, vertical, or slanted fragment taken from the letter (e.g., I in H,–in F, etc.). Subjects first fixated the letter context (mean exposure duration = 23 ms) and then were shown a two-alternative forced-choice fragment display. The results indicated that subjects were more likely to choose the fragment that was part of the target letter string, compared to a visually matched fragment. Hence, not only does word level information influence the detection of letters, as indicated by the word superiority effect, but also letter level information influences the detection of the lines that make up the letters.

Weinstein and Harris (1974) found a similar finding with two- and three-dimensional structures. They found that subjects detected a line segment faster when it was embedded in a meaningful three-dimensional structure as compared to a less-meaningful two-dimensional structure. In this study "meaningfulness" was operationally defined along Gestalt dimensions. Basically the results indicated that the more *unitary* a particular display appeared to the subject, the more accurately they could identify a target line segment embedded in that display. This object superiority effect is quite intriguing in the present context, because it extends the meaning influence on perceptual processing to pictorial stimuli. Hence, as discussed below, the impact of meaning in perceptual processing may not simply be tied to lexical strings but may be a general characteristic of the pattern recognition system.

Finally, Virzi and Egeth (1984) reported two experiments that address the impact of meaning-level information on the occurrences of illusory conjunctions. Illusory conjunctions involve the incorrect joining of two or more features from separate items in an array. Treisman and her colleagues (see Treisman & Gormican, 1988, for a review of this literature) have argued that such conjunctions involve early perceptual codes that have undergone relatively little processing, and that neither meaning assignment nor object recognition has occurred. Virzi and Egeth provided evidence that meaning can influence the probability of the occurrence of such conjunctions. They found evidence for meaning-level illusory conjunctions in an experimental paradigm used by Treisman and Schmidt (1982) to demonstrate purely perceptual conjunctions. The meaning variable in the Virzi and Egeth study was either the color of a word or the color that the word represented. For example, if the word *RED* was presented in blue ink and the word *ALONE* was presented in green ink, subjects would sometimes report the color word *BLUE* or the color *RED*. Neither of these stimuli were directly presented, but both could be produced by meaning-based illusory conjunctions. These results are quite intriguing because they suggest that phenomena that presumably reflect early integration of featural information, i.e., illusory conjunctions, can also be influenced by meaning level information.

In sum, the studies reviewed in this section suggest that there may be meaning-level effects in nonlexical aspects of perception. Hence, the meaning-level effects in the identification of words may not be an isolated characteristic of lexical processing, but may be a more general characteristic of the perceptual system.

GENERAL DISCUSSION

We have now reviewed the literature on the impact of meaning variables on early perceptual, primarily lexical, processing. We believe that there is sufficient evidence to reconsider models of lexical processing that place primary emphasis on processes that lead up to a measurable point in time, referred to as word identification, that is devoid of meaning access. We have argued for such a reconsideration on two grounds. First, the tasks that are used to measure a premeaning word identification stage are not devoid of what would appear to be post-lexical processing. Second, even if one assumes that the available tasks are windows into only premeaning lexical identification processes, the general thrust of the literature involving these tasks (displayed in Table 8.1) is inconsistent with a premeaning word identification stage of processing.

Of course, it would be useful to provide an alternative modeling framework that would allow early meaning-level influences. We now turn to a brief discussion of such a framework. This is followed by a discussion of how this framework might handle the meaning-level influences reviewed earlier.

How Could Access of Meaning Occur Before Lexical Identification?

At one level, there appears to be a logical inconsistency in our arguments. Very simply, how could a reader know the meaning of the stimulus before the reader has identified the stimulus? The answer to this question is rather simple, and has been used in the past to answer a similar question produced by the word-superiority effect. In the latter case, the question is how can one know what the word is before one recognizes the letters that make up the word? The obvious answer in both cases is to rely on notions of cascadic processes and partial activation. That is, all one needs to assume is that there is partial activation of word-level or, in the present case, meaning-level units which in turn partially activate the representations that produced those partial activations. This of course is simply a slight modification of the basic interactive activation framework originally proposed by McClelland and Rumelhart (1981; Rumelhart & McClelland, 1982) to account for the word-superiority effect. As shown in Fig. 8.1,

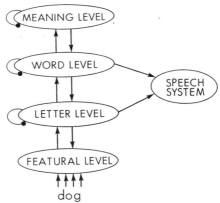

FIG. 8.1. Potential interactive activation framework for word recognition including meaning-level influences.

we are simply adding an additional level referring to meaning-level analyses to this framework. We see nothing inherently different between adding meaning-level information to this framework and adding word-level information to this framework (similar extensions can be made to other models of lexical processing, see Balota, 1990).

There are two points to note about this framework. First, this framework primarily involves a serial structure. That is, there is primarily a bottom-up flow of information from features, to letters, to words, to meanings. Meaning- and word-level information can have a reinforcing effect at lower levels only *after* earlier aspects of the processing system have been sufficiently activated to pass on activation to these higher levels. Second, the model relies quite heavily on the notion of continuous flow of activation. That is, activation does not need to accumulate at a given level before it spreads to a higher or lower level. This, of course, simply reflects the cascadic nature of the system.

The addition of meaning-level influences within such a framework provides the basis for some intriguing empirical questions. For example, once one has clearly established a meaning-level effect (e.g., contextual availability in lexical decision), then one might wish to limit the time for meaning level information to play a role. In this way one should be able to track the time-course of such information, as McClelland and Rumelhart did with respect to the time-course of word-level information. Second, it would be interesting to determine whether there is an analog of neighborhood effects at the meaning level. Specifically, McClelland and Rumelhart provided evidence that orthographically similar neighbors at the word level worked in consort to influence letter recognition. It would be interesting to determine whether words that share meanings with other words produce similar influences. We return to this possibility below.

Accounting for Meaning-Level Effects

Of course, a more important question that needs to be addressed is why one finds the particular pattern of meaning-level effects obtained in past studies. Up to this point, we have simply described studies that have demonstrated such an impact, without specifying why one might expect a particular pattern. We now turn to a brief discussion of such an account.

First, if there is an impact of concreteness above-and-beyond familiarity and contextual availability, as Bleasdale has argued, one may appeal to the notion that concrete words have an "extra" (or possibly stronger) imaginal representation compared to abstract words. This extra meaning representation should serve as an extra top-down source of activation. Such a possibility is consistent with the data and arguments presented by Day (1977). This account simply is based on the assumption that *more-means-better* when considering the impact of meaning on word recognition. In addition, the impact of contextual availability and polysemy may be accounted for in a similar manner. That is, in both the case of contextual availability and polysemy the evidence suggests that words with more meaning representations are recognized more quickly. Again, the premise of *more-means-better* is instantiated.

Second, the impact of meaning without conscious word identification (threshold semantic priming effects) simply reflects the continuous activation aspect of the framework. That is, meanings are partially activated even though sufficient information has not been activated for the subject to make a presence/absence decision. Part of this effect is probably due to the attentional disruption produced by the pattern mask at the visual level codes that are necessary in making the presence/absence decision. Threshold semantic priming effects simply suggest that there is partial information transfer before the subject can fully access such codes.

Third, the predictive power of associative response latency for lexical decision performance may simply reflect the fact that the ease of accessing a meaning level representation is reflected by the associative response latency measure. If this were the case, then one would expect more of a top-down influence for words that have meaning information readily accessible. Thus, one should expect associative response latency to be a strong predictor of lexical decision performance, as reported by Chumbley and Balota.

Finally, the impact of adding meaning to a nonword string, could be accounted for by the *more-means-better* principle. The notion here is that the addition of meaning would provide a level of representation that would benefit both word processing (Forster, 1985) and letter processing (Whittlesea & Cantwell, 1987).

Of course, it is not surprising that the *more-means-better* assumption would be useful in providing a surface-level account for the reviewed literature. However, one might argue that in some cases *more* could produce meaning-level inhibition. For example, it would appear counterproductive for both meanings of an ambiguous word to be simultaneously activated. Interestingly, this appears to be dependent upon the time–course of activation at the meaning level. For example, in his review of the literature on lexical ambiguity resolution, Simpson (1984) has argued for automatic ordered (by frequency of usage) access of multiple interpretations of ambiguous words, but then selective access of the contextually determined interpretation. Moreover, Simpson and Burgess (1985) have provided evidence that at longer intervals a selected interpretation can inhibit a nonselected interpretation of an ambiguous word. As indicated, both of these patterns of data appear to be highly dependent upon the time-course of activation. Thus, the *more-means-better* principle, at least with respect to polysemous items, may primarily reflect processes early in word recognition. The importance of this observation is very simple. In order to adequately model the semantic impact in word identification, it appears crucial to include assumptions regarding the temporal course of activation across levels within the system.

What Might the Meaning Representation for Words Involve?

Of course, one must address what *more* means in the present context. The topic of meaning representation is quite controversial and has been at the center of considerable theoretical debate. For example, one consistent problem that has occurred in the literature on word meaning is whether it should be represented as a single core meaning or a list of semantic features. Under both approaches it would appear that the meaning of a word involves a core set of semantic information that is, in some sense, different from the individual episodic experiences with a given word.

We would support an alternative approach to meaning representation that follows from suggestions made by Hintzman (1986, also see Medin & Schaffer, 1978; Schwanenflugel & Shoben, 1983). Although Hintzman's model was primarily developed to account for prototype learning, it can also be extended to meaning representations. Hintzman presents an alternative approach to account for the classic Posner and Keele (1968) findings regarding prototype abstraction. He argues that each of the episodic experiences with the instances of a prototype produces a *unique* episodic memory trace that consists of a list of primitive features. The higher delayed recognition memory that Posner and Keele found for nonpresented prototypes, compared to presented exemplars, simply reflects the retrieval process when the test item is presented. Hintzman argues that when the test item is presented it partially activates "all" of the episodic traces. The result of this activation process is an echo that represents all of the episodic traces in memory. If there is sufficient overlap between the echo and the test item, the item is recognized. In some cases, it is possible that the similarity of the echo to the test item may be stronger when a prototype is presented that partially overlaps with many episodic traces (i.e., the instances), than when an instance is presented that strongly overlaps with a single episodic trace. Thus, the culmination of many different, but related, episodic memory traces can produce the relatively high recognition confidence for a stimulus (i.e., the prototype) that was never directly presented.

It is important to emphasize here that this model suggests that meaning is produced at retrieval via the interaction of all previously stored memory traces. Meaning of a word is not simply a static representation that is represented by (a) a set of semantic features, (b) a prototype representation, or (c) the definition that the subjects look up in their mental dictionary, but rather, involves the accumulation of individual episodic traces that are produced by individual experiences with the word. Each of these experiences (i.e., the word and its context) contributes to the evolving meaning that we attribute to a given word.

There are a number of important implications of this approach. First, one does not have to appeal to different memory systems to account for different *apparent* memory types. That is, all experiences produce episodic traces, and the stability of some information, such as general definitions of categories (e.g., *Fruit, Animal, Mineral, etc.*) are simply due to the convergence of these episodic traces, as opposed to the abstraction of core meanings. In addition, this framework nicely handles the contextual dependency that we find in language (e.g., see Roth & Shoben, 1983). Static notions concerning meaning representation have difficulty handling such contextual dependency. Of course, one may be able to argue that different static meanings are accessed in different contexts but then it seems that one has to specify a different meaning whenever one provides a different context. The account here for contextual dependency is simply that when a target word and its context is presented it produces a unique echo. The echo from these episodic traces *is* the meaning. This meaning will primarily be a function of the context that the word has most typically been embedded within.

Of course, there are many questions that need to be addressed if the Hintzman-type approach would be extended to word meaning. For example, one must define what is encoded in an episodic trace. Are there primitive dimensions of such traces and, if so, how is this different from semantic features? Although there are clearly many questions that need to be resolved, we believe that the notion that word meaning is a constantly evolving characteristic of episodic traces is an intriguing and potentially fruitful approach to word meaning.

Implications for the Modularity of the Language Processing System

Our contention that meaning influences word recognition is problematic for models that assume a modular (strictly encapsulated) word processing system that limits meaning analyses to associative connections between words within a lexical network. However, we should point out that the processing system displayed in Fig. 8.1 does have an overall serial structure. Thus, although we allow for top-down influences from meaning-level analyses, we do not wish to argue against the importance of a highly structured language processing architecture. In this sense, the more important issue is the *degree* of interaction among the various levels. Moreover, in order to understand the degree of interaction, as noted before, one must consider the time-course of such an interaction. In this light, hopefully, the present chapter helps to frame useful empirical and theoretical questions regarding the temporal course of meaning-level variables in word recognition.

CONCLUSION

One of the major motivations for the present chapter has been functional in nature. That is, researchers in the area of word recognition have developed models that primarily emphasize orthographic and phonological aspects of lexical processing, that are relatively devoid of meaning-level impacts. We believe that the available evidence suggests that meaning may contribute to early processes in word identification. Because of this current state of affairs, we feel that it is prudent to begin considering models that allow meaning-level influences in word identification. That is, we believe that the more important issue in word recognition research is to provide an accurate model of how words convey meaning than how orthography and phonology lead to the magical word identification point.

ACKNOWLEDGMENTS

We thank Christine Chiarello and Paula Schwanenflugel for their helpful comments on an earlier version of this chapter. This work was, in part, supported by NIA grant RO1 A607406.

REFERENCES

Balota, D. A. (1983). Automatic semantic activation and episodic memory encoding. *Journal of Verbal Learning and Verbal Behavior, 22,* 88–104.

Balota, D. A. (1990). The role of meaning in word recognition. In D. A. Balota, G. B. Flores d'Arcais, & K. Rayner (Eds.), *Comprehension processes in reading* (pp. 9–32), Hillsdale, NJ: Lawrence Erlbaum Associates.

Balota, D. A., Boland, J. E., & Shields, L. (1989). Priming in pronunciation: Beyond pattern recognition and onset latency. *Journal of Memory and Language, 28,* 14–36.

Balota, D. A., & Chumbley, J. I. (1984). Are lexical decisions a good measure of lexical access? The role of word frequency in the neglected decision stage. *Journal of Experimental Psychology: Human Perception and Performance, 10,* 340–357.

Balota, D. A., & Chumbley, J. I. (1985). The locus of word-frequency effects in the pronunciation task: Lexical access and/or production? *Journal of Memory and Language, 24,* 89–106.

Balota, D. A., & Duchek, J. M. (1991). Semantic priming effects, lexical repetition effects, and contextual disambiguation effects in healthy aged individuals and individuals with Senile Dementia of the Alzheimer Type. *Brain and Language,* in press.

Balota, D. A., & Lorch, R. F. (1986). Depth of automatic spreading activation: Mediated priming effects in pronunciation but not in lexical decision. *Journal of Experimental Psychology: Learning, Memory and Cognition, 12,* 336–345.

Becker, C. A. (1980). Semantic context effects in visual word recognition: An analysis of semantic strategies. *Memory & Cognition, 8,* 493–512.

Besner, D., & McCann, R. S. (1987). Word frequency and pattern distortion in visual word identification and production: An examination of four classes of models. In M. Coltheart (Ed.), *Attention and performance XII: The psychology of reading* (pp. 201–219). Hillsdale, NJ: Lawrence Erlbaum Associates.

Bleasdale, F. A. (1987). Concreteness-dependent associative priming: Separate lexical organization for concrete and abstract words. *Journal of Experimental Psychology: Learning, Memory, & Cognition, 13,* 582–594.

Boles, D. B. (1983). Dissociated imageability, concreteness, and familiarity in lateralized word recognition. *Memory & Cognition, 11,* 511–519.

Boles, D. B. (1989). Word attributes and lateralization revisited: Implications for dual coding and discrete versus continuous processing. *Memory & Cognition, 17,* 106–114.

Carr, T. H., & Dagenbach, D. C. (1990). Semantic priming and repetition priming from masked words: Evidence for a center-surround attentional mechanism in perceptual recognition. *Journal of Experimental Psychology: Learning, Memory, & Cognition, 16,* 341–350.

Catlin, J. (1973). In defense of sophisticated guessing theory. *Psychological Review, 80,* 412–416.

Chumbley, J. I., & Balota, D. A. (1984). A word's meaning affects the decision in lexical decision. *Memory & Cognition, 12,* 590–606.

Clark, H. H. (1973). The language-as-fixed-effect fallacy: A critique of language statistics in psychological research. *Journal of Verbal Learning & Verbal Behavior, 12,* 335–359.

Coltheart, M. (1980). Reading, phonological reading, and deep dyslexia. In M. Coltheart, K. Patterson, & J. C. Marshall (Eds.), *Deep dyslexia* (pp. 22–47). London: Routledge & Kegan Paul.

Coltheart, M., Patterson, K., & Marshall, J. C. (1980). *Deep dyslexia.* London: Routledge & Kegan Paul.

Connine, C., Mullennix, J., Shernoff, E., Yelen, J. (1990). Word familiarity and frequency in visual and auditory word recognition. *Journal of Experimental Psychology: Learning, Memory and Cognition, 16,* 1084–1096.

Dallas, M., & Merikle, P. M. (1976). Response processes and semantic-context effects. *Bulletin of the Psychonomic Society, 8,* 441–444.

Dagenbach, D., Carr, T. H., & Wilhelmsen, A. (1989). Task-induced strategies and near-threshold priming: Conscious influences on unconscious perception. *Journal of Memory & Language, 28,* 412–443.

Day, J. (1977). Right-hemisphere language processing in normal right-handers. *Journal of Experimental Psychology: Human Perception and Performance, 3,* 518–528.

DeGroot, A. M. B. (1983). The range of automatic spreading activation in word priming. *Journal of Verbal Learning and Verbal Behavior, 22,* 417–436.

DeGroot, A. M. B. (1989). Representational aspects of word imageability and word frequency as assessed through word associations. *Journal of Experimental Psychology: Learning, Memory & Cognition, 15,* 824–845.

Forster, K. I. (1979). Levels of processing and the structure of the language processor. In W. E. Cooper & E. Walker (Eds.), *Sentence processing: Psychological studies presented to Merrill Garrett* (pp. 27–85), Hillsdale, NJ: Lawrence Erlbaum Associates.

Forster, K. I. (1985). Lexical acquisition and the modular lexicon. *Language and Cognitive Processes, 1,* 87–108.

Forster, K. I., & Bednall, E. S. (1976). Terminating and exhaustive search in lexical access. *Memory & Cognition, 4,* 53–61.

Fowler, C. A., Wolford, G., Slade, R., & Tassinary, L. (1981). Lexical access with and without awareness. *Journal of Experimental Psychology: General, 110,* 341–362.

Gernsbacher, M. A. (1984). Resolving 20 years of inconsistent interactions between lexical familiarity and orthography, concreteness, and polysemy. *Journal of Experimental Psychology: General, 113,* 256–280.

Hintzman, D. L. (1986). Schema abstraction in a multiple-trace memory model. *Psychological Review, 93,* 411–428.

Holender, D. (1986). Semantic activation without conscious identification in dichotic listening, parafoveal vision, and visual masking: A survey and appraisal. *The Behavioral and Brain Sciences, 9,* 1–66.

James, C. T. (1975). The role of semantic information in lexical decisions. *Journal of Experimental Psychology: Human Perception and Performance, 1,* 130–136.

Jastrzembski, J. E. (1981). Multiple meanings, number of related meanings, frequency of occurrence, and the lexicon. *Cognitive Psychology, 13,* 278–305.

Jastrzembski, J. E., & Stanners, R. F. (1975). Multiple word meanings and lexical search speed. *Journal of Verbal Learning & Verbal Behavior, 14,* 534–537.

Keefe, D. E., & Neely, J. H. (1990). Semantic priming in the pronunciation task: The role of prospective prime-generated expectancies. *Memory & Cognition, 18,* 289–298.

Kellas, G., Ferraro, F. R., & Simpson, G. B. (1988). Lexical ambiguity and the timecourse of attentional allocation in word recognition. *Journal of Experimental Psychology: Human Perception & Performance, 14,* 601–609.

Kellas, G., Simpson, G. B., & Ferraro, F. R. (1988). Aging and performance: A mental workload analysis. In P. Whitney & R. B. Ochsman (Eds.), *Psychology & productivity* (pp. 35–49). New York: Plenum Press.

Kroll, J. F., & Merves, J. S. (1986). Lexical access for concrete and abstract words. *Journal of Experimental Psychology: Learning, Memory, and Cognition, 12,* 92–107.

Lorch, R. F., Balota, D. A., & Stamm, E. G. (1986). Locus of inhibition effects in the priming of lexical decision: Pre- or post-lexical access? *Memory & Cognition, 14,* 95–103.

Marcel, A. J. (1983). Conscious and unconscious perception: Experiments on visual masking and word recognition. *Cognitive Psychology, 15,* 197–237.

Marshall, J. C., & Newcombe, F. (1980). The conceptual status of deep dyslexia: An historical perspective. In M. Coltheart, K. Patterson, & J. C. Marshall (Eds.), *Deep dyslexia* (pp. 1–21). London: Routledge & Kegan Paul.

McClelland, J. L., & Rumelhart, D. E. (1981). An interactive activation model of context effects in letter perception: Part 1. An account of basic findings. *Psychological Review, 88,* 375–407.

Medin, D. L., & Schaffer, M. M. (1978). Context theory of classification learning. *Psychological Review, 85,* 207–238.

Midgley-West, L. (1979). *Phonological encoding and subject strategies in skilled reading.* Unpublished doctoral thesis. University of London, Birkbeck College.

Millis, M. L., & Button, S. B. (1989). The effect of polysemy on lexical decision time: Now you see it, now you don't. *Memory & Cognition, 17,* 141–147.

Morton, J. (1969). The interaction of information in word recognition. *Psychological Review, 76,* 165–178.

Neely, J. H. (1990). Semantic priming effects in visual word recognition: A selective review of current findings and theories. In D. Besner & G. Humphreys (Eds.), *Basic processes in reading: Visual word recognition.* (pp. 264–336) Hillsdale, NJ: Lawrence Erlbaum Associates.

Neely, J. H., & Keefe, D. E. (1989). Semantic context effects on visual word processing: A hybrid prospective/retrospective processing theory. In G. H. Bower (Ed.), *The psychology of learning and motivation: Advances in research and theory* (Vol. 24, pp. 207–248), New York: Academic Press.

Neely, J. H., Keefe, D. E., & Ross, K. L. (1989). Semantic priming in the lexical decision task: Roles of prospective prime-generated expectancies and retrospective semantic matching. *Journal of Experimental Psychology: Learning, Memory, and Cognition, 15,* 1003–1019.

Norris, D. (1986). Word recognition: Context effects without priming. *Cognition, 22,* 93–136.

Paivio, A., & O'Neill, B. J. (1970). Visual recognition thresholds and dimensions of word meaning. *Perception and Psychophysics, 8,* 273–275.

Posner, M. I., & Keele, S. W. (1968). On the genesis of abstract ideas. *Journal of Experimental Psychology, 77,* 353–363.

Reicher, G. M. (1969). Perceptual recognition as a function of meaningfulness of stimulus material. *Journal of Experimental Psychology, 81,* 274–280.

Richards, L. G. (1976). Concreteness as a variable in word recognition. *American Journal of Psychology, 89,* 707–718.

Richardson, J. T. E. (1975a). Further evidence on the effect of word imageability in dyslexia. *Quarterly Journal of Experimental Psychology, 27,* 445–449.

Richardson, J. T. E. (1975b). The effect of word imageability in acquired dyslexia. *Neuropsychologia, 13,* 281–288.

Richardson, J. T. E. (1976). The effects of stimulus attributes upon latency of word recognition. *British Journal of Psychology, 67*, 315–325.

Roth, E. M., & Shoben, E. J. (1983). The effect of context on the structure of categories. *Cognitive Psychology, 15*, 346–378.

Rubenstein, H., Garfield, L., & Millikan, J. A. (1970). Homographic entries in the internal lexicon. *Journal of Verbal Learning & Verbal Behavior, 9*, 487–494.

Rubenstein, H., Lewis, S. S., & Rubenstein, M. (1971). Homographic entries in the internal lexicon: Effects of systematicity and relative frequency of meanings. *Journal of Verbal Learning & Verbal Behavior, 10*, 57–62.

Rumelhart, D. E., & McClelland, J. L. (1982). An interactive activation model of context effects in letter perception: Part 2. The contextual enhancement effect and some tests and extensions of the model. *Psychological Review, 89*, 60–94.

Saffran, E. M., Bogyo, L. C., Schwartz, M. F., & Marin, O. S. M. (1980). Does deep dyslexia reflect right-hemisphere reading? In M. Coltheart, K. Patterson, & J. C. Marshall (Eds.) *Deep dyslexia* (pp. 381–406). London: Routledge & Kegan Paul.

Schendel, J. D., & Shaw, P. (1976). A test of the generality of the word-context effect. *Perception & Psychophysics, 19*, 383–393.

Schwanenflugel, P. J., Harnishfeger, K. K., & Stowe, R. W. (1988). Context availability and lexical decisions for abstract and concrete words. *Journal of Memory and Language, 27*, 499–520.

Schwanenflugel, P. J., & Shoben, E. J. (1983). Differential context effects in the comprehension of abstract and concrete verbal materials. *Journal of Experimental Psychology: Learning, Memory & Cognition, 9*, 82–102.

Seidenberg, M. S., Tanenhaus, M. K., Leiman, J. L., & Bienkowski, M. (1982). Automatic access of the meanings of ambiguous words in context: Some limitations on knowledge-based processing. *Cognitive Psychology, 14*, 489–537.

Seidenberg, M. S., Waters, G. S., Sanders, M., & Langer, P. (1984). Pre- and post-lexical loci of contextual effects on word recognition. *Memory & Cognition, 12*, 315–328.

Seymour, M. K. J. (1990). Semantic processing in dyslexia. In D. A. Balota, G. B. Flores d'Arcais, & K. Rayner (Eds.), *Comprehension processes in reading* (pp. 581–602). Hillsdale, NJ: Lawrence Erlbaum Associates.

Shallice, T., & Warrington, E. K. (1975). Word recognition in a phonemic dyslexic patient. *Quarterly Journal of Experimental Psychology, 27*, 187–199.

Shallice, T., & Warrington, E. K. (1980). Single and multiple component central dyslexic syndromes. In M. Coltheart, K. Patterson, & J. C. Marshall (Eds.), *Deep dyslexia* (pp. 119–145). London: Routledge & Kegan Paul.

Simpson, G. B. (1984). Lexical ambiguity and its role in models of word recognition. *Psychological Bulletin, 96*, 316–340.

Simpson, G. B., & Burgess, C. (1985). Activation and selection processes in the recognition of ambiguous words. *Journal of Experimental Psychology: Human Perception and Performance, 11*, 28–39.

Swinney, D. A. (1979). Lexical access during sentence comprehension: (Re) consideration of context effects. *Journal of Verbal Learning & Verbal Behavior, 18*, 645–659.

Tabossi, P. (1988). Accessing lexical ambiguity in different types of sentential contexts. *Journal of Memory & Language, 27*, 324–340.

Triesman, A. M., & Gormican, S. (1988). Feature analysis in early vision: Evidence from search asymmetries. *Psychological Review, 95*, 15–48.

Triesman, A. M., & Schmidt, H. (1982). Illusory conjunctions in the perception of objects. *Cognitive Psychology, 14*, 107–141.

Virzi, R. A., & Egeth, H. E. (1984). Is meaning implicated in illusory conjunctions? *Journal of Experimental Psychology: Human Perception & Performance, 10*, 573–580.

Weinstein, N., & Harris, C. S. (1974). Visual detection of line segments: An object-superiority effect. *Science, 186*, 752–755.

West, R. F., & Stanovich, K. E. (1982). Source of inhibition in experiments on the effect of sentence context on word recognition. *Journal of Experimental Psychology: Learning, Memory and Cognition, 8,* 385–399.

Wheeler, D. D. (1970). Processes in word recognition. *Cognitive Psychology, 1,* 59–85.

Whittlesea, B. W. A., & Cantwell, A. L. (1987). Enduring influence of the purpose of experiences: Encoding-retrieval interactions in word and pseudoword perception. *Memory & Cognition, 15,* 465–472.

Winnick, W. A., & Kressel, K. (1965). Tachistoscopic recognition thresholds, paired-associate learning, and free recall as a function of abstractness-concreteness and word frequency. *Journal of Experimental Psychology, 70,* 163–168.

9 Why are Abstract Concepts Hard to Understand?

Paula J. Schwanenflugel
University of Georgia

Most of us possess the intuitive feeling that abstract word concepts are harder to understand than concrete word concepts. If you ask people why this is do, their answer would most likely reflect the belief that abstract words are hard to understand because they lack the fairly direct sensory referents that concrete words have. In fact, in cognitive psychology, it has long been assumed that it is this difference between these two concept types that makes abstract concepts harder to understand, process, acquire, remember, and so on than concrete ones. In this chapter, I use *concreteness* as a generic term to refer generally to the constellation of variables that distinguish abstract words from concrete words. However, the term is used merely as a convenience for differentiating among word types and, by itself, should not be taken to imply that abstract words are harder to understand than concrete words because they lack direct sensory referents. Instead, my purpose here is to evaluate that basic explanation.

Understanding the representational, developmental, and processing differences between abstract and concrete words is critical to developing an understanding of word meanings in general. There is a considerable amount of evidence that concreteness represents a fundamental semantic distinction among words. Concreteness invariably emerges as an important variable that differentiates words in large factor analytic studies (DiVesta & Walls, 1970; Paivio, 1968; Rubin, 1980). Yet, most current theories of word meaning do not directly address this basic distinction. A full theory of word meaning must include information regarding how words may differ in their representations, how these differences are acquired developmentally, and how such variations are reflected in verbal processing. The study of concreteness effects should help us move toward this ultimate goal.

In this first section, I review the evidence that abstract words *are* harder to understand than concrete words in order to establish that there is, indeed, something important that a theory of word meaning must explain. As we shall see, although concreteness effects in verbal processing are ubiquitous, they are not uniformly obtained. Despite this nonuniformity, however, some regularities are discernible. Following that, I describe and evaluate various theories that have been proposed to account for why abstract words are hard to understand. Such theories are important to the development of a psychology of word meaning because of the varying claims they make with regard to representations and processes associated with the meanings of words.

ARE ABSTRACT WORDS HARDER TO UNDERSTAND THAN CONCRETE WORDS?

There are several different kinds of evidence that are relevant to deciding whether abstract words are harder to discern than concrete words. Some of this evidence revolves around the initial processing of abstract and concrete verbal materials. Other evidence involves memory for abstract and concrete verbal materials after they have already been processed and stored in long-term memory. There are several recent reviews of research on concreteness effects in verbal memory by Marschark, Richman, Yuille, and Hunt (1987) and by Paivio (1986). These reviews highlight the fact that 25 years of research has shown us that concreteness effects in verbal memory are often large and reasonably consistent, but that the cause of these concreteness effects in long-term memory is not as yet fully understood. Instead, this review focuses on studies examining the initial processing, development, and representation of abstract and concrete verbal materials and does not deal extensively with studies examining memory for abstract and concrete verbal information.

The evidence regarding concreteness effects occurring early in verbal processing takes several forms. Some of this research focuses on the timed comprehension of abstract and concrete sentences. Other studies center on lexical processing of abstract and concrete words using tasks such as lexical decision and naming. Still other research examines the acquisition of abstract and concrete words in children's oral and reading vocabularies. I examine each of these in turn.

The Comprehension of Abstract and Concrete Sentences

If abstract words are harder to understand than concrete words, then it would seem to follow that sentences composed of abstract words should also be harder to understand than those composed of concrete words. This greater difficulty in comprehension for abstract sentences should be reflected in generally longer processing times for abstract than concrete sentences. Such evidence might be important for deciding the general issue of whether abstract concepts are more difficult to understand than concrete words.

There are two tasks that have been used to gain evidence regarding the issue of whether abstract sentences are harder to understand: (1) sentence verification, and (2) timed sentence comprehension. The most commonly used task in examining concreteness effects in sentence comprehension has been the sentence verification task. In this task, persons are asked to make some kind of timed meaningfulness judgment regarding the abstract or concrete sentence. Faster verification times are assumed to reflect faster comprehension. However, it is important to note that sentence verification actually involves both the comprehension of the sentence and a decision regarding its truth value (Glass, Millen, Beck, & Eddy, 1985). Thus, we can't be sure whether the finding of concreteness effects in sentence verification reflect processes operating during comprehension or during the decision regarding the truth value of a sentence already comprehended. On the other hand, Lorch (1982) has noted similar semantic processing in a category verification task (which is similar to the sentence verification task in that it requires a decision) and an instance naming task (which does not involve such a decision). To some degree, then, studies on the verification of abstract and concrete sentences might provide some initial insight into the question of whether abstract verbal materials are harder to understand.

Sentence Verification.   Studies comparing the verification of abstract and concrete sentences have ranged from those using simple semantic statements of the sort typically used in standard semantic memory experiments (e.g., Glass & Holyoak, 1975; Smith, 1978) to those using more complex, but ordinary sentences. For example, in a highly cited study by Jorgensen and Kintsch (1973), subjects were asked to verify high and low imagery statements such as "Truck has oil" (low imagery) and "Book has cover" (high imagery). Despite the fact that all of the content words used in all the statements were very concrete, some sentences were considered low imagery because subjects had rated the statements taken as a whole to be less imageable than their high imagery counterparts. In that study, high imagery true statements were verified 571 ms faster than the low imagery true statements. Thus, imageability was concluded to have a beneficial effect on retrieving information from semantic memory.

This early conclusion regarding the role of imagery in semantic verification has been questioned by Holyoak (1974), however, who suggested that the faster verification times of the Jorgensen and Kintsch (1973) study might be accounted for by factors other than imagery. His subjects rated the low imagery sentences used by Jorgensen and Kintsch as being less easy to comprehend, having more difficult verbs, and having more semantically related predicates than the high imagery sentences. Furthermore, because all the sentences used in the study possessed highly concrete content words, it does not completely address the issue of whether semantic verification is more difficult for abstract sentences than concrete sentences.

Glass, Eddy, and Schwanenflugel (1980, Experiment 2) attempted to address more directly the issue of whether simple semantic verifications for abstract statements are harder to make than for concrete statements by comparing the verification of abstract sentences such as "Every idea is a thought" with concrete sentences such as "Every shotgun is a weapon." Their study attempted to minimize the influence of possible confounding variables such as perceived comprehensibility, intersubject agreement in truth value, and semantic relatedness of subjects and predicates. They found semantic verifications to be no faster for concrete than abstract statements, although accuracy was higher for the concrete statements. Thus, these studies using simple semantic verification have proven to be indeterminate with regard to the issue of whether abstract verbal materials are harder to understand than concrete ones, but are in the direction of suggesting a concreteness advantage.

Other studies have asked people to verify the general meaningfulness of more elaborate, ordinary abstract and concrete sentences in order to examine the question of whether abstract sentences are harder to understand than concrete ones. Klee and Eyesenck (1973), for example, asked subjects to decide whether concrete sentences like "The veteran soldier rode the lame horse" and abstract sentences such as "The wrong attitude caused a major loss" were meaningful, plausible sentences. They found an overall 420 ms benefit for concrete over abstract sentences, although many of the plausible abstract sentences used in that study have also been criticized for not being very plausible (Holmes & Langford, 1976; Moeser, 1974). Moreover, subjects were asked to perform the verifications with a memory load.

A study by Belmore, Yates, Bellack, Jones, and Rosenquist (1982) examined the verification of three kinds of statements derived from abstract and concrete sentences that subjects had just encoded: (1) identical statements in which subjects were represented with the original encoded sentence, (2) paraphrase statements in which subjects were presented with a paraphrase of the original encoded statement, and (3) inference statements which were reasonable from the original encoded statement. Overall, verifications took longer for abstract sentences than concrete sentences for all types of verification statements with the difference being larger in the paraphrase and inference cases.

Probably the clearest case for the position that abstract sentences are verified more slowly than concrete sentences comes from a well-controlled study by Holmes and Langford (1976). In that study, abstract and concrete target sentences of varying syntactic form that were highly plausible and meaningful were used and, yet, a 183 ms concreteness benefit was noted.

The cumulative evidence from all of these studies tells us that abstract sentences are, indeed, harder to verify than concrete ones. But this does not mean that *all* concrete sentences are easier to verify. Glass and his colleagues (Glass et al., 1980; Glass et al., 1985) point out that we may need to distinguish between two types of concrete sentences: (a) concrete sentences that seem to *require* the explicit formation of images for their verification, and (b) concrete sentences that do not require such image formation. For example, the concrete sentence "A pool table has six pockets" intuitively seems more likely to evoke imagery formation as a potential verification strategy than does an equally concrete sentence such as "A canary has wings."

This distinction between sentences requiring imagery and sentences not requiring imagery for verification seems an important one for identifying processes that may become involved in verification but not comprehension. In several studies, highly concrete sentences requiring imagery formation have been found to take longer to *verify* than other concrete sentences even though they do not necessarily take longer to *comprehend* (Glass et al., 1985). Consequently, it is important to distinguish between truly abstract sentences and different kinds of concrete sentences in deciding the issue of whether abstract sentences are harder to verify than concrete sentences. However, for most ordinary concrete sentences, it does appear that concrete sentences are verified faster than abstract sentences.

Sentence Comprehension. Given that sentence verification entails extra processes beyond simple comprehension, it seems reasonable to continue to ask whether abstract sentences are specifically more difficult to comprehend than concrete sentences. The problem with asking this question directly is that comprehension is not a precisely defined concept. Can we say that comprehension has occurred when one has merely skimmed a sentence to get the vaguest sense of its gist? Or do we wish to use a more stringent criteria for determination of comprehension such as being able to remember or answer questions about the materials some time later? How we ask this question may determine whether we find a concreteness advantage in sentence comprehension.

Two experiments conducted at the extremes of this question uniquely illustrate this point. In an early study on the question of whether concreteness influences the on-line comprehension of abstract and concrete sentences, Paivio and Begg (1971) instructed subjects simply to "release the button when they understood the sentence." In that study, the approximately 300 ms difference between abstract and concrete sentences was not significant. On the other hand, it should be noted that relatively small numbers of subjects were used and also that sentence comprehension times correlated quite highly with sentence imaging times questioning the reliability of this nonsignificant effect. At the other extreme is a study by Moeser (1974). Subjects in that study were asked to read the sentences in order to detect meaning or wording changes in an upcoming test. Comprehension times were quite long (around 10 seconds), but a significant 2850 ms concreteness benefit was found. Clearly, in this latter study, subjects were both comprehending and attempting to encode the sentences into long-term memory, leaving the precise locus of the concreteness effects unclear.

This distinction between comprehending for later recall and comprehending for possibly marginal understanding emerges clearly in a study by Marschark (1979). In that study, some subjects were simply asked to comprehend the abstract versus concrete passages and others were asked to read it to be able to recall the passages. In the cases where subjects had to read for simple comprehension, only marginally significant concreteness benefits were found (and subsequent recall was also very low). When the task was to recall the materials later, large and significant concreteness benefits were found.

Most studies have opted for some middle ground with regard to the goal of the comprehension task, ensuring that subjects read with comprehension without enforcing unusual memory encoding demands. For example, Haberlandt and Graesser (1985) asked people to be prepared to complete a multiple choice task after reading the passages and found that sentence imagery was negatively related to comprehension time. Similarly, Schwanenflugel and Shoben (1983) asked their subjects to perform an immediate verification of a simple partial paraphrase following the comprehension of abstract and concrete sentences presented in isolation. Again, they also found that abstract sentences take longer to comprehend than concrete sentences.

In sum, most studies find that persons take longer to comprehend abstract than concrete sentences. However, the degree to which this is true is probably affected by the way comprehension is defined in the experiment.

Conclusion.   What conclusions can we draw from these disparate findings regarding concreteness effects in sentence verification and comprehension? Overall, I think we see a decided trend for abstract sentences to be both harder to comprehend and to verify than concrete sentences. In most cases, even when abstract sentences do not take significantly longer to comprehend, the means are almost invariably in the direction of their taking longer to comprehend. However, it is also clear that task demands will influence the degree to which these effects surface. For example, when persons deem imaging to be strategically necessary to complete verification, this additional transformational and constructive imaging may cause concrete sentences actually to take longer to verify than abstract sentences. When abstract and concrete sentences are to be encoded into long-term memory, we see that the processing of abstract sentences particularly suffers, producing especially longer comprehension times.

To the degree that we can isolate a specific comprehension stage in processing, then, it does appear that abstract sentences take longer to comprehend than concrete sentences. Whereas we might infer that abstract words are harder to understand than concrete words from this evidence, it is also important to realize that sentence comprehension is likely to engage processes that understanding the meanings of words alone does not. To the degree that these other sentence-level processes are also differentially affected by the concreteness of the lexical items within sentences, evidence regarding the comprehension of abstract and concrete sentences only serves as indirect evidence for the proposition that abstract words are harder to understand.

Concreteness and Lexical Processing

More direct evidence for the view that abstract words are hard to understand might be expected to come from studies specifically examining lexical processing of abstract and concrete words. In this section, I focus on studies using one of two target tasks: (1) the lexical decision task, and (2) the naming (sometimes called pronunciation) task. In the lexical decision task, subjects are presented with abstract or concrete target words and are asked simply to decide whether each item represents a real English word as quickly and as accurately as possible. In the naming task, subjects are also presented with abstract or concrete words, but instead are asked to name them quickly. It is important to note that neither task requires the subjects to retrieve the meaning of the words they are naming or making lexical decisions for. Yet, as we shall see, very often concreteness effects emerge in lexical decision and naming. Therefore, to the degree that such basic semantic differences surface in such tasks, it would mean that concreteness has its effects at a very early stage in lexical processing and that retrieval of word meaning occurs regardless of the explicit demands of the task.

In order to address the question of whether there are concreteness effects in early processing, I focus on evidence from studies examining the processing of abstract and concrete words presented either in isolation or in semantically neutral contexts. Focusing on such studies will provide us with the most direct case for deciding the issue of whether abstract words are generally difficult to understand. On the other hand, it is important to keep in mind that the issue is likely to turn out quite differently when studies examining the processing of abstract and concrete words in meaningful contexts are also included. However, as we shall see later, this distinction between the processing of abstract and concrete words in context or in isolation may be useful for deciding between various theories of concreteness effects.

Lexical Decision.   The evidence regarding whether abstract words take longer to process than concrete words is quite mixed for lexical decision. Some researchers have found that abstract words have longer lexical decision times than concrete words (Akin & Schwanenflugel, 1990; Bleasdale, 1987; deGroot, 1989; Howell & Bryden, 1987; James, 1975, Experiments 1 and 2; Kroll & Mervis, 1986, Experiment 2; Rubin, 1980; Schwanenflugel, Harnishfeger, & Stowe, 1988; Schwanenflugel & Shoben, 1983; Whaley, 1978), whereas others have not (Gernsbacher, 1984; James, 1975, Experiments 3 and 4; Kroll & Mervis, 1986, Experiment 1; Richardson, 1976). As we see below, it is not entirely clear what the contributors are to these diverse findings.

Some experimenters have taken a correlational approach to the question of whether abstract words take longer to understand than concrete ones. In these studies, subjects are presented with a random variety of words ranging on many dimensions along with concreteness and no attempt is made to select words only from the extremes of the concreteness and imagery scales. From the subjects' point of view, the task is simply to decide whether a particular item is or is not a real English word. They are not told of the various characteristics of the items they will be making decisions about. Nor are they told that they should try to retrieve the meanings of the various words as they make their decisions. Usually, lexical decision times for particular words are averaged across subjects and these are then correlated with concreteness and imagery ratings, among other variables.

In almost all of such studies conducted to date, rated concreteness and, especially, imagery have been found to be significantly correlated with lexical decision time. Whaley (1978) noted a correlation of $-.41$ between imageability and lexical decision time, and a somewhat smaller correlation of $-.22$ for concreteness. Similarly, Rubin (1980) reported a significant correlation of $-.27$ between imagery and lexical decision, and a correlation of $-.19$ for concreteness. Howell and Bryden (1987) report correlations between imageability and lexical decision time ranging from $-.19$ to $-.32$, when word length and word frequency were partialed out of both variables. Moreover, the size of these correlations did not vary consistently as a function of the visual field in which the words are presented. Schwanenflugel, Harnishfeger, and Stowe (1988) found a significant correlation between lexical decision time and imageability ($r = -.15$, $p < .05$), but not concreteness ($r = -.11, p > .05$), when word length and word frequency was partialed out. Thus, there seems to be an overall small, but significant relationship between the imageability of the concept to which the word refers and the time it takes people to make a lexical decision.

Other studies have taken an experimental approach attempting to control for or manipulate potential nuisance variables that are associated with lexical imageability. A number of both experimental and lexical variables have been implicated in the appearance and disappearance of concreteness effects in lexical decisions.

One experimental variable that has been associated with the appearance of concreteness effects in lexical decisions is distractor type. James (1975) has argued that, when pronounceable distractors are used, subjects will have a greater tendency to retrieve semantic information surrounding a word as a way of providing evidence for the lexical decision. He showed that the use of pronounceable nonwords as distractors is associated with the finding of significant concreteness effects, but the use of unpronounceable distractors is not. However, Richardson (1976) also compared lexical decisions for abstract and concrete words embedded in an experimental context of pronounceable or unpronounceable distractors and did not find significant concreteness effects in lexical decisions in either case. Neither was such an effect of distractor type revealed in a study by Gernsbacher (1984), who also did not find concreteness effects. On the other hand, both the Richardson and Gernsbacher studies employed very small numbers of subjects in each condition, so it is not clear how reliable their findings might be. Consequently, it is not clear what the influence of distractor pronounceability is, if any.

Another experimental factor that has been implicated in the appearance and disappearance of concreteness effects in lexical decision is whether the abstract and concrete items are presented in a blocked manner or in randomly intermixed trials. Kroll and Merves (1986) showed that, when abstract and concrete items are blocked, concreteness effects are much less evident than when they are intermixed. This is particularly true if a block of abstract words is completed first. Exactly how this blocking by concreteness works to influence the kind of information subjects retrieve for making lexical decision is not yet clear.

Several lexical factors have also been implicated in the appearance and disappearance of concreteness effects in lexical decision. Among these lexical factors is word frequency. One proposal is that concreteness effects in lexical decision are noticeable only for low frequency words. Thus, one would expect to find larger concreteness effects for low frequency than high frequency words. This basic trend has been noted in several studies. For examples, James (1975) found larger concreteness effects for low frequency words when pronounceable nonwords were used. Kroll and Merves (1986) found a similar interaction between concreteness and word frequency when abstract and concrete words were presented in an intermixed experimental setting. DeGroot (1989) also found this interaction between word imageability and frequency in lexical decision. Thus, it seems that the degree to which marked concreteness effects are displayed in lexical decision is related to the frequency with which a lexical item appears in the language.

Of these lexical factors, several related semantic factors have been implicated in the appearance and disappearance of concreteness effects. One of these is experiential familiarity. In a study by Gernsbacher (1984), subjects rated a set of abstract and concrete words on their familiarity with the word's referent in daily experience. Then, abstract and concrete words rated similarly on this variable were presented in a lexical decision study. No significant difference in lexical decision time between abstract and concrete words was found. On the other hand, there were two potential problems with this study. First, the experiments suffered from a low number of subjects which might influence the reliability of the findings. Second, controls for word frequency and word length were not reported, so we cannot be sure that the abstract words used in the study did not have higher overall actual frequency than concrete words.

Another semantic variable implicated in the appearance and disappearance of concreteness effects in lexical decisions is what has been termed context availability. In an early unpublished study conducted on this topic in my laboratory, I asked subjects to rate a large number of nouns on the ease with which they could think of a context or circumstance in which each word could appear. I believe these ratings reflect the ease with which persons are able to retrieve associated information from long-term memory for each word. These ratings showed that lexical concreteness is highly correlated with rated context availability, so that people usually find it harder to think of associated contextual information for abstract than concrete words. I, then, identified a set of the abstract and concrete words for which this confound did not seem to apply (that is, words that had been rated similarly on context availability and not differing on word length and frequency) and presented them in a lexical decision task. No concreteness effect in lexical decision surfaced in that study. However, given the somewhat spotty history of concreteness effects in lexical processing, it seemed necessary to demonstrate that concreteness effects *are* obtainable when concreteness also covaries with context availability, as they do for most abstract and concrete nouns. In a follow-up study (Schwanenflugel et al., 1988), we were able to show that concreteness effects appear only when lexical concreteness is confounded with rated context availability. We have since been able to demonstrate this effect for abstract and concrete words acquired early and for 10-year-old children (Akin, 1989; Akin & Schwanenflugel, 1990).

One problem with taking the approach of controlling for nuisance semantic factors associated with lexical concreteness is that, very often, by controlling for such factors, we have eliminated part of the difference that makes abstract words distinguishable from concrete words. Lexical concreteness is significantly correlated with numerous semantic variables. In fact, factor analytic studies by Rubin (1980) and Paivio (1968) show fairly conclusively that lexical concreteness reflects a constellation of semantic variables that covary. If part of the goal of studying abstract and concrete words is to discern how they differ semantically and how those semantic differences affect their processing, then examination of these correlated variables might also be used to enhance our understanding of why abstract words are harder to understand than concrete words.

All in all, then, it does appear that lexical decisions for abstract words take longer to make than concrete words. However, it seems that subtle characteristics of the experimental situation may also influence the degree to which such concreteness effects are shown.

Naming.   In recent years, it has become clear that the task of naming upcoming words has somewhat different properties than lexical decision. Lexical decision times have been shown to reflect both a lexical access component and a decision component (Seidenberg, Waters, Sanders, & Langer, 1984; Tanenhaus, Carlson, & Seidenberg, 1985), whereas naming times seem to reflect primarily the lexical access component. It is possible that the concreteness effects shown in those studies are the result of the decision component of lexical decision, and not the lexical access component. For example, lexical decisions appear to be highly affected by semantic information (Balota & Chumbley, 1984; Balota & Lorch, 1986; Chumbley & Balota, 1984). Therefore, it is a reasonable possibility that lexical concreteness influences the decision component of lexical decisions rather than the lexical access component.

In fact, the evidence with regard to the issue of whether lexical concreteness affects the naming of words is quite mixed, perhaps more than it is for lexical decisions. Whereas some studies have found significant concreteness effects in naming (Bleasdale, 1987; deGroot, 1989; Rubin, 1980; Shoben, Wilson, & Schwanenflugel, 1990; Schwanenflugel & Stowe, 1989), about as many have not (Brown & Watson, 1987; Coltheart, Laxton, & Keating, 1988; Richardson, 1976; Supraner & Kroll, cited in Kroll & Merves, 1986). Moreover, when significant concreteness effects in naming are found, they are sometimes quite small. For example, the effect was only 7 ms in the deGroot (1989) study and 11 ms in the Bleasdale (1987) study. On the other hand, Shoben, Wilson, and Schwanenflugel (1990) have not found concreteness effects to vary as a function of task. It currently is not quite clear why some studies show significant concreteness benefits and others do not.

Surveying these studies, it seems that one potential contributor to the finding of concreteness effects in naming is the tendency of the experimental context to encourage semantic processing of the words that are named. For example, in many studies conducted in my laboratory, we typically present abstract and concrete words alternately in meaningful and neutral contexts. We have found concreteness benefits in naming for the abstract and concrete words presented in neutral contexts to be generally greater than 40 ms in size (Schwanenflugel & Stowe, 1989; Shoben, Wilson, & Schwanenflugel, 1990). Moreover, we have also found that the presence of unrelated or incongruous context trials seems to reduce significantly the size of the concreteness effects displayed in both naming and lexical decision (Shoben, Wilson, & Schwanenflugel, 1990). I have also noted such a trend in my previous lexical decision studies. For example, in the Schwanenflugel et al. (1988) study, a very small correlation between lexical imageability and lexical decision time was noted when words were presented in isolation ($r = -.15$ for Experiment 2). However, when some trials engaged subjects in meaningful sentence processing, we found the correlation between lexical imageability and lexical decision time to increase marginally for the abstract and concrete words presented in a neutral context ($r = -.31$ for Experiment 3). In the literature, all studies noting nonsignificant concreteness effects in naming have been ones in which words were always presented in isolation and in which no trials engaged subjects in meaningful contextual processing. Thus, the experimental context may serve to influence the degree to which people retrieve lexical meaning as part of the naming task. Consequently, we can tentatively conclude that when the experimental context encourages meaningful processing, concreteness effects in naming are more likely to be found.

Conclusion. In the majority of studies examining concreteness effects in lexical processing, it seems that most find reliable concreteness effects on processing time. However, four factors do seem implicated in the finding of significant context effects in lexical processing. First, blocking by concreteness seems to have not well understood effects on the presence of concreteness effects. Second, low word frequency seems to make the occurrence of concreteness effects more likely. Third, when subjects are engaged in processing meaningful contexts on some trials, the occurrence of concreteness effects in neutral trials is more likely. Last, concreteness effects in lexical processing seem to be more prevalent in lexical decision tasks than naming tasks.

These last three factors seem to suggest that, when meaning retrieval is required by the task, concreteness effects in lexical processing are likely to be displayed. That is, it would seem to be a reasonable strategy to attempt to retrieve some disambiguating semantic information while processing low frequency words, particularly in a lexical decision task. Similarly, when meaningful semantic processing is stressed in many of the experimental trials (as it is in studies examining context effects in lexical processing), it is likely that persons will continue to attempt to retrieve semantic information in the processing of abstract and concrete words presented in contextually neutral trials as well. Last, the tendency of persons to retrieve disambiguating semantic information in the decision component of lexical decision is widely agreed upon, and reflects itself here in the tendency of concreteness effects to surface in lexical decisions over naming. Thus, as for the discussion of concreteness effects in sentence processing, it can be concluded that concreteness effects are likely to appear in lexical processing when deeper semantic processing is required by the task.

Concreteness Effects and Vocabulary Acquisition

Another source of evidence that abstract concepts are harder to understand than concrete concepts is the observation that abstract words are acquired later than concrete words developmentally (Brown, 1957). This evidence comes from studies examining both the development of a spoken vocabulary, the acquisition of a reading vocabulary, and the understanding of basic meaning categories (called ontological categories) in children. I discuss each of these in turn below.

The Acquisition of Abstract and Concrete Words in Spoken Vocabulary. The tendency for young children to acquire words referring to concrete entities in their spoken vocabulary prior to words referring to abstract concepts is incontestible. Children's first nouns invariably refer to concrete objects in their environment. A survey of the early infant language corpuses assembled by Gentner (1982) and by Nelson (1973) makes it clear that none of the early nouns acquired by children refer to abstract concepts of any sort.

This same tendency towards the acquisition of concrete over abstract words continues throughout early childhood. In a classic study on this topic, Brown (1957) compared the lexical productions of 1st-grade children and adults in order to discern whether children possessed a bias toward naming concrete actions and objects. To compare the overall concreteness of children's vocabulary with adults', he compared the 1000 words most often used by 1st-grade children as defined by the Rinsland (1945) count with the 1000 words most often used by adults as defined by the Thorndike-Lorge (1944) count. The Rinsland corpus, the only existing corpus of its kind, was derived from conversations, letters, and stories from a large number of 1st- through 8th-grade children. Because of its emphasis on children's productions rather than children's reading materials (which are largely written by adults), it provides a unique window into the productive vocabularies of children. In the Brown study, a word was considered concrete if its common referent had a "characteristic visual contour and size" (in the case of nouns) or named "animal (including human) movement" (in the case of verbs; p. 2). He found that a full 75% of these most often used children's nouns and 67% of the verbs were concrete, whereas only 28% of the most often used adult nouns and 33% of the verbs were concrete. This suggests that there is a wide disparity between adults and children in their relative use of abstract and concrete words.

Unfortunately, these dramatic results do not tell us much about how long these disparities in word use between adults and children persist developmentally. In order to examine this issue, I determined the typical age of acquisition as defined by the Rinsland corpus for the 365 nouns used in the concreteness norms reported by Schwanenflugel et al. (1988). Specifically, I selected the 198 nouns that had an adult word frequency of greater than 30 per million in the Kucera and Francis (1967) adult corpus, with the view that words of such frequency are likely to be at least heard by children. These 198 nouns were compared with the Rinsland corpus for grades 1 through 8 and the word was classified as acquired if the item appeared at least twice in the corpus for each grade. Concrete words were defined as those words that had a rated imagery value of greater than 4.5 (on a 7-point scale) and abstract words were defined as those that had ratings of less than 4.5. The proportion of words acquired for each word type at each grade level can be found in Fig. 9.1.

What is clear from this analysis is that the disparity in the acquisition of abstract and concrete words persists developmentally until early adolescence. For these relatively high frequency words, the acquisition of concrete nouns is nearly 80% complete by 1st grade, showing very little vocabulary growth thereafter. On the other hand, the acquisition of abstract words does not achieve a similar level until around Grade 7.

A similar developmental trend is reported by West, Martindale, and Sutton-Smith (1985) in their study of children's spontaneous fantasy narratives. Even though fantasy narratives would seem to encourage the use of highly imageable, concrete nouns and verbs at all ages, they found a significant correlation between age and noun and verb concreteness. That is, as children got older, the nouns and verbs they used tended to be less and less concrete. Thus, this trend toward greater lexical abstractness with age is a highly reliable and long-lasting developmental progression.

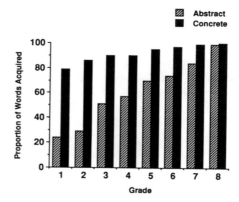

Fig. 9.1. The percentage of high frequency abstract and concrete words acquired by children in Grades 1 through 8 as defined by Rinsland (1945) child language corpus.

Acquisition of a Reading Vocabulary for Abstract and Concrete Words. Another type of evidence that abstract words are acquired later than concrete words comes from studies of the development of reading vocabularies in early elementary school children. Some of these have been controlled teaching studies in which young children were first instructed on a set of abstract and concrete words that they did not possess in their initial reading vocabulary, and then tested on the degree to which the words had entered the children's reading vocabulary (Kiraly & Furlong, 1974; Richmond & McNinch, 1977; Yore & Ollila, 1985). In the Richmond and McNinch (1977) study, 1st-grade children were taught four abstract and four concrete words. No significant difference was found in the number of trials to criterion needed to acquire the abstract and concrete words, but the means were in the direction of a concreteness advantage. In a very similar study, Kiraly and Furlong (1974) did find a concreteness advantage in learning to read concrete over abstract words. Yore and Ollila (1985), using a larger number of words of each type, also found a significant 6.4% concreteness benefit in acquiring concrete words over abstract words in 1st-grade children's reading vocabularies. Thus, of the few studies that have been conducted on this topic, early readers have generally found abstract words harder to learn to read than concrete words.

Other evidence suggests that this difference in reading vocabulary for common abstract and concrete words may be fairly persistent developmentally. In a study of the reading behavior of 10-year-old children, Coltheart, Laxton, and Keating (1988) noted a 6% difference in the reading accuracy of high frequency abstract and concrete words, with this concreteness benefit being larger for poor readers than good readers. Moreover, Akin and Schwanenflugel (1990; Akin, 1989) found that, even for words that children did know, concreteness effects in lexical processing time were considerably larger for 8- and 10-year-olds than adults (see also Wolf & Gow, 1986).

The Development of Basic Meaning Categories.   Another source of evidence related to the proposition that children acquire the meaning of concrete words prior to abstract words comes from studies examining the development of ontological knowledge in children. Ontological knowledge is defined as "people's beliefs about what the basic categories of existence are" (Keil, 1983, p. 104). An ontological category is distinguished by the kinds of predicates it can take. For example, the ontological category Living Things (such as birds and flowers) can take potential predicates such as "is dead," "needs food," which could never be true for Nonliving Things (such as houses or bricks) or Abstract Concepts (such as truth or happiness). Keil (1979) reported an interesting series of studies examining the degree to which children understood that various kinds of nouns could take particular kinds of predicates and showed that young children often confuse abstract concepts as being able to take predicates associated with object categories and living things. Consequently, it appears that children do not have the distinct ontological knowledge associated with abstract concepts as a whole and that such knowledge is acquired rather late in development.

Conclusion.   There is substantial evidence that children take longer to acquire abstract concepts and words than concrete ones. Indeed, the differential acquisition of abstract and concrete words is quite large even for high frequency words and is quite persistent developmentally. This trend seems to be true for the acquisition of both spoken and reading vocabulary. Moreover, the understanding of how abstract concepts may operate as an ontological group is not appreciated until fairly late in development. Consequently, it might be inferred that abstract words are harder overall for children to understand than concrete words.

Summary

In this section, I have outlined three sources of evidence that abstract words presented in isolation are, indeed, harder to understand that concrete words. Abstract sentences take longer to understand and verify than concrete sentences. Abstract words are certainly more difficult to make lexical decisions for and probably more difficult to name than concrete words. Abstract words are acquired later in childhood than concrete words and maintain an inferiority in processing long after children have presumably acquired their meanings. Although the evidence for the proposition that abstract words are harder to understand than concrete words has been by no means unanimous for all tasks and observations, the bulk of it has suggested that the degree to which the various tasks require a deeper, more meaning-oriented processing of verbal materials is also the degree to which concreteness effects in understanding will surface.

THEORIES FOR WHY ABSTRACT WORDS
ARE HARD TO UNDERSTAND

Over the years, a large number of positions and theories have been put forth in an attempt to explain the general processing superiority of concrete verbal materials over abstract materials. Such theories are important for the light they may shed on the representation, development, and processing of word meaning. To be complete, theories of word meaning must also include information regarding how words vary in their representations and how these representational distinctions are related to known developmental and processing differences.

In this section, I concentrate on what I feel have been the three most successful theories or hypotheses concerning why abstract word concepts are harder to understand than concrete concepts: the Dual-Coding Theory, the Age-of-Acquisition Hypothesis, and the Context Availability Model. The Dual-Coding Theory formalizes the basic notion that abstract words are hard to understand because they lack the direct sensory referents associated with concrete words. The Age-of-Acquisition and Context Availability views posit other, nonsensory explanations for why abstract words are harder to understand than concrete words. In what follows, I discuss what each theory has to say about the representation, development, and processing of abstract and concrete words.

Dual-Coding Theory

The Dual-Coding Theory by Paivio and his colleagues (Paivio, 1971, 1986) is probably the best known of all the theories on concreteness effects in verbal processing. Its strength (and the task for which it was originally developed) is its relative ability account for the highly pervasive effects of concreteness effects in verbal memory (but see Marschark et al., 1987). The theory was specifically developed to describe the representational differences between abstract and concrete words that cause concrete verbal materials to be remembered so much better than abstract materials.

Dual-Coding Theory (Paivio, 1986) posits the existence of a structurally and functionally distinct verbal system (called the logogen system) and image system (called the imagen system). The logogen system is said to be set up as a system of logogens, corresponding roughly to words, which are interconnected in an associative network of relations. These associative networks are acquired as a direct function of associative experience, that is, as a function of the natural word-to-word associations that come about with language experience. Logogens are said to be most directly and immediately activated by written or spoken language. The imagen system, on the other hand, is a system of sensory images that maintain the characteristics of the original modalities from which they arise. The imagery system contains various configurations of part-whole relations that arise from sensory experience. The imagens are said to be most directly activated by visual-spatial information (in the visual sensory case).

These representational systems can act either together or separately in language processing. The logogen and imagen systems are tied together by cross-referential links that enable one system to activate the other. Concrete words are said to have stronger referential connections to the imagen system than abstract words have, although the verbal associative linkages are said to be similar for the two word types (Paivio, 1986, p. 128). Therefore, in reading or listening to linguistic materials, then, the logogen system must be activated, but the imagen system might also be activated in some cases, particularly by concrete verbal materials. As Paivio (1986) puts it, "precisely which images or descriptions will be activated at any moment depends upon the stimulus context interacting with the relative functional strength of the different referential connections" (p. 63).

The theory vacillates with regard to whether concreteness effects should be displayed in verbal comprehension and exactly which form they should take. Paivio and Begg's (1971) early work on sentence comprehension suggested that concreteness effects were not to be found in the initial stages of comprehension. They reasoned that the imagen system was not involved in comprehension because imagery formation to sentences took longer to evoke than simple comprehension did. However, as noted earlier in this chapter, further research has suggested that concreteness effects do occur in comprehension and (most of the time) seem to facilitate sentence and word processing. Paivio (1986) concludes from this work that ". . . referential and associative imagery reactions are more likely to be part of the comprehension of concrete than abstract material" (p. 218). He further notes that "The contribution of imagery is supplemented by effects that are attributable to verbal processes . . . The effects of imagery and verbal processes are additive, both in a positive and negative sense" (p. 222). Thus, it seems that the involvement of the imagery system in language comprehension may either assist comprehension (causing shorter reaction times), or may slow comprehension (causing longer reactions times).

Assuming that the imagen system usually acts to assist in sentence and word processing, and that these effects are additive, it would seem that this theory would have difficulty explaining why it is that concreteness effects in comprehension usually disappear when abstract and concrete verbal materials are presented in a meaningful verbal context. For example, Schwanenflugel and Shoben (1983) showed that although there were large differences between abstract and concrete sentences in neutral contexts, the comprehension time differences between those sentences disappeared when they were presented in a meaningful paragraph context. Several other studies in my laboratory have shown similar results for abstract and concrete words presented in meaningful compared with neutral sentence contexts (Schwanenflugel et al., 1988; Schwanenflugel & Shoben, 1983; Schwanenflugel & Stowe, 1989). In meaningful, supportive contexts, abstract sentences and words are comprehended as quickly as concrete ones.

The problem for the dual-coding theory is this: The finding that abstract materials take longer to understand than concrete materials when they are presented in isolation suggests that the imagen system is involved in comprehending concrete verbal materials. If so, and if the effects of the imagery and verbal associative processes are additive, then it would seem that concreteness effects should be found both when the materials are presented in context as without. Moreover, for a number of studies, abstract materials were always presented in an abstract verbal context to rule out the possibility that the context merely served to activate the imagen system for abstract words. Thus, concrete materials always had better access to the imagen system than abstract materials both in and out of context and, yet, concreteness effects were not displayed when the verbal materials were presented in context. If the imagen system is to be involved early in the comprehension of words, then the dual-coding theory needs to have a mechanism to account for why the concreteness effects disappear in context. If the imagen system is not to be involved, then the theory needs to have another mechanism for accounting for why abstract words take longer to process than concrete words when they are presented in isolation.

The dual-coding theory does discuss the development of the representational differences between abstract and concrete words. The view is that nonverbal representations precede verbal ones and that the verbal representations arise out of nonverbal representations. This claim is not unique to the theory and can be found in most cognitive developmental theories including that of Piaget (Piaget & Inhelder, 1971), Bruner (1966), and Fischer (Fischer, Hand, & Russell, 1984). The general view is that concrete ideas are easier for children to acquire than abstract ideas because they bear a more direct relationship to their real world, sensory counterparts.

This theory is generally able to account for the finding that concrete words are acquired sooner than abstract words developmentally. However, it is unable to account for a developmental trend we have noticed in our laboratory (Akin, 1989; Akin & Schwanenflugel, 1990). Usually, younger readers find abstract words particularly difficult to make lexical decisions for. Concreteness effects for 3rd graders are large (around 250 ms) and highly reliable. However, in two experiments, we have found that, by 10 years old, children begin to differentiate between various kinds of abstract and concrete words in a manner displayed by adults in the Schwanenflugel et al. (1988) study. Specifically, lexical decisions for abstract words are made as fast as for concrete words by 10-year-olds when the abstract and concrete words are similar in context availability (as defined by either their own or adults' ratings). This suggests that the processing difficulty usually associated with abstract words is minimized for certain abstract words over others. Currently, the dual-coding theory treats abstract and concrete words as relatively undifferentiated classes of words and, as a result, cannot account for developmental differences among various types of abstract and concrete words.

In sum, the strength of this theory is that it makes a strong statement with regard to the differing representations of abstract and concrete words. However, given that the dual-coding theory does not make strong predictions as to what the relative contributions of the verbal and imagen system will be in on-line language comprehension, it is difficult to say how well it does or does not do in accounting for concreteness effects occurring early in comprehension. The conditions under which the imagen system will necessarily be involved have never been specified. This means that, whenever concreteness effects are displayed, it can always be argued *ad hoc* that imagery was invoked. Similarly, when concreteness effects are not displayed, it can also be argued that imagen system was not involved. As a result, the current theory is virtually untestable with regard to issues of comprehension and lexical processing. The theory is more successful, however, in describing relative trends in the development of abstract and concrete word meanings (although it must be noted that it does so more by postulate than by any inherent feature of the theory itself).

Age-of-Acquisition Hypothesis

The age-of-acquisition hypothesis (Gilhooly & Gilhooly, 1979) was not developed as a theory of concreteness effects and is, therefore, less well developed than the dual-coding hypothesis for describing such effects. The theory is, however, designed to describe the kinds of trends that are seen in lexical decision and comprehension studies. The theory states simply that the concreteness effects typically displayed in lexical retrieval tasks are merely cumulative word frequency effects. It is argued that the usual word frequency indices that are obtained from objective measures of written and spoken English (such as the written word frequency index by Kucera and Francis, 1967, and the spoken word frequency index by Svartvik and Quirk, 1980) are inappropriate measures of the phenomenological frequency of abstract and concrete words because they do not take into account differential acquisition rates of the two word types. Because concrete words are acquired so much earlier in development than abstract words, they have effectively been experienced more often. They have correspondingly lower thresholds of activation, making them faster to retrieve associated lexical information for than abstract words. Moreover, adults apparently are able to judge with some accuracy the relative ages at which they learned various words (Gilhooly & Gilhooly, 1980), although just how they make this decision is not quite clear. It can be inferred from the hypothesis that the differences in the representation between abstract and concrete words can be isolated at the differing thresholds of activation for the two word types. Thus, lexical concreteness effects occurring early in lexical processing are said to be merely age-of-acquisition effects.

This view does reasonably well in explaining concreteness effects for words occurring in isolation. In fact, Brown and Watson (1987) have shown age-of-acquisition ratings to be better predictors of naming times than lexical familiarity, imageability, and written or spoken frequency measures. Similarly, Coltheart, Laxon, and Keating (1988) found no difference in naming times between abstract and concrete words rated similarly on age-of-acquisition. My studies have found age-of-acquisition to be as good, but no worse, a predictor of lexical decision time as imageability, once objective word length and word frequency is partialed out (Schwanenflugel et al., 1988). Thus, age-of-acquisition seems to be a reasonable candidate for explaining why abstract words and sentences take longer to process than concrete materials presented in isolation.

The hypothesis has some difficulty explaining why the differences in comprehension between abstract and concrete verbal materials tend to disappear when they are presented in a supportive context. Although the hypothesis makes no statements with regard to the influence of context on lexical processing, it would seem that the influence of context would have to be treated similarly to the context and word frequency interactions that have been noted in the literature (see Stanovich & West, 1983). That is, it has often been noted that the difference in processing time between low frequency and high frequency words is minimized when such words are presented in a meaningful context. While it is true that the previous research generally supports the finding of diminished word frequency effects when words are presented in context, it does not support the finding that such frequency effects should disappear completely in context. Consequently, to the degree that context does not completely override the influence of frequency in the processing of upcoming words, the age-of-acquisition hypothesis cannot account for the absence of concreteness effects when abstract and concrete verbal materials are presented in a supportive context.

Finally, the age-of-acquisition hypothesis does not have a position on why abstract words take longer for children to acquire than concrete words. It merely asserts that, because they do, processing is slowed for such words in adulthood.

In sum, the age-of-acquisition hypothesis does reasonably well in accounting for comprehension time differences between abstract and concrete verbal materials presented in isolation. It fares less well in accounting for the elimination of concreteness effects when abstract and concrete words are presented in a supportive context and in explaining exactly why it is that abstract words are acquired later than concrete words.

Context Availability Model

The context availability model (Bransford & McCarrell, 1974; Kieras, 1978; Schwanenflugel & Shoben, 1983) is a variant of a more general model of comprehension that has been extended to account for concreteness effects in comprehension. This model views comprehension as being an interaction between the comprehender's knowledge base and external stimulus context. According to the model, comprehension is aided fundamentally by the addition of contextual information to the materials that are to be understood. This contextual information may come either from the comprehender's knowledge base or from the external stimulus context. This contextual information serves to enable comprehenders to make the necessary interrelations between concepts needed for subjective feeling of comprehension. If persons are unable to retrieve relevant information from prior knowledge to supplement the incoming message, then comprehension is difficult and a subjective sense of comprehension may not take place. Thus, the emphasis in the theory is placed on the relative retrievability of information from knowledge base and how the availability of such information influences comprehension.

Concreteness effects for abstract and concrete verbal materials presented in isolation are dealt with in this model by assuming that the retrieval of information from knowledge base is more difficult for some concepts than others. Generally, abstract materials are said to be more difficult to understand than concrete materials because persons find it more difficult to retrieve the associated contextual information from knowledge base needed to augment comprehension for abstract concepts than concrete concepts. Therefore, the main representational difference between abstract and concrete words is that abstract words possess weaker connections to associated contextual information in knowledge base than concrete words do.

Abstract words could possess weaker connections to associated contextual information than concrete words for a number of reasons. One way that an abstract word might come to have weaker connections to knowledge base is by appearing in a great diversity of contexts (Galbraith & Underwood, 1973). Another way is by simply being relatively unfamiliar (that is, by appearing so seldomly that the person cannot connect any contextual information at all with the word). What is important to this view is not how abstract words come to have weaker connections to contextual information from knowledge base, but only that they generally do.

Because contextual information retrieval is usually slower for abstract concepts than for concrete concepts, abstract sentences and words normally take longer to comprehend than concrete words when they are presented in isolation. Thus, for example, when persons read an abstract sentence such as "Many factors affected the crucial decision," they may attempt to retrieve a plausible circumstance from prior knowledge in which such a sentence might be embedded (say, in a decision about which graduate school to attend) and may have difficulty doing so. On the other hand, for a similar concrete sentence like "Many sailors deserted the sinking vessel," they may have a somewhat easier time retrieving such contextual information (say, in a war story) and would be correspondingly faster to comprehend such sentences. The finding of longer lexical decision times for abstract and concrete words would be interpreted in much the same way. The model claims that, in making a lexical decision, persons also attempt to retrieve related information from prior knowledge. The ease with which they are able to do so would be reflected in longer lexical decision times for abstract than concrete words. Similar predictions would also be made for naming to the degree to which persons process words for meaning in that task.

The model also makes explicit predictions regarding what should happen when abstract and concrete verbal materials are presented in meaningful, highly supportive contexts. The model predicts that abstract and concrete words should be equally easy to understand when presented in a supportive context because context serves to preactivate related information in prior knowledge. This preactivation of contextual knowledge helps to override the relative difficulty in retrieving such knowledge for abstract words, making them as easy to comprehend as concrete words. Concrete words, because they already have highly available contextual knowledge associated with them, do not benefit nearly as much from being presented in a supportive context as abstract words do. Thus, context effects should be larger for abstract than concrete sentences and words.

A number of studies have supported such a claim about the influence of context on abstract and concrete words. For example, Schwanenflugel and Shoben (1983) found that, when abstract and concrete sentences were presented in meaningful paragraph contexts, concreteness effects in comprehension times disappeared. (Wattenmaker & Shoben, 1987, extended this finding to sentence recall; see also Marschark, 1985). Schwanenflugel et al. (1988) and Schwanenflugel and Shoben (1983) have noted the elimination of lexical decision time differences for abstract and concrete words embedded in sentence contexts. Schwanenflugel and Stowe (1989) have also shown that naming times and meaningfulness judgment times do not differ for abstract and concrete words presented in sentence contexts. Thus, across a wide array of tasks, the processing difficulty usually associated with abstract materials has been shown to disappear when those materials are presented in highly supportive contexts.

Another finding supporting this view of concreteness effects in comprehension is that subjects' ratings of context availability (in which subjects are asked to rate the relative difficulty of retrieving associated contextual information for isolated abstract and concrete words) are significantly correlated with ratings of imagery and concreteness. Moreover, context availability is also correlated with lexical decision (Schwanenflugel et al., 1988) and sentence comprehension times (Schwanenflugel & Shoben, 1983). In fact, context availability has been found to be a better predictor of lexical decision times than imagery, concreteness, or age-of-acquisition ratings. Furthermore, when rated context availability is controlled for, lexical decision times for abstract and concrete words do not differ (Akin, 1989; Akin & Schwanenflugel, 1990; Schwanenflugel et al., 1988).

At present, there is one exception to the general trend that the processing time differences between abstract and concrete words disappear when presented in a meaningful context. Specifically, Bleasdale (1987) found equivalent priming effects for abstract and concrete words in a word prime lexical decision task, yielding significant concreteness effects both in and out of context. We (Shoben, Wilson, & Schwanenflugel, 1990) have recently replicated Bleasdale's basic findings. Although we did find differential priming for abstract and concrete words both in a naming and lexical decision task, concreteness effects did not completely disappear when the words were presented in a word prime context. Although we are not sure why the findings diverge for word prime contexts, at least two possibilities are plausible. First, in word prime studies, the degree of associative and semantic relatedness between word primes and their targets tend to be weaker than they are for sentence-target pairs. Second, sentence contexts in general may operate differently than word prime contexts, if for no other reason than that sentence contexts are more like normal text. Sentence contexts have been shown to produce larger contextual benefits than word primes alone (West & Stanovich, 1988). Consequently, it seems that abstract words need a considerable amount of contextual support to be processed similarly to concrete words.

Currently, the context availability model makes no statements with regard to the development of the representational differences between abstract and concrete words. However, I have compared the relative contributions of imageability and context availability on the acquisition of abstract and concrete words. Specifically, I correlated the typical age of acquisition as defined by the Rinsland corpus (1945) and for the 198 nouns used in the analysis featured in Fig. 9.1 with adult ratings of context availability. This analysis showed context availability to be as good a predictor of age of acquisition as rated imagery. That is, words that adults rate as easy to think of contextual information for are typically acquired earlier than words they find difficult to retrieve associated contextual information for. Thus, early acquired words tend not only to be concrete and imageable, but are also relatively easy to retrieve contextual information for in adulthood.

On the other hand, lexical imageability may be important early in language development beyond the contributions of context availability. In a recent study, Akin and Schwanenflugel (1990) found that 8-year-olds (but not 10-year-olds and adults) still took longer to make lexical decisions for acquired abstract words than acquired concrete words even when the two word types were controlled on rated context availability. For 8-year-olds, imageability ratings were better predictors of reaction times than context availability times, although the reverse was true for adults. Consequently, it does seem that younger readers may attempt to retrieve sensory, imaginal information to make lexical decisions.

In sum, the context availability model describes the representational differences between abstract and concrete words in terms of differences in strength of connections between concepts and associated knowledge base. However, some abstract words may be relatively strongly connected to their associated contextual information and some concrete words less so and, therefore, their lexical decision times should vary accordingly. The model does reasonably well in accounting for comprehension times, lexical decision, and naming times for words appearing in isolation. It also accounts for the disappearance of concreteness effects when the items are presented in a supportive context. It currently does not have any systematic position regarding how the representational differences between the two word types come about.

CONCLUSION

In this chapter, I have outlined the current status of concreteness effects occurring early in the comprehension of abstract and concrete verbal materials. In general, it has been found that greater concreteness is associated with faster processing times for both sentences and words presented in isolation. However, these concreteness effects in comprehension typically disappear when the verbal materials are presented in a meaningful, supportive context. Furthermore, concrete words are acquired earlier developmentally than abstract words, and maintain their superiority in processing long after their meaning is acquired.

Currently, none of the existing theories is able to explain all the related findings regarding concreteness effects in comprehension. The dual-coding theory does reasonably well in describing the processing of abstract and concrete words presented in isolation and in accounting for developmental trends in their acquisition. It also makes the strongest statements regarding the representational distinctions between the two word types. The age-of-acquisition hypothesis does very well in accounting for the processing of isolated abstract and concrete words, but does less well in describing their development and their processing in meaningful contexts. The context availability model, on the other hand, accounts reasonably well for findings regarding comprehension of abstract and concrete verbal materials both in and out of context. However, it currently lacks mechanisms for describing how and why the representational differences between abstract and concrete words come about developmentally.

On the other hand, I feel the context availability model has an important advantage over the other views because it is in basic agreement with current discussions about the nature of concepts and word meanings in general. Specifically, these recent views (e.g., Barsalou, 1987; Brooks, 1987; Roth & Shoben, 1983) have focused on the episodic, contextually based character of word meaning. There is a general movement away from thinking of concepts as having fixed, definitional cores that become activated on all instances of word use. The context availability model, with its emphasis on the retrieval of contextual information from prior knowledge, also emphasizes this contextually based character of word meanings. The demonstration that even the processing of words in isolation requires the retrieval of contextual information from prior knowledge further supports this general view of the nature of word meanings. Moreover, it also suggests that word meanings may never become completely decontextualized from their contexts of prior use.

These views of word meaning (Barsalou, 1982; Greenspan, 1986) point out that not all knowledge associated with concepts is equally accessible during every instance of word use. Some knowledge is said to be context-dependent (accessible only in particular contexts) and other knowledge is said to be context-independent (accessible in all contexts of word use). It is possible that words rated low in context availability largely possess context-dependent knowledge which is relatively inaccessible when the words are presented in isolation. However, when such words are presented in supportive contexts, this context-dependent information becomes highly available for deriving meaning, eliminating potential differences in comprehension between abstract and concrete words.

Although none of the theories can currently account for all the phenomena related to concreteness effects in comprehension, I have highlighted the kinds of information that a theory of concreteness effects will have to account for in order to be a comprehensive description of concreteness and word meaning. It is clear that a comprehensive theory of concreteness effects in word meaning will be a necessary feature of a complete theory of the structures and processes engaged in a psychology of word meanings.

ACKNOWLEDGMENTS

I thank Mike Martin, Alan Roth, and Ed Shoben for their helpful comments on an earlier draft of this chapter.

REFERENCES

Akin, C. E. (1989). *Context availability and the developmental use of imagery.* Unpublished doctoral dissertation, University of Georgia, Athens, GA.

Akin, C. E., & Schwanenflugel, P. J. (1990). *Context availability and developmental trends in the processing of abstract and concrete words.* Unpublished manuscript, University of Georgia, Athens, GA.

Balota, D. A., & Chumbley, J. I. (1984). Are lexical decisions a good measure of lexical access? The role of word-frequency in the neglected decision stage. *Journal of Experimental Psychology: Human Perception and Performance, 10,* 340–357.

Balota, D. A., & Lorch, R. F., Jr. (1986). Depth of automatic spreading activation: Mediated priming effects in pronunciation but not in lexical decision. *Journal of Experimental Psychology: Learning, Memory, & Cognition, 12,* 336–345.

Barsalou, L. W. (1982). Context-independent and context-dependent information in concepts. *Memory & Cognition, 11,* 629–654.

Barsalou, L. W. (1987). The instability of graded structure: Implications for the nature of concepts. In U. Neisser (Ed.), *Concepts and conceptual development: Ecological and intellectual factors in categorization* (pp. 101–140). New York: Cambridge University Press.

Belmore, S. M., Yates, J. M., Bellack, D. R., Jones, S. N., & Rosenquist, S. E. (1982). Drawing inferences from concrete and abstract sentences. *Journal of Verbal Learning and Verbal Behavior, 21,* 338–351.

Bleasdale, F. A. (1987). Concreteness dependent associative priming: Separate lexical organization for concrete and abstract words. *Journal of Experimental Psychology: Learning, Memory, and Cognition, 13,* 582–594.

Bransford, J. D., & McCarrell, N. S. (1974). A sketch of a cognitive approach to comprehension: Some thoughts on what it means to comprehend. In W. Weimer & D. Palermo (Eds.), *Cognition and the symbolic processes* (pp. 189–230). Hillsdale, NJ: Lawrence Erlbaum Associates.

Brooks, L. (1987). Decentralized control of categorization: The role of prior processing episodes. In

U. Neisser (Ed.), *Concepts and conceptual development: Ecological and intellectual factors in categorization* (pp. 141–174). New York: Cambridge University Press.

Brown, G. D. A., & Watson, F. L. (1987). First in, first out: Word learning age and spoken word frequency as predictors of word familiarity and word naming latency. *Memory & Cognition, 15,* 208–216.

Brown, R. W. (1957). Linguistic determinism and the part of speech. *Journal of Abnormal and Social Psychology, 55,* 1–5.

Bruner, J. S. (1966). *Toward a theory of instruction.* New York: W. W. Norton.

Coltheart, V., Laxon, V. J., & Keating, C. (1988). Effects of word imageability and age of acquisition on children's reading. *British Journal of Psychology, 79,* 1–11.

DeGroot, A. M. B. (1989). Representational aspects of word imageability and word frequency as assessed through word association. *Journal of Experimental Psychology: Learning, Memory, and Cognition, 15,* 824–845.

DiVesta, F. J., & Walls, R. T. (1970). Factor analysis of the semantic attributes of 487 words and some relationships to the conceptual behavior of fifth-grade children. *Journal of Educational Psychology Monograph, 61*(6, Pt. 2).

Fischer, K. W., Hand, H. H., & Russell, S. (1984). The development of abstractions in adolescence and adulthood. In M. L. Commons, F. A. Richards, & C. Armon (Eds.), *Beyond formal operations: Late adolescent and adult cognitive development.* New York: Prager.

Galbraith, R. C., & Underwood, B. J. (1973). Perceived frequency of concrete and abstract words. *Memory & Cognition, 1,* 56–60.

Gentner, D. (1982). Why nouns are learned before verbs: Linguistic relativity versus natural partitioning. *Center for the Study of Reading: Technical Report No. 257.* Urbana, IL: University of Illinois at Urbana-Champaign.

Gernsbacher, M. A. (1984). Resolving 20 years of inconsistent interactions between lexical familiarity and orthography, concreteness, and polysemy. *Journal of Experimental Psychology: General, 113,* 256–281.

Gilhooly, K. J., & Gilhooly, M. L. (1979). Age-of-acquisition effects in lexical and episodic tasks. *Memory & Cognition, 7,* 214–223.

Gilhooly, K. J., & Gilhooly, M. L. (1980). The validity of age-of-acquisition ratings. *British Journal of Psychology, 71,* 105–110.

Gilhooly, K. J., & Watson, F. L. (1981). Word age-of-acquisition effects: A review. *Current Psychological Reviews, 1,* 269–286.

Glass, A. L., Eddy, J. K., & Schwanenflugel, P. J. (1980). The verification of high and low imagery sentences. *Journal of Experimental Psychology: Human Learning and Memory, 6,* 692–704.

Glass, A. L., & Holyoak, K. J. (1975). Alternative conceptions of semantic memory. *Cognition, 3,* 313–319.

Glass, A. L., Millen, D. R., Beck, L. G., & Eddy, J. K. (1985). Representation of images in sentence verification. *Journal of Memory and Language, 24,* 539–557.

Greenspan, S. L. (1986). Semantic flexibility and referential specificity of concrete nouns. *Journal of Memory and Language, 25,* 539–557.

Haberlandt, K. F., & Graesser, A. C. (1985). Component processes in text comprehension and some of their interactions. *Journal of Experimental Psychology: General, 114,* 357–375.

Holmes, V. M., & Langford, J. (1976). Comprehension and recall of abstract and concrete sentences. *Journal of Verbal Learning and Verbal Behavior, 15,* 559–566.

Holyoak, K. J. (1974). The role of imagery in the evaluation of sentences: Imagery or semantic factors. *Journal of Verbal Learning and Verbal Behavior, 13,* 163–166.

Howell, J. R., & Bryden, M. P. (1987). The effects of word orientation and imageability on visual half-field presentations with a lexical decision task. *Neuropsychologia, 25,* 527–538.

James, C. T. (1975). The role of semantic information in lexical decisions. *Journal of Experimental Psychology: Human Perception and Performance, 104,* 130–136.

Jorgensen, C. C., & Kintsch, W. (1973). The role of imagery in the evaluation of sentences. *Cognitive Psychology, 4,* 110–116.

Keil, F. C. (1979). *Semantic and conceptual development: An ontological perspective.* Cambridge, MA: Harvard University Press.

Keil, F. C. (1983). Semantic inferences and the acquisition of word meaning. In T. Seiler & W. Wannenmacher (Eds.), *Concept development and the development of word meaning* (pp. 103–124). Berlin: Springer-Verlag.

Kieras, D. (1978). Beyond pictures and words: Alternative information processing models for imagery effects in verbal memory. *Psychological Bulletin, 85,* 532–554.

Kiraly, J., & Furlong, A. (1974). Teaching words to kindergarten children with picture, configuration, and initial sound cues in a prompting procedure. *Journal of Educational Research, 67,* 295–298.

Klee, H., & Eyesenck, M. W. (1973). Comprehension of concrete and abstract sentences. *Journal of Verbal Learning and Verbal Behavior, 12,* 522–529.

Kroll, J. F., & Merves, J. S. (1986). Lexical access for concrete and abstract words. *Journal of Experimental Psychology: Learning, Memory, and Cognition, 12,* 92–107.

Kucera, H., & Francis, W. H. (1967). *Computational analysis of present-day American English.* Providence, RI: Brown University Press.

Lorch, R. F. (1982). Priming and search processes in semantic memory: A test of three models of spreading activation. *Journal of Verbal Learning and Verbal Behavior, 21,* 468–492.

Marschark, M. (1979). The syntax and semantics of comprehension. In G. Prideaux (Ed.), *Perspectives in experimental linguistics.* Amsterdam: John Benjamins B. V.

Marschark, M. (1985). Imagery and organization in the recall of high and low imagery prose. *Journal of Memory and Language, 24,* 734–745.

Marschark, M., Richman, C. L., Yuille, J. C., & Hunt, R. R. (1987). The role of imagery in memory: On shared and distinctive information. *Psychological Bulletin, 102,* 28–41.

Moeser, S. D. (1974). Memory for meaning and wording in concrete and abstract sentences. *Journal of Verbal Learning and Verbal Behavior, 13,* 682–697.

Nelson, K. (1973). Structure and strategy in learning to talk. *Monographs of the Society for Research in Child Development, 38* (Serial No. 149).

Paivio, A. (1968). A factor-analytic study of word attributes and verbal learning. *Journal of Verbal Learning and Verbal Behavior, 7,* 41–49.

Paivio, A. (1971). *Imagery and verbal processes.* New York: Holt, Rinehart, & Winston.

Paivio, A. (1986). *Mental representations: A dual coding approach.* Oxford, England: Oxford University Press.

Paivio, A., & Begg, I. (1971). Imagery and comprehension latencies as a function of sentence concreteness and structure. *Perception & Psychophysics, 10,* 408–412.

Piaget, J., & Inhelder, B. (1971). *Mental imagery in the child.* New York: Basic Book.

Prior, M. R., Cumming, G., & Hendy, J. (1984). Recognition of abstract and concrete words in a dichotic listening paradigm. *Cortex, 20,* 149–157.

Richardson, J. T. E. (1976). The effects of stimulus attributes upon latency of word recognition. *British Journal of Psychology, 67,* 315–325.

Richmond, M. G., & McNinch, G. (1977). Word learning: Concrete vs. abstract acquisition. *Perceptual and Motor Skills, 45,* 292–294.

Rinsland, H. D. (1945). *A basic vocabulary of elementary school children.* New York: Macmillan.

Roth, E. H., & Shoben, E. J. (1983). The effect of context on the structure of categories. *Cognitive Psychology, 15,* 346–378.

Rubin, D. C. (1980). 51 properties of 125 words: A unit analysis of verbal behavior. *Journal of Verbal Learning and Verbal Behavior, 19,* 736–755.

Schwanenflugel, P. J., Harnishfeger, K. K., & Stowe, R. W. (1988). Context availability and lexical decisions for abstract and concrete words. *Journal of Memory and Language, 27,* 499–520.

Schwanenflugel, P. J., & Shoben, E. J. (1983). Differential context effects in the comprehension of abstract and concrete verbal materials. *Journal of Experimental Psychology: Learning, Memory, & Cognition, 9,* 82–102.

Schwanenflugel, P. J., & Stowe, R. W. (1989). Context availability and the processing of abstract and concrete words. *Reading Research Quarterly, 24,* 114–126.

Seidenberg, M. S., Waters, G. S., Sanders, M., & Langer, P. (1984). Pre- and post-lexical loci of contextual effects on word recognition. *Memory & Cognition, 12,* 315–328.

Shoben, E. J., Wilson, T., & Schwanenflugel, P. J. (1990). *The influence of lexical primes on the processing of abstract and concrete words.* Unpublished data, University of Georgia, Athens, GA.

Smith, E. E. (1978). Theories of semantic memory. In W. K. Estes (Ed.), *Handbook of learning and cognitive processes* (Vol. 6). Hillsdale, NJ: Lawrence Erlbaum Associates.

Stanovich, K. E., & West, R. F. (1983). On priming by a sentence context. *Journal of Experimental Psychology: General, 112,* 1–36.

Svartvik, J., & Quirk, R. (1980). *A corpus of English conversation.* Lund, Sweden: Gleerup.

Tanenhaus, M. K., Carlson, G. N., & Seidenberg, M. S. (1985). Do listeners compute linguistic representations? In A. Zwicky, L. Kartunnen, & D. Dowty (Eds.), *Natural language parsing: Psycholinguistic, theoretical, and computational perspectives* (pp. 359–408). Cambridge: Cambridge University Press.

Thorndike, E. L., & Lorge, I. (1944). *The teacher's word book of 30,000 words.* New York: Teachers College, Columbia University.

Wattenmaker, W. D., & Shoben, E. J. (1987). Context and the recallability of concrete and abstract sentences. *Journal of Experimental Psychology: Learning, Memory, and Cognition, 13,* 140–150.

West, A., Martindale, C., & Sutton-Smith, B. (1985). Age trends in the content of children's spontaneous fantasy narratives. *Genetic Psychology Monographs, 111,* 389–405.

West, R. F., & Stanovich, K. E. (1988). How much of sentence priming is word priming? *Bulletin of the Psychonomic Society, 26,* 1–4.

Whaley, C. P. (1978). Word-nonword classification times. *Journal of Verbal Learning and Verbal Behavior, 17,* 143–154.

Wolf, M., & Gow, D. (1986). A longitudinal investigation of gender differences in language and reading development. *First Language, 6,* 81–110.

Yore, L. D., & Ollila, L. O. (1985). Cognitive development, sex, and abstractness in grade one word recognition. *Journal of Educational Research, 78,* 242–247.

10 Interpretation of Word Meanings by the Cerebral Hemispheres: One is Not Enough

Christine Chiarello
Syracuse University

INTRODUCTION

The field of cognitive psychology has had a great deal of success in understanding the mind as an abstract information processing system, without regard to its actual instantiation in the human nervous system. One benefit of this approach is that principles articulated in terms of information can then be implemented on any sort of hardware, and this surely has facilitated the rapid development of artificial intelligence systems. However, as psychologists, our primary interest is in human cognition which is mediated by a specific piece of hardware, the brain. Because our brain is the result of evolutionary pressures that select for biological fitness and reproductive success we can expect that the human mind will have some design features that may not be predictable from an information engineering standpoint. Thus, the most elegant model of some cognitive process, even if it predicts a range of behavioral data, may not be the right model unless it is also *neurologically plausible*.

A neurologically plausible model is one which, in addition to explaining the relevant experimental data, is consistent with what is known about the structure and function of the human nervous system. One approach is to develop models that take into account the massively parallel architecture of the brain (Rumelhart & McClelland, 1986; Seidenberg & McClelland, 1989). Such models are plausible at the level of microstructure since both the model and the brain consist of huge numbers of basic processing elements which are richly interconnected and function in parallel. Thus far such connectionist models of cognition make no claim about instantiation in the brain: the proposed architectures at present cannot

251

be mapped onto actual neural circuits. Nevertheless, it is likely that such models have a better "fit" than those which do not explicitly posit parallelism.

One can also take a systems approach to neurological plausibility by focusing on the macrostructural level. The human brain has a high degree of regional specificity, and brain lesions typically impair some functions while leaving others unaffected. The functional dissociations that occur after brain injury, or when different anatomical systems (such as the two cerebral hemispheres) are selectively stimulated, reveal separable components of the cognitive system, and also provide clues to their instantiation in the brain (see Kosslyn, 1987; Posner, Inhoff, Friedrich, & Cohen, 1987 for examples). Theoretical models that are neurologically plausible will be able to accommodate such distinctions in a motivated way.

This chapter employs the macrostructural approach to neurological plausibility by considering how the study of cerebral hemisphere asymmetry can contribute to the psychology of word meanings. The left and right cerebral hemispheres, although grossly symmetrical in appearance, are known to differ biochemically (Glick, Ross, & Hough, 1982), in the size of intrahemispheric regions such as the planum temporale (Geschwind & Levitsky, 1968), in the ratio of grey-to-white matter (Gur et al., 1980), in cytoarchitecture (Galaburda, Sanides, & Geschwind, 1978), and perhaps also in their sensitivity to various hormones (Geschwind & Galaburda, 1987). It would be surprising if this neural differentiation had no consequences for cognitive functions (such as language) which are cortically mediated.

It is argued here that each hemisphere has its own semantic system and that both are required during on-line comprehension for the proper interpretation of word meanings in context. The current data suggest that presenting a word initiates parallel, but distinct, word recognition and semantic activation processes in each hemisphere. As these processes unfold over time, different meanings may become available to each hemisphere. I argue that the partial separation of these semantic systems in different hemispheres allows for the segregation of potentially conflicting operations. This design may permit a wider range of semantic processes to be flexibly deployed in thinking and language comprehension than would be possible with a single semantic processor.

I begin by mentioning some relevant historical background and then describe the visual half-field method for investigating cerebral asymmetries in neurologically normal persons. Next, I review what has been learned about hemisphere differences in word recognition and semantic priming using such techniques. This leads to a proposal about hemisphere-specific semantic interpretation processes which argues for an important role for the right cerebral hemisphere. Data from right-hemisphere lesioned patients is then examined from this point of view. Finally, I offer some speculations about how the existence of two distinct, but interacting, semantic systems may permit a range of linguistic and cognitive processes resulting from the access to word meanings.

CEREBRAL ASYMMETRY FOR LANGUAGE

Study of the neurological basis of language processing flowered in the 19th century with the investigation of brain injured patients (Broca, 1863; Wernicke, 1874). Since frank aphasias occurred with overwhelming frequency after unilateral left, but not right, hemisphere damage, it seemed obvious that only one hemisphere (the left) was responsible for language processing. This view was unchallenged for more than a century until the split-brain operation of Sperry and colleagues permitted the left and right hemispheres to be tested independently (Sperry, Gazzaniga, & Bogen, 1969). Investigation of the surgically isolated hemispheres soon revealed that while the left hemisphere alone could produce speech (Gazzaniga & Hillyard, 1971), the right hemisphere had a surprising capacity for word recognition and semantic interpretation (Zaidel, 1976, 1978, 1982). For example, using manual rather than vocal responses, Zaidel demonstrated that the isolated right hemisphere could perform lexical decisions, and comprehend a variety of word meanings as well as some basic sentences. Simple semantic judgments can also be performed by the disconnected right hemisphere (Sidtis & Gazzaniga, 1983).

Although in every case the linguistic ability of the left hemisphere of the split-brain exceeded that of the right hemisphere, such data provided a powerful demonstration that the right hemisphere had at least rudimentary lexical-semantic capacities. For the first time it became plausible to entertain the idea that the human mind consists of not one, but two linguistic semantic systems. Such findings produced a new and intriguing set of questions for neurological investigations of language. Which linguistic processes are strictly lateralized to the left hemisphere, and which are equally available to either half-brain? Are there any language functions that depend on unique right hemisphere processing? How are these variously lateralized subprocesses coordinated during ongoing language use? The position to be articulated here is that the answers to these questions are important not only for understanding the neurobiology of language, but also for the development of models of cognition which attain neurological plausibility.

The split-brain studies also provided an experimental paradigm that could be used to investigate hemisphere asymmetries in neurologically intact persons. The anatomy of the visual system is such that stimuli presented in the left half-field of vision (LVF) are directly transmitted only to the right visual cortex, and vice versa. Thus, by lateralizing visual input to one half-field one can selectively stimulate the opposite cerebral hemisphere. In the intact brain lateralized information will eventually be available to either hemisphere via the cerebral commissures and subcortical structures. However, the "head-start" on processing afforded the directly stimulated hemisphere provides a glimpse at hemisphere-specific processing. When performance is qualitatively different depending on visual field (i.e., when VF interacts with some experimental variable), it is reasonable to infer that this reflects differential processing by the hemisphere of input.[1] More than a decade of visual half-field research has revealed distinctively different profiles for word recognition and semantic processing in each cerebral hemisphere (reviewed by Chiarello, 1988).

WORD RECOGNITION IN THE INTACT HEMISPHERES

It is not surprising that word recognition is faster and more accurate when stimuli are directly presented to the left hemisphere for lexical decision or pronunciation responses. Several findings suggest that much of the left hemisphere advantage can be attributed to poorer word encoding processes used by the right hemisphere. Moscovitch (1983) investigated noise and pattern masking functions for words displayed in left or right visual fields. With unstructured noise masks similar functions were obtained in each VF/hemisphere. However, words presented to the right hemisphere required a greater stimulus-mask interval to escape the effects of a pattern mask than did the same words presented to the left hemisphere. Moscovitch (1983) argued that while early sensory processes were comparable over the hemispheres, the right hemisphere required more time than the left to extract the perceptual features needed for word recognition.

Word length also has differential effects across the hemispheres. Over the range of lengths typically used in visual half-field research, left hemisphere performance is unaltered, while right hemisphere word recognition declines as word length increases (Young & Ellis, 1985; Ellis, Young, & Anderson, 1988). When nonwords are presented, however, comparable word length effects are found in each hemisphere. Young and Ellis (1985) were able to rule out acuity gradients and other nonhemispheric interpretations of their findings. Thus, it appears that while words are rapidly recognized in the left hemisphere as lexical units, right hemisphere word recognition depends on serial letter identification processes. This view is supported by the absence of word superiority effects in the right hemisphere (Besner, 1983; Kreuger, 1975). Whereas lexical context assists letter identification in the left hemisphere, this is not found in the right hemisphere. This suggests that lexical codes are not available to the right hemisphere before letter identification has been completed. In other words, top-down feedback from lexical to orthographic units (McClelland & Rumelhart, 1981) is only present in the left hemisphere.

Thus, initial word identification processes differ in the two hemispheres, and put the right hemisphere at a disadvantage. In contrast, word frequency effects are comparable for words input to either hemisphere (Boles, 1983; Bradshaw & Gates, 1978). It can be argued that word frequency affects lexical access (Mon-

---

[1]If language information presented to the right hemisphere were transferred to the left hemisphere for processing, this should entail a constant increment in accuracy/response time and thus no VF interactions (see Hellige, 1983; Zaidel, 1983).

sell, Doyle, & Haggard, 1989) as well as post-access processes (Balota & Chumbley, 1984, 1985). Given the repeated failures to find visual field X frequency interactions, over a range of experimental conditions (see Chiarello, 1988), it is reasonable to conclude that frequency-dependent aspects of lexical processing, whatever their locus, do not differ regardless of which hemisphere initiates word recognition processes.

Hemisphere differences are present, however, in some decision/response processes. There is little evidence that the right hemisphere can produce speech and thus, even though words may be identified by the right hemisphere, pronunciation will require left hemisphere participation. It is not clear when the left hemisphere is accessed to pronounce a word which has been presented to the right hemisphere, but some findings suggest that this occurs very late (Chiarello, Nuding, & Pollock, 1988). With respect to lexical decision, hemisphere differences are present in both detectability (d') and decision bias (beta) (Chiarello, et al., 1988; Chiarello, Senehi, Soulier, 1986). The latter finding implies that the outcome of lexical access process is evaluated differently by each hemisphere, with the left hemisphere employing a laxer criterion for lexicality.

Even this cursory review suggests that word recognition processes proceed differently in each hemisphere (for a more thorough consideration of these issues see Chiarello, 1988). With this background we can now turn to the issue of semantic access in each hemisphere.

SEMANTIC PRIMING IN LEFT AND RIGHT HEMISPHERES

Most of the data regarding semantic processing in the intact hemispheres comes from studies employing single word priming paradigms. Virtually all studies have used lexical decision rather than pronunciation tasks in order to minimize any requirement for left hemisphere processing of words presented to the LVF/RH. While there are numerous theories of semantic priming (Neely, 1990), nearly all acknowledge at least two processes that can account for such effects in lexical decision: automatic spreading activation and post-access semantic integration[2] (but see Ratcliff & McKoon, 1988 for a recent alternative). Priming

---

[2]Neely and colleagues (Neely, 1990; Neely, Keefe, & Ross, 1989) have recently shown that it is possible to separate the effects of semantic expectancy and post-access semantic integration in lexical priming paradigms. Thus, there may well be at least three different semantic priming mechanisms (automatic activation, expectancy, and post-semantic integration) potentially operating in lexical decision. However, none of the VF priming investigations conducted to date was designed to differentiate between expectancy and post-access processing. That is, whenever the relatedness proportion was high (low) the nonword ratio was likewise high (low). Thus, although I continue to refer to nonautomatic priming as due to semantic integration processes, it should be kept in mind that expectancy and/or attentional processing may also be contributing to these effects.

attributed to automatic activation is thought to occur as a consequence of the connections between related meanings in a semantic network. Recognition of the prime word activates its meaning(s) and this activation spreads to related meanings, temporarily making them more accessible.[3] In addition, recognition of a semantic relationship between prime and target strings provides good evidence that the target is a word. Thus semantic relatedness can influence lexical decision performance after lexical-semantic access but prior to the response. Although post-access priming processes sometimes have been viewed as an "artifact" of the lexical decision task, semantic processing does not end with access to word meanings. The fact that post-access priming occurs at all may reflect the ubiquity of semantic integration processes in normal language comprehension. Therefore it seems reasonable to assume that at least some aspects of normal semantic integration are observable using single word priming paradigms.

While there is no foolproof way to separate the effects of automatic activation and post-access integration in lexical decision priming, there are some conditions under which post-access effects can be minimized. For example, when the primes are pattern-masked, when there is a low proportion of related trials in the experiment, or when the prime-target stimulus onset asynchrony (SOA) is very brief, priming should be largely due to the automatic activation of related word meanings. On the other hand, when primes are clearly visible, and long SOAs or high relatedness proportions are used, more strategic post-access processes are likely to contribute to the observed priming effect. When one differentiates those visual field priming experiments that should primarily measure automatic meaning activation from those which should include a prominent contribution of post-access processing, a number of interesting findings emerge. I will consider each set of findings separately before discussing how the combined results converge on the view that parallel, yet distinctive, semantic processes occur in each hemisphere as word meanings are accessed and integrated for further processing.

In all the studies reviewed here, a RVF/left hemisphere advantage in response time (RT) and accuracy was obtained for lexical decision, reflecting the left hemisphere's more efficient word recognition processes. Despite this, priming effects are not invariably larger in the left hemisphere. In fact, not one study that putatively investigated automatic meaning activation by employing either brief pattern-masked primes (Marcel & Patterson, 1978), a low proportion of related primes (Chiarello, 1985; Chiarello, Senehi, & Nuding, 1987; Chiarello, Burgess, Richards, & Pollock, 1990; Eglin, 1987), or brief SOAs (Burgess & Simpson, 1988—for dominant associates; Eglin, 1987; Michimata, 1987; Walker & Ceci, 1985) obtained greater semantic priming for words presented to the left hemisphere. Although most of these studies reported equivalent priming in each

---

[3]This description begs the question as to whether meanings are best represented as concept nodes or in a more distributed fashion as weighted sets of semantic features. Although this is an important theoretical issue, for our purposes either interpretation will suffice as a first approximation.

VF, in three cases significantly greater priming was found in the LVF/right hemisphere (Chiarello, 1985; Chiarello et al., 1990; Michimata, 1987). Examining the latter three studies more closely allows us to draw some interesting inferences about similarities and differences in automatic meaning activation in the two hemispheres.

Experimenters generally select stimuli for priming tasks from published word association norms (e.g., Postman & Keppel, 1970). By definition the word pairs will be highly associated, but many will also share a large number of other semantic properties. For example, the pairs CAT-DOG, DOCTOR-NURSE, and ARM-LEG are members of the same superordinate categories, and have a high degree of semantic feature overlap. However, in my 1985 study I happened to use as stimuli words which shared category membership, but were not strongly associated (e.g., KING-DUKE, ARM-NOSE), and obtained substantial priming (with low proportion related) only for words presented to the RH. Several years later Michimata (1987) used these stimuli, as well as some additional pairs, and also obtained significant priming (with 200 ms SOA) only for words presented to the RH. In contrast, all other previous studies which had obtained equal hemispheric priming used "associated" words. Such findings imply that categorically related, but nonassociated meanings are automatically activated only in the right hemisphere.

Chiarello et al. (1990) performed the obvious parametric experiment, using a low proportion of related primes, in which the same subjects were shown categorical associates (CAT-DOG), noncategorical associates (BEE-HONEY), and categorical nonassociates (DOG-GOAT). Priming in this study was characterized by facilitation for related targets without inhibition for unrelated targets (Posner & Snyder, 1975). While CAT-DOG priming was equivalent over VFs/hemispheres, DOG-GOAT priming was only obtained in the LVF/right hemisphere. These results were also replicated with a pronunciation task. Our findings indicate that a different set of meanings is activated when a word is selectively presented to the left or right hemisphere. In the left hemisphere other members of the same category will be activated only if they are strongly related, while in the right hemisphere it appears that a wider range of category members is activated. This implies that more distantly related meanings are activated only in the right hemisphere. But what does distance refer to here?

There are at least two ways in which CAT-DOG and DOG-GOAT differ: the presence/absence of an associative relation and the amount of semantic feature overlap. For example, in addition to being associated, CAT and DOG share some properties (e.g., pets, live indoors) that DOG and GOAT do not. Fortuitously, the results of Chiarello et al. (1990) were able to distinguish between the association and feature overlap interpretations. When primes were laterally presented no priming was obtained for noncategorical associates such as BEE-HONEY (however, robust priming was obtained when these primes were centrally presented which indicates that the stimuli were not idiosyncratic). Since purely associative priming could not be obtained under our experimental conditions, it is reasonable to presume that the associative relation contributed little to the priming we observed for categorical associates such as CAT-DOG. Thus, we argue that the amount of semantic feature overlap between prime and target determines whether or not there are hemisphere differences in automatic meaning activation; primes will activate meanings with a high degree of semantic overlap in either hemisphere, but meanings with more moderate overlap will be activated only in the right hemisphere. I will consider the implications of this finding in due course. For the moment, it is sufficient to emphasize that a wider range of meanings is activated in the right than in the left hemisphere as a consequence of word recognition.

The priming results reviewed so far allow us to rule out two possible interpretations that might otherwise seem feasible. First, the finding of unique priming for some semantic relations in the LVF undermines any possibility of attributing LVF/RH word recognition in these experiments to interhemispheric transfer to the left hemisphere. If all word stimuli, regardless of VF of presentation, are processed by the left hemisphere, then it is logically impossible to obtain any linguistic effect (such as priming for nonassociated category members) for stimuli presented to the LVF/right hemisphere, unless it also occurs for stimuli directed to the RVF/left hemisphere. Yet this is exactly the result obtained in three independent studies of automatic semantic priming (Chiarello, 1985; Chiarello et al., 1990; Michimata, 1987). Thus, there is strong evidence that the effects described here are a true reflection of differential processing by left and right hemispheres.

Second, it could be argued that greater priming for words presented to the right hemisphere would be expected given its less efficient word recognition processes. It is known that semantic priming effects are larger for words that are difficult to recognize, due to visual degradation (Durgunoglu, 1988) or low frequency of occurrence (Becker, 1979), than for more easily recognized words. Since it is assumed that the semantic context supplied by the prime provides greater benefit to the more inaccessible stimuli, it follows that words processed by the right hemisphere should obtain more priming than those processed by the left hemisphere. However this view predicts that greater RH priming should occur across all prime relations. Yet we have seen that there is no evidence for greater RH priming when strongly related primes (categorical associates) are used. Thus, it appears that the differential hemisphere priming effect is telling us something about the semantic organization of the hemispheres, rather than being a by-product of less specialized right hemisphere word decoding processes.

Thus far I have reviewed evidence that, while meanings are automatically activated in both hemispheres, a wider range of meanings is facilitated in the right hemisphere. However, the mere activation of related meanings is not sufficient for adequate comprehension of a word, nor can the integration of word meanings in context be accomplished via simple activation processes. There must be some additional processes which select for further processing only those meanings which are appropriate in the current context. This may well involve the suppression of some meanings that were initially activated. Determination of which meanings are currently appropriate requires comparison of the current word meaning to meanings accessed in the preceding context. In real world language comprehension context includes immediately preceding words as well as meanings and expectations derived from the entire discourse, and the goal of post-access processing is to build an integrated meaning representation. In single word priming paradigms, the context is necessarily more impoverished, consisting only of the preceding prime word and any expectations the subject has gleaned about the experiment itself (e.g., that prime and target words are, or are not, likely to be related). The goal of post-access processing in this case is to determine whether the target is likely to be a word.

Despite the obvious differences between these two situations it is argued here that post-access priming in the lexical decision task can reflect some of the same semantic integration processes used in natural comprehension. It is highly unlikely that subjects will, *de novo*, create unique semantic operations to assist them in the lexical decision task. It is much more likely that they will adapt normal comprehension processes to the admittedly artificial experimental situation. Thus post-access priming in lexical decision may allow us to observe some of the same processes recruited for natural language comprehension. We can now consider the results of VF priming experiments which should include more strategic post-access priming operations (i.e., those employing a high proportion of related primes/high nonword ratio and/or long SOAs—see also footnote 3). These data paint a very different picture of left and right hemisphere contributions to semantic processing than do the priming experiments reviewed above, one which suggests that the left hemisphere predominates for post-access meaning selection and integration.

Four studies have varied either proportion related (Chiarello, 1985; Chiarello et al., 1987) or SOA (Burgess & Simpson, 1988; Michimata, 1987) to contrast automatic and post-access priming mechanisms in the cerebral hemispheres. Recall that Chiarello (1985) and Michimata (1987) both obtained evidence for automatic activation of categorical nonassociates only in the RH. However, under more strategic priming conditions, both studies obtained significantly greater priming when the same stimuli were presented to the left hemisphere. In addition, while Chiarello et al. (1987) found equivalent automatic priming over VFs, when the proportion of related trials was increased priming was significantly greater in the RVF/left hemisphere (for abstract primes). These data suggest that some aspect of post-access semantic processing is performed much more efficiently by the left hemisphere.

There is some evidence to suggest that inhibition of unrelated meanings occurs only in the left hemisphere. Separation of the overall priming effect into facilitatory and inhibitory processes has been hindered by the inability to obtain a stable neutral prime condition in some VF studies (see Burgess & Simpson, 1988; Chiarello, 1985). However, both Chiarello et al. (1987) and Michimata (1987) found, as would be predicted by some theories (Neely, 1977; Posner & Snyder, 1975), that inhibition occurred only under conditions that would encourage strategic post-access priming (long SOA, high proportion related). More importantly, the inhibition was restricted to trials in which stimuli were presented to the left hemisphere. In other words, while a related prime can facilitate lexical decisions in either hemisphere, unrelated primes may inhibit performance only within the left hemisphere.

What do such findings indicate about hemisphere differences in semantic comprehension processes? Post-access theories of semantic priming (de Groot, 1984; Neely, Keefe, & Ross, 1989) claim that, following semantic access, the meaning of prime and target strings are compared to determine whether any relationship is present. If so, a rapid "word" response can be made; if not, additional processing is required before an accurate lexical decision can be made. Thus processing is slowed (inhibited) when no relation is detected. Similar processes may well play a role in ongoing language comprehension. As word meanings are accessed they must be integrated with prior meanings in the discourse. This should occur rapidly whenever the meaning(s) of the current word are congruent with the context. However, whenever the meaning of the current word is inconsistent with the prior context, additional processing will be needed either to revise the discourse model or to reinterpret the current word. In either case processing will be slowed (inhibited) when the current word is not related to previously accessed meanings.

Thus it is not too far-fetched to suggest that left hemisphere post-access processing may function to integrate meanings within the current model of the discourse and to detect semantic anomalies. In contrast, within the right hemisphere semantic integration may not occur, or it may occur in such a way that irrelevant meanings do not disrupt processing. Note that I am not claiming that post-access processing does not occur in the right hemisphere. Indeed, the word recognition evidence reviewed earlier suggests that the right hemisphere employs different criteria for making word/nonword decisions than does the LH. Rather, it appears that semantic relatedness does not influence lexical decision criteria to any great extent in the right hemisphere. By extrapolation, we can conjecture that obligatory integration of the meanings of successive words in context does not take place within the right hemisphere.

So far I have discussed post-access semantic processes as if their only role is to integrate a single activated meaning with prior context. However, most words have more than one meaning. Studies that use ambiguous words as primes suggest that all meanings are initially activated, but that eventually only the dominant or contextually appropriate sense remains (Seidenberg, Tanenhaus, Leiman, & Bienkowski, 1982; Swinney, 1979). This implies that, following exhaustive access, some mechanism exists to select the most appropriate meaning and suppress irrelevant alternative meanings so that only the relevant sense is integrated with prior context (see also Simpson & Kellas, 1988; Simpson, Kreuger, & Beyer, 1989). An important study by Burgess and Simpson (1988) indicates that the cerebral hemispheres are differentially involved in the activation and selection of ambiguous word meanings.

In their study, ambiguous homograph primes (e.g., BANK) were paired with targets related to either dominant (MONEY) or subordinate (RIVER) meanings. SOAs of 35 and 750 ms were used. For targets presented to the right hemisphere, at the brief SOA priming was obtained for the dominant associate only, while at the longer SOA both meanings were primed. In contrast, when targets were presented to the left hemisphere both dominant and subordinate senses were initially primed.[4] However, with the 750 ms SOA only the dominant meaning was facilitated in the left hemisphere, while the subordinate meaning was inhibited (i.e., related subordinate targets were recognized more slowly than unrelated targets in the RVF/LH). In other words, at the longest SOA the subordinate meaning was activated in the right hemisphere, but suppressed in the left hemisphere! Furthermore, evidence for meaning selection was only obtained in the left hemisphere. At a relatively late time in processing the RH maintained both meanings, while the LH had selected one (dominant) meaning and inhibited the other.

The Burgess and Simpson (1988) results confirm and extend the view of hemispheric-specific semantic processing articulated here. First, their findings provide additional evidence that, at some moments of processing, different meanings may be activated in each cerebral hemisphere. At the 750 ms SOA, subordinate meanings were facilitated in the right hemisphere, but inhibited in the left hemisphere. This implies that a meaning can be facilitated in one hemisphere at the same time that it is inhibited in the other, which provides compelling support for the existence of separate semantic systems in each hemisphere. A single meaning representation, whatever its locus, cannot be in two contradictory states at the same time. However, such a result would be possible if the two hemispheres represent parallel, and partially independent, semantic systems. Below I discuss some situations in which it may be advantageous to permit such conflicting semantic processes to coexist.

Second, the Burgess and Simpson (1988) data suggest that the time course of meaning resolution differs over the cerebral hemispheres. Their findings imply

---

[4]Note that, at the 35 ms SOA, subordinate meanings were activated in the left, but not the right, hemisphere. This is the only case I know of in which a meaning was automatically available in the left, but not the right, hemisphere. However, this does not indicate a slower onset of meaning activation in general in the RH. When dominant associates (Burgess & Simpson, 1988, 35 ms SOA) or primary associates (Eglin, 1987, 0 ms SOA) are used, equivalent priming is obtained in either VF at the shortest SOAs tested. Thus, if there is a hemisphere difference in the rate at which semantic activation builds up, this may only affect more weakly associated meanings (see Burgess & Simpson, 1988 for further discussion).

that the left hemisphere makes a rapid commitment to a particular meaning. In contrast, the right hemisphere appears to maintain alternate meanings for a longer time period. At present we do not know whether the right hemisphere maintains multiple senses indefinitely (i.e., until passive decay processes reduce activation of both meanings to baseline) or whether RH meaning selection ultimately occurs at some later time. In the latter case there are two possibilities. The RH may, like the LH, eventually select the dominant or most contextually appropriate sense. However, since RH selection, if it occurs at all, is delayed until after the LH has selected a meaning, the RH might also function to selectively maintain just those meanings that the LH has selected against. In the case of ambiguous homographs this would result in RH selective maintenance of subordinate senses. Investigations similar to that of Burgess and Simpson, but employing SOAs of 1000 ms or more, will be needed to distinguish among these possibilities. In any case the current findings suggest that meaning selection occurs rapidly in the left, but not the right, hemisphere.

Third, the ambiguity results confirm those reviewed earlier, that left hemisphere predominance for semantic processing is not tied to automatic meaning activation, but rather emerges after lexical-semantic access has occurred. It is reasonable to propose that left hemisphere processes are important for the selection, from among a set of activated meanings, of the most relevant sense in a given context, and the inhibition of irrelevant meanings. If this is the case, we might also expect to see LH predominance for other effects which result from the necessity to select one response from others that are simultaneously activated. Perhaps it is not surprising, then, that Stroop color-word interference is significantly larger for stimuli presented to the LH (Hugdahl & Franzon, 1985; Schmit & Davis, 1974; Tsao, Feustelk, & Soseos, 1981). This result implies that activation of an irrelevant color word interferes with selection of the appropriate color name response primarily in the left hemisphere. In addition, Lupker and Sanders (1982) demonstrated that picture-word interference in the RVF (i.e., LH) was potentiated when the distractor word was semantically related to the picture, whereas in the LVF (i.e., RH) interference due to a semantically related word was no greater than that observed for any letter string. This suggests that interference based on competing semantic information occurs primarily in the LH. Semantic interference effects would not be expected to take place in the RH if, as hypothesized, selection from among several activated meanings does not occur here.

In summary, the semantic priming results, taken as a whole, suggest that there are important differences in how the two cerebral hemispheres process word meanings. Under conditions that should allow us to observe automatic meaning activation, equivalent hemispheric priming is obtained as long as very strongly related stimuli are used. However, more weakly related stimuli (such as non-associated category members) yield greater priming in the right hemisphere. In contrast, greater left hemisphere priming is obtained under experimental conditions which encourage strategic and/or post-access prime processing, and inhibition for unrelated words may only occur within the left hemisphere. When primes are ambiguous words, priming of subordinate meanings is maintained for a longer period in the right hemisphere, than in the left hemisphere where subordinate meanings are rapidly suppressed. It is now appropriate to place these findings in a broader framework.

HEMISPHERIC PROCESSING OF WORD MEANINGS: A SYNTHESIS

If, as suggested here, different processes unfold in each hemisphere as word meanings are activated, selected, and integrated with prior context, then it is necessary to articulate how the two semantic systems are coordinated in ongoing language comprehension. In this section I attempt to synthesize the experimental results reviewed earlier with this goal in mind. Much of this discussion is admittedly speculative. However, filling in the available empirical sketch allows one to derive predictions for further research. I then examine the literature on semantic processing in right hemisphere lesioned patients from this perspective. If the portrait drawn here is grossly accurate, certain language disturbances should occur when the right hemisphere semantic system is disrupted.[5]

When a word is encountered in some linguistic context the following processes are hypothesized to occur in each hemisphere. In the left hemisphere specialized word encoding processes are available to rapidly resolve the perceptual input as a lexical string. Semantic access results in the automatic activation of all meanings of the word, as well as meanings that are strongly related to the target concept. However, based on the current context, one meaning is rapidly selected and integrated into the current discourse model. Once meaning selection has occurred, other plausible candidates are actively suppressed (i.e., their semantic representations are inhibited). Semantic integration will proceed smoothly as long as the selected meaning "fits" with the given discourse model. However, an anomaly will be detected when the selected meaning does not fit (as, for example, with a garden path sentence). In order to recover, some semantic reanalysis would be needed. If one were relying solely on the resources of the left hemisphere, this would require the access to meanings which had just been inhibited. It's unclear what would be required to "disinhibit" a semantic representation, but it would presumably be a rather costly process.

Now consider what is hypothesized to be occurring simultaneously in the right

---

[5]Patients with unilateral LH injury are likely to have multiple linguistic deficits, involving phonology and syntax as well as the lexical and semantic functions under consideration here. For this reason, it is more useful to examine data from RH-injured patients, because their linguistic dysfunctions are much more circumscribed.

hemisphere. Due to the lack of specialized lexical encoding processes, perceptual analysis of words will be much less efficient than that of the LH. Nevertheless RH word recognition will entail the automatic activation of multiple word meanings (although subordinate senses may not be available as rapidly as dominant senses, see Burgess and Simpson, 1988). A rather broad range of related meanings will also be activated, including concepts only moderately related to the target concept. There is presently little evidence for RH meaning selection. Rather it appears that alternate meanings are maintained for some indefinite period, and decay rather than inhibition may be the primary mechanism for "clearing" the semantic system. Furthermore, semantic integration either does not occur or occurs in such a way that semantic "misfits" are not discerned. Thus, semantic anomalies would be difficult to detect.[6] The right hemisphere, then, while it may have access to a quite wide range of word meanings, lacks the mechanisms needed to *build* the one semantic model that best fits the current context. However, given the right hemisphere propensity to maintain a wide set of related meanings, it is possible that the right hemisphere may play some role in *maintaining* the discourse model which is constructed on-line in the left hemisphere.

Thus, the semantic consequences of word recognition may be quite different in each hemisphere: the RH maintains a range of plausible meanings at the same time that the LH has selected for one particular meaning (and selected *against* other potentially relevant meanings). It is not controversial to suggest that the left hemisphere is required for high level comprehension processes. However, the analysis offered here suggests that a "blind spot" may result from the LH's rapid commitment to a single interpretation. To the extent that semantic selection produces the suppression of discarded candidate meanings, it will be difficult to recover such meanings if it becomes necessary to revise an initial interpretation. Furthermore, it is difficult to see how such a system could mediate those aspects of comprehension that require the simultaneous consideration of more than one plausible meaning. Verbal humor, for example, often turns on the ability to interpret the same message in two inconsistent ways.

However, if alternate interpretations are maintained by the right hemisphere, it would not be necessary to reaccess representations inhibited in the LH in order to revise an interpretation. A semantic anomaly detected by the LH could be repaired by accessing candidates still activated in the RH. In addition, nonselective right hemisphere semantics seems particularly well-suited to the comprehension of words/messages where several levels of meaning must be simultaneously

---

[6]This position is not contradicted by the finding that N400 is larger when recorded over the RH (Kutas, Van Petten, & Besson, 1988). Although this evoked potential component is sensitive to the presence of semantic and nonsemantic incongruities (Kutas & Van Petten, 1988), there is no direct evidence that it reflects anomaly *detection*. It is equally plausible that it indexes incongruity *resolution* processes. The latter interpretation is more compatible with the view articulated here.

considered. Because the right hemisphere appears to maintain word meanings for some indefinite period, it may also be involved in the continued activation of discourse level meaning. Finally, we might expect the RH to mediate the availability of concepts that are somewhat related to words heard or read, but that are not directly relevant to understanding the current message. (Recall that words with only moderate semantic feature overlap were automatically activated in the right, but not the left, hemisphere.) In this case, the RH would not be contributing to language comprehension in the strictest sense, but rather to cognitive processes which may be triggered by the linguistic message (i.e., keeping related concepts "in mind" even if they are not necessary to actually decode the linguistic message).

Thus I am arguing that each cerebral hemisphere plays a role in the interpretation of word meanings, broadly construed. The current proposal hypothesizes that an extensive range of semantic processes arises from the dynamic interaction between two, potentially conflicting, semantic systems. To date there is no technique available that would permit us to track which semantic system is being utilized at a given moment in processing. However, current experimental data casts doubt on one potential interpretation. One might argue that, since the left hemisphere is specialized for most linguistic processes, it dominates in all linguistic behavior. Semantic processing that we observe via selective stimulation of the right hemisphere, then, at best would represent a potentiality that is never realized in normal language comprehension (i.e., when both hemispheres have equal access to stimulus information). However, studies of hemispheric metacontrol indicate that the most efficient hemisphere does not always dominate performance, even when both hemispheres have equal access to the stimuli and response systems (Hellige, Jonsson, & Michimata, 1988; Levy & Trevarthen, 1976). Such findings raise the more interesting possibility that, under some conditions, the less specialized hemisphere contributes uniquely to behavior *precisely because it is not so highly specialized.* In the present case, less precise RH semantic processing may be valuable whenever rapid LH semantic integration and selection processes fail to produce a sufficiently rich semantic representation.

Although it is not possible to test the more dynamic aspects of the present proposal, we can consider whether right hemisphere brain injury produces impairment consistent with the above view. Patients with RH injury should behave as if the LH semantic system were functioning without some or all of the support provided by RH semantics. Specifically, we would expect such patients to have difficulty in any situation requiring semantic reanalysis, that is, whenever an initial interpretation requires revision. We would also expect difficulty in ability to appreciate ambiguity, and other aspects of language which may depend on the continued activation of multiple meanings. We can now examine the literature on RH injured patients to determine whether such effects are present.

SEMANTIC INTERPRETATION
IN RH-LESIONED PATIENTS

Patients with RH brain injury do not present with obvious linguistic difficulties. Their speech is fluent and grammatical, and they do not differ significantly from normal on standardized reading and auditory comprehension tests. Nevertheless, investigators have noted subtle alterations in semantic/pragmatic aspects of language unlike those which characterize LH-injured aphasic patients. A review of the literature on language interpretation after RH-injury reveals three, partially overlapping deficits:[7] abnormalities in the interpretation of linguistic units which have alternate meanings, an inability to revise an initial interpretation, and a more difficult to characterize deficit which seems to involve a failure to use broad contextual information in the interpretation of narratives and other types of connected discourse. After first reviewing the evidence for each of these deficits, I attempt to integrate this data with the theoretical proposals offered earlier. It should be noted, however, that markedly different paradigms have been used to investigate semantic processing in the intact and lesioned hemispheres. Therefore, any attempt to integrate findings across these populations must necessarily take place at a rather abstract level of analysis.

The most widely documented linguistic deficit that accompanies RH-injury involves the processing of single words, phrases, and narratives that have multiple meanings, particularly when these forms can have literal as well as figurative interpretations. Brownell, Potter, Michelow, and Gardner (1984) examined the processing of adjectives such as "warm" which have connotative as well as denotative senses. A clustering analysis revealed that while normal individuals were sensitive to both dimensions, RH-lesioned patients (henceforth RH patients) relied almost exclusively on the denotative meaning in making similarity judgments. (LH patients showed the converse, with near exclusive reliance on connotative meaning.) In a subsequent study (Brownell, Simpson, Bihrle, Potter, & Gardner, 1990), word triads consisting of an ambiguous word ("kid"), a synonym of its subordinate meaning ("goat"), and a nonsimilar associate of its dominant meaning ("schoolhouse") were presented and subjects were asked to select the two words that were most similar in meaning. In contrast to normal controls, RH patients were impaired at grouping the ambiguous word with its subordinate synonym. In addition, this impairment was significantly worse when the ambiguous word was an adjective with a metaphoric alternate meaning (e.g., "dull" was paired more frequently with "butter knife" than with "stupid" by these patients). At a minimum these findings indicate that connotative, meta-

---

[7]To date there is insufficient data to localize any of these symptoms to particular regions within the RH. Yet it is unlikely that the RH deficits reflect non-specific symptoms of brain injury in general, because such deficits are not seen in patients with unilateral LH injury.

phoric, and/or subordinate meanings are much less salient when the right hemisphere is dysfunctional.

Similar deficits have been uncovered in the interpretation of phrasal metaphors and idioms. When presented with phrases such as "He has a heavy heart" (Winner & Gardner, 1977) or "He's living high on the hog" (Van Lancker & Kempler, 1987), RH patients were more likely than LH patients or controls to select pictures representing the literal, rather than figurative, interpretation to represent the meaning of the phrase. Furthermore, even when supporting context is given, in the form of a preceding short story that should bias the figurative meaning of idioms such as "face the music," RH patients were significantly more likely than LH patients or controls to select the incorrect literal interpretation (Myers & Linebaugh, 1981).

RH patients are also impaired in the correct interpretation of sarcastic remarks (Tompkins & Mateer, 1985). In this case tone of voice was used to convey sarcastic intent. RH patients were unable to discriminate the intent of positive statements read with normal or sarcastic intonation. In a subsequent experiment, the sarcastic remark was preceded by a paragraph which (for normal subjects) biased a literal or sarcastic interpretation of the final comment. Once again, even with a supporting context, RH patients were unable to appreciate that the interpretation of an utterance could be the opposite of its literal meaning. As in the studies reviewed above, messages with "double meanings" present inordinate difficulty when the right cerebral hemisphere is dysfunctional.

Finally, RH injury prevents the proper interpretation of indirect requests such as "Can you close the window?". RH patients were presented with short vignettes which concluded with such questions and a response, and were asked to judge whether the given response was appropriate (Foldi, 1987; see also Hirst, LeDoux, & Stein, 1984). Some of the questions were to be interpreted as direct requests, and others as indirect requests. RH patients performed normally in judging direct requests, but unlike LH patients and controls, they preferred literal responses to the indirect requests. In a somewhat different task, subjects heard a paragraph that biased the reading of a final question as a literal or indirect request, and were asked to select the proper response from four alternatives (Weylman, Brownell, Roman, & Gardner, 1989). In this study, RH patients were much less likely than normal controls to use the paragraph context to correctly determine whether literal or indirect readings were appropriate.

Ambiguous words, connotations, metaphors, idioms, sarcasm, and indirect requests represent an eclectic set of linguistic forms. Yet they constitute a class in that each possesses multiple, and sometimes contradictory, levels of meaning. Consideration of multiple levels of meaning also becomes important when an initial interpretation of an utterance or discourse must be revised in light of subsequent, inconsistent information. Such reanalysis requires at least two different processes to be successful. First, there must be some mechanism which detects an anomaly or inconsistency. Second, the anomaly must be repaired, presumably by considering viable alternate interpretations. A number of studies document reanalysis deficits after RH injury, and point to the second process as the locus of the impairment.

Perhaps the strongest evidence for a reanalysis deficit comes from a study utilizing two sentence "stories" (Brownell, Potter, Bihrle, & Gardner, 1986). The stories were constructed such that the two sentences in conjunction made one interpretation likely, while one of the sentences, in isolation, would encourage a different interpretation. (Ex.: "Barbara became too bored to finish the history book. She had already spent five years writing it.") The position of the misleading sentence was varied over the items. When the misleading information was presented first (as in the above example), RH patients, unlike controls, made many more errors in answering true/false questions about the story. Their errors were indicative of a rigidity of interpretation, in that they could not revise the interpretation implied by the first, misleading sentence. It is important to note that RH patients do not have inference deficits per se. Such patients are able to make bridging inferences, as long as these do not require reinterpretation (e.g., Joanette & Goulet, 1987; McDonald & Wales, 1986). In a related vein, Tompkins and Mateer (1985) noted that RH patients could infer a character's implicit attitude (positive or negative) when it was not directly stated. The same patients could not, however, correctly interpret a character's attitude when a final statement, in its literal form, contradicted expectations built up from earlier information.[8] In such cases, the final statement is best interpreted sarcastically. RH patients apparently could not draw this inference because they could not revise their original literal interpretation of the final comment.

A reanalysis deficit can also be found in studies of verbal humor processing. Brownell, Birhle and colleagues have discussed impairments of humor interpretation in RH patients within a two process model of humor comprehension (Birhle, Brownell, Powelson, & Gardner, 1986; Bihrle, Brownell, & Gardner, 1988; Brownell, Michel, Powelson, & Gardner, 1983). The first process requires the detection of a discrepancy between expectations built up by the body of the joke which are then violated by the punchline (i.e., surprise). The second process requires a revision of one's interpretation in order to resolve the incongruity. This must involve finding an alternate meaning for the originally presented information which will then be coherent with the punchline. In a series of experiments these investigators localized the RH humor impairment to the second process. Subjects were given the body of a joke and asked to select, from among several alternatives, the appropriate punchline. Included among the choices were nonsequitur endings which preserved the element of surprise, but did not cohere with

---

[8]In this study (Tompkins & Mateer, 1985, Exp. II), subjects read paragraphs. Thus no intonation cues were present. In order to correctly interpret the final sarcastic comment one must discard its literal interpretation, and reinterpret it as having the opposite meaning.

the preceding context. The RH patients were much more likely to select the nonsequitur endings than were LH patients or normal controls. They appeared to realize that jokes required a surprising ending, but they were unable to forge a reinterpretation of the message that would make the punchline the correct choice.

There is also some evidence that the RH reanalysis deficit extends to the (re)assignment of syntactic roles, which represent the scaffolding upon which sentence meaning is built. Right and left hemisphere injured patients were given a complete sentence and an additional word which they were asked to insert into the sentence (Schneiderman & Saddy, 1988). Not unexpectedly the LH aphasic patients showed an across the board deficit in this task. In contrast, the RH patients were only impaired when the correct insertion required that the syntactic role of some word in the sentence be reassigned. Once words were assigned to syntactic roles (in the original sentence) the RH patients were unable to see how they might be reinterpreted to accommodate an additional word.

Thus, there is evidence that damage to the right hemisphere entails impairments in an array of situations that require an initial interpretation to be revised. It is important to note that a number of investigators have remarked that these patients are able to detect the presence of incongruities (Bihrle et al., 1986; Brownell et al., 1983; Gardner, Brownell, Wapner, & Michelow, 1983; Schneiderman & Saddy, 1988; Wapner, Hamby, & Gardner, 1981). What is missing, then, is the means to repair the anomaly, that is, to construct a viable alternate interpretation.

A final deficit attributable to RH dysfunction may be described as an inability to bring to bear upon a current message meanings (in the very broadest sense) derived from the entire discourse context. For example, the proper interpretation of indirect requests requires that the utterance be interpreted in light of the entire communicative setting. It is possible that an inability to keep this information in mind may underlie the difficulties RH patients experience with indirect speech acts. Such patients also have difficulty in extracting the moral of the story or the abstract motivation of characters in a narrative despite an adequate "factual" understanding (Gardner et al., 1983; Wapner et al., 1981). An inability to appreciate the wider context (even though more basic comprehension processes are intact) could contribute to this failure. In addition, RH patients find it very difficult to arrange individual sentences into a coherent story (Delis, Wapner, Moses, & Gardner, 1983; Gardner et al., 1983; Wapner et al., 1981). The extent to which this deficit relates to impaired interpretive processes is unclear. However, the sentence arrangement task would place a high demand on discourse level semantic processes. In addition, it might also require that various sentence combinations be "tried out" and revised if a nonsensical combination results. Thus, an inability to consider alternate interpretations would make sentence arrangement difficult.

Although these high level deficits are difficult to characterize, one gets the impression in each case that RH patients simply fail to "get the big picture." No doubt there are a number of impaired processes contributing. Nevertheless, it is worth considering whether an inability to maintain discourse level meaning for an extended period might produce symptoms similar to some of those noted here. This view would posit a role for the RH in "long-term" meaning activation even in cases where ambiguity is not involved.

Before attempting to integrate the RH patient findings with the cerebral lateralization data, we need to consider some of their potential limitations. First, our hypotheses about hemisphere asymmetries in semantic processing were derived from single word priming studies, yet the RH patient deficit seems to extend to higher levels of semantic/pragmatic processes. Although some impairments have been documented with single words or word-like phrases (i.e., idioms), other deficits clearly involve processes which extend over sentences within a particular discourse context. Yet even these higher level deficits are broadly consistent with the views of right and left hemisphere processing which were derived from the study of single word meanings. Next, I explore the possibility that the lateralized mechanisms identified in the single word priming studies may also contribute to the proper interpretation of figurative language and discourse/narrative level meaning.

A potentially more serious limitation of the RH patient data is the reliance on tasks that often involve metalinguistic judgments as well as more basic comprehension processes. It is unclear, for example, whether RH patients are unable to *comprehend* idioms, or whether they merely *prefer* their literal interpretations.

I am only aware of two reaction time studies that examined linguistic processing in RH patients (Gagnon, Goulet, & Joanette, 1989; Tompkins, in press). Both utilized single word priming in lexical decision and attempted to measure automatic meaning activation (low proportion related, brief SOA). Normal semantic priming was reported. Since Gagnon et al. (1989) used categorically related words, but did not control for associative relatedness, normal priming in RH patients is not unexpected. (Recall that Chiarello et al., 1990, found facilitation of categorical associates in either hemisphere; the only type of facilitation specific to the RH, and thus likely to be disrupted after RH injury, was that for nonassociated category members.) Tompkins (in press) reported normal priming for "metaphoric" pairs, such as "sharp-smart." This might suggest that figurative meanings are automatically activated after RH injury, casting doubt on whether the findings of Brownell et al. (1984, 1990) reflect true interpretative disorders. However, Tompkins' conclusions were based on only three "metaphoric" stimulus pairs, and critical target words were repeated at least 15 times in the experiment. Thus, the generalizability of the results are uncertain, and one cannot rule out strategic factors in this priming study. Furthermore, one can question whether figurative meaning is involved here at all, since "sharp-smart" pairs are near synonyms (a denotative relation).

Thus, we cannot yet ascertain the extent to which the RH semantic/pragmatic disorders reviewed here are due to failures in basic semantic comprehension processes. Further study with online measures of comprehension are clearly needed. Although their source cannot be conclusively specified, the linguistic symptomatology of RH patients is well-defined. Patients with RH injury are deficient in the interpretation of nonliteral language of various sorts (connotation, metaphor, idioms, sarcasm, indirect requests), in situations that require meaning reanalysis or simultaneous access to multiple levels of meaning, and in some aspects of discourse processing. I argue next that these interpretive disorders are just the sort that would be expected if the continued maintenance of alternate meanings were not possible.

SEMANTIC PROCESSING WITHOUT THE RIGHT HEMISPHERE: A CONJECTURE

On the basis of visual half-field research I proposed that word meanings in context are analyzed simultaneously by each cerebral hemisphere. Within the left hemisphere word meanings are accessed rapidly, resulting in the temporary activation of a small set of highly related concepts. Meaning selection also occurs rapidly, entailing the suppression of candidate meanings which are not deemed immediately relevant. Selected meanings are then integrated with the current semantic representation of the sentence or discourse. However, if the selected meaning does not "fit," an anomaly is detected and repair (reanalysis) processes must be initiated. Word meaning access also takes place in the right hemisphere, but a larger set of related meanings is activated and meaning selection either does not occur, or occurs much later than within the left hemisphere. The continued maintenance of a wide set of meanings in the RH may represent contextual meaning of a very broad and diffuse sort, whereas context within the LH may be much more local (perhaps restricted to the current and just previous sentence). Thus it is argued that while the LH is specialized to make a rapid commitment to a single local analysis, the RH, devoid of such specialized mechanisms, de facto maintains broader contextual information as well as alternate meanings for individual words and word-like units.

Under this scenario what would be the consequence of a loss of the RH semantic system? Certainly there would be no across-the-board comprehension problem. LH activation, selection, and integration processes would still proceed normally. However, there are at least two situations in which problems should arise. First, if LH meaning selection processes are obligatory, absence of RH semantic processes should result in interpretive difficulties whenever multiple levels of meaning convey important information. Not all examples of multiple meaning (i.e., ambiguity) require selection. It can be argued that most types of figurative language require simultaneous access to both literal and nonliteral senses in order to be properly appreciated. Consider, for example, the use of sarcasm. If, after hearing a colleague's productivity being lavishly praised, I remark, "Yeah, he's always been a loafer," this does not convey the same meaning as the straightforward statement "Yeah, he's always been a hard work-er." The use of sarcasm in the first instance not only conveys my agreement with the idea that my colleague is productive, but simultaneously communicates other messages (e.g., I think his rate of productivity is really extraordinary; I think this is a positive thing; I am probably envious of him). Thus the use of figurative language here conveys more than one meaning, and it cannot be adequately paraphrased by a single literal statement. To fully appreciate sarcasm requires the recognition of several simultaneously conveyed meanings.[9]

Sarcasm may be the most subtle example requiring simultaneous recognition of multiple meanings. Appreciation of a word's connotation is another example. Recently, Glucksberg and Cacciari (1989) have proposed that in order to cor-rectly use and interpret idioms (arguably the most "frozen" type of figurative language) literal as well as nonliteral meanings must be available. And, as discussed earlier, one can only appreciate verbal humor by recognizing that a given statement has more than one meaning. In each of these cases, focusing on only one meaning (regardless of which one is selected) cannot produce correct interpretation of the nonliteral senses.

It cannot be a coincidence that the very words and phrases that RH patients have difficulty interpreting are just those that possess multiple meanings: ambig-uous words, metaphor and idioms, indirect requests, sarcasm, and jokes. Further, the particular difficulty with nonliteral meaning, which has by now been amply documented, may be attributable to the inability to keep in mind more than one meaning at a time. If we assume that the RH normally functions to maintain multiple meanings, loss of this semantic system would provide a plausible, unifying explanation for the interpretive deficits shown by RH patients.

Greater than normal reliance on the LH semantic system could also account for the second major linguistic deficit shown by RH patients: the inability to revise an initial interpretation, despite an apparent awareness that something is amiss. If, as hypothesized, LH processing results in the suppression of candidate meanings that were selected against, subsequent recovery of these meanings would be very difficult, unless the RH semantic system could be accessed. Since these candidates are likely to be still activated in the RH, recovery of an alternate interpretation could be readily achieved, as long as the RH system remained accessible. In the case of pronounced RH injury, however, initial interpretations would be rigidly adhered to, even if they were shown to be no longer appropriate. This is because in the remaining intact (left) hemisphere, the representations needed to recover an alternate interpretation would be in a highly inaccessible state. Recall that it was earlier posited that LH integrative processes would detect

---

[9]It also presumably requires that the utterance's literal meaning be discarded in favor of an opposite meaning. Thus the RH reanalysis deficit would also contribute to the inability of RH patients to appreciate sarcasm.

an anomaly, but that meanings still activated in the RH would be needed to adequately repair a misinterpretation once detected. This view is consistent with the reports that RH patients are often aware that a particular interpretation is no longer appropriate, yet are at a loss to come up with a viable alternative.

Altered meaning activation processes may also contribute to the third interpretive deficit shown by RH patients, problems in the comprehension of narrative/discourse level meaning. However, the link here is more tenuous. Given the wide ranging narrative impairments reported for RH patients, it is likely that there are several deficits involved. Nevertheless, if the RH normally functions to maintain word meanings for an extended period, it is possible that discourse level meanings are also held in the RH as the LH continues to process incoming information. In addition, it has been argued here that the RH activates a broad set of related meanings in the course of word recognition. Although moderately related meanings may be irrelevant locally (i.e., for sentence comprehension), some may be used to construct the global (i.e., discourse) context. Loss of these normal RH functions might render discourse level meanings unusually transient, which could contribute to the difficulties RH patients have in narrative/discourse comprehension.

Thus, the views on hemisphere differences in semantic processing which were derived from the visual half-field research can be extended to account for the effects of RH injury. This, however, requires us to assume that the activation and selection mechanisms used in the processing of single words are also applicable to sentence and discourse level meanings. This is not an unreasonable assumption, but one which will need to be verified by research that bridges word meaning activation with higher order comprehension processes.

CONCLUSION

I began this chapter with the contention that models of human cognitive processes should be neurologically plausible as well as being consistent with a range of empirical data. On the basis of two areas of neuropsychological research (normal cerebral lateralization and the effects of unilateral brain injury) one is left with the view that the human mind consists of not one, but two, semantic systems that are used in the interpretation of linguistic meaning. This is not a position that one would come to based on the data typically reported in the cognitive psychology literature, nor is it the most parsimonious interpretation possible. However, it is a position worth contemplating if we take seriously the constraints imposed on human cognition by the structure and function of the nervous system.

It is a fact that most cognitive processes require cortical mediation, and that the human cerebral cortex has as a prominent feature structural and functional asymmetry. When we consider the range of cognitive functions attributed to each hemisphere, it becomes apparent that each hemisphere must have access to some semantic system. It is obvious that LH language comprehension requires access to a rich system of meanings. But it is equally true that functions known to be within the competence of the RH (e.g., object and face recognition) also require access to meaning, and that these functions are not lost when the RH no longer has access to LH systems (as in commissurotomy patients). Thus, it is hardly controversial to suggest that each hemisphere possesses some sort of semantic system. Dual semantic systems, then, are part of our biological endowment. When viewed from this vantage point it is surprising that models of cognition typically assume, without comment, that there is a single system of meaning and then proceed from this premise.[10] Yet this is not a neurologically plausible architecture.

Thus, the evidence described in this chapter is not needed to support the view that there are two semantic systems. Rather, it supports the more controversial proposition that right, as well as left, hemisphere semantics contribute to language comprehension. As articulated here, the anatomical separation of the cerebral hemispheres permits the segregation of potentially conflicting semantic processes. A meaning which has been selected against (i.e., inhibited) in the left hemisphere in the course of local sentence comprehension, may still be available in the right hemisphere for other cognitive processes. In addition, the rapid recovery from semantic garden paths (of all types, including humor appreciation) which characterizes normal language comprehension is easily accommodated within a neurologically plausible model that permits meaning selectivity and alternate meaning activation to coexist. Finally, the interpretation of linguistic units that may require the simultaneous consideration of multiple levels of meaning need not have an impact on other processes that demand rapid meaning selection and integration, if these distinct processes are mediated by anatomically separate systems.

In sum, a consideration of the available neuropsychological data leads one to the view that processes subserved by each of the two cerebral hemispheres are necessary for the proper interpretation of words in context. One is not enough.

ACKNOWLEDGMENTS

The preparation of this chapter was supported by NIMH grant MH43868. I wish to thank D. Balota, C. Burgess, and P. Schwanenflugel for their helpful comments on an earlier version of this manuscript.

---

[10]One possible exception is the literature comparing word and object recognition, where it is sometimes argued that there are verbal and nonverbal semantic systems (e.g., Te Linde, 1982). But even these discussions do not consider that nonverbal semantics must be dually represented in each hemisphere.

REFERENCES

Balota, D. A., & Chumbley, J. I. (1984). Are lexical decisions a good measure of lexical access? The role of word frequency in the neglected decision stage. *Journal of Experimental Psychology: Human Perception and Performance, 10*, 340–357.

Balota, D. A., & Chumbley, J. I. (1985). The locus of word-frequency effects in the pronunciation task: Lexical access and/or production? *Journal of Memory and Language, 24*, 89–106.

Becker, C. A. (1979). Semantic context and word frequency effects in visual word recognition. *Journal of Experimental Psychology: Human Perception and Performance, 3*, 389–401.

Besner, D. (1983). Deep dyslexia and the right hemisphere hypothesis: Evidence from the U.S.A. and U.S.S.R. *Canadian Journal of Psychology, 37*, 565–571.

Bihrle, A. M., Brownell, H. H., & Gardner, H. (1988). Humor and the right hemisphere: A narrative perspective. In H. A. Whitaker (Ed.), *Contemporary reviews in neuropsychology* (pp. 109–126). New York: Springer-Verlag.

Bihrle, A. M., Brownell, H. H., Powelson, J., & Gardner, H. (1986). Comprehension of humorous and non-humorous materials by left and right brain-damaged patients. *Brain and Cognition, 5*, 399–412.

Boles, D. B. (1983). Dissociated imageability, concreteness, and familiarity in lateralized word recognition. *Memory and Cognition, 11*, 511–519.

Bradshaw, J. L., & Gates, E. A. (1978). Visual field differences in verbal tasks: Effects of task familiarity and sex of subject. *Brain and Language, 5*, 166–187.

Broca, P. (1863). Localisation des fonctions cerebrales siege du langage articule. *Bulletins de la Societe d'anthropologie, 4*, 200–204.

Brownell, H. H., Michel, D., Powelson, J., & Gardner, H. (1983). Surprise but not coherence: Sensitivity to verbal humor in right-hemisphere patients. *Brain and Language, 18*, 20–27.

Brownell, H. H., Potter, H. H., Bihrle, A. M., & Gardner, H. (1986). Inference deficits in right brain-damaged patients. *Brain and Language, 27*, 310–321.

Brownell, H. H., Potter, H. H., Michelow, D., & Gardner, H. (1984). Sensitivity to lexical denotation and connotation in brain-damaged patients: A double dissociation? *Brain and Language, 22*, 253–265.

Brownell, H. H., Simpson, T. L., Bihrle, A. M., Potter, H. H., & Gardner, H. (1990). Appreciation of metaphoric alternative word meanings by left and right brain-damaged patients. *Neuropsychologia, 28*, 375–384.

Burgess, C., & Simpson, G. B. (1988). Cerebral hemispheric mechanisms in the retrieval of ambiguous word meanings. *Brain and Language, 33*, 86–103.

Chiarello, C. (1985). Hemisphere dynamics in lexical access: Automatic and controlled priming. *Brain and Language, 26*, 146–172.

Chiarello, C. (1988). Lateralization of lexical processes in the normal brain: A review of visual half-field research. In H. A. Whitaker (Ed.), *Contemporary reviews in neuropsychology* (pp. 36–76). New York: Springer-Verlag.

Chiarello, C., Burgess, C., Richards, L., & Pollock, A. (1990). Semantic and associative priming in the cerebral hemispheres: Some words do, some words don't . . . sometimes, some places. *Brain and Language, 38*, 75–104.

Chiarello, C., Nuding, S., & Pollock, A. (1988). Lexical decision and naming asymmetries: Influence of response selection and response bias. *Brain and Language, 34*, 302–314.

Chiarello, C., Senehi, J., & Nuding, S. (1987). Semantic priming with abstract and concrete words: Differential asymmetry may be postlexical. *Brain and Language, 31*, 43–60.

Chiarello, C., Senehi, J., & Soulier, M. (1986). Viewing conditions and hemisphere asymmetry for the lexical decision. *Neuropsychologia, 24*, 521–530.

de Groot, A. M. B. (1984). Primed lexical decision: Combined effects of the proportion of related prime-target pairs and the stimulus-onset asynchrony of prime and target. *Quarterly Journal of Experimental Psychology, 36A*, 253–280.

275

Delis, D. C., Wapner, W., Moses, J. A., & Gardner, H. (1983). The contribution of the right hemisphere to the organization of paragraphs. *Cortex, 19,* 43–50.

Durgunoglu, A. Y. (1988). Repetition, semantic priming, and stimulus quality: Implications for the interactive-compensatory reading model. *Journal of Experimental Psychology: Learning, Memory, and Cognition, 14,* 590–603.

Eglin, M. (1987). Interference and priming within and across visual fields in a lexical decision task. *Neuropsychologia, 25,* 613–625.

Ellis, A. W., Young, A. W., & Anderson, C. (1988). Modes of word recognition in the left and right cerebral hemispheres. *Brain and Language, 35,* 254–273.

Foldi, N. S. (1987). Appreciation of pragmatic interpretations of indirect commands: Comparison of right and left hemisphere brain-damaged patients. *Brain and Language, 31,* 88–108.

Gagnon, J., Goulet, P., & Joanette, Y. (1989). Activation automatique et controlee du savoir lexico-semantique chez les cerebroleses droits. *Langages, 96,* 95–111.

Galaburda, A. M., Sanides, F., & Geschwind, N. (1978). Human brain: Cytoarchitectonic left-right asymmetries in the temporal speech region. *Archives of Neurology, 35,* 812–817.

Gardner, H., Brownell, H. H., Wapner, W., & Michelow, D. (1983). Missing the point: The role of the right hemisphere in the processing of complex linguistic materials. In E. Perecman (Ed.), *Cognitive processes in the right hemisphere* (pp. 169–191). New York: Academic Press.

Gazzaniga, M. S., & Hillyard, S. A. (1971). Language and speech capacity of the right hemisphere. *Neuropsychologia, 9,* 273–280.

Geschwind, N., & Galaburda, A. M. (1987). *Cerebral lateralization: Biological mechanisms, associations, and pathology.* Cambridge: MIT Press.

Geschwind, N., & Levitsky, W. (1968). Human brain: Left-right asymmetries in temporal speech region. *Science, 161,* 186–187.

Glick S. D., Ross, D. A., & Hough, L. B. (1982). Lateral asymmetry of neurotransmitters in human brain. *Brain Research, 234,* 53–63.

Glucksberg, S., & Cacciari, C. (1989). *Contributions of word meanings to idiomatic meanings.* Presented at 30th annual meeting, Psychonomic Society, Atlanta.

Gur, R. C., Packer, I. K., Hungerbuhler, J. P., Reivich, M., Obrist, W. D., Amarnek, W. S., & Sackheim, H. A. (1980). Differences in the distribution of gray and white matter in human cerebral hemispheres. *Science, 207,* 1226–1228.

Hellige, J. B. (1983). Hemisphere X task interaction and the study of laterality. In J. B. Hellige (Ed.), *Cerebral hemisphere asymmetry: Method, theory, and application* (pp. 411–443). New York: Praeger.

Hellige, J. B., Jonsson, J. E., & Michimata, C. (1988). Processing from LVF, RVF and BILATERAL presentations: Examinations of metacontrol and interhemispheric interaction. *Brain and Cognition, 7,* 39–53.

Hirst, W., LeDoux, J., & Stein, S. (1984). Constraints on the processing of indirect speech acts: Evidence from aphasiology. *Brain and Language, 23,* 26–33.

Hugdahl, K., & Franzon, M. (1985). The incongruent color-words paradigm and language lateralization: An EEG-study. *Scandanavian Journal of Psychology, 26,* 321–326.

Joanette, Y., & Goulet, P. (1987). *Inference deficits in right-brain-damaged right-handers: Absence of evidence.* Paper presented at 10th European meeting of International Neuropsychological Society, Barcelona.

Kosslyn, S. M. (1987). Seeing and imaging in the cerebral hemispheres: A computational approach. *Psychological Review, 94,* 148–175.

Kreuger, L. E. (1975). The word-superiority effect: Is its locus visual-spatial or verbal. *Bulletin of the Psychonomic Society, 6,* 465–468.

Kutas, M., & Van Petten, C. (1988). Event-related brain potential studies of language. *Advances in Psychophysiology, 3,* 139–187.

Kutas, M., Van Petten, C., & Besson, M. (1988). Event-related potential asymmetries during the reading of sentences. *Encephalography and Clinical Neurophysiology, 69,* 218–233.

Levy, J., & Trevarthen, C. (1976). Metacontrol of hemispheric function in human split-brain patients. *Journal of Experimental Psychology: Human Perception and Performance, 2,* 299–312.

Lupker, S. J., & Sanders, M. (1982). Visual field differences in picture-word interference. *Brain and Cognition, 1,* 381–398.

Marcel, A. J., & Patterson, K. E. (1978). Word recognition and production: Reciprocity in clinical and normal studies. In J. Requin (Ed.), *Attention and performance VII* (pp. 209–226). Hillsdale, NJ: Lawrence Erlbaum Associates.

McDonald, S., & Wales, R. (1986). An investigation of the ability to process inferences in language following right hemisphere brain damage. *Brain and Language, 29,* 68–80.

McClelland, J. L., & Rumelhart, D. E. (1981). An interactive activation model of context effects in letter perception: Part 1. An account of basic findings. *Psychological Review, 88,* 375–407.

Michimata, C. (1987). *Lateralized effects of semantic priming in lexical decision tasks: Examinations of the time course of semantic activation build-up in the left and right cerebral hemispheres.* Doctoral dissertation, University of Southern California.

Monsell, S., Doyle, M. C., & Haggard, P. N. (1989). Effects of word frequency on visual word recognition tasks: Where are they? *Journal of Experimental Psychology: General, 118,* 43–71.

Moscovitch, M. (1983). Laterality and visual masking: Interhemispheric communication and the locus of perceptual asymmetries for words. *Canadian Journal of Psychology, 37,* 85–106.

Myers, P. S., & Linebaugh, C. W. (1981). Comprehension of idiomatic expressions by right-hemisphere-damaged adults. In R. H. Brookshire (Ed.), *Clinical aphasiology: Conference proceedings* (pp. 254–261). Minneapolis: BRK Publishers.

Neely, J. H. (1977). Semantic priming and retrieval from lexical memory: Roles of inhibitionless spreading activation and limited-capacity attention. *Journal of Experimental Psychology: General, 106,* 226–254.

Neely, J. H. (1990). Semantic priming effects in visual word recognition: A selective review of current findings and theories. In D. Besner & G. Humphreys, (Eds.), *Basic processes in reading: Visual word recognition.* Hillsdale, NJ: Lawrence Erlbaum Associates.

Neely, J. H., Keefe, D. E., & Ross, K. (1989). Semantic priming in the lexical decision task: Roles of prospective prime-generated expectancies and retrospective semantic matching. *Journal of Experimental Psychology: Learning, Memory, and Cognition, 15,* 1003–1019.

Posner, M. I., Inhoff, A., Friedrich, F. J., & Cohen, A. (1987). Isolating attentional systems: A cognitive-anatomical analysis. *Psychobiology, 15,* 107–121.

Posner, M. I., & Snyder, C. R. R. (1975). Attention and cognitive control. In R. L. Solso (Ed.), *Information processing and cognition: The Loyola symposium* (pp. 55–85). Hillsdale, NJ: Lawrence Erlbaum Associates.

Postman, L., & Keppel, G. (1970). *Norms of word association.* New York: Academic Press.

Ratcliff, R., & McKoon, G. (1988). A retrieval theory of priming in memory. *Psychological Review, 95,* 385–408.

Rumelhart, D. E., & McClelland, J. L. (1986). *Parallel distributed processing: Volume 1.* Cambridge, MA: MIT Press.

Schmit, V., & Davis, R. (1974). The role of hemispheric specialization in the analysis of Stroop stimuli. *Acta Psychologica, 38,* 149–158.

Schneiderman, E. I., & Saddy, J. D. (1988). A linguistic deficit resulting from right-hemisphere damage. *Brain and Language, 34,* 38–53.

Seidenberg, M. S., & McClelland, J. L. (1989). A distributed, developmental model of word recognition and naming. *Psychological Review, 96,* 523–568.

Seidenberg, M. S., Tanenhaus, M. K., Leiman, J. M., & Bienkowski, M. (1982). Automatic access of the meanings of ambiguous words in context: Some limitations of knowledge-based processing. *Cognitive Psychology, 14,* 489–537.

Sidtis, J. J., & Gazzaniga, M. S. (1983). Competence vs performance after callosal section: Looks can be deceiving. In J. B. Hellige (Ed.), *Cerebral hemisphere asymmetry: Method, theory, and application* (pp. 152–176). New York: Praeger.

Simpson, G. B., & Kellas, G. (1988). *Repetition priming of homograph meanings*. Presented at 29th annual meeting, Psychonomic Society, Chicago.

Simpson, G. B., Krueger, M. A., & Beyer, R. L. (1989). *Lexical access and meaning suppression*. Presented at the 30th annual meeting, Psychonomic Society, Atlanta.

Sperry, R. W., Gazzaniga, M. S., & Bogen, J. E. (1969). Interhemispheric relationships: the neocortical commissures; syndromes of hemisphere disconnection. In P. J. Vinken & G. W. Bruyn (Eds.), *Handbook of clinical neurology* (pp. 273–290). New York: Wiley-Interscience.

Swinney, D. (1979). Lexical access during sentence comprehension: (re)consideration of context effects. *Journal of Verbal Learning and Verbal Behavior, 14,* 645–660.

Te Linde, J. (1982). Picture-word differences in decision latency: A test of common coding assumptions. *Journal of Experimental Psychology: Learning, Memory and Cognition, 8,* 584–598.

Tompkins, C. A. (in press). Knowledge and strategies for processing lexical metaphor after right brain damage. *Journal of Speech and Hearing Research.*

Tompkins, C. A., & Mateer, C. A. (1985). Right hemisphere appreciation of prosodic and linguistic indications of implicit attitude. *Brain and Language, 24,* 185–203.

Tsao, Y., Feustelk, T., & Soseos, C. (1979). Stroop interference in the left and right visual fields. *Brain and Language, 8,* 367–371.

Van Lancker, D. R., & Kempler, D. (1987). Comprehension of familiar phrases by left- but not right-hemisphere damaged patients. *Brain and Language, 32,* 265–277.

Walker, E., & Ceci, S. J. (1985). Semantic priming effects for stimuli presented to the right and left visual fields. *Brain and Language, 25,* 144–159.

Wapner, W., Hamby, S., & Gardner, H. (1981). The role of the right hemisphere in the apprehension of complex linguistic materials. *Brain and Language, 14,* 15–33.

Wernicke, C. (1874). *Der Aphasische Symptomencomplex*. Breslau: Cohn & Weigart.

Weylman, S. T., Brownell, H. H., Roman, M., & Gardner, H. (1989). Appreciation of indirect requests by left- and right-brain-damaged patients: The effects of verbal context and conventionality of wording. *Brain and Language, 36,* 580–591.

Winner, E., & Gardner, H. (1977). The comprehension of metaphor in brain-damaged patients. *Brain, 100,* 717–729.

Young, A. W., & Ellis, A. W. (1985). Different methods of lexical access for words presented in the left and right visual hemifields. *Brain and Language, 24,* 326–358.

Zaidel, E. (1976). Auditory vocabulary of the right hemisphere following brain bisection or hemidecortication. *Cortex, 12,* 191–211.

Zaidel, E. (1978). Lexical organization in the right hemisphere. In P. Buser & A. Rougeul-Buser (Eds.), *Cerebral correlates of conscious experience* (pp. 177–197). Amsterdam: Elsevier.

Zaidel, E. (1982). Reading by the disconnected right hemisphere: An aphasiological perspective. In Y. Zotterman (Ed.), *Dyslexia: Neurological, cognitive, and linguistic aspects* (pp. 76–91). Wenner-Glen Symposium Series, Vol. 35. Oxford: Pergamon Press.

Zaidel, E. (1983). Disconnection syndrome as a model for laterality effects in the normal brain. In J. B. Hellige (Ed.), *Cerebral hemisphere asymmetry: Method, theory, and application* (pp. 95–151). New York: Praeger.

Author Index

Subject Index